Honey Hunt

1 story and art by Miki Aihara

Honey Hunt 1

CONTENTS

Hey, did you know one of the girls in the senior class...
...is the daughter of Yukari Shiraki?!
Are you serious?! That means she's also the daughter of the world-famous musician Onozuka! A celebrity in our school!!
Wasn't he the first Japanese composer to receive an Academy Award? I love that car commercial song he wrote.
She's so lucky! She gets to live with Yukari Shiraki and Takayuki Onozuka.
Let's go check it out. Which room is she in? I want to see what she looks like. Is she pretty? Does she look famous?
Well, I heard she's not what you'd think. She's more average and, like, normal looking.
Honey Hunt
CHAPTER 1

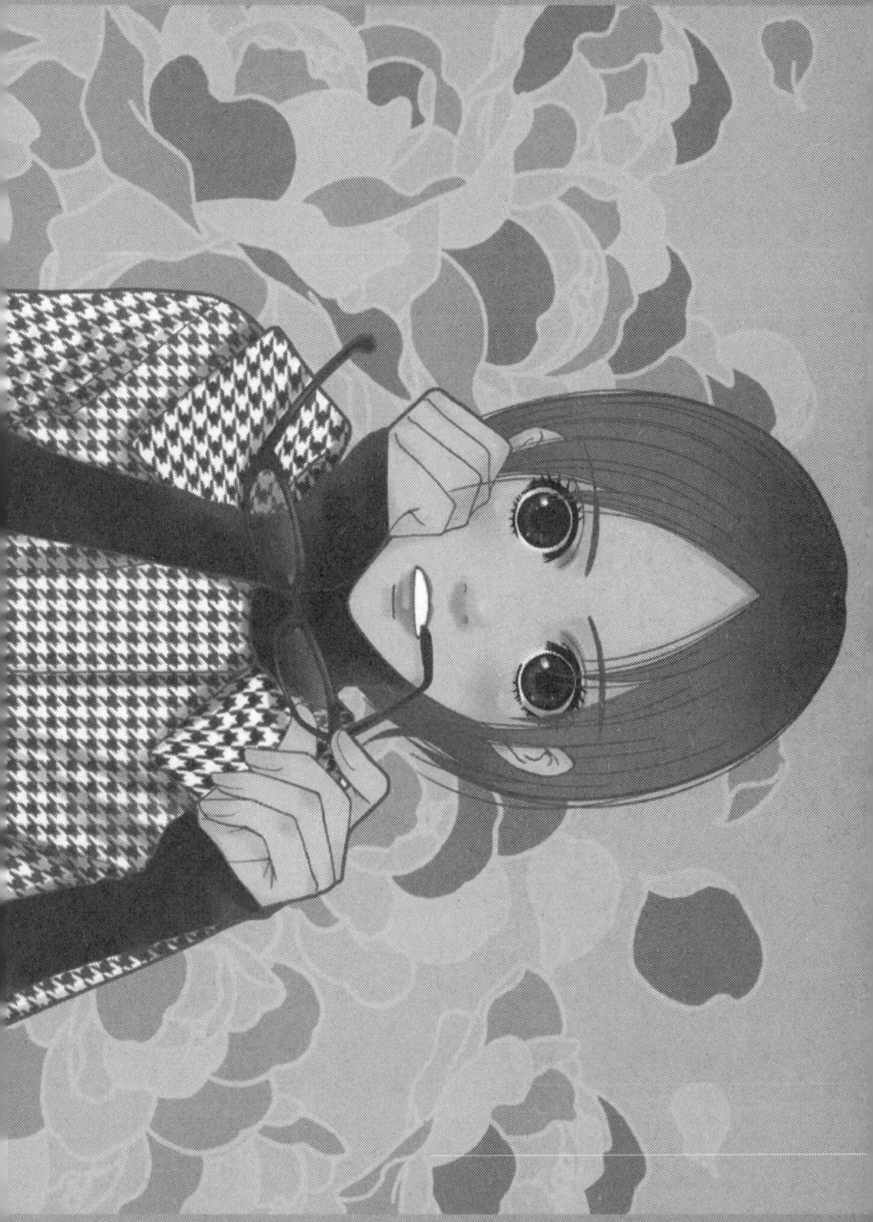

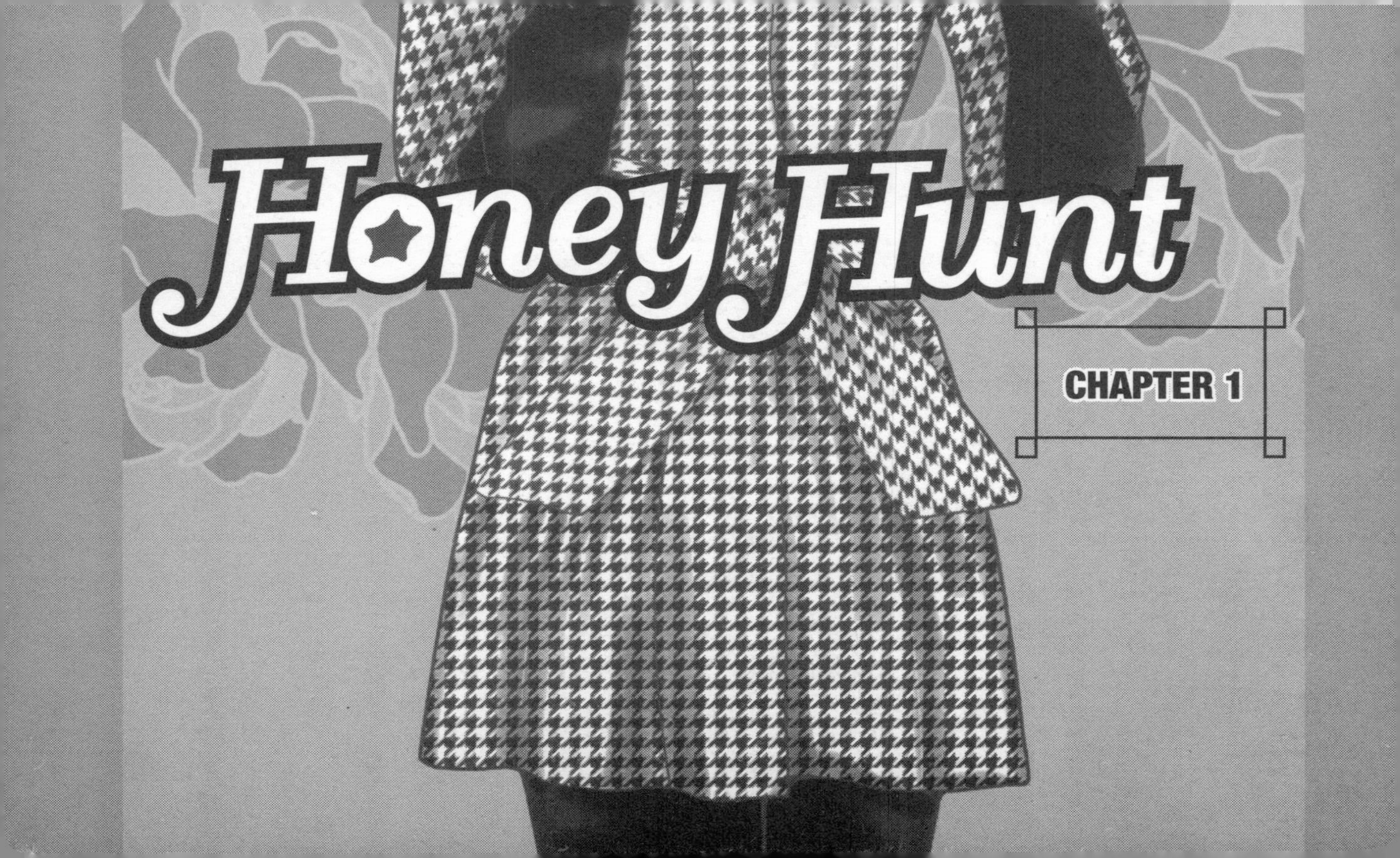
Honey Hunt
CHAPTER 1

Honey Hunt 01

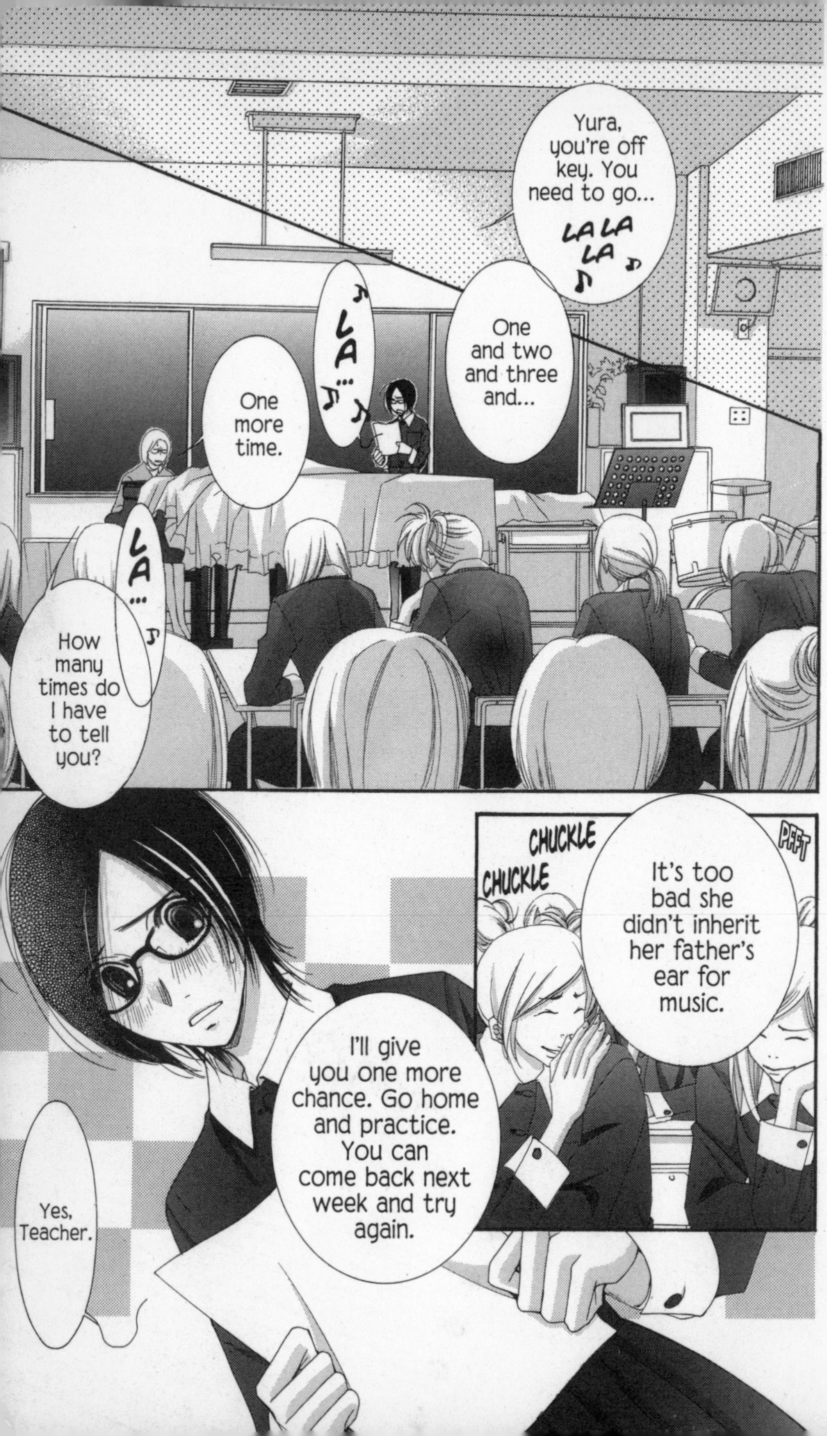
Yura, you're off key. You need to go...
LA LA LA ♪
One and two and three and...
♪ LA... ♪
One more time.
LA... ♪
How many times do I have to tell you?
PFFT
CHUCKLE
CHUCKLE
It's too bad she didn't inherit her father's ear for music.
I'll give you one more chance. Go home and practice. You can come back next week and try again.
Yes, Teacher.

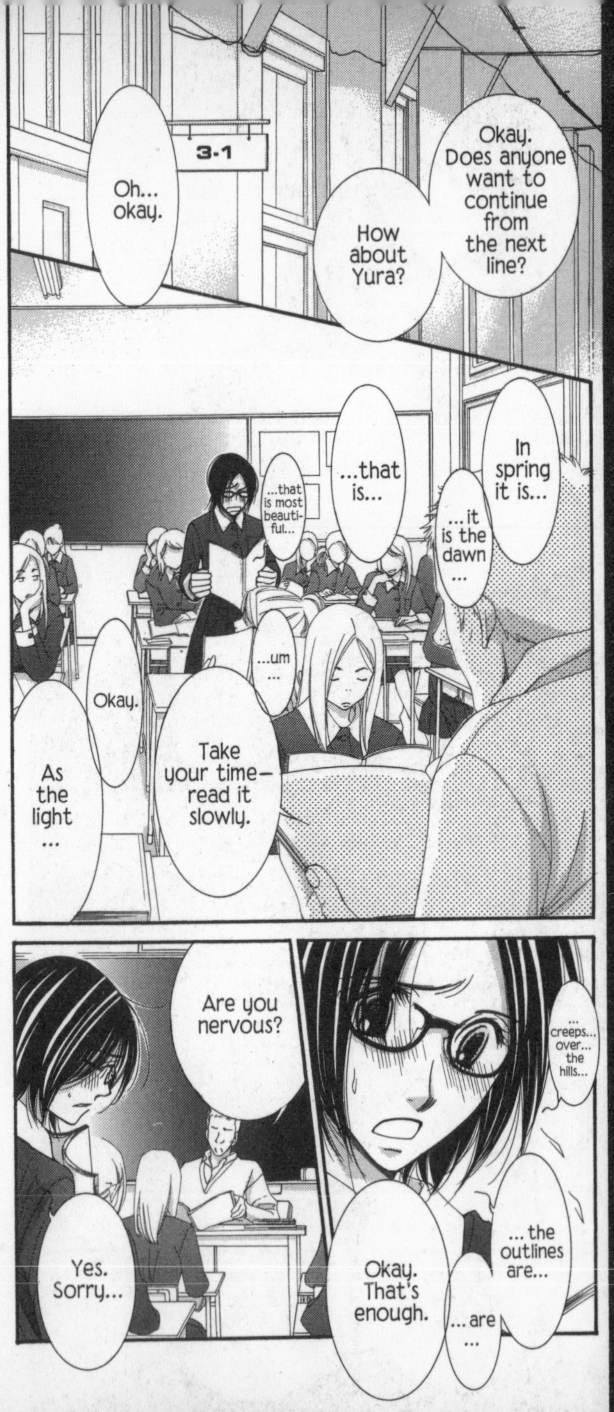
Okay. Does anyone want to continue from the next line?
How about Yura?
3-1
Oh... okay.
In spring it is...
...it is the dawn...
...that is...
...that is most beauti-ful...
...um...
Okay.
Take your time—read it slowly.
As the light...
...creeps... over... the hills...
...the outlines are...
...are...
Okay. That's enough.
Are you nervous?
Yes. Sorry...

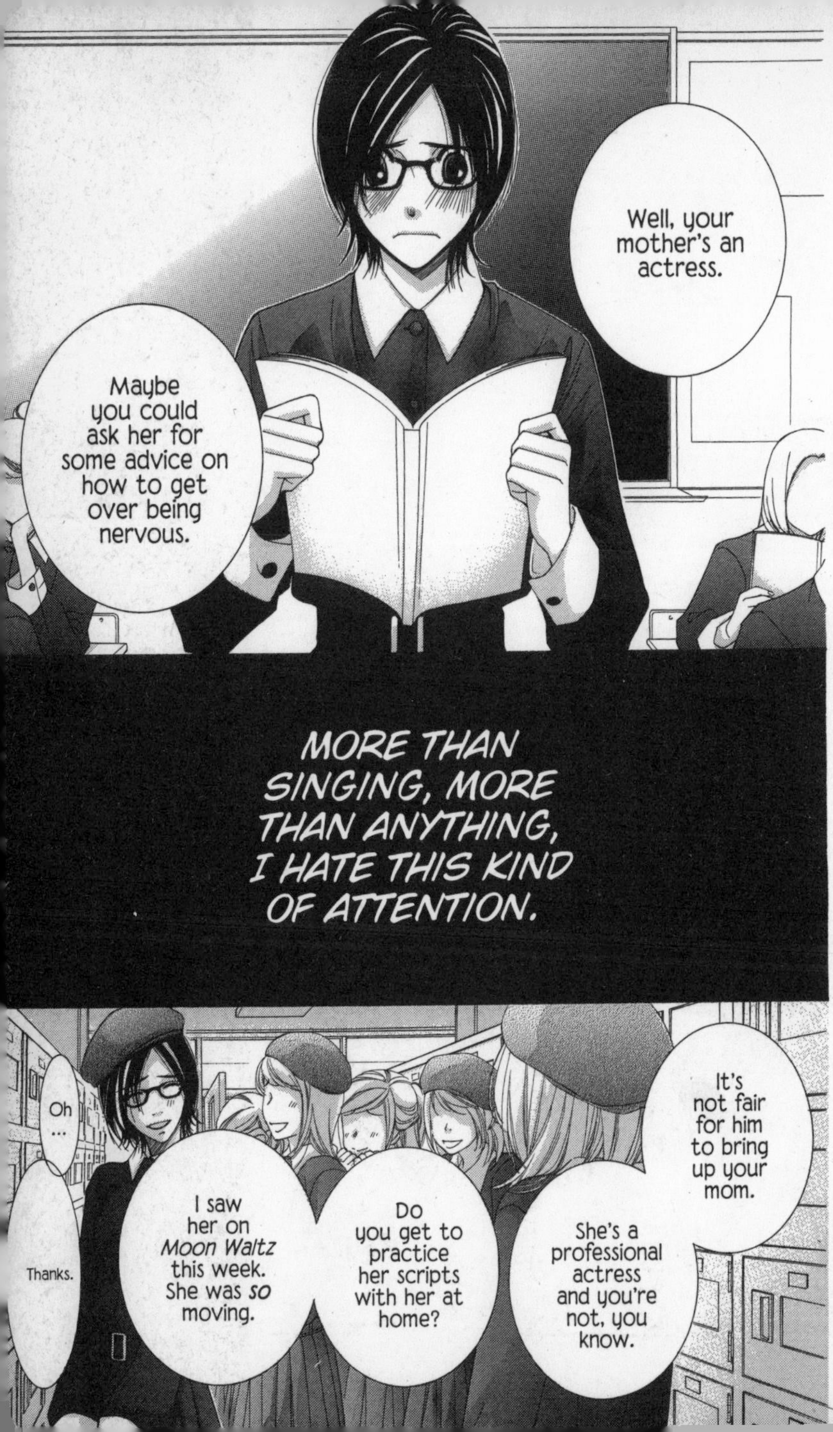
Well, your mother's an actress.
Maybe you could ask her for some advice on how to get over being nervous.
MORE THAN SINGING, MORE THAN ANYTHING, I HATE THIS KIND OF ATTENTION.
It's not fair for him to bring up your mom.
She's a professional actress and you're not, you know.
Do you get to practice her scripts with her at home?
I saw her on *Moon Waltz* this week. She was *so* moving.
Oh ...
Thanks.

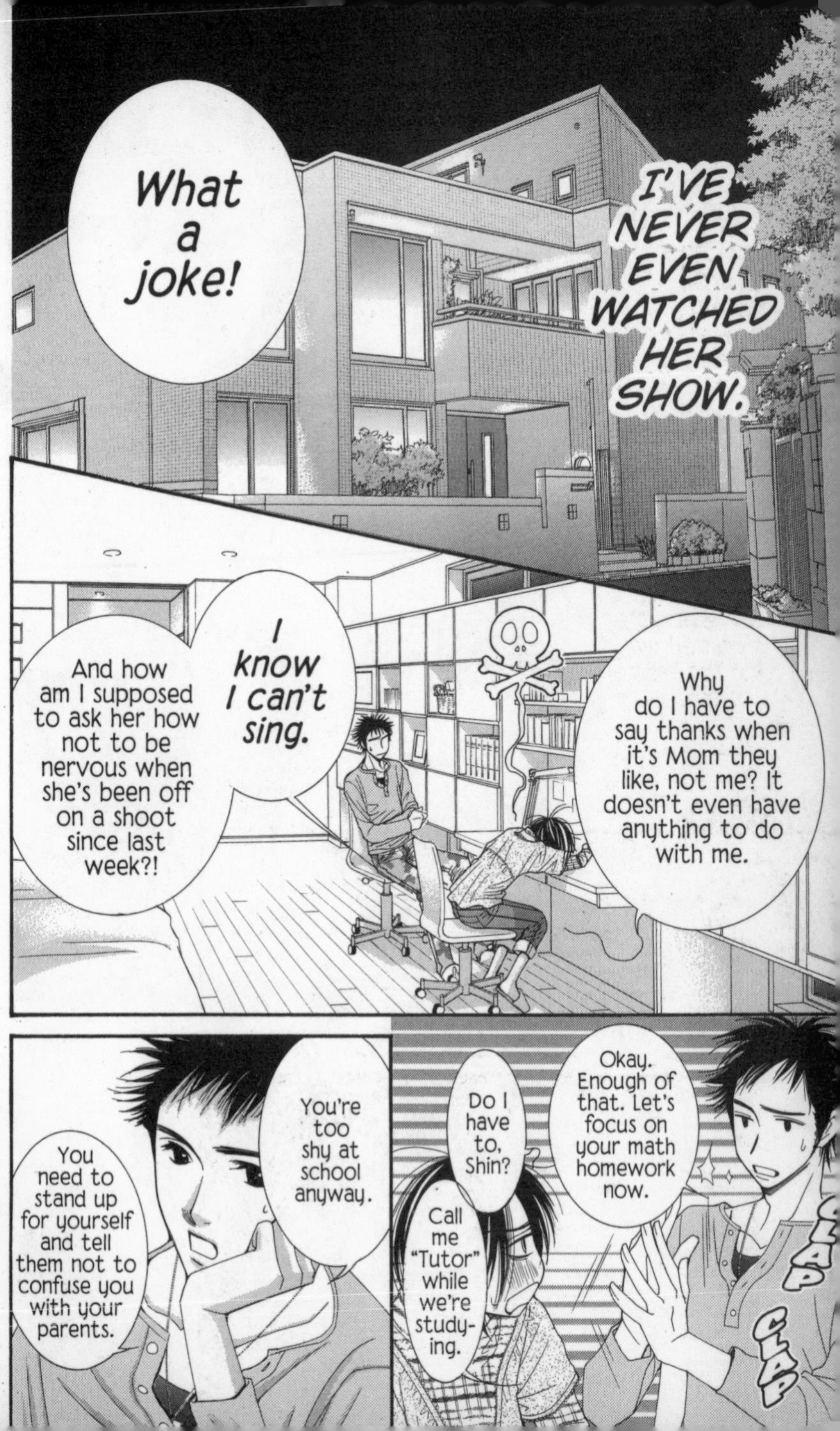
I'VE NEVER EVEN WATCHED HER SHOW.
What a joke!
Why do I have to say thanks when it's Mom they like, not me? It doesn't even have anything to do with me.
I know I can't sing.
And how am I supposed to ask her how not to be nervous when she's been off on a shoot since last week?!
Okay. Enough of that. Let's focus on your math homework now.
CLAP
CLAP
Do I have to, Shin?
Call me "Tutor" while we're study-ing.
You're too shy at school anyway.
You need to stand up for yourself and tell them not to confuse you with your parents.

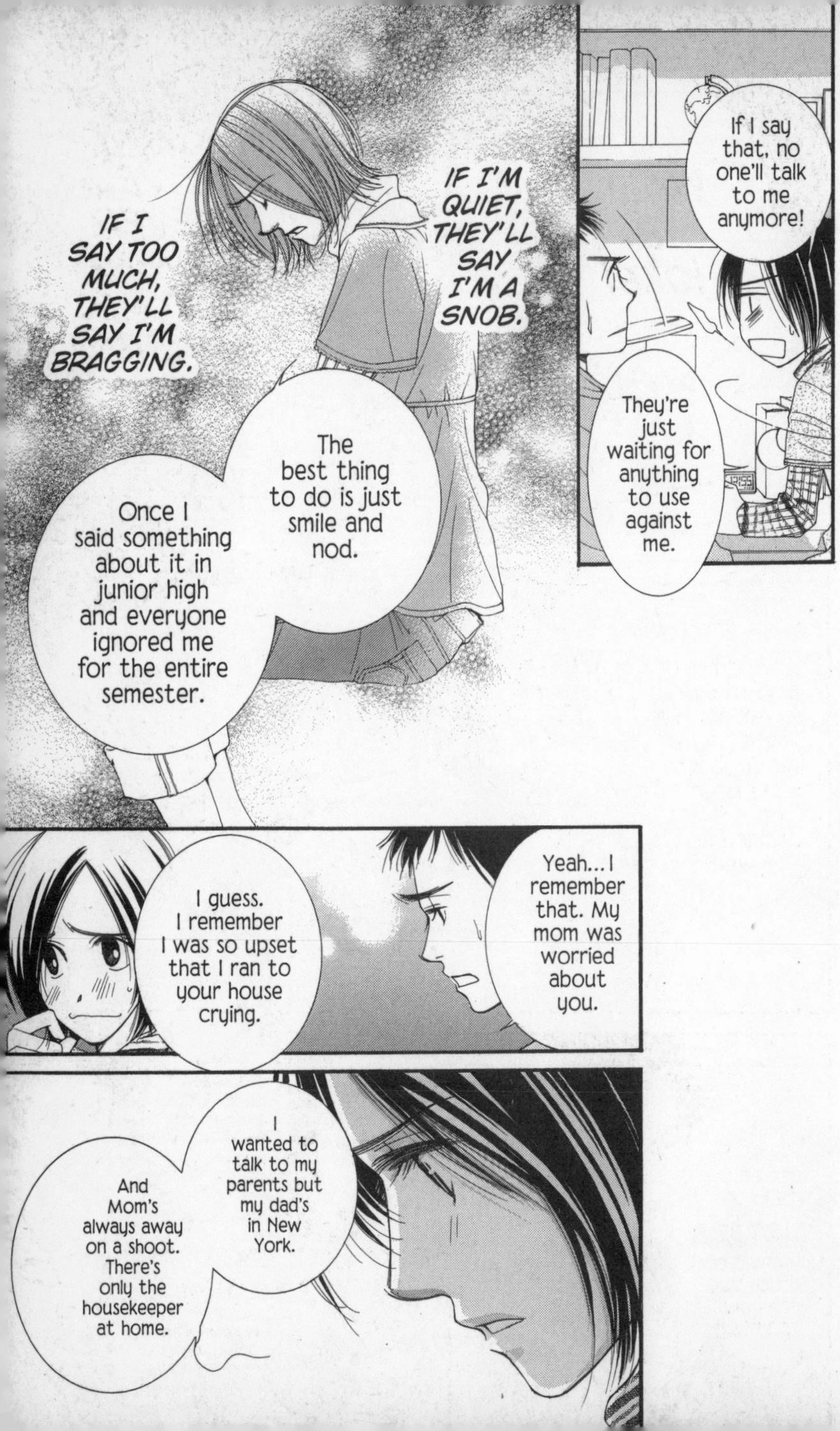
If I say that, no one'll talk to me anymore!
They're just waiting for anything to use against me.
IF I'M QUIET, THEY'LL SAY I'M A SNOB.
IF I SAY TOO MUCH, THEY'LL SAY I'M BRAGGING.
The best thing to do is just smile and nod.
Once I said something about it in junior high and everyone ignored me for the entire semester.
Yeah... I remember that. My mom was worried about you.
I guess. I remember I was so upset that I ran to your house crying.
I wanted to talk to my parents but my dad's in New York.
And Mom's always away on a shoot. There's only the housekeeper at home.

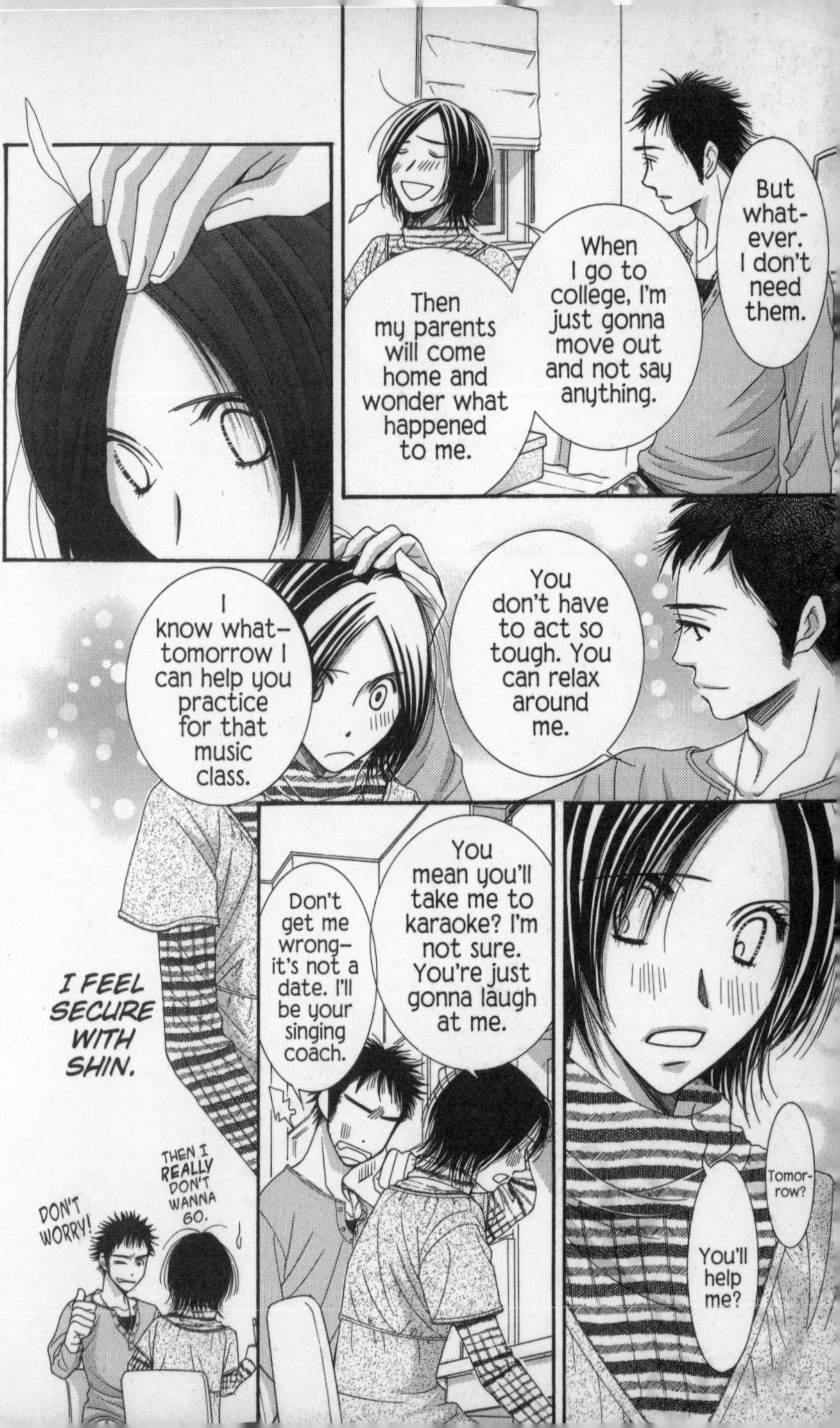
But whatever. I don't need them.
When I go to college, I'm just gonna move out and not say anything.
Then my parents will come home and wonder what happened to me.
You don't have to act so tough. You can relax around me.
I know what—tomorrow I can help you practice for that music class.
Tomorrow?
You'll help me?
You mean you'll take me to karaoke? I'm not sure. You're just gonna laugh at me.
Don't get me wrong—it's not a date. I'll be your singing coach.
I FEEL SECURE WITH SHIN.
THEN I REALLY DON'T WANNA GO.
DON'T WORRY!

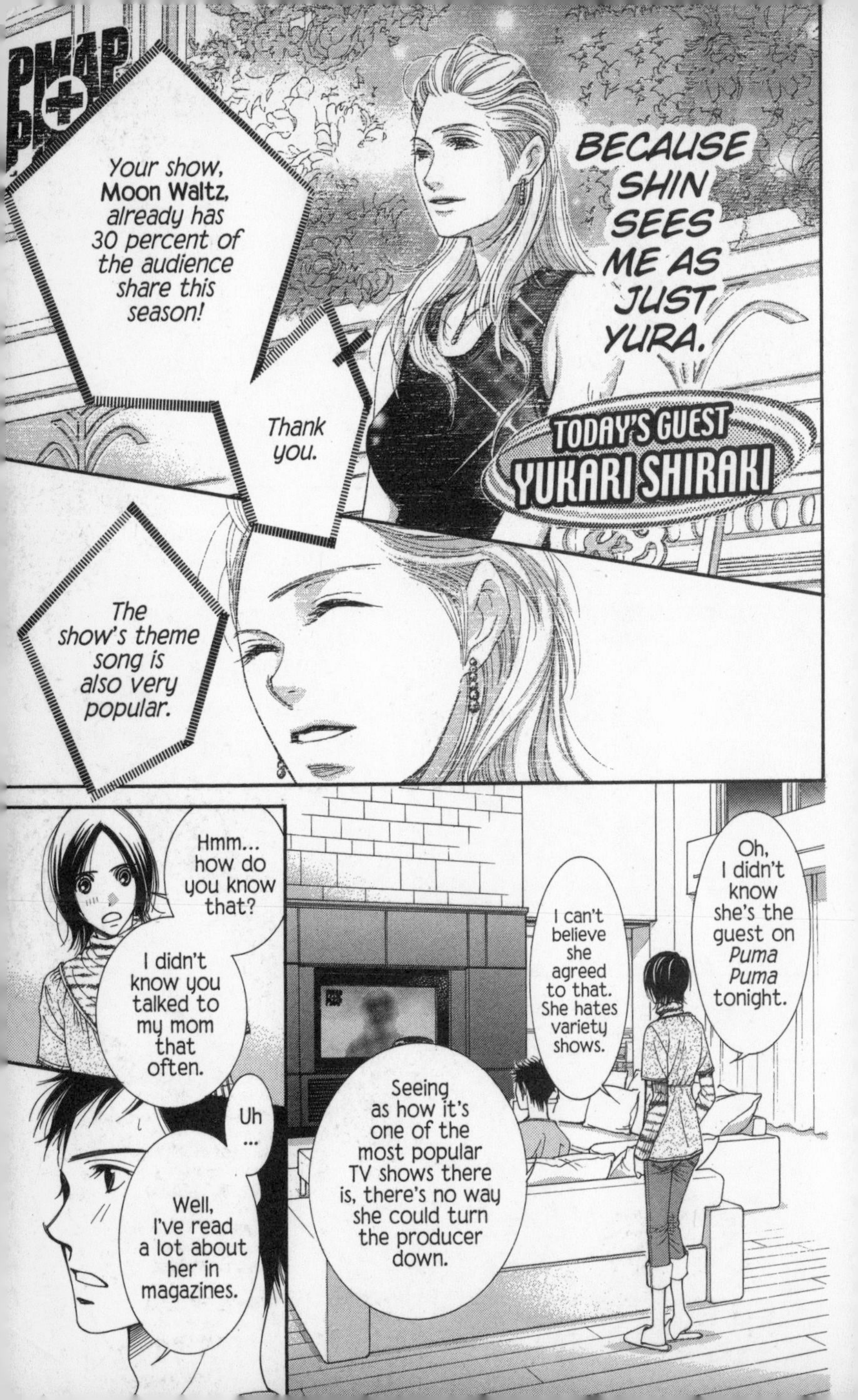
PMAP
BECAUSE SHIN SEES ME AS JUST YURA.
TODAY'S GUEST YUKARI SHIRAKI
Your show, Moon Waltz, already has 30 percent of the audience share this season!
Thank you.
The show's theme song is also very popular.
Oh, I didn't know she's the guest on Puma Puma tonight.
I can't believe she agreed to that. She hates variety shows.
Seeing as how it's one of the most popular TV shows there is, there's no way she could turn the producer down.
Hmm... how do you know that?
I didn't know you talked to my mom that often.
Uh ...
Well, I've read a lot about her in magazines.

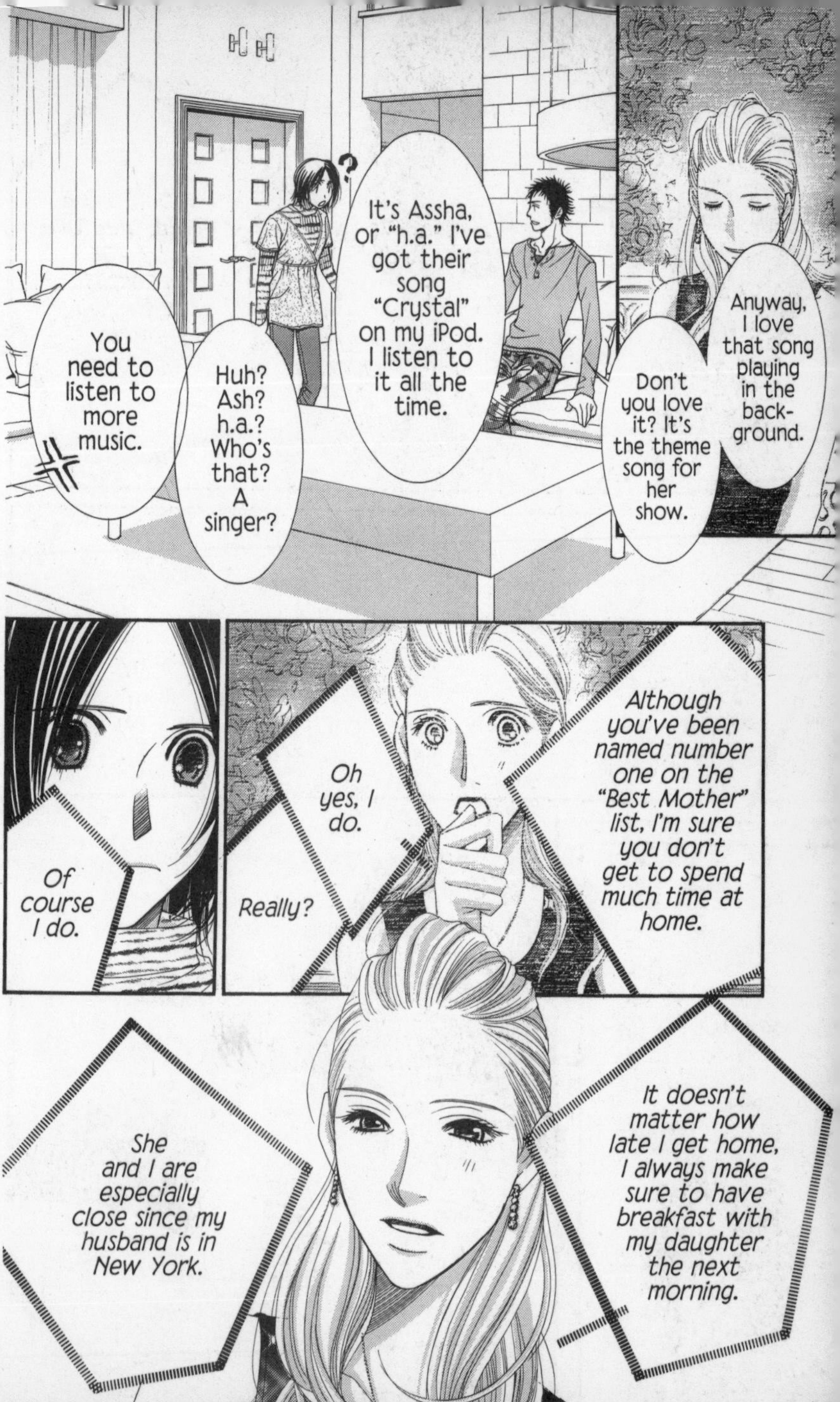
Anyway, I love that song playing in the back-ground.
Don't you love it? It's the theme song for her show.
It's Assha, or "h.a." I've got their song "Crystal" on my iPod. I listen to it all the time.
Huh? Ash? h.a.? Who's that? A singer?
You need to listen to more music.
Although you've been named number one on the "Best Mother" list, I'm sure you don't get to spend much time at home.
Oh yes, I do.
Really?
Of course I do.
It doesn't matter how late I get home, I always make sure to have breakfast with my daughter the next morning.
She and I are especially close since my husband is in New York.

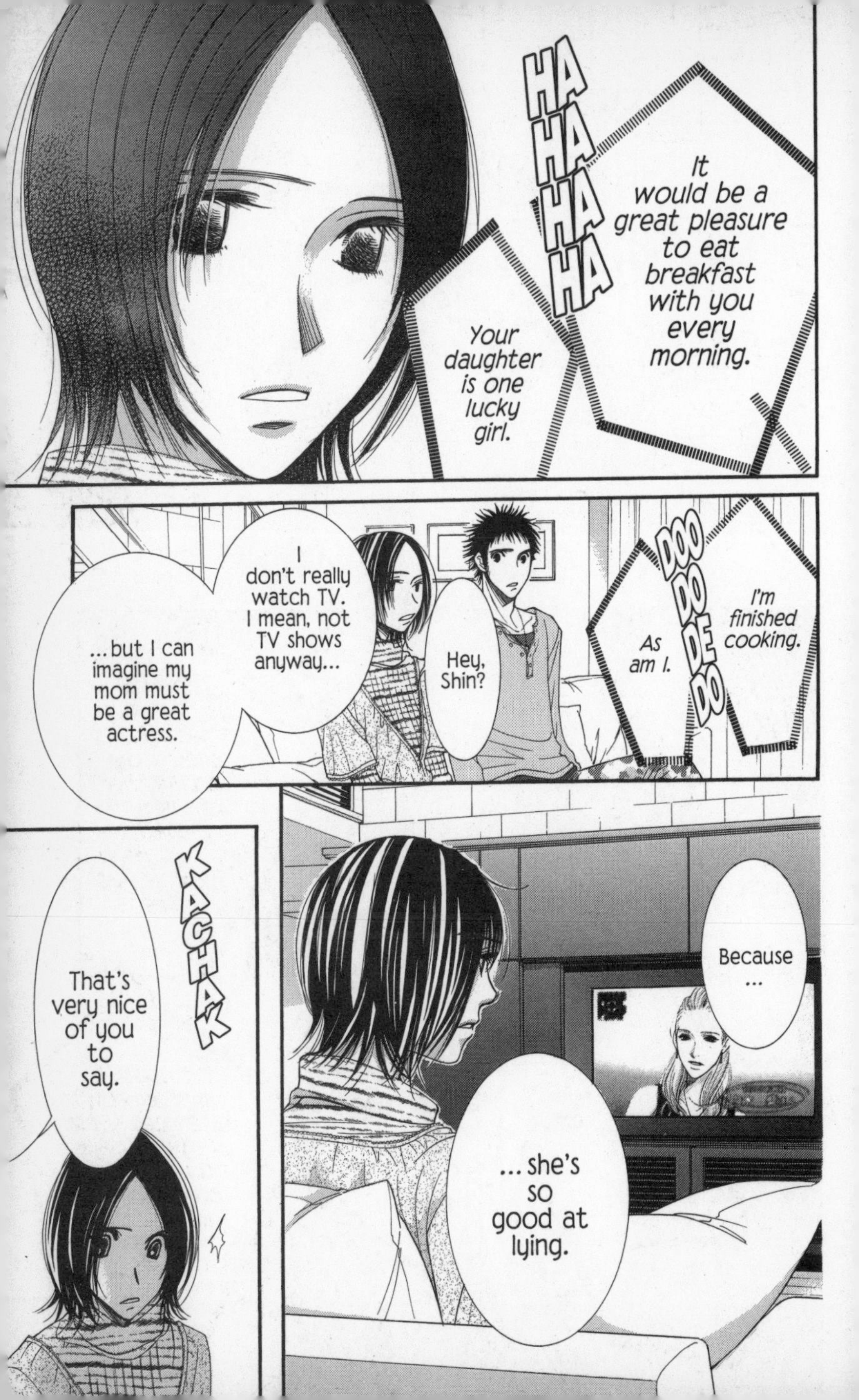
It would be a great pleasure to eat breakfast with you every morning.
HAHAHAHA
Your daughter is one lucky girl.
I'm finished cooking.
DOO DO DE DO
As am I.
Hey, Shin?
I don't really watch TV. I mean, not TV shows anyway...
...but I can imagine my mom must be a great actress.
Because ...
... she's so good at lying.
KACHAK
That's very nice of you to say.

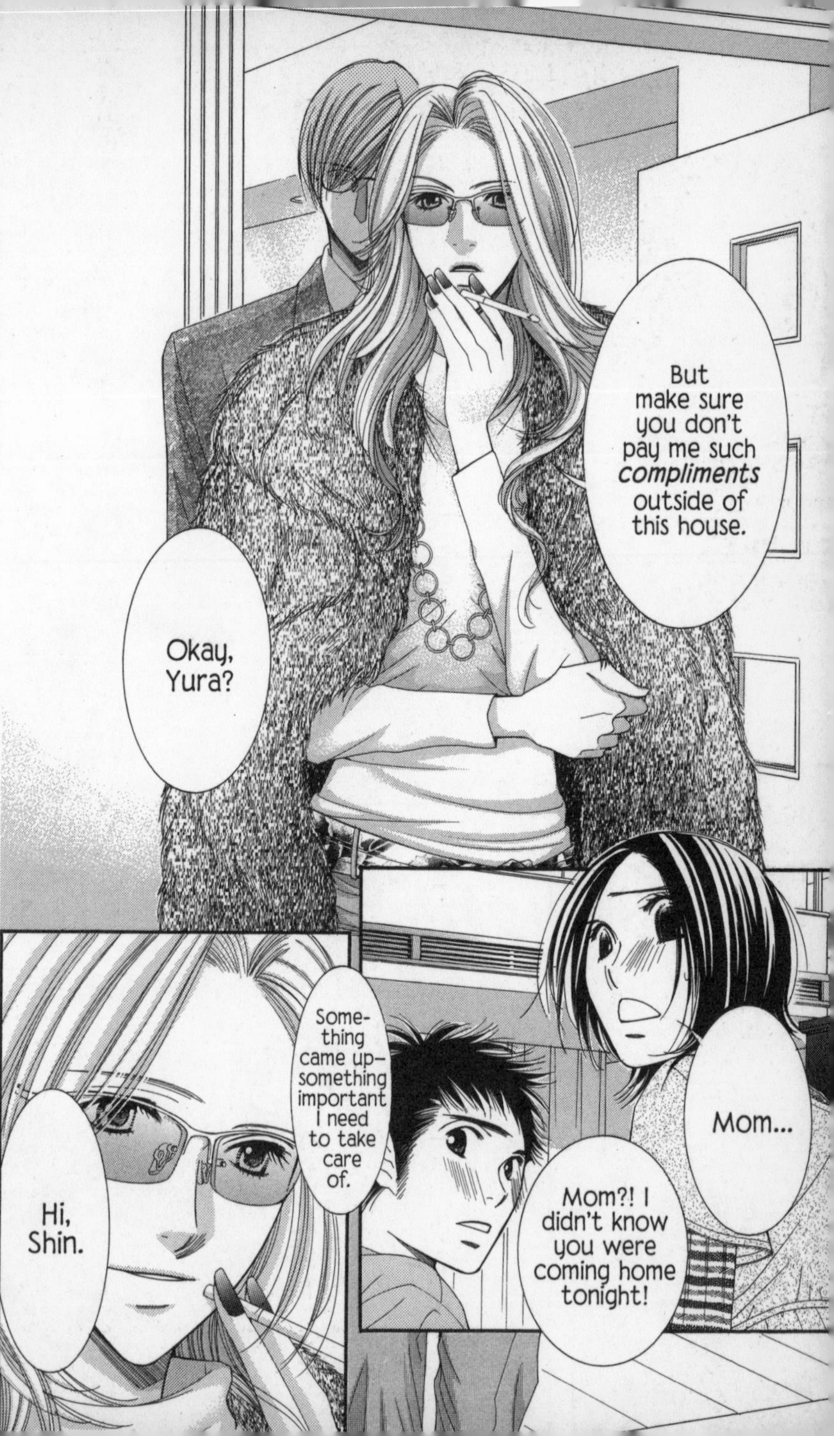
But make sure you don't pay me such *compliments* outside of this house.
Okay, Yura?
Mom...
Mom?! I didn't know you were coming home tonight!
Some-thing came up-something important I need to take care of.
Hi, Shin.

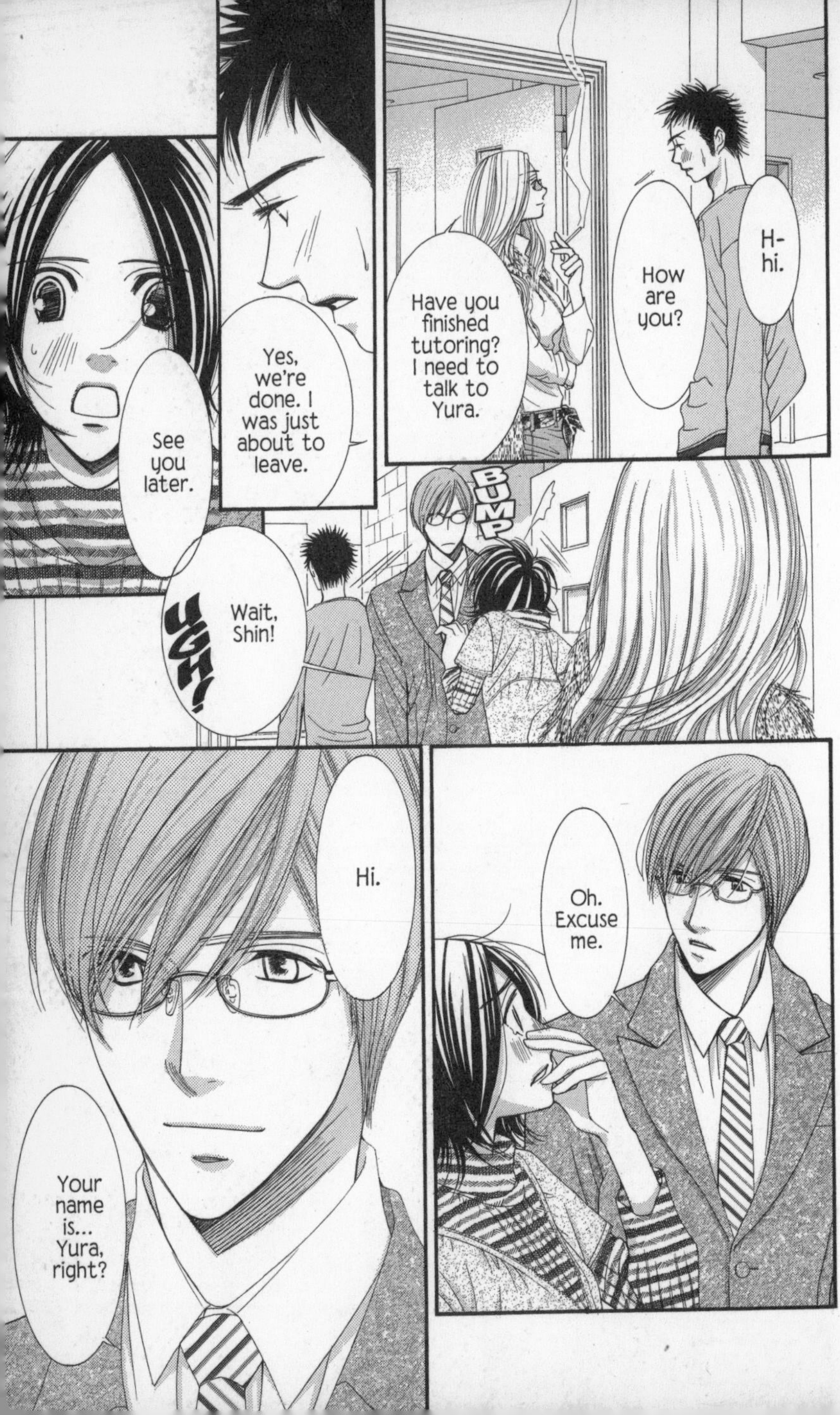
H-hi.
How are you?
Have you finished tutoring? I need to talk to Yura.
Yes, we're done. I was just about to leave.
See you later.
BUMP
Wait, Shin!
UGH!
Oh. Excuse me.
Hi.
Your name is... Yura, right?

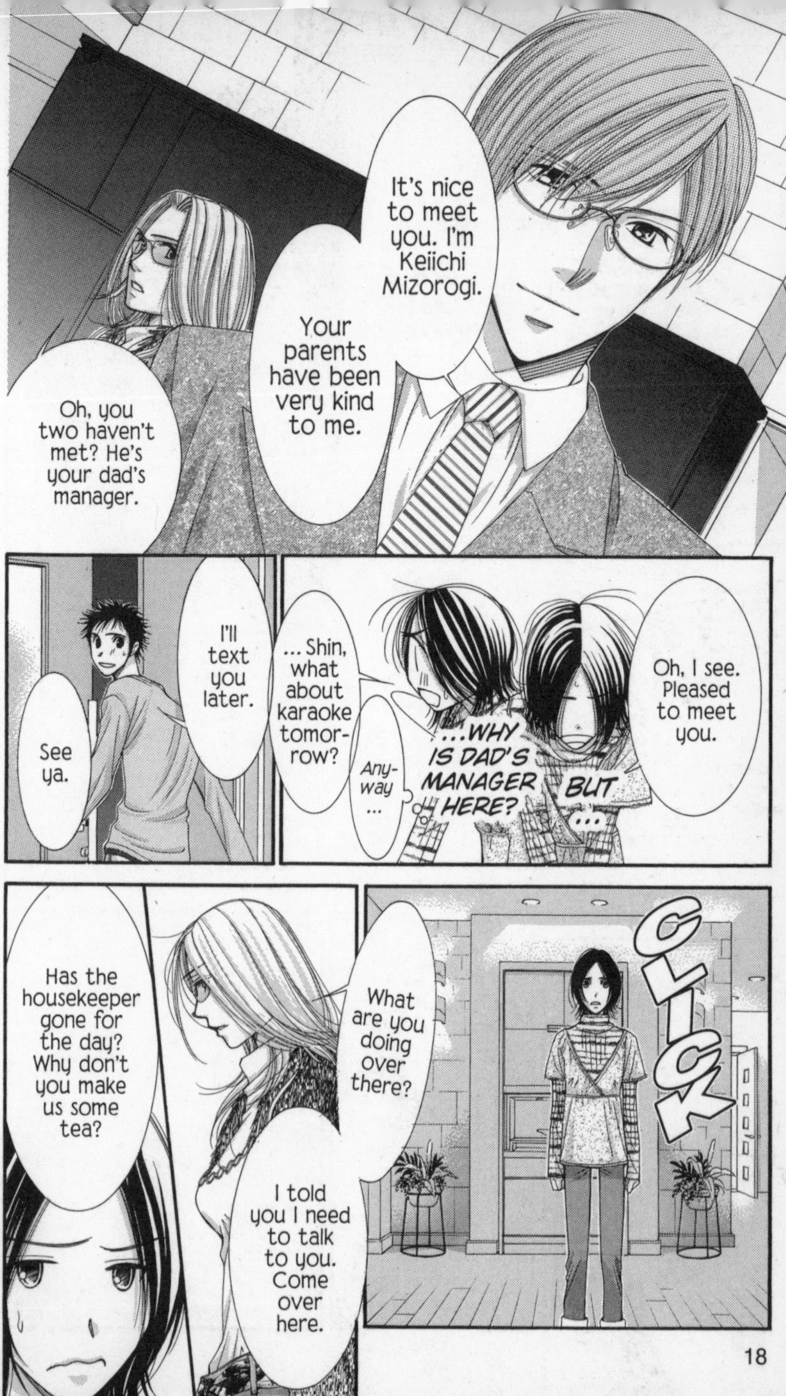
It's nice to meet you. I'm Keiichi Mizorogi.
Your parents have been very kind to me.
Oh, you two haven't met? He's your dad's manager.
Oh, I see. Pleased to meet you.
BUT...
...WHY IS DAD'S MANAGER HERE?
...Shin, what about karaoke tomorrow?
Anyway...
I'll text you later.
See ya.
CLICK
What are you doing over there?
I told you I need to talk to you. Come over here.
Has the housekeeper gone for the day? Why don't you make us some tea?

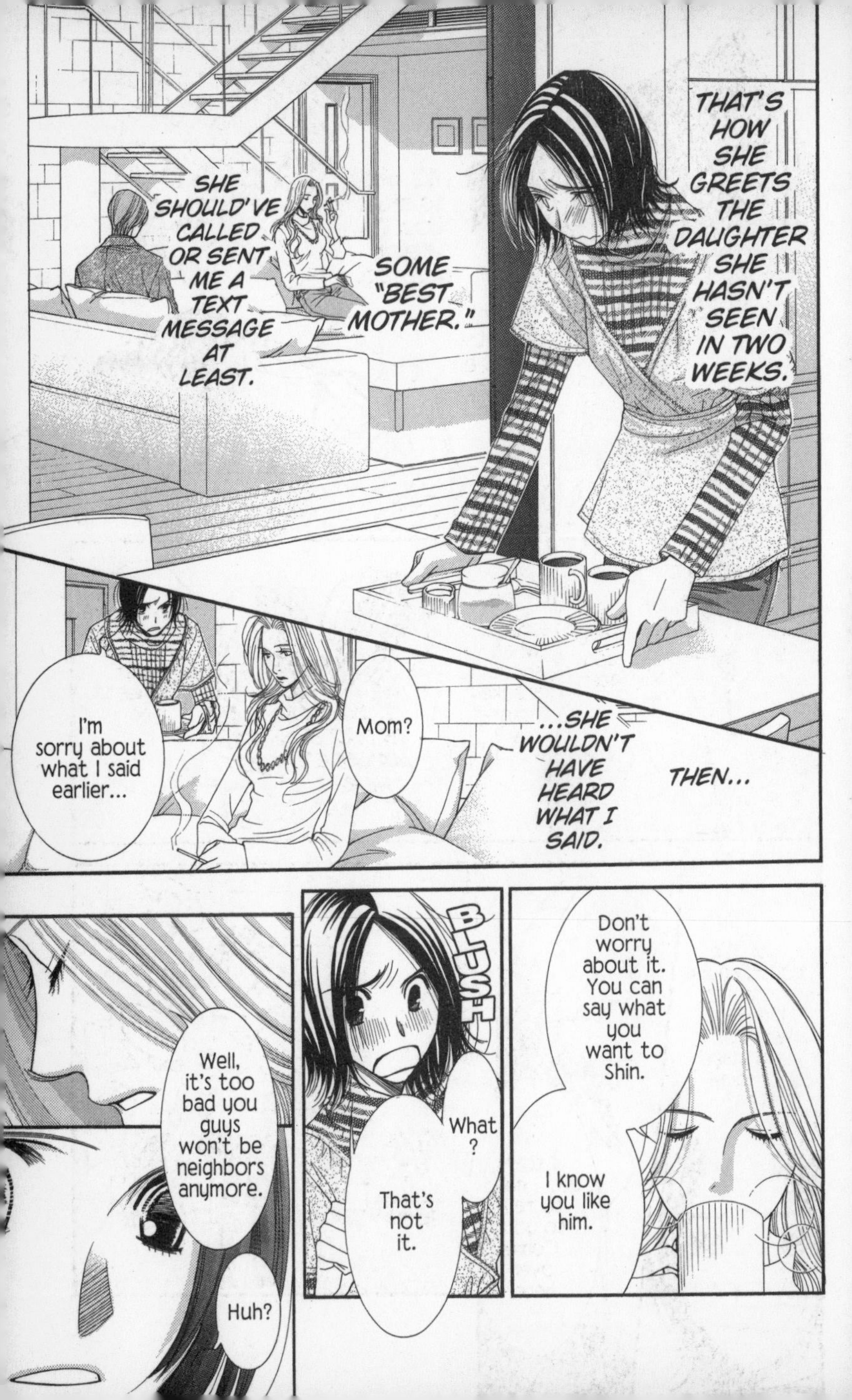
THAT'S HOW SHE GREETS THE DAUGHTER SHE HASN'T SEEN IN TWO WEEKS.
SOME "BEST MOTHER."
SHE SHOULD'VE CALLED OR SENT ME A TEXT MESSAGE AT LEAST.
THEN...
...SHE WOULDN'T HAVE HEARD WHAT I SAID.
Mom?
I'm sorry about what I said earlier...
Don't worry about it. You can say what you want to Shin.
I know you like him.
BLUSH
What?
That's not it.
Well, it's too bad you guys won't be neighbors anymore.
Huh?

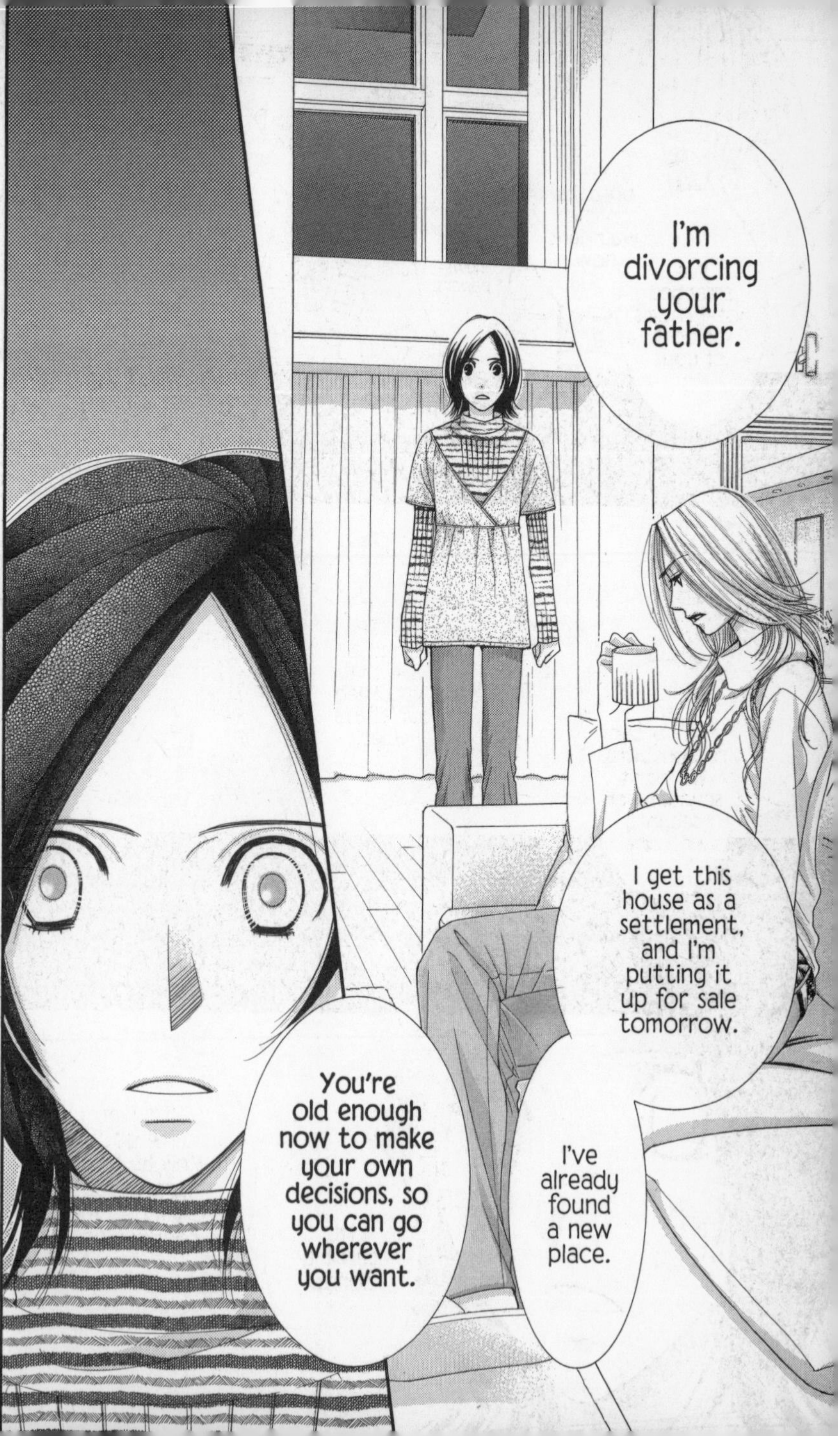
I'm divorcing your father.
I get this house as a settlement, and I'm putting it up for sale tomorrow.
I've already found a new place.
You're old enough now to make your own decisions, so you can go wherever you want.

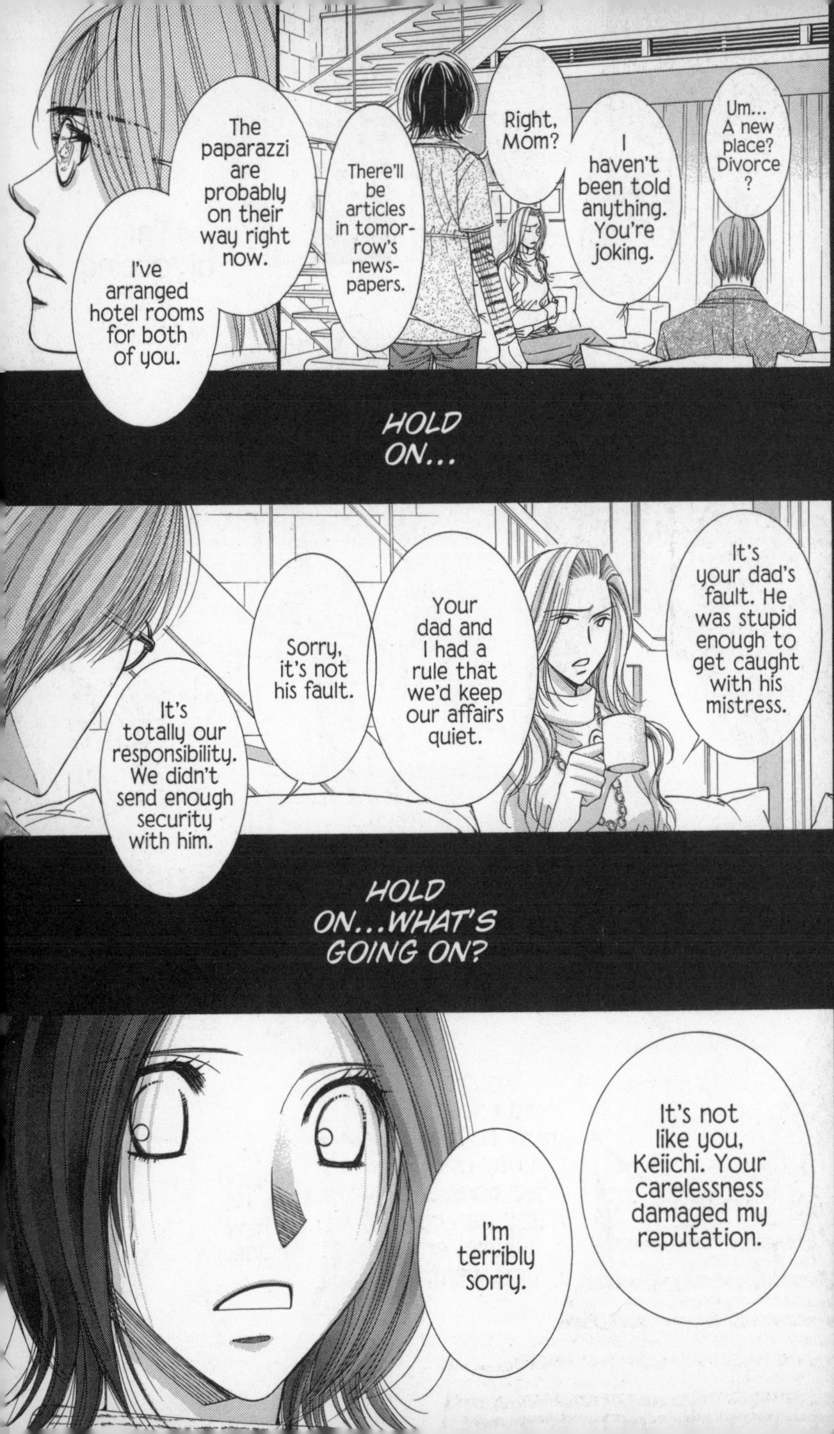
Um... A new place? Divorce?
I haven't been told anything. You're joking.
Right, Mom?
There'll be articles in tomorrow's newspapers.
The paparazzi are probably on their way right now.
I've arranged hotel rooms for both of you.
HOLD ON...
It's your dad's fault. He was stupid enough to get caught with his mistress.
Your dad and I had a rule that we'd keep our affairs quiet.
Sorry, it's not his fault.
It's totally our responsibility. We didn't send enough security with him.
HOLD ON...WHAT'S GOING ON?
It's not like you, Keiichi. Your carelessness damaged my reputation.
I'm terribly sorry.

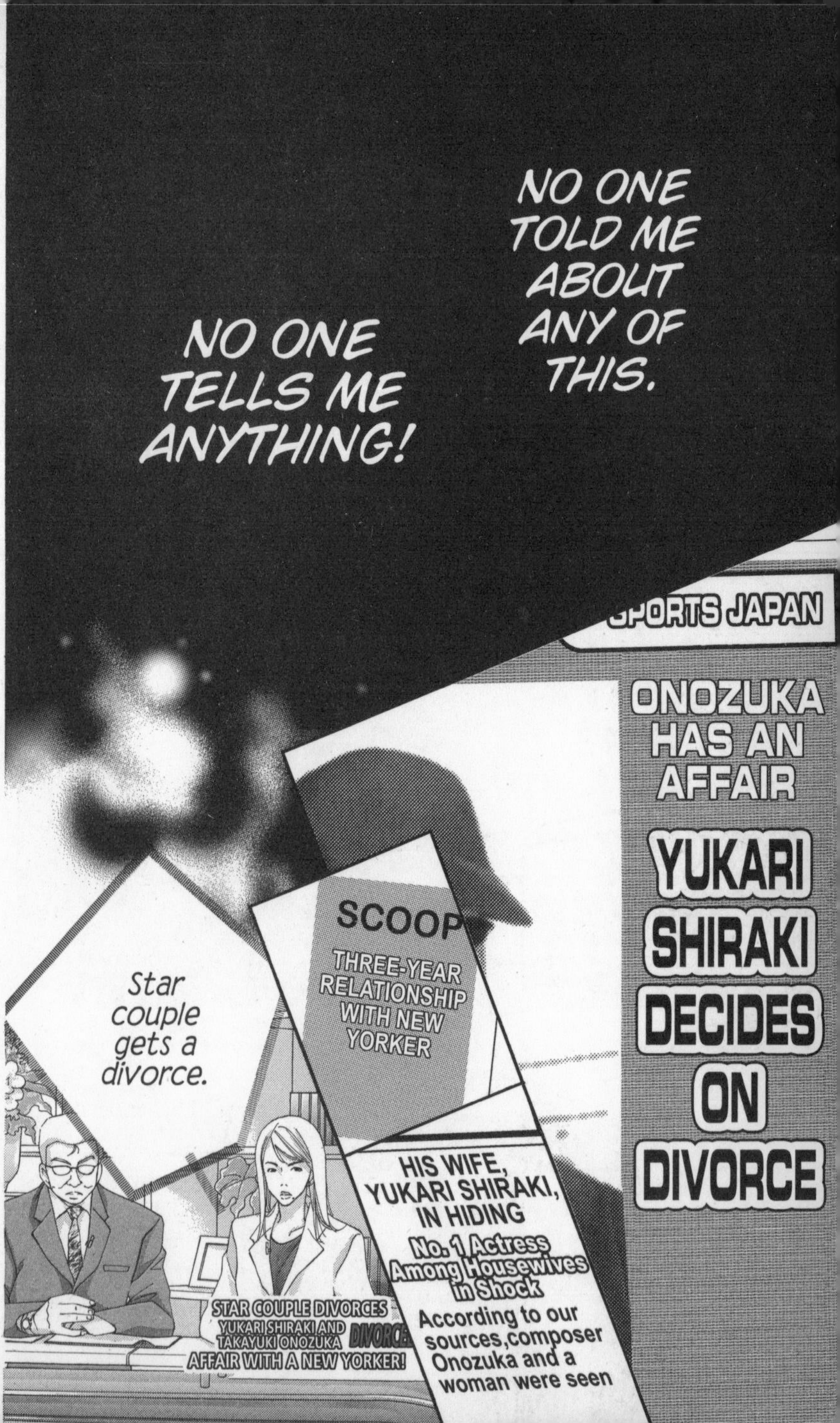
NO ONE TOLD ME ABOUT ANY OF THIS.
NO ONE TELLS ME ANYTHING!
SPORTS JAPAN
ONOZUKA HAS AN AFFAIR
YUKARI SHIRAKI DECIDES ON DIVORCE
SCOOP
THREE-YEAR RELATIONSHIP WITH NEW YORKER
HIS WIFE, YUKARI SHIRAKI, IN HIDING
No. 1 Actress Among Housewives in Shock
According to our sources, composer Onozuka and a woman were seen
Star couple gets a divorce.
STAR COUPLE DIVORCES
YUKARI SHIRAKI AND TAKAYUKI ONOZUKA
DIVORCE
AFFAIR WITH A NEW YORKER!

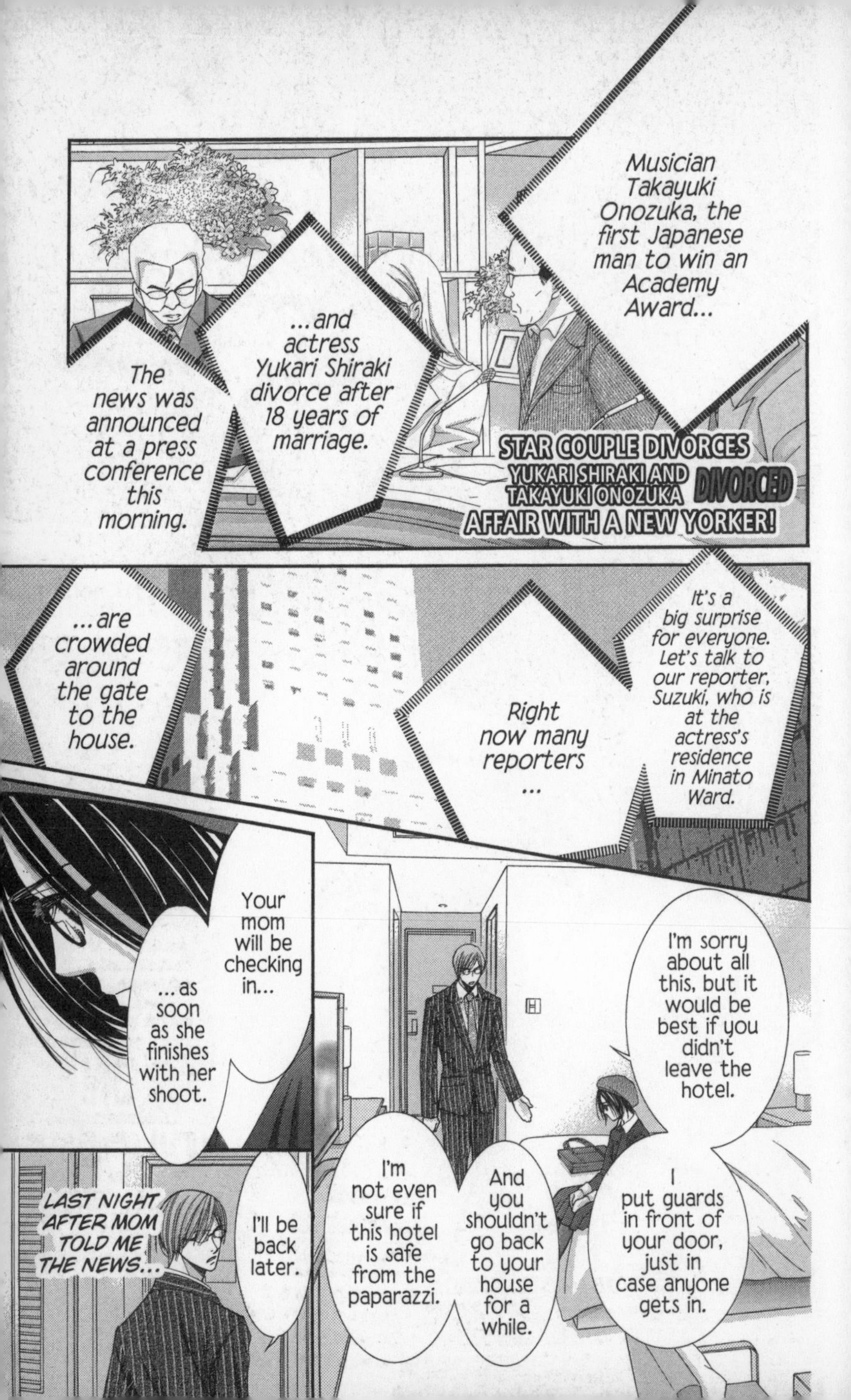

Musician Takayuki Onozuka, the first Japanese man to win an Academy Award...
...and actress Yukari Shiraki divorce after 18 years of marriage.
The news was announced at a press conference this morning.
STAR COUPLE DIVORCES
YUKARI SHIRAKI AND TAKAYUKI ONOZUKA
DIVORCED
AFFAIR WITH A NEW YORKER!
It's a big surprise for everyone. Let's talk to our reporter, Suzuki, who is at the actress's residence in Minato Ward.
Right now many reporters...
...are crowded around the gate to the house.
I'm sorry about all this, but it would be best if you didn't leave the hotel.
I put guards in front of your door, just in case anyone gets in.
And you shouldn't go back to your house for a while.
I'm not even sure if this hotel is safe from the paparazzi.
Your mom will be checking in...
...as soon as she finishes with her shoot.
I'll be back later.
LAST NIGHT AFTER MOM TOLD ME THE NEWS...

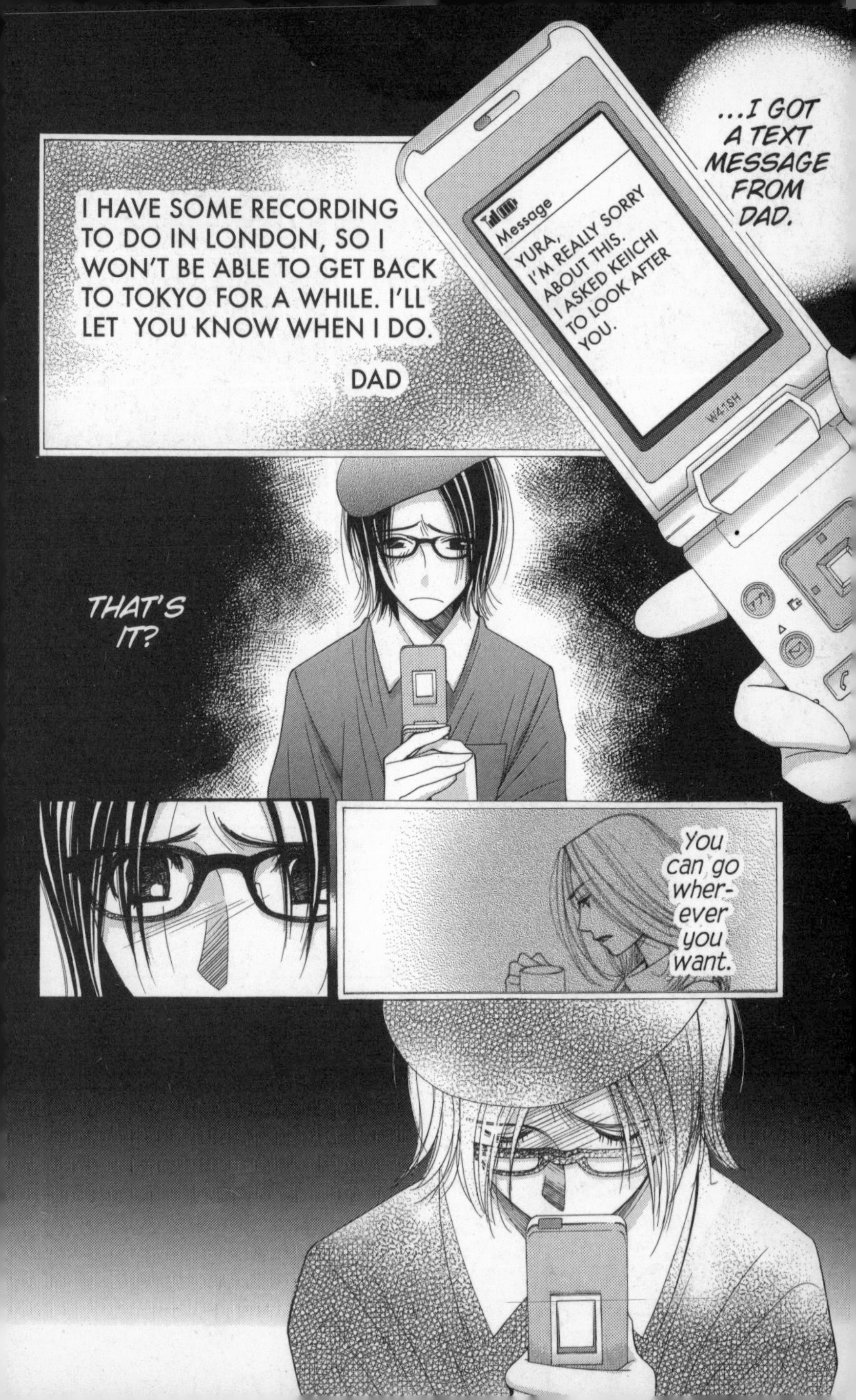
...I GOT A TEXT MESSAGE FROM DAD.
Message
YURA, I'M REALLY SORRY ABOUT THIS. I ASKED KEIICHI TO LOOK AFTER YOU.
I HAVE SOME RECORDING TO DO IN LONDON, SO I WON'T BE ABLE TO GET BACK TO TOKYO FOR A WHILE. I'LL LET YOU KNOW WHEN I DO.
DAD
THAT'S IT?
You can go wher-ever you want.

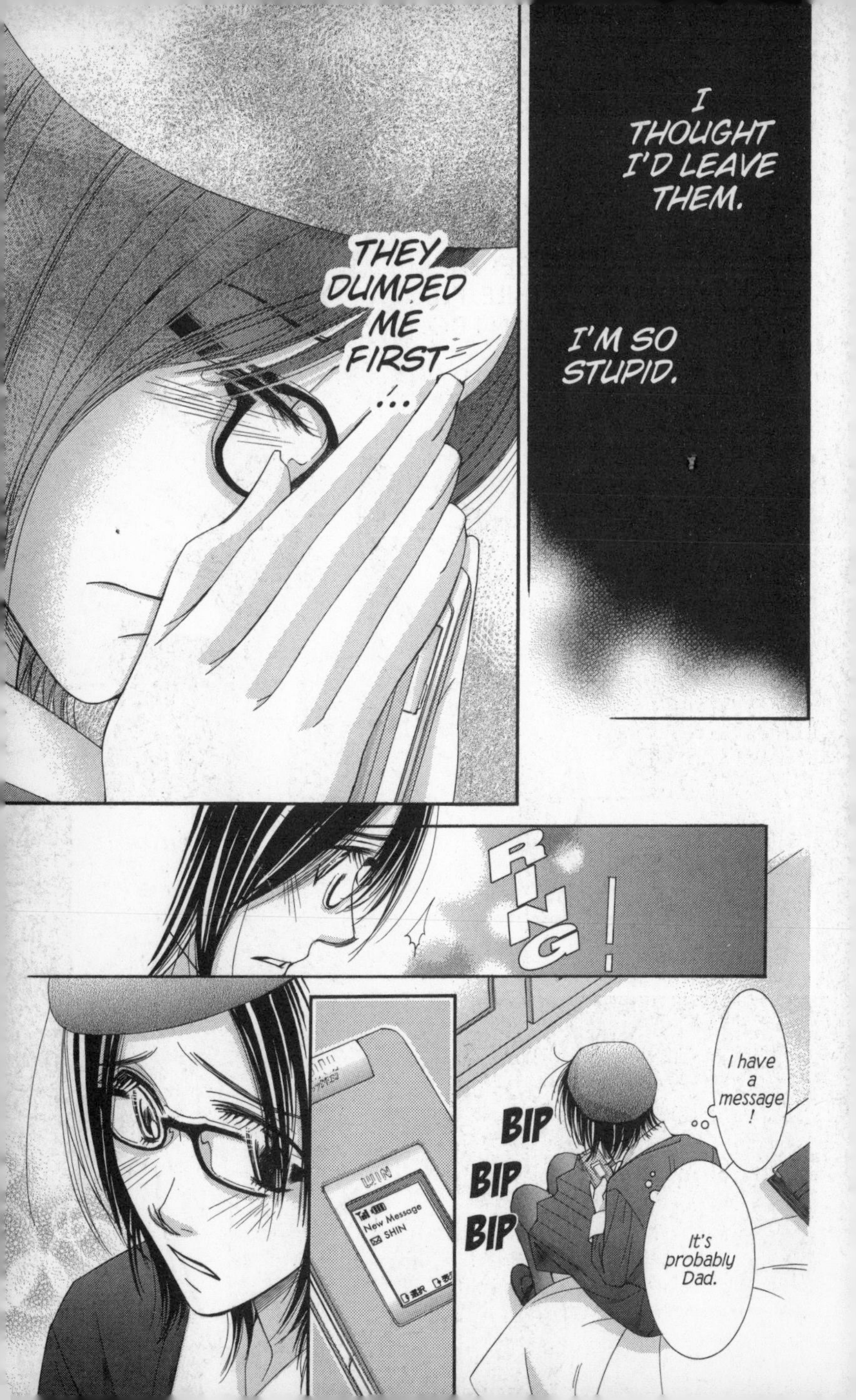
I THOUGHT I'D LEAVE THEM.
I'M SO STUPID.
THEY DUMPED ME FIRST ...
RING !
BIP
BIP
BIP
I have a message !
It's probably Dad.
New Message
SHIN

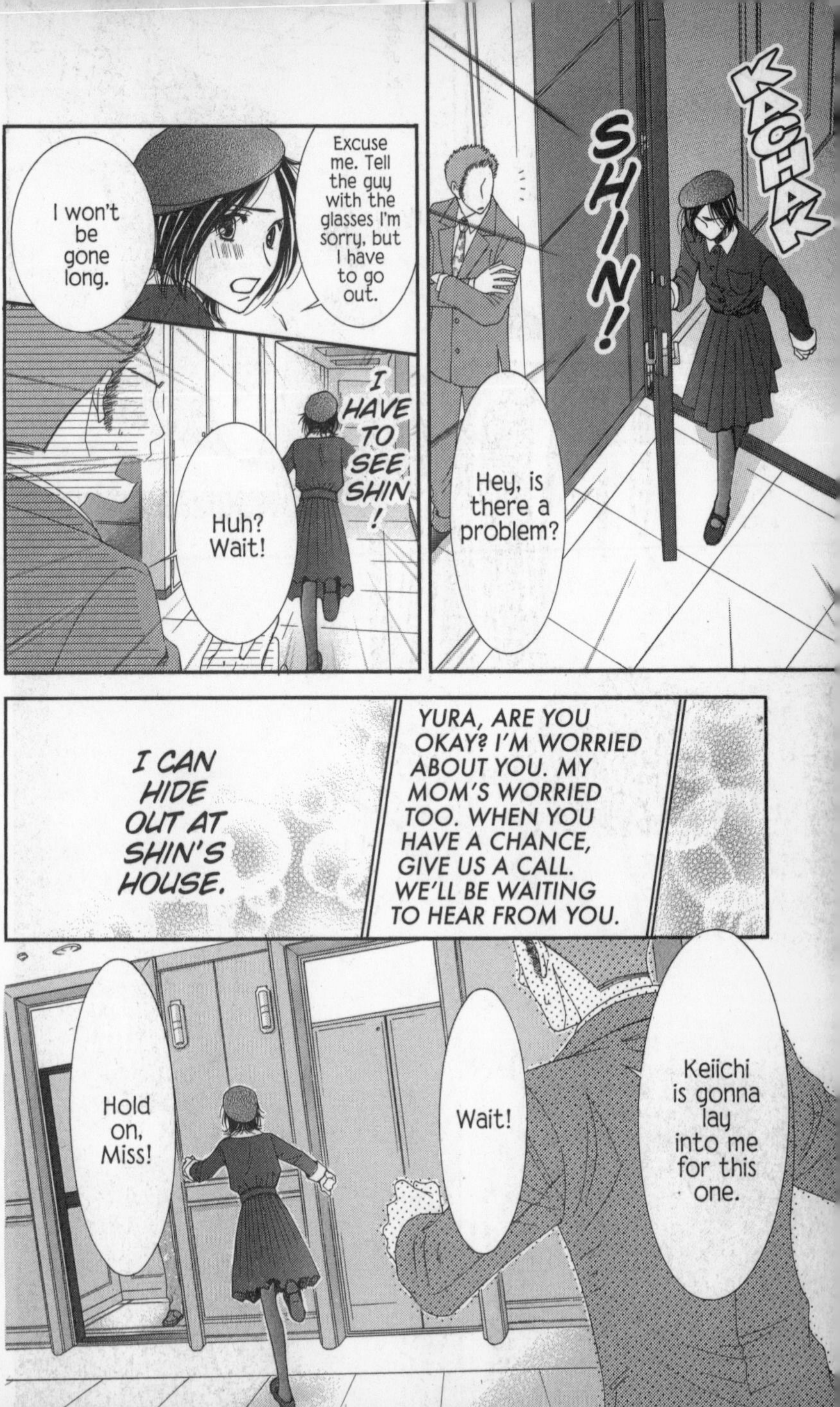
KACHAK
SHIN!
Hey, is there a problem?
Excuse me. Tell the guy with the glasses I'm sorry, but I have to go out.
I won't be gone long.
I HAVE TO SEE SHIN!
Huh? Wait!
YURA, ARE YOU OKAY? I'M WORRIED ABOUT YOU. MY MOM'S WORRIED TOO. WHEN YOU HAVE A CHANCE, GIVE US A CALL. WE'LL BE WAITING TO HEAR FROM YOU.
I CAN HIDE OUT AT SHIN'S HOUSE.
Keiichi is gonna lay into me for this one.
Wait!
Hold on, Miss!

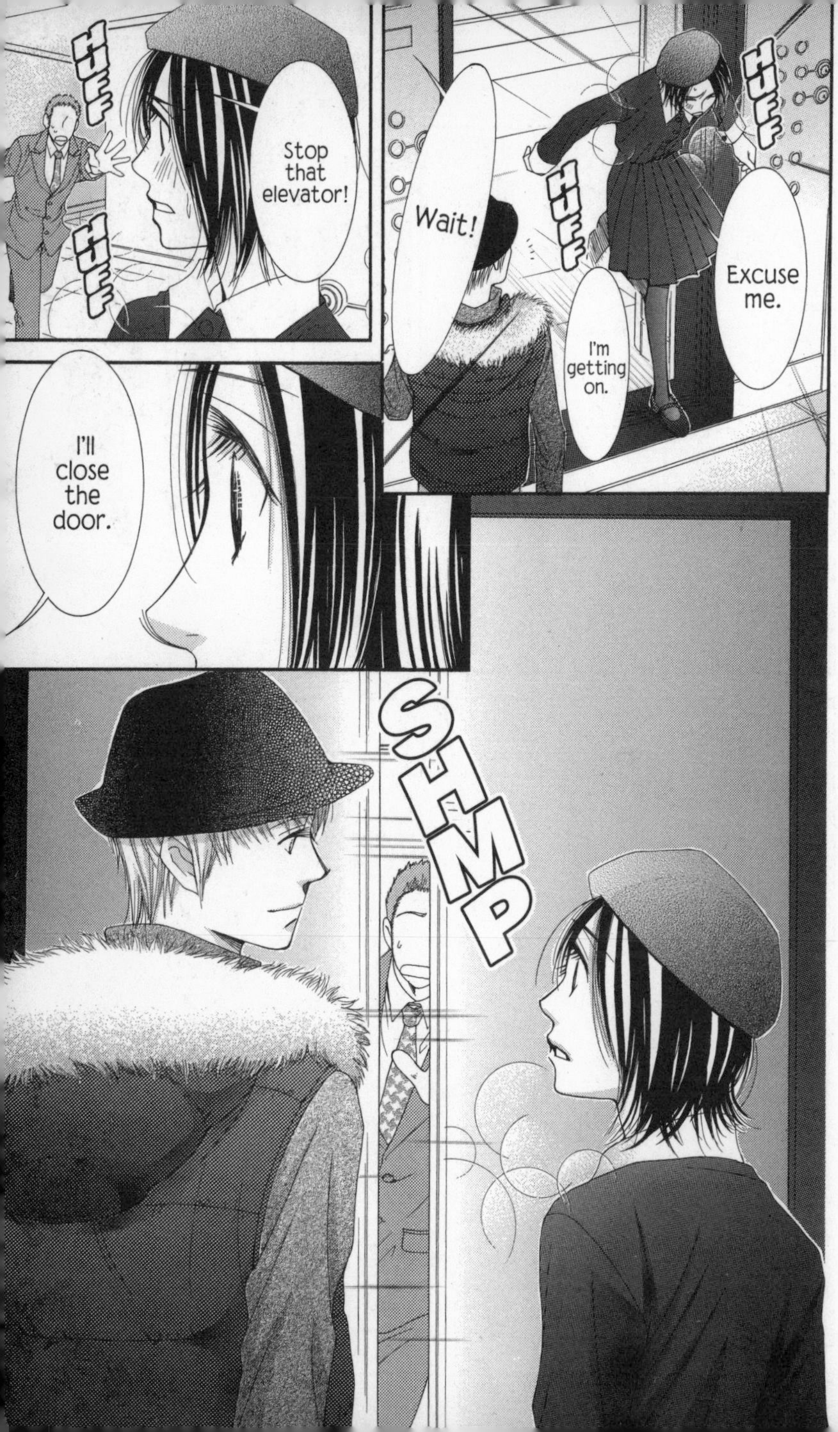

HUFF
HUFF
Excuse me.
I'm getting on.
Wait!
Stop that elevator!
HUFF
HUFF
I'll close the door.
SHMP

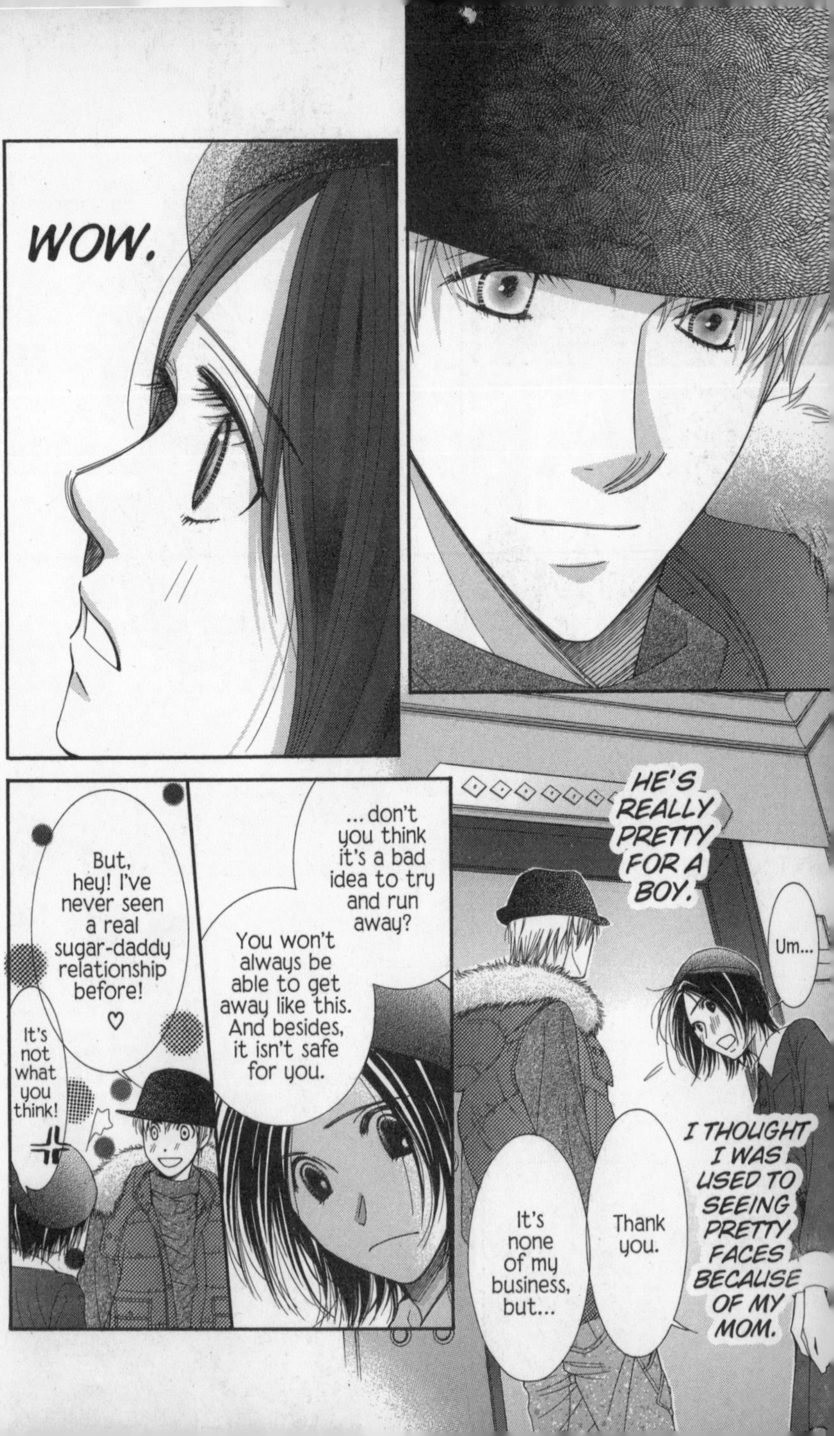
WOW.
HE'S REALLY PRETTY FOR A BOY.
Um...
I THOUGHT I WAS USED TO SEEING PRETTY FACES BECAUSE OF MY MOM.
Thank you.
It's none of my business, but...
...don't you think it's a bad idea to try and run away?
You won't always be able to get away like this. And besides, it isn't safe for you.
But, hey! I've never seen a real sugar-daddy relationship before! ♡
It's not what you think!

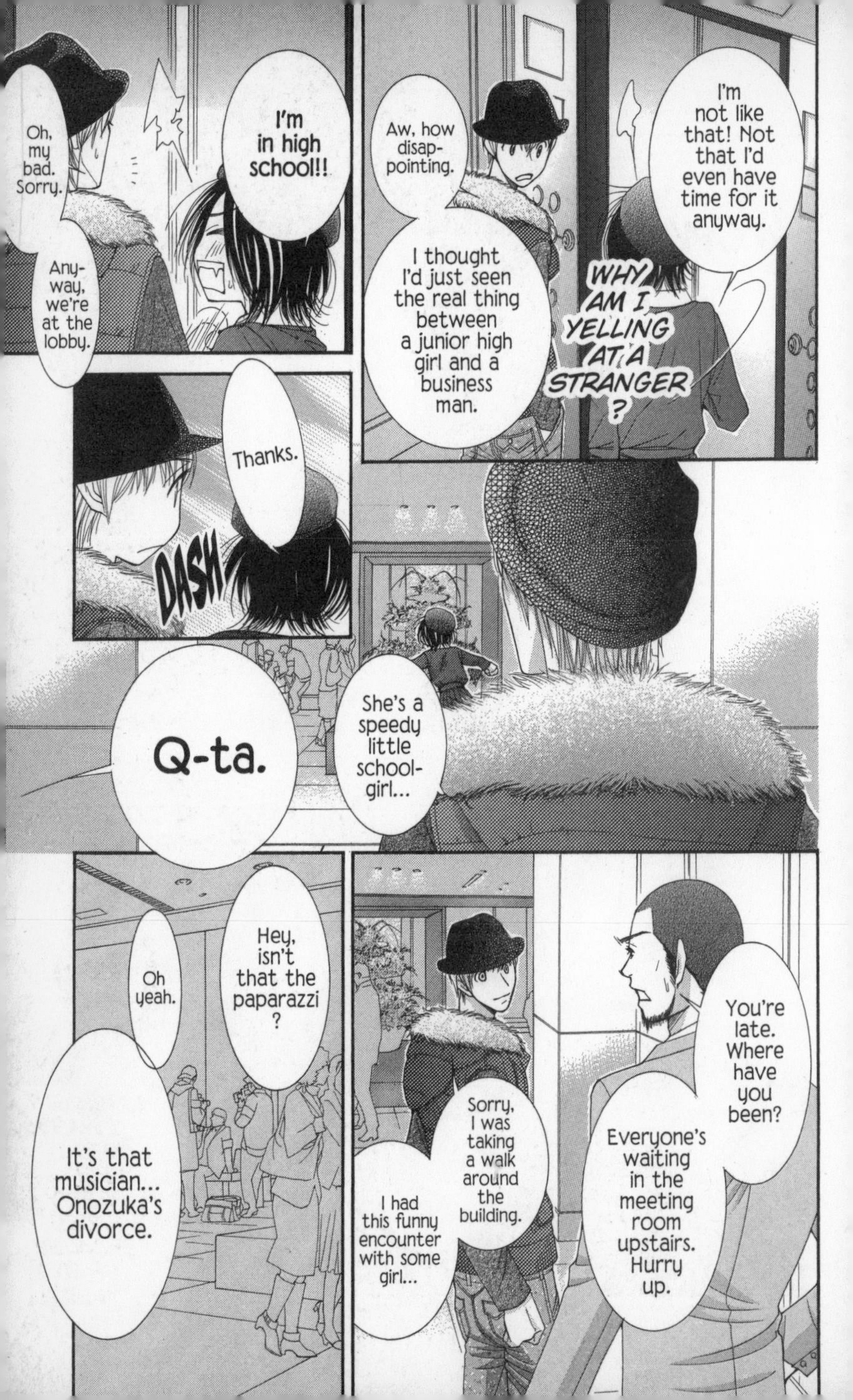
I'm not like that! Not that I'd even have time for it anyway.
WHY AM I YELLING AT A STRANGER?
Aw, how disap-pointing.
I thought I'd just seen the real thing between a junior high girl and a business man.
I'm in high school!!
Oh, my bad. Sorry.
Any-way, we're at the lobby.
Thanks.
DASH
She's a speedy little school-girl...
Q-ta.
You're late. Where have you been?
Everyone's waiting in the meeting room upstairs. Hurry up.
Sorry, I was taking a walk around the building.
I had this funny encounter with some girl...
Hey, isn't that the paparazzi?
Oh yeah.
It's that musician... Onozuka's divorce.

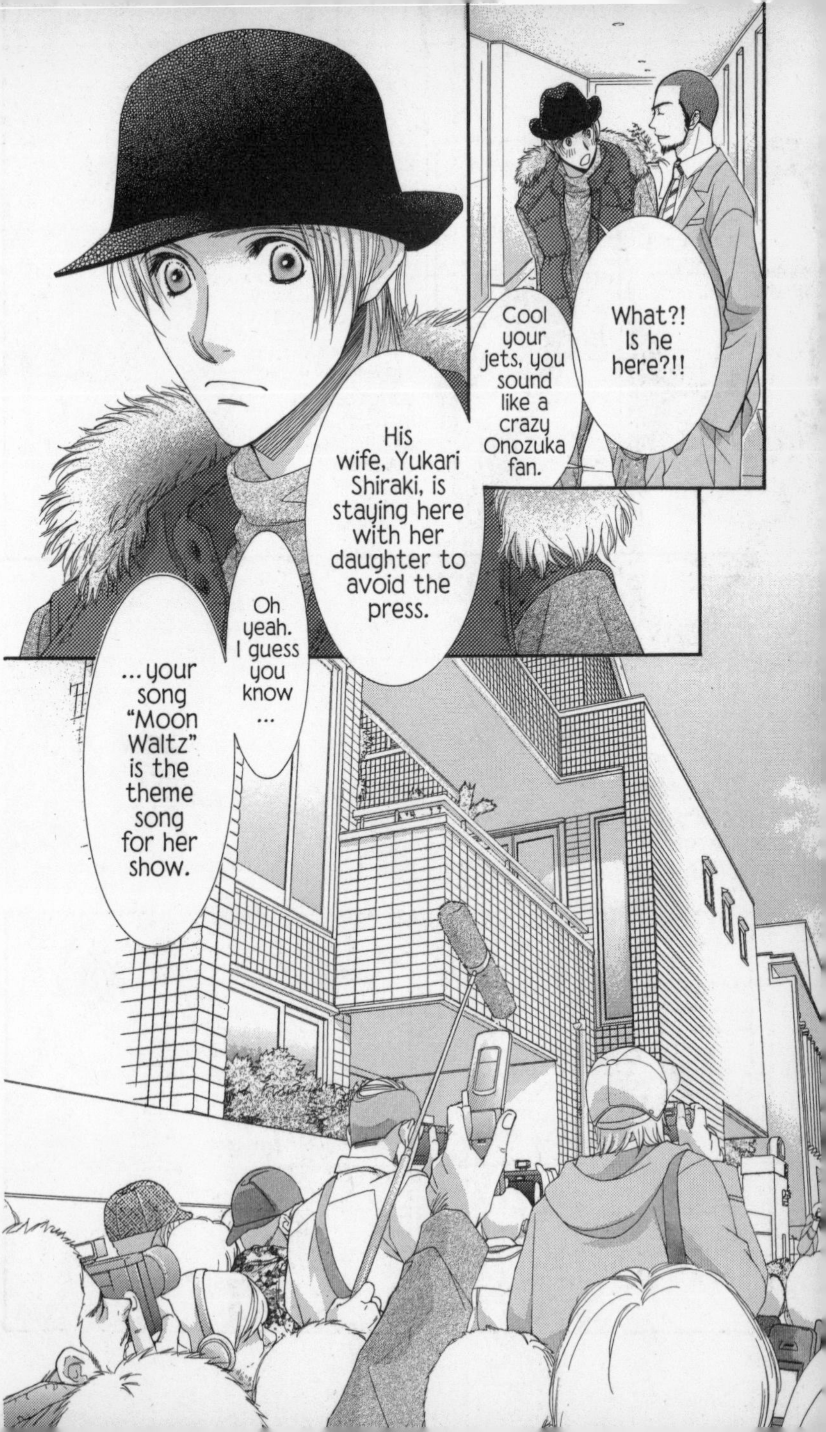
What?! Is he here?!!
Cool your jets, you sound like a crazy Onozuka fan.
His wife, Yukari Shiraki, is staying here with her daughter to avoid the press.
Oh yeah. I guess you know...
...your song "Moon Waltz" is the theme song for her show.

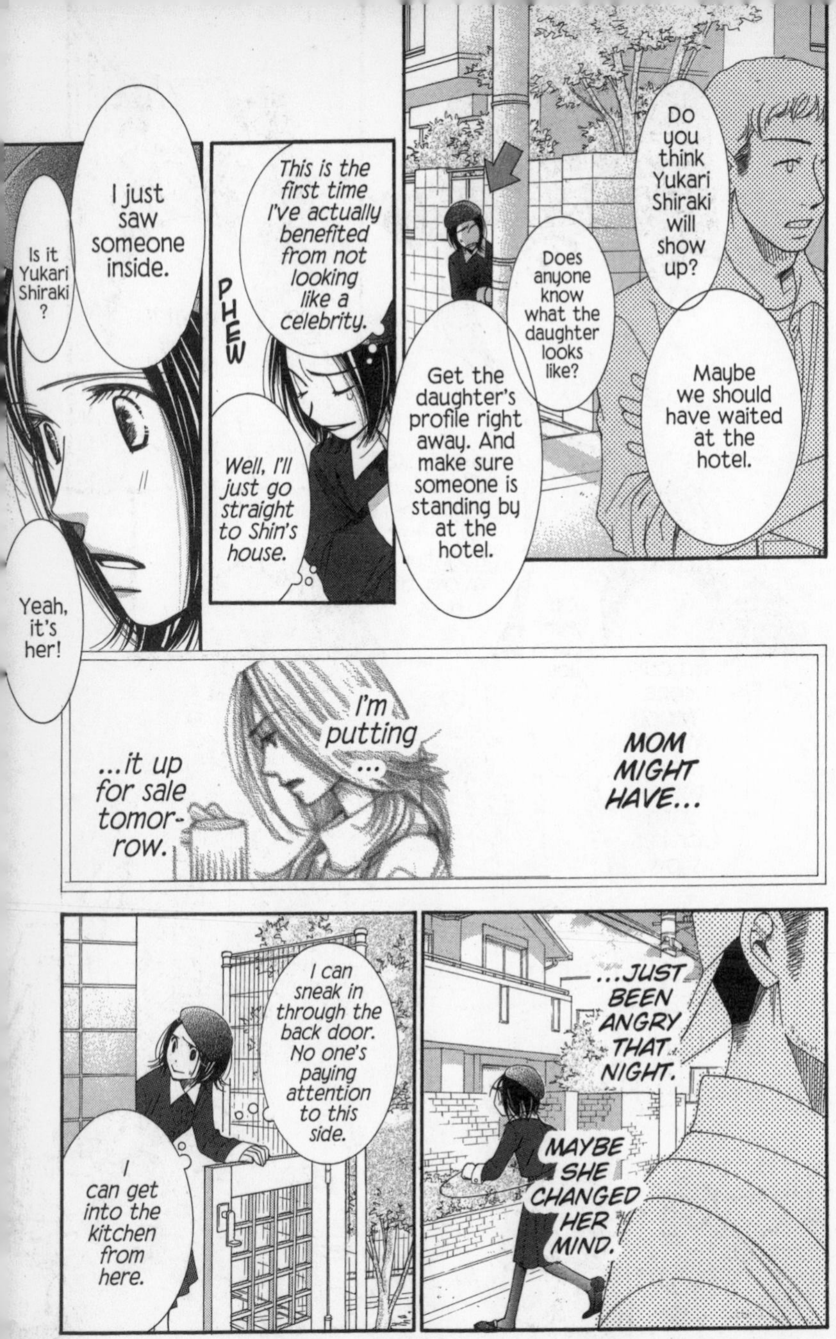
Do you think Yukari Shiraki will show up?
Maybe we should have waited at the hotel.
Does anyone know what the daughter looks like?
Get the daughter's profile right away. And make sure someone is standing by at the hotel.
This is the first time I've actually benefited from not looking like a celebrity.
PHEW
Well, I'll just go straight to Shin's house.
I just saw someone inside.
Is it Yukari Shiraki?
Yeah, it's her!
MOM MIGHT HAVE...
I'm putting...
...it up for sale tomorrow.
...JUST BEEN ANGRY THAT NIGHT.
MAYBE SHE CHANGED HER MIND.
I can sneak in through the back door. No one's paying attention to this side.
I can get into the kitchen from here.

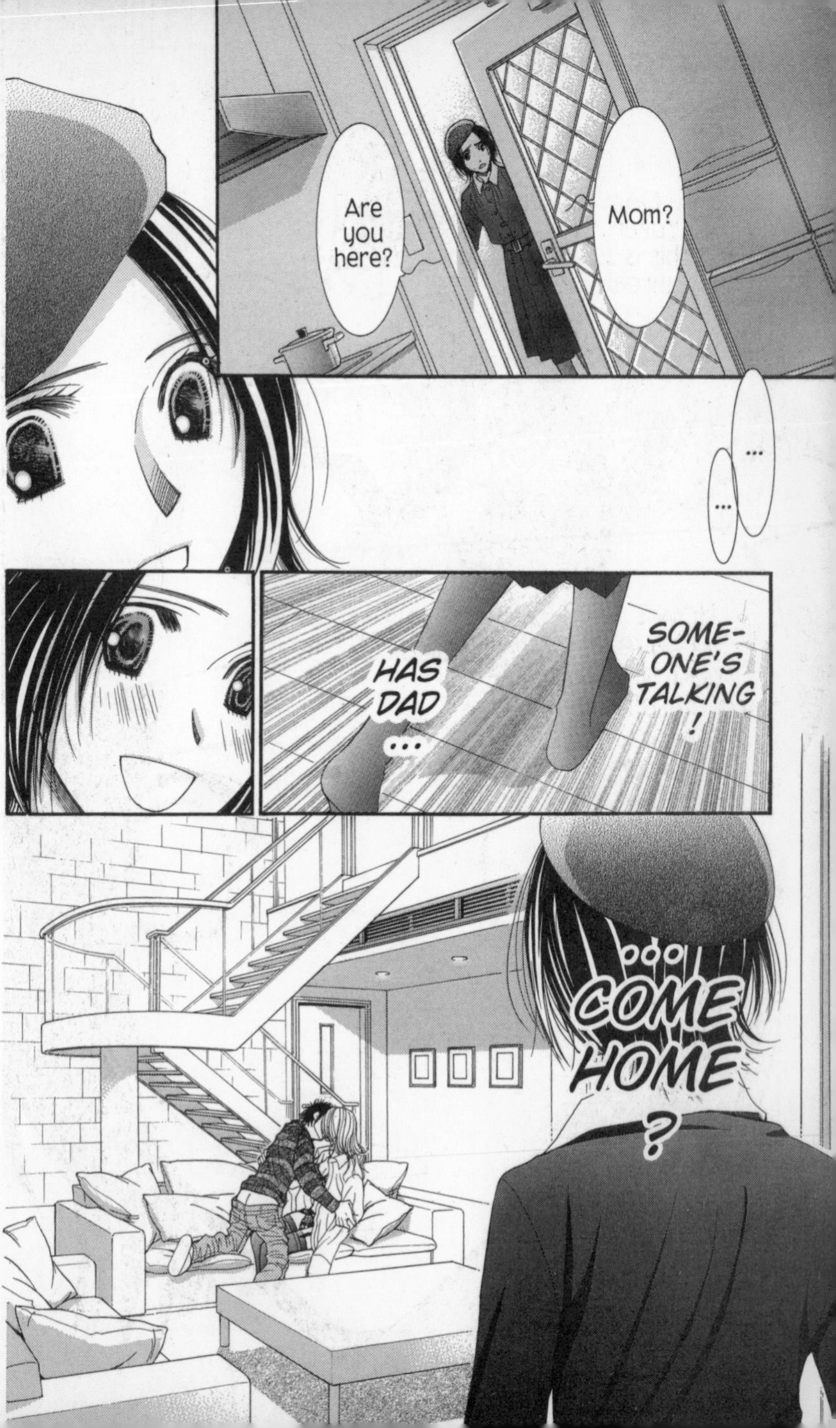
Mom?
Are you here?
...
...
SOME-ONE'S TALKING!
HAS DAD ...
...COME HOME?

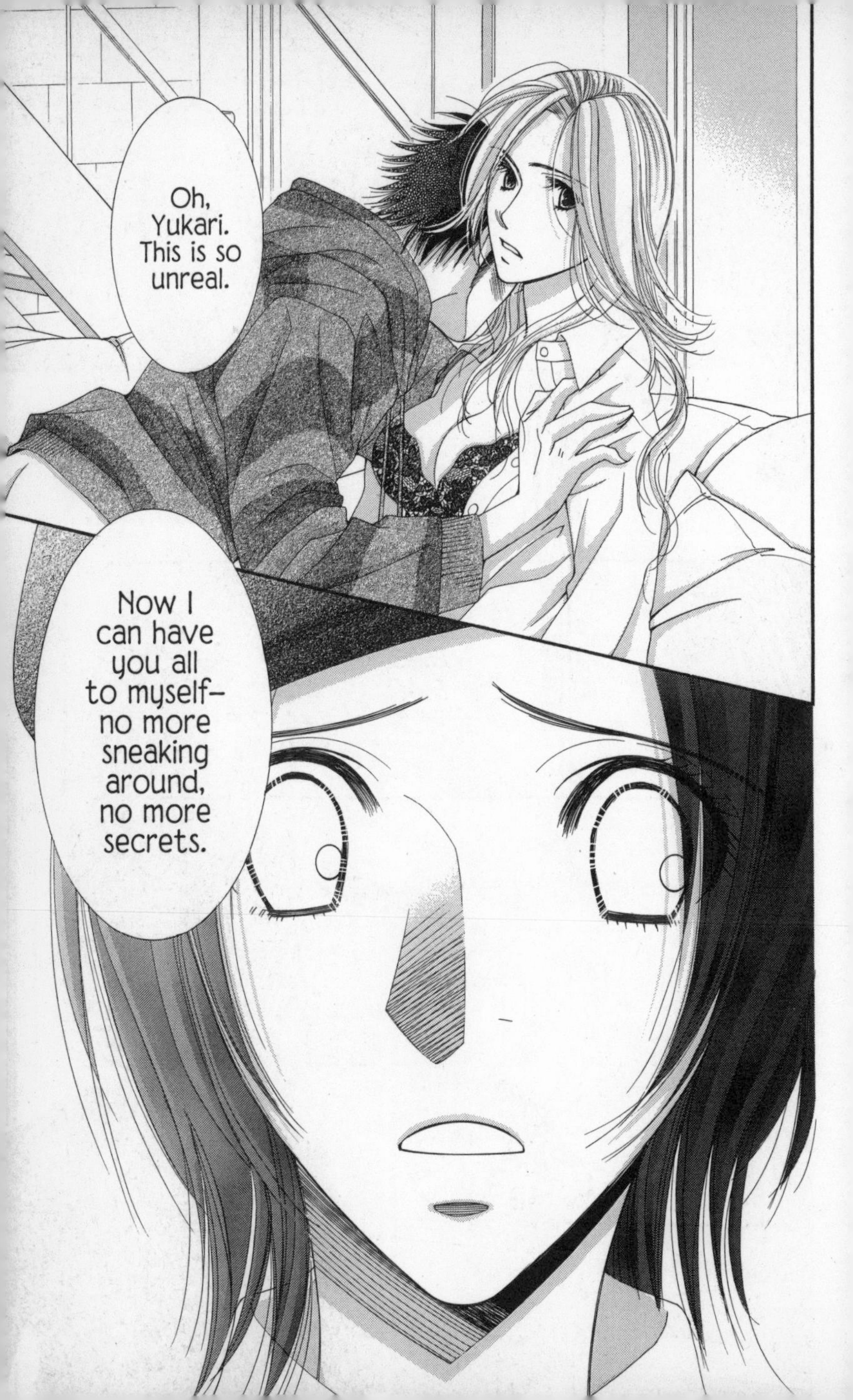
Oh, Yukari. This is so unreal.
Now I can have you all to myself– no more sneaking around, no more secrets.

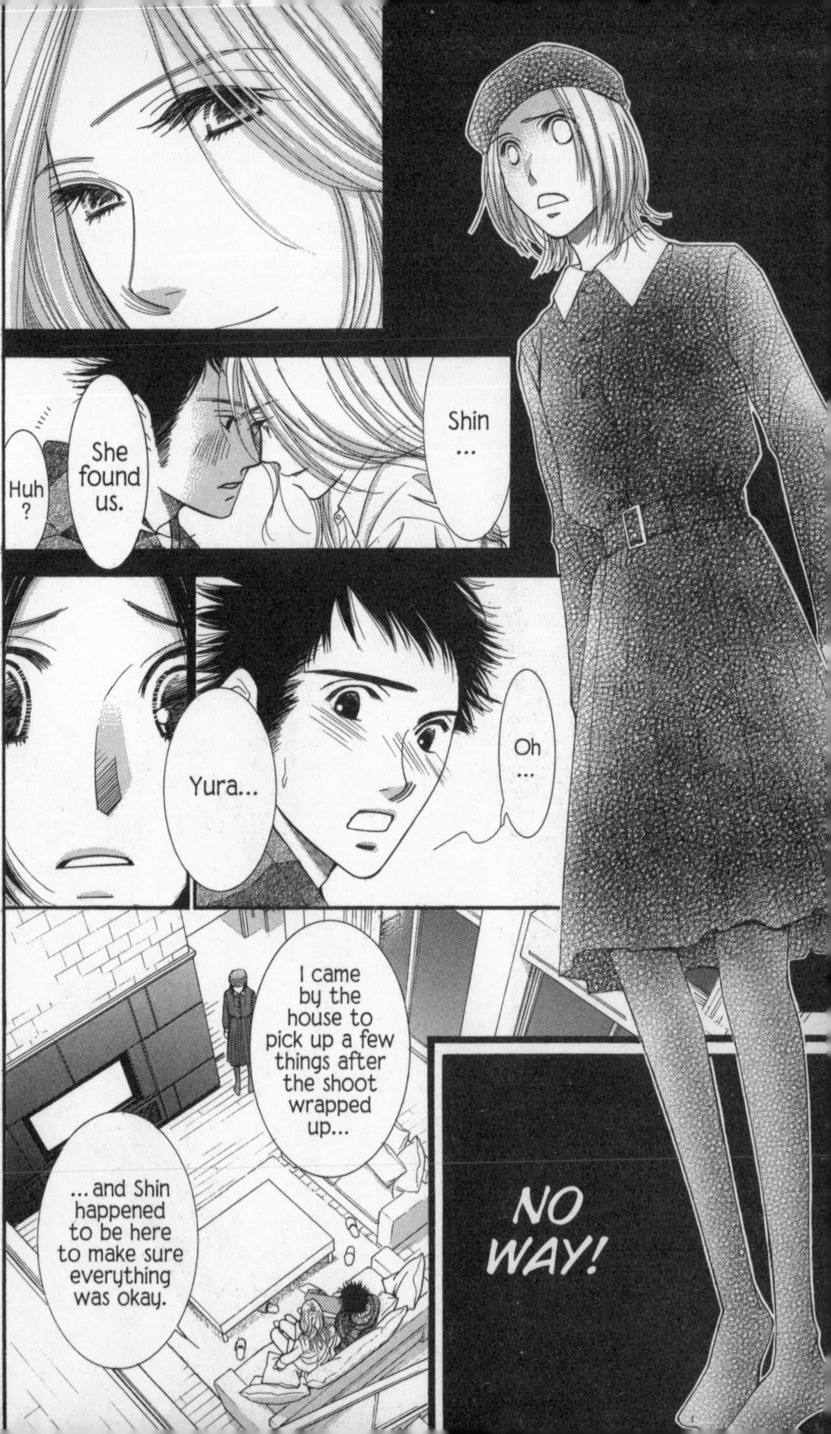
NO WAY!
Shin ...
She found us.
Huh ?
Oh ...
Yura...
I came by the house to pick up a few things after the shoot wrapped up...
... and Shin happened to be here to make sure everything was okay.

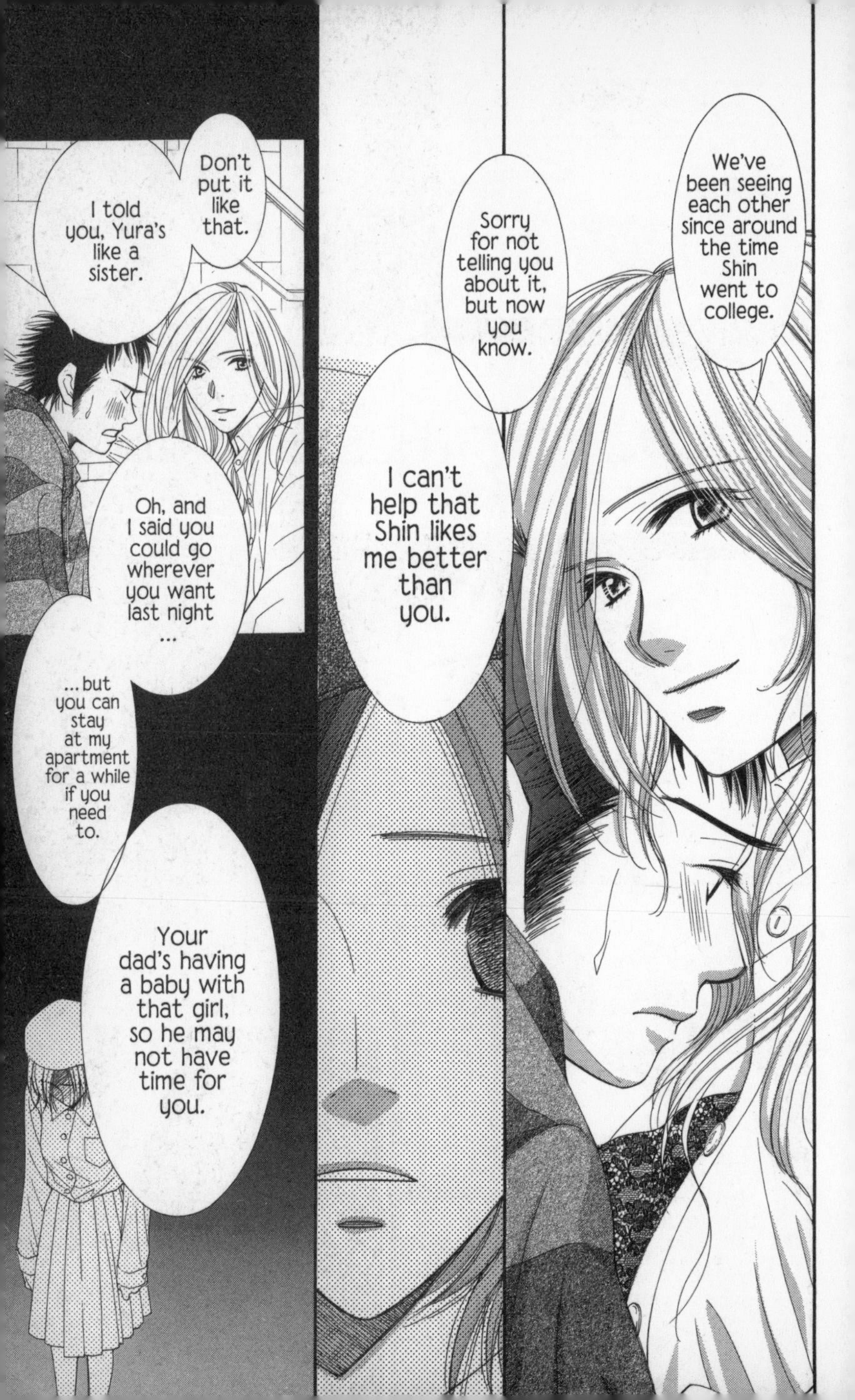
We've been seeing each other since around the time Shin went to college.
Sorry for not telling you about it, but now you know.
I can't help that Shin likes me better than you.
Don't put it like that.
I told you, Yura's like a sister.
Oh, and I said you could go wherever you want last night ...
... but you can stay at my apartment for a while if you need to.
Your dad's having a baby with that girl, so he may not have time for you.

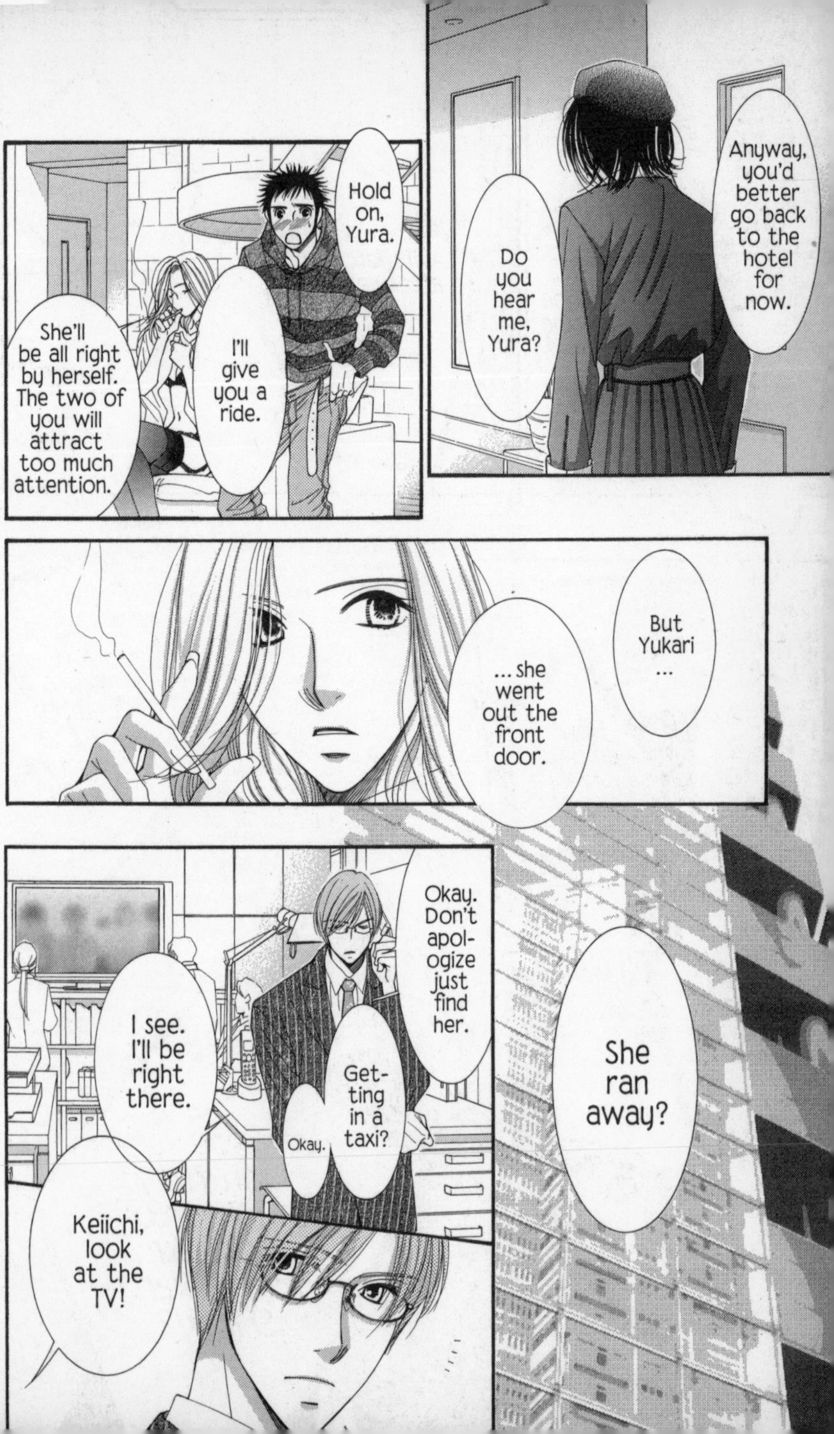
Anyway, you'd better go back to the hotel for now.
Do you hear me, Yura?
Hold on, Yura.
I'll give you a ride.
She'll be all right by herself. The two of you will attract too much attention.
But Yukari ...
... she went out the front door.
She ran away?
Okay. Don't apologize just find her.
Getting in a taxi?
Okay.
I see. I'll be right there.
Keiichi, look at the TV!

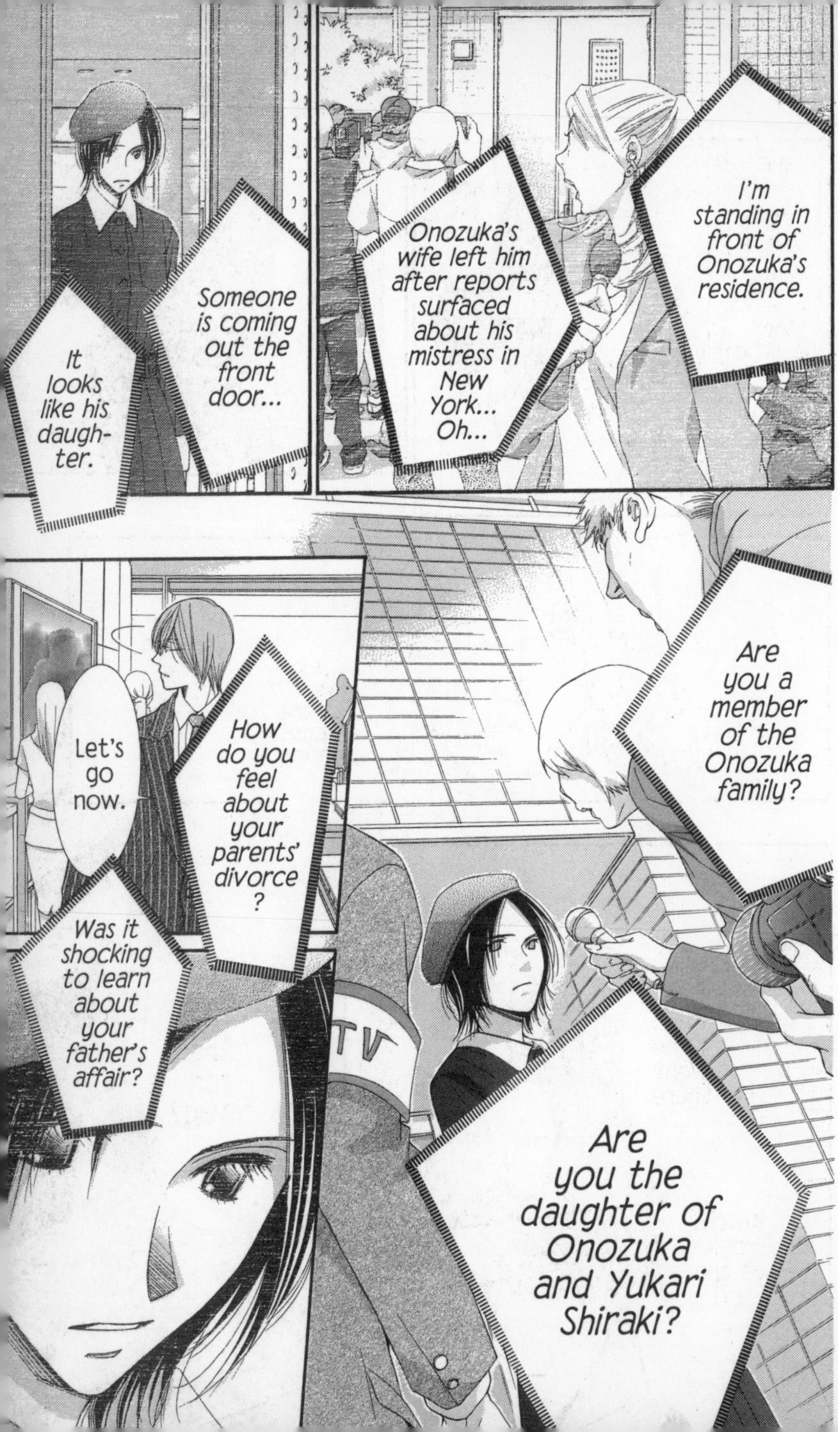
I'm standing in front of Onozuka's residence.
Onozuka's wife left him after reports surfaced about his mistress in New York... Oh...
Someone is coming out the front door...
It looks like his daughter.
Are you a member of the Onozuka family?
Are you the daughter of Onozuka and Yukari Shiraki?
How do you feel about your parents' divorce?
Let's go now.
Was it shocking to learn about your father's affair?

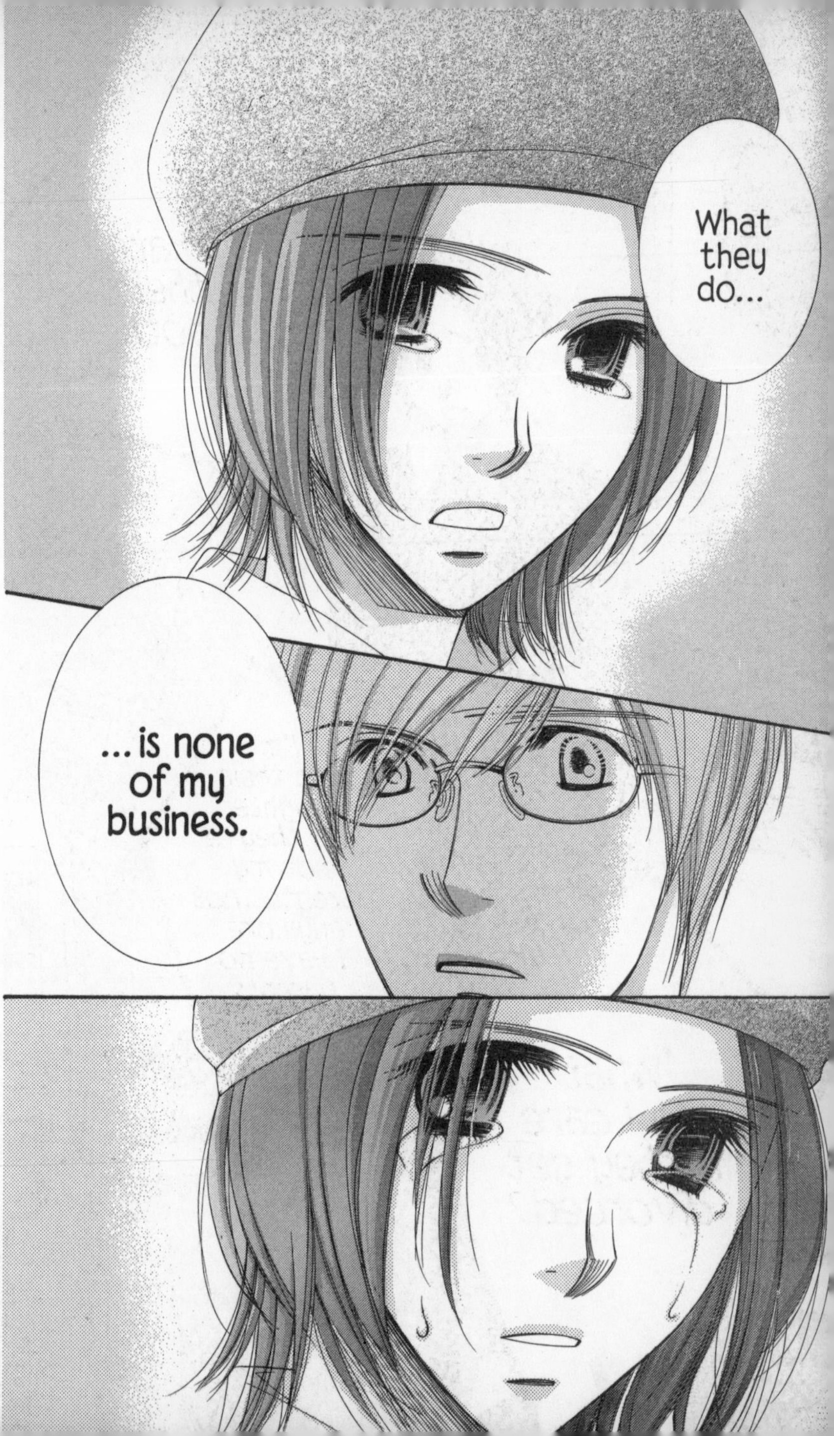
What they do...
...is none of my business.

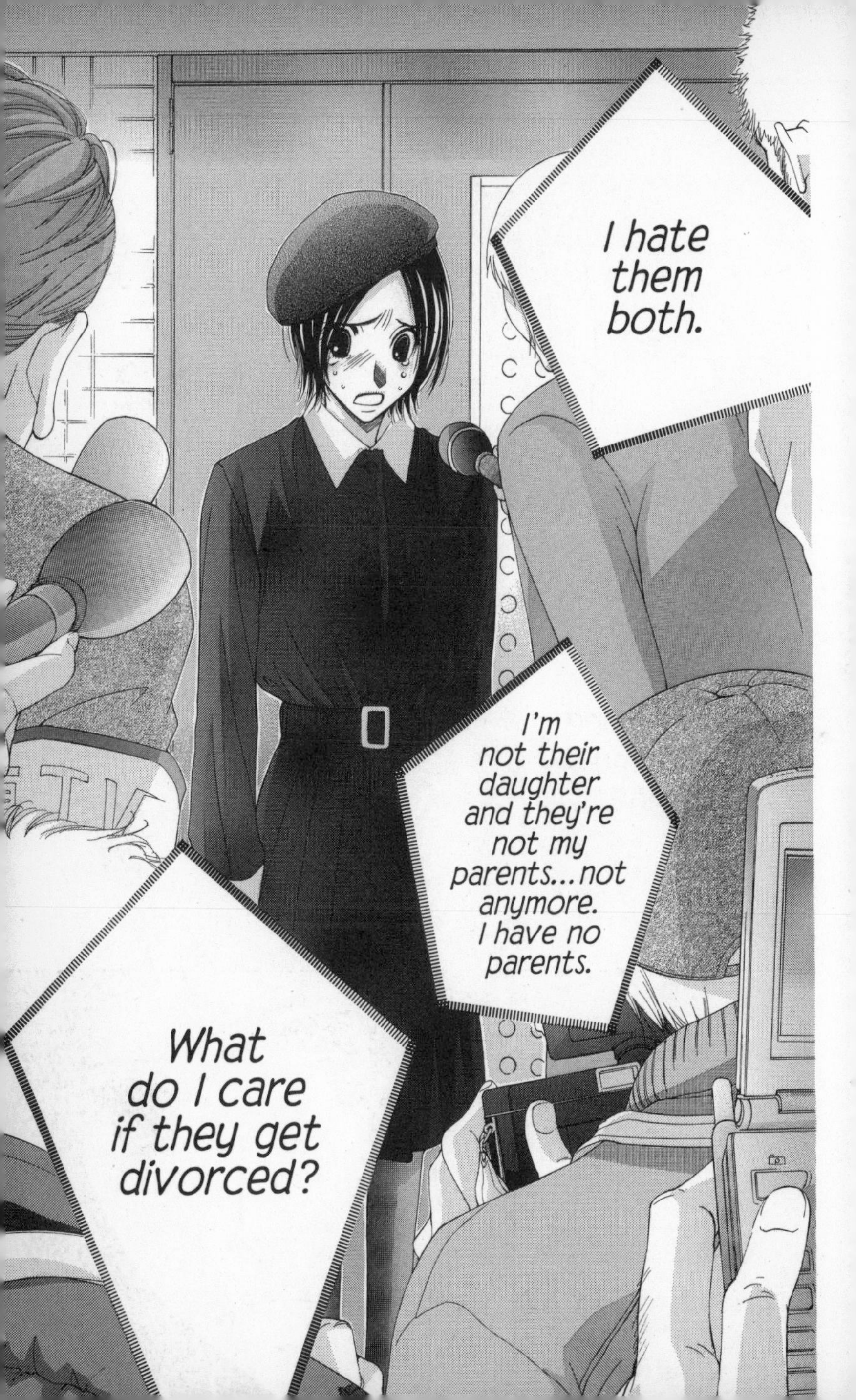
I hate them both.
I'm not their daughter and they're not my parents...not anymore. I have no parents.
What do I care if they get divorced?

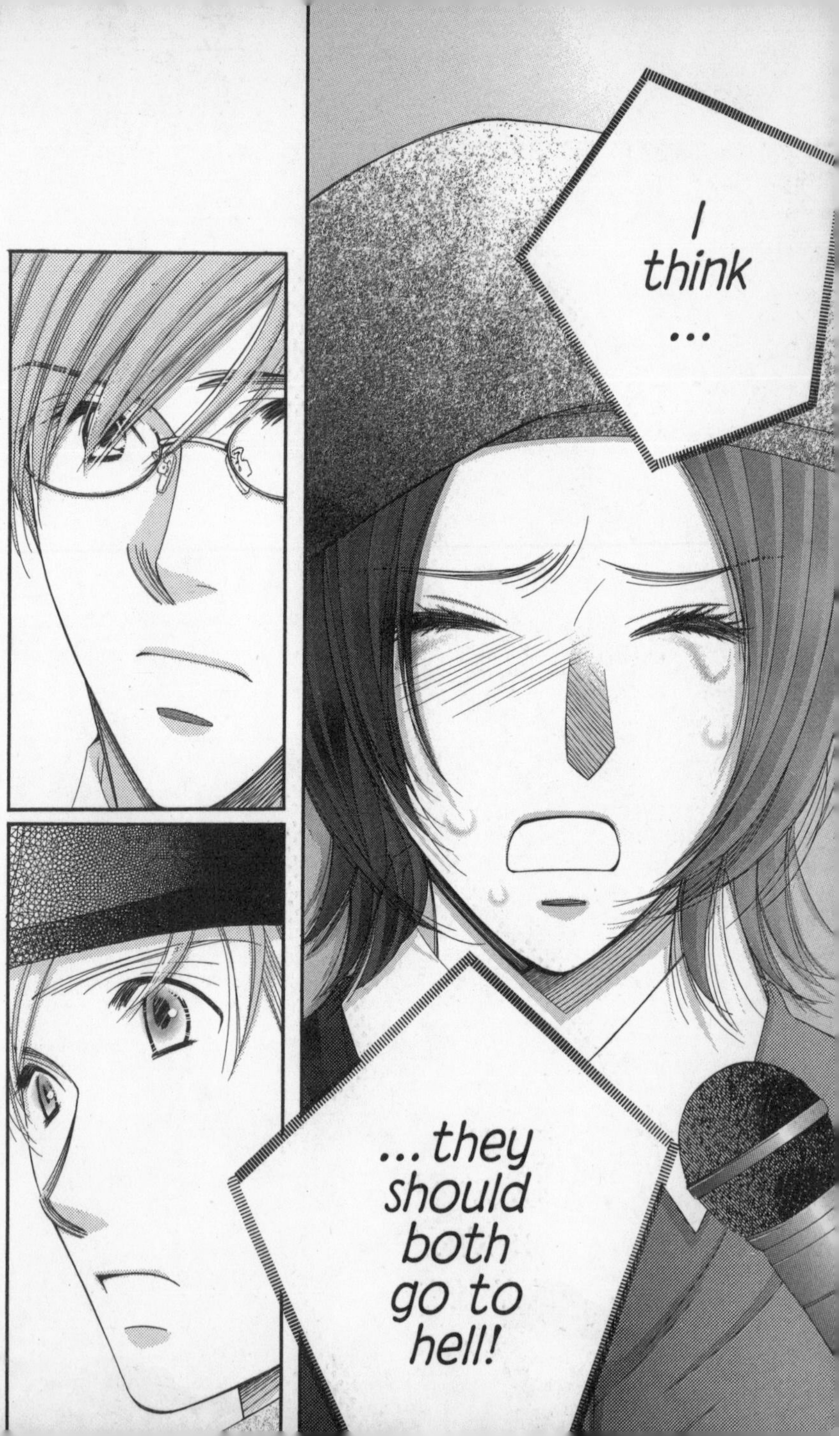
I think ...
...they should both go to hell!

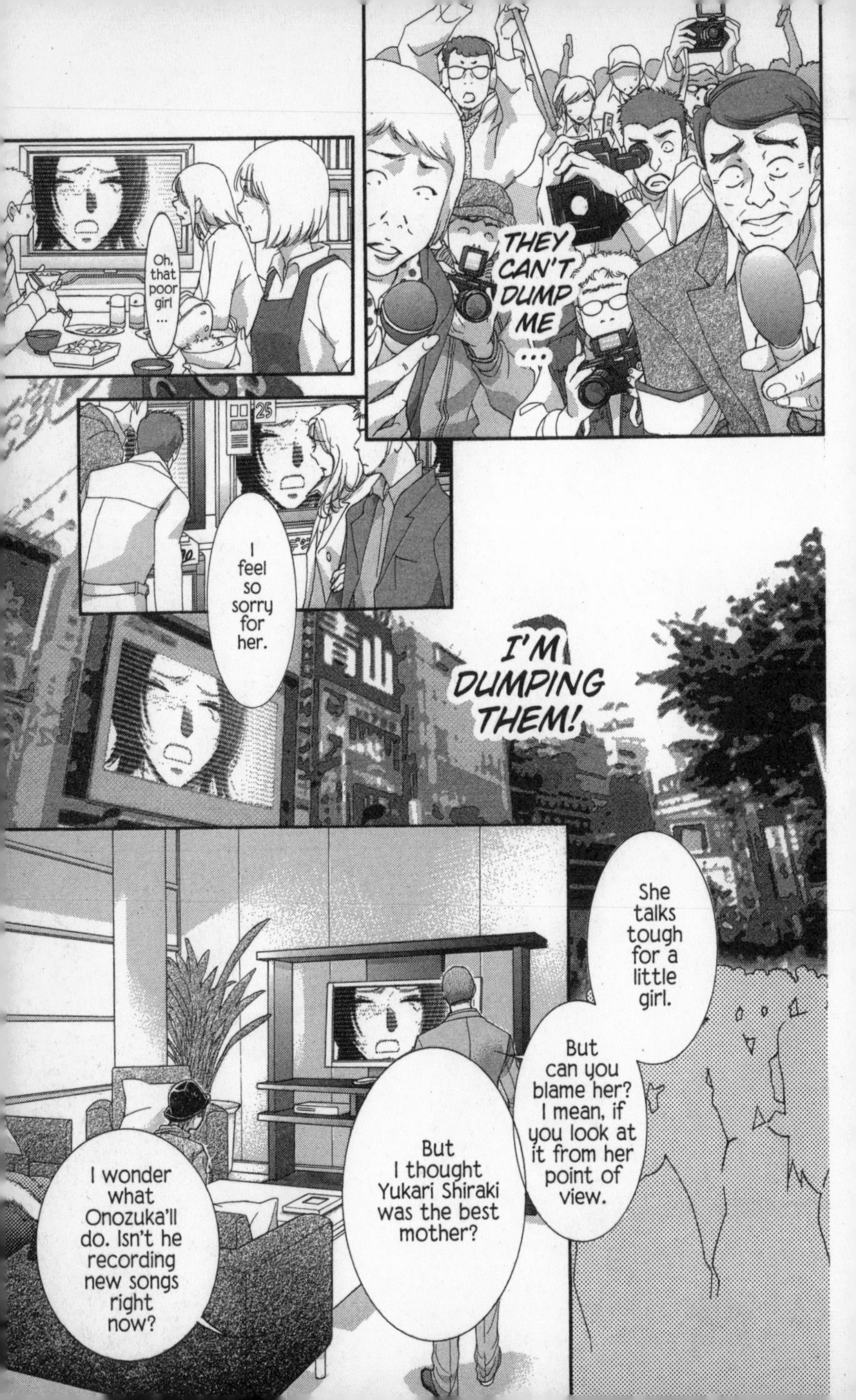
THEY CAN'T DUMP ME...
Oh, that poor girl...
I feel so sorry for her.
I'M DUMPING THEM!
She talks tough for a little girl.
But can you blame her? I mean, if you look at it from her point of view.
But I thought Yukari Shiraki was the best mother?
I wonder what Onozuka'll do. Isn't he recording new songs right now?

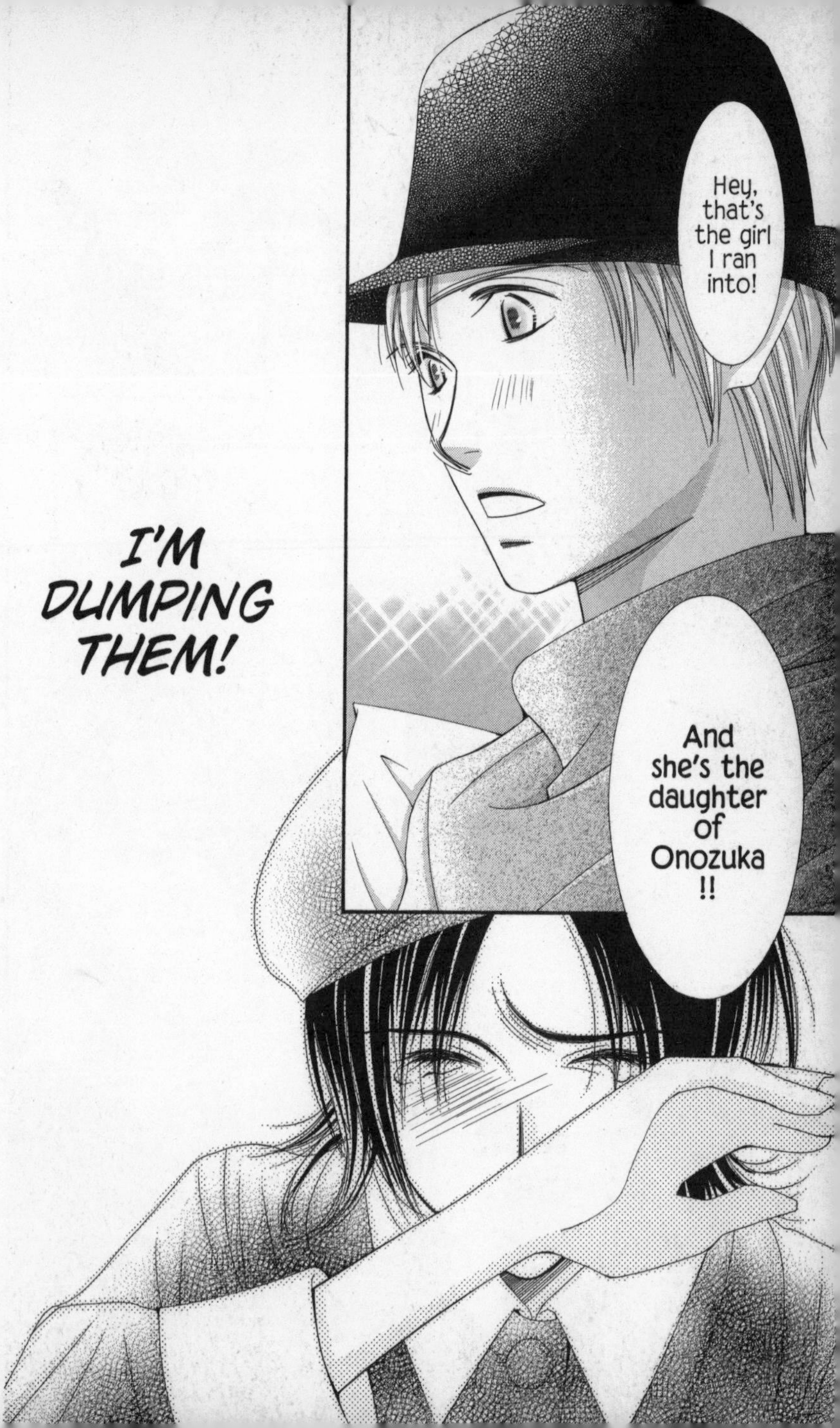
Hey, that's the girl I ran into!
And she's the daughter of Onozuka!!
I'M DUMPING THEM!

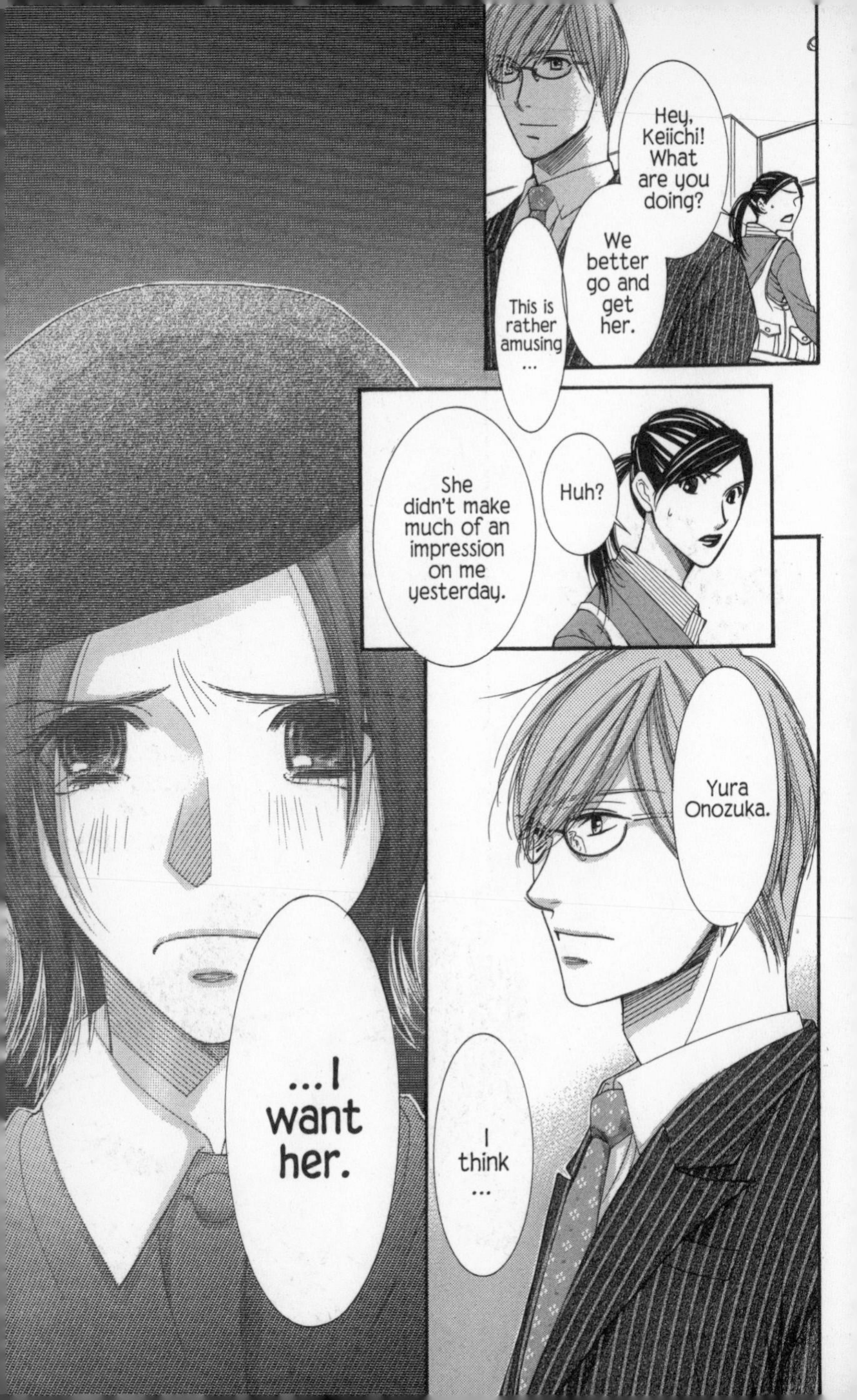
Hey, Keiichi! What are you doing?
We better go and get her.
This is rather amusing...
Huh?
She didn't make much of an impression on me yesterday.
Yura Onozuka.
I think...
...I want her.

Yura Onozuka
Senior high school student
(17 years old)
Blood type A

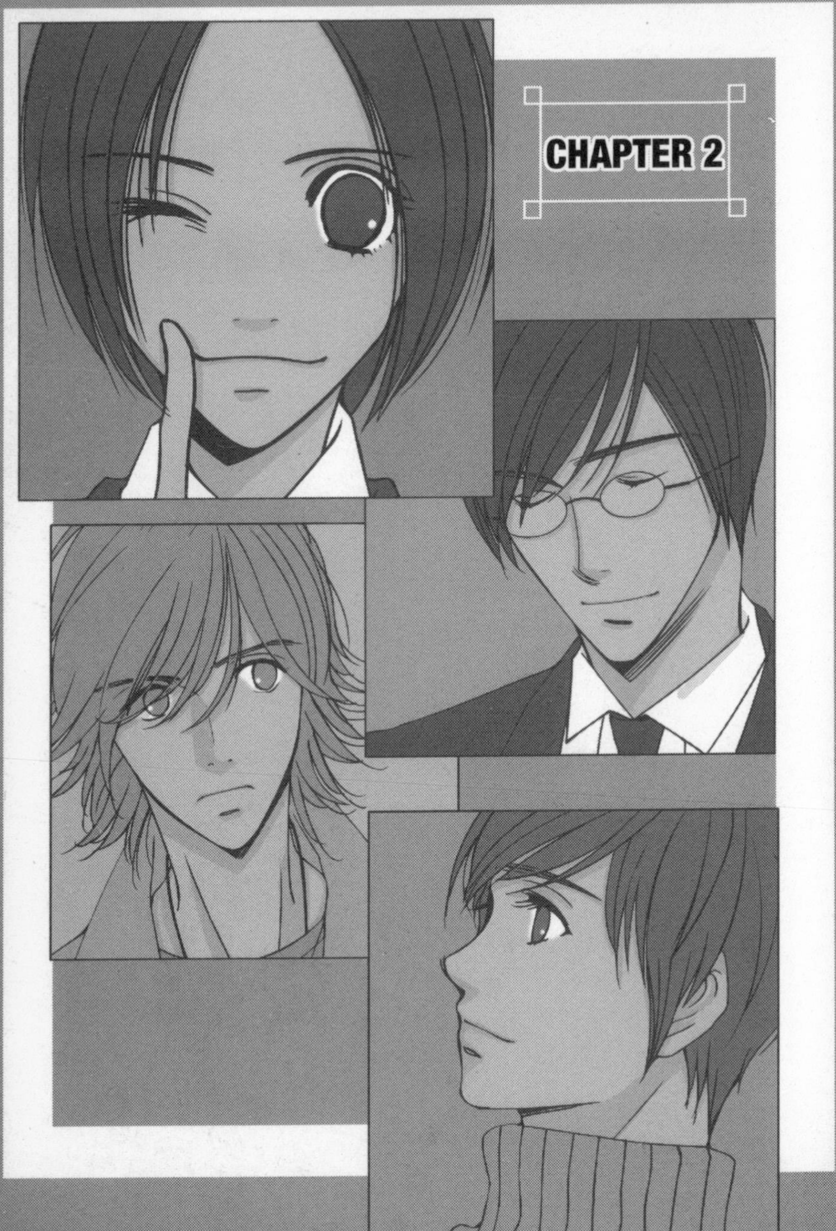
CHAPTER 2

Keiichi Mizorogi
32 years old
Blood type AB

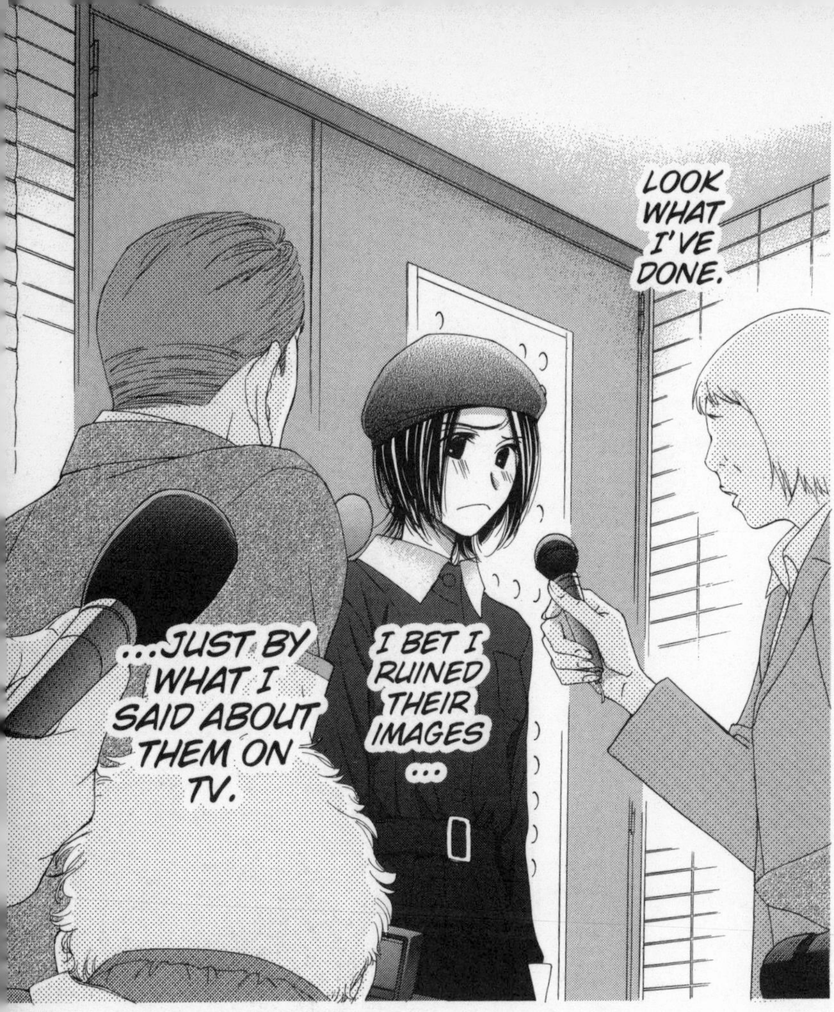
LOOK WHAT I'VE DONE.
I BET I RUINED THEIR IMAGES...
...JUST BY WHAT I SAID ABOUT THEM ON TV.

Honey Hunt

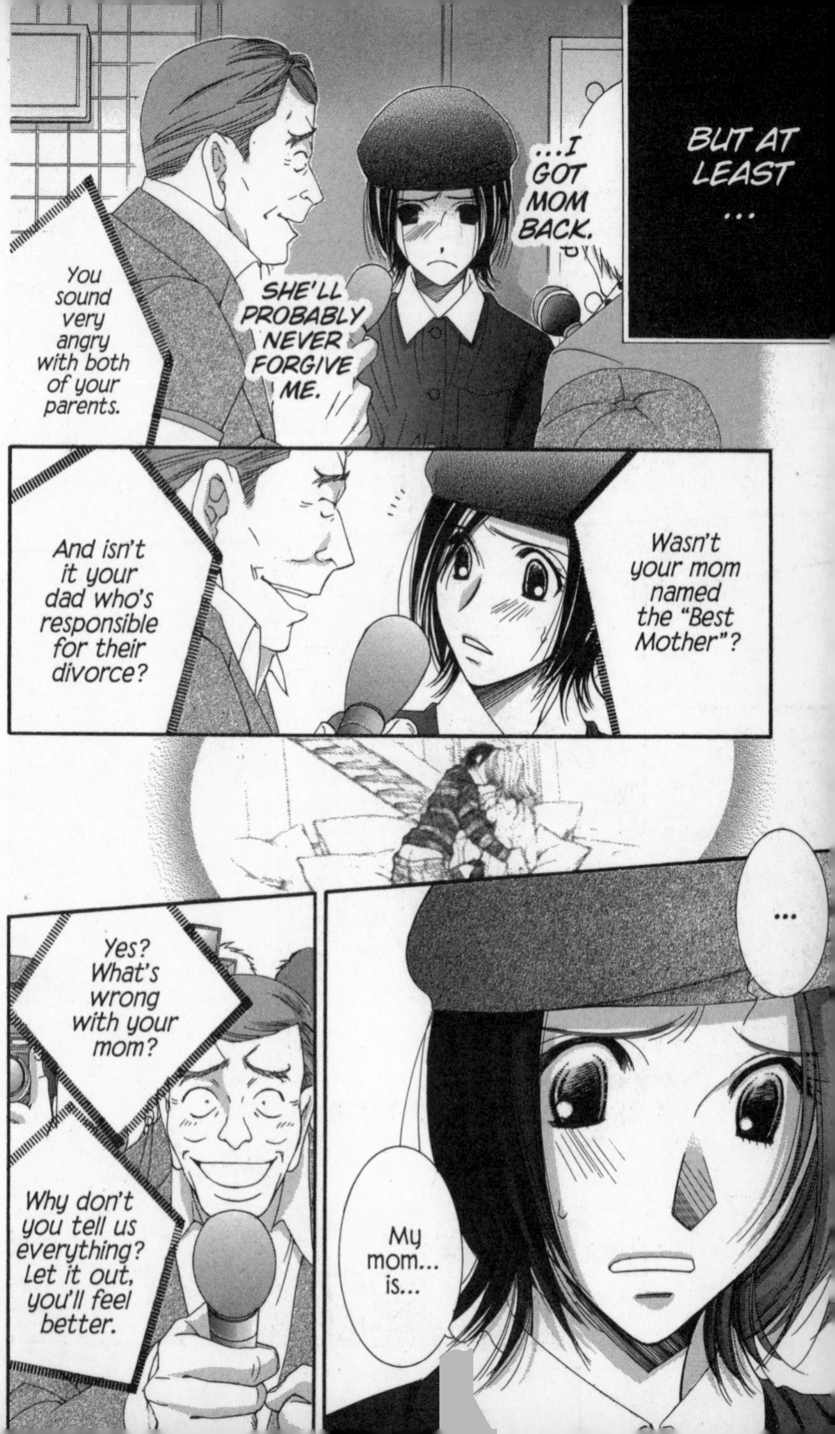
BUT AT LEAST...
...I GOT MOM BACK.
SHE'LL PROBABLY NEVER FORGIVE ME.
You sound very angry with both of your parents.
Wasn't your mom named the "Best Mother"?
And isn't it your dad who's responsible for their divorce?
...
My mom... is...
Yes? What's wrong with your mom?
Why don't you tell us everything? Let it out, you'll feel better.

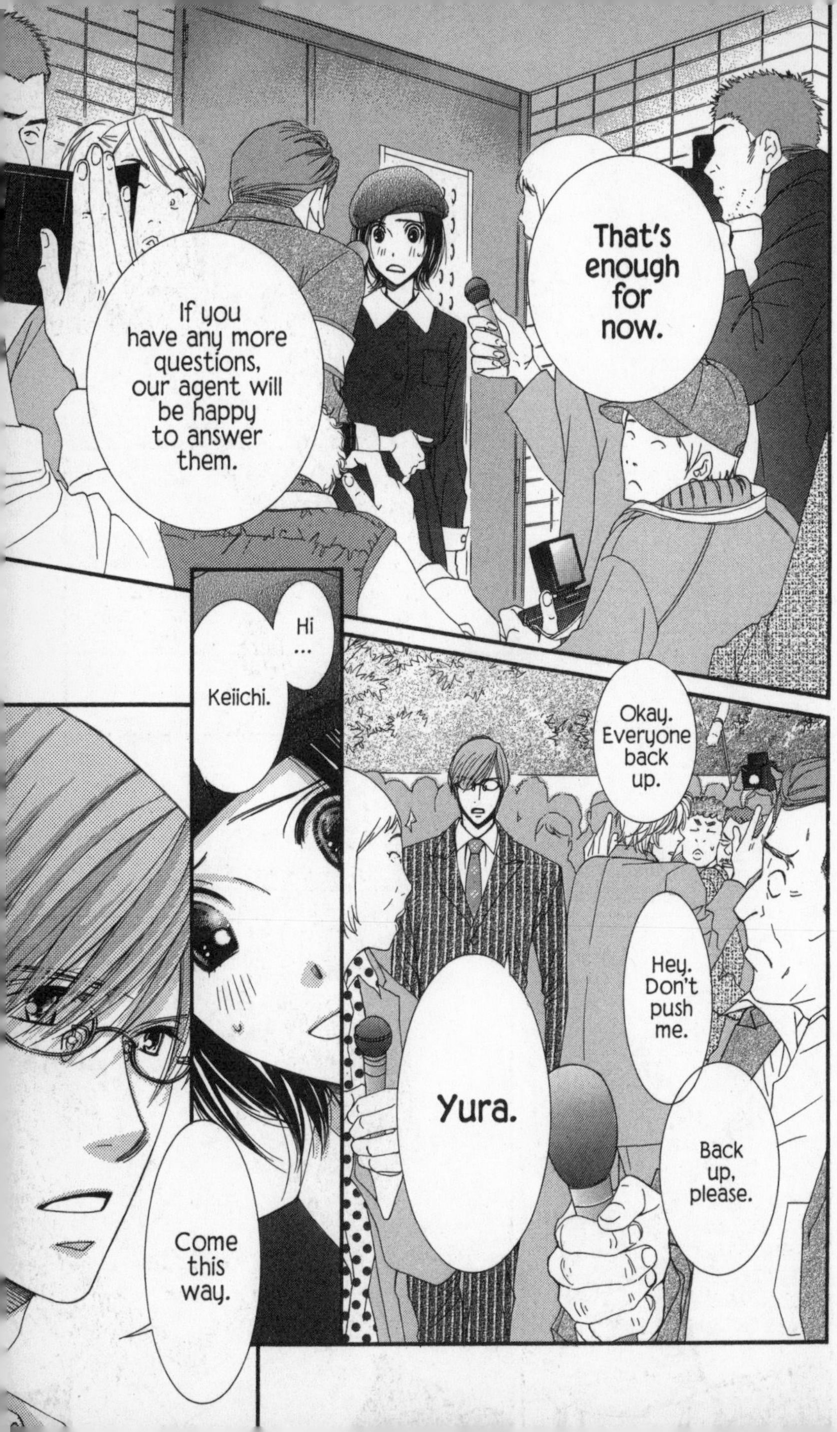

That's enough for now.
If you have any more questions, our agent will be happy to answer them.
Okay. Everyone back up.
Hey. Don't push me.
Back up, please.
Yura.
Hi ... Keiichi.
Come this way.

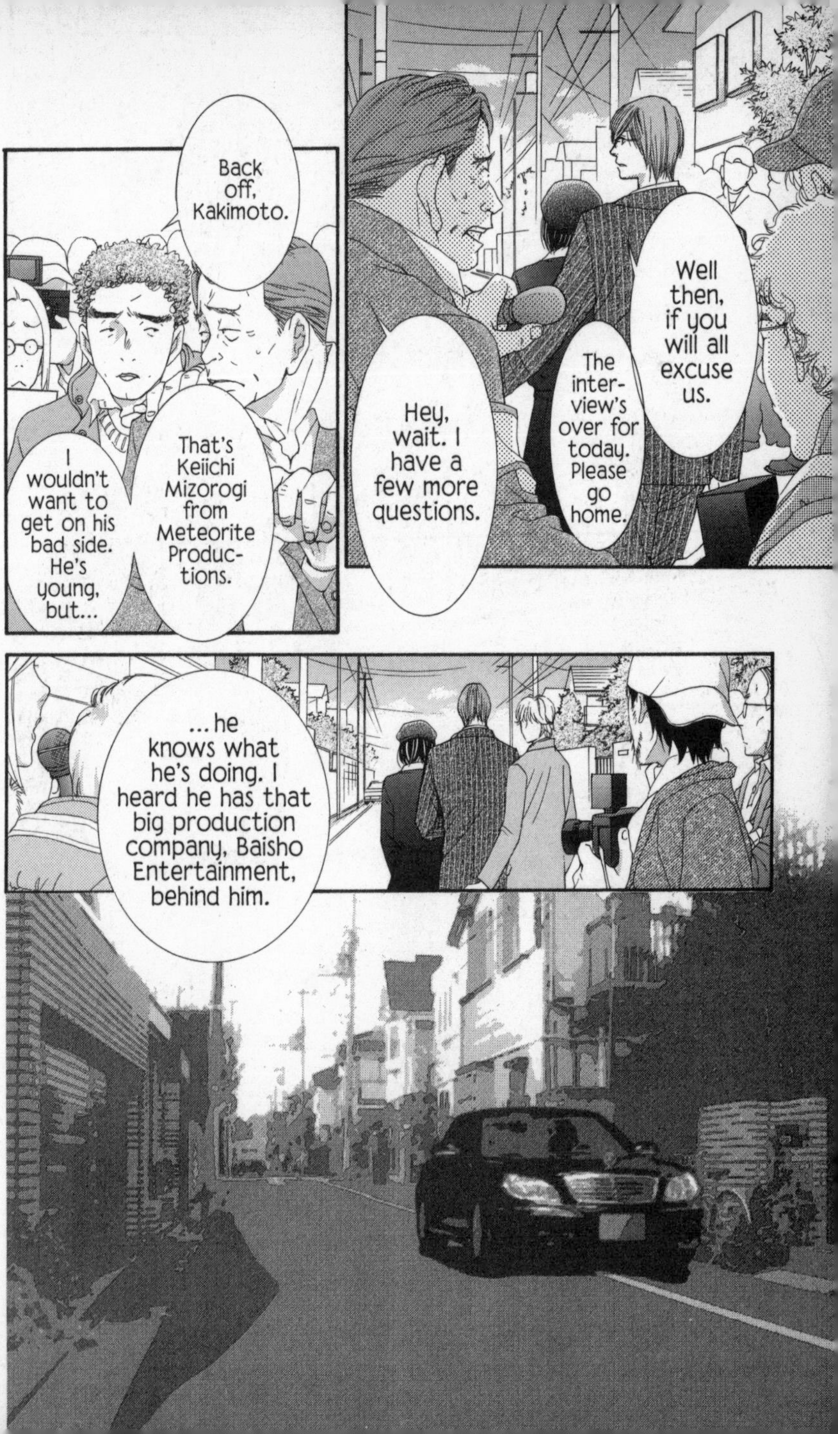
Well then, if you will all excuse us.
The interview's over for today. Please go home.
Hey, wait. I have a few more questions.
Back off, Kakimoto.
That's Keiichi Mizorogi from Meteorite Productions.
I wouldn't want to get on his bad side. He's young, but...
...he knows what he's doing. I heard he has that big production company, Baisho Entertainment, behind him.

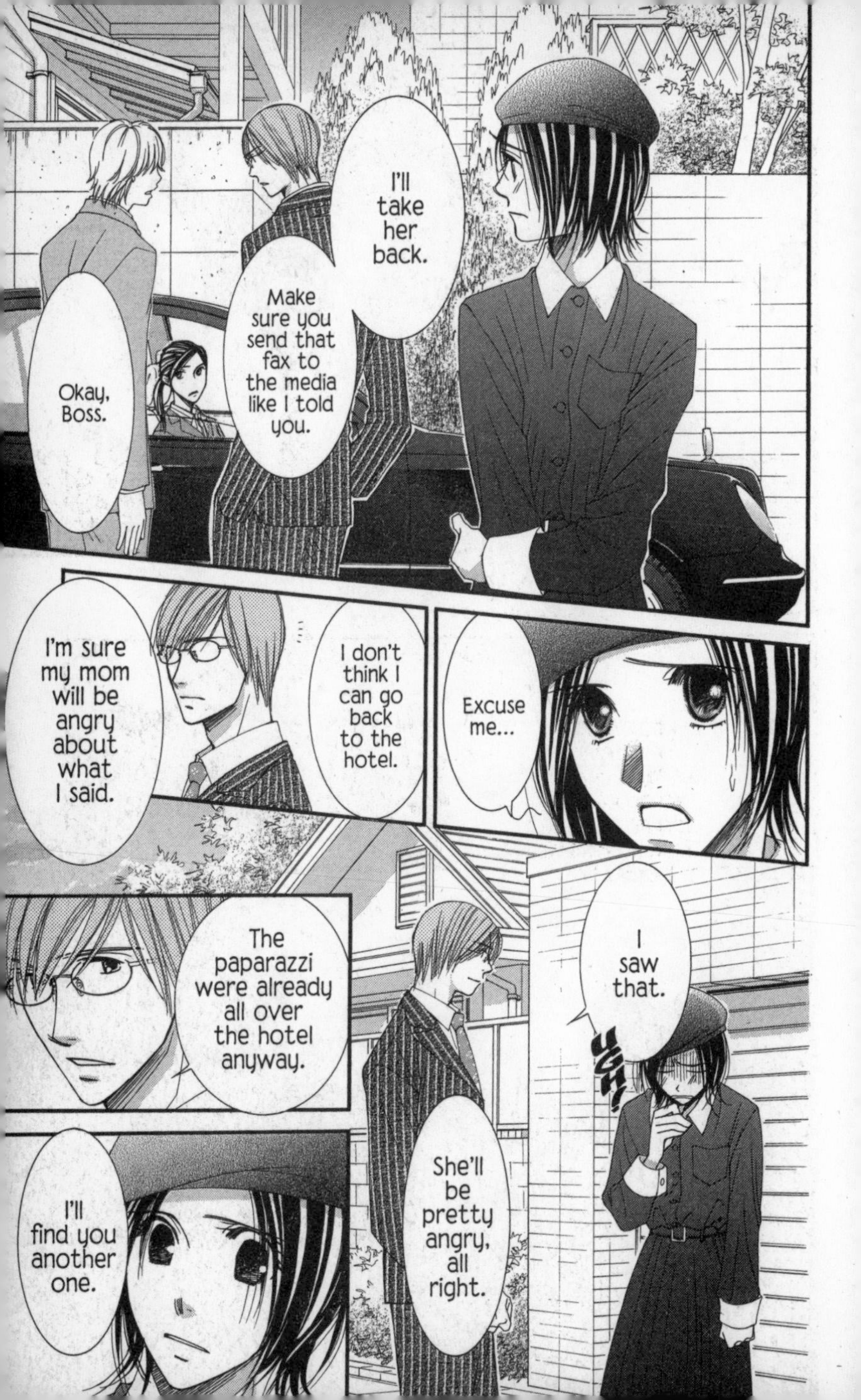
I'll take her back.
Make sure you send that fax to the media like I told you.
Okay, Boss.
Excuse me...
I don't think I can go back to the hotel.
I'm sure my mom will be angry about what I said.
I saw that.
UGH!
She'll be pretty angry, all right.
The paparazzi were already all over the hotel anyway.
I'll find you another one.

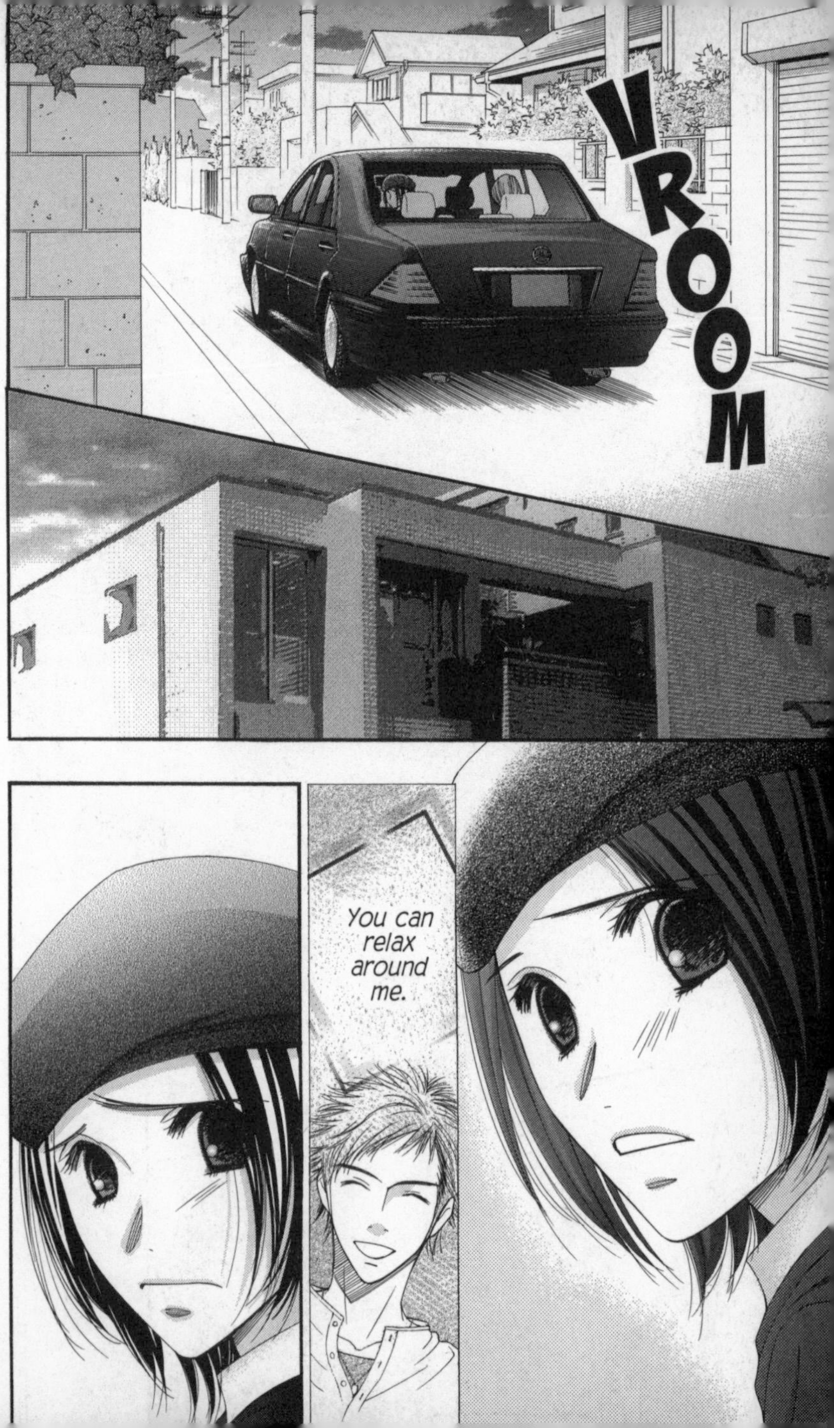
VROOM
You can relax around me.

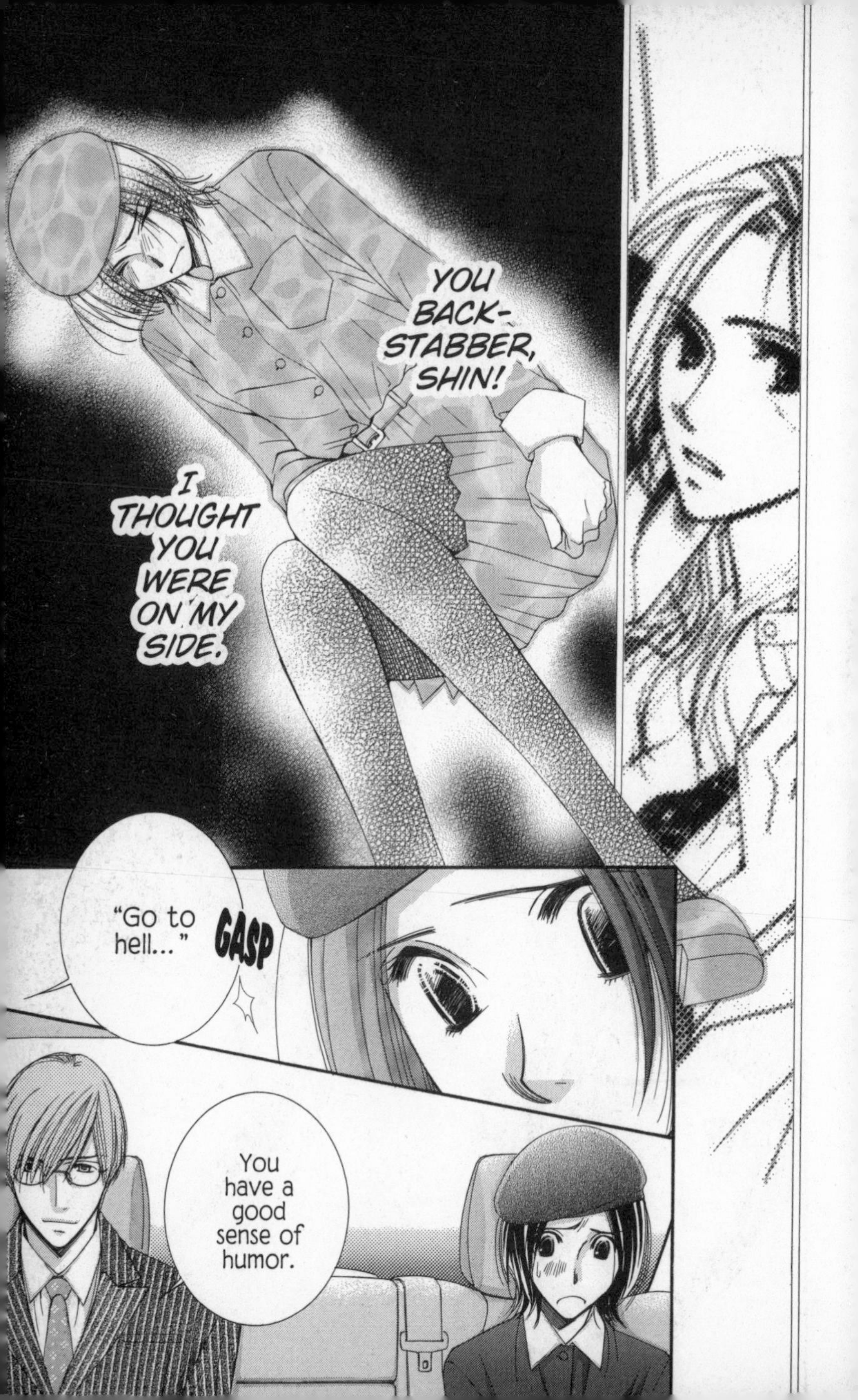
YOU BACK-STABBER, SHIN!
I THOUGHT YOU WERE ON MY SIDE.
"Go to hell..."
GASP
You have a good sense of humor.

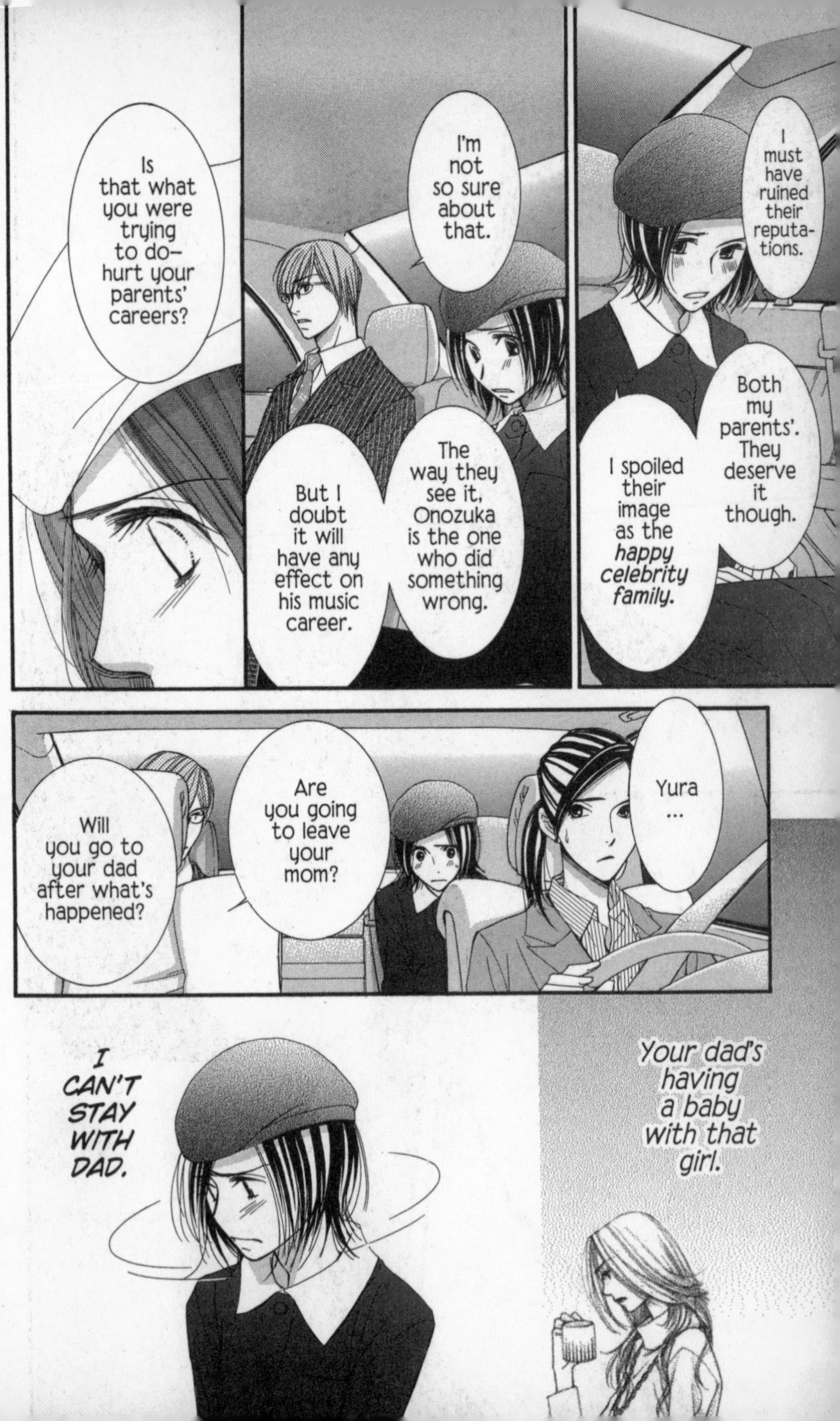
I must have ruined their reputations.
Both my parents'. They deserve it though.
I spoiled their image as the *happy celebrity family.*
I'm not so sure about that.
The way they see it, Onozuka is the one who did something wrong.
But I doubt it will have any effect on his music career.
Is that what you were trying to do— hurt your parents' careers?
Yura ...
Are you going to leave your mom?
Will you go to your dad after what's happened?
Your dad's having a baby with that girl.
I CAN'T STAY WITH DAD.

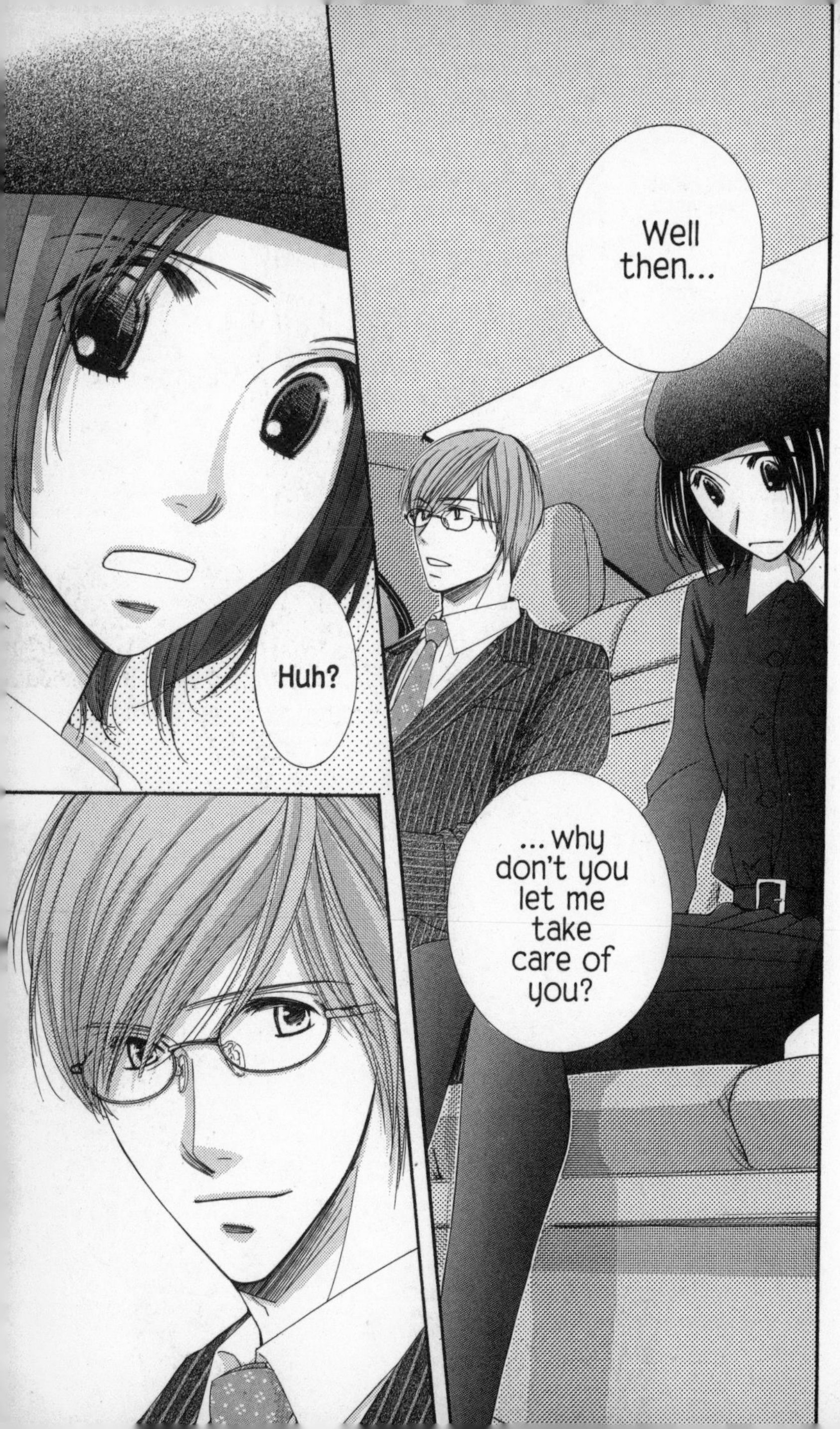
Well then...
...why don't you let me take care of you?
Huh?

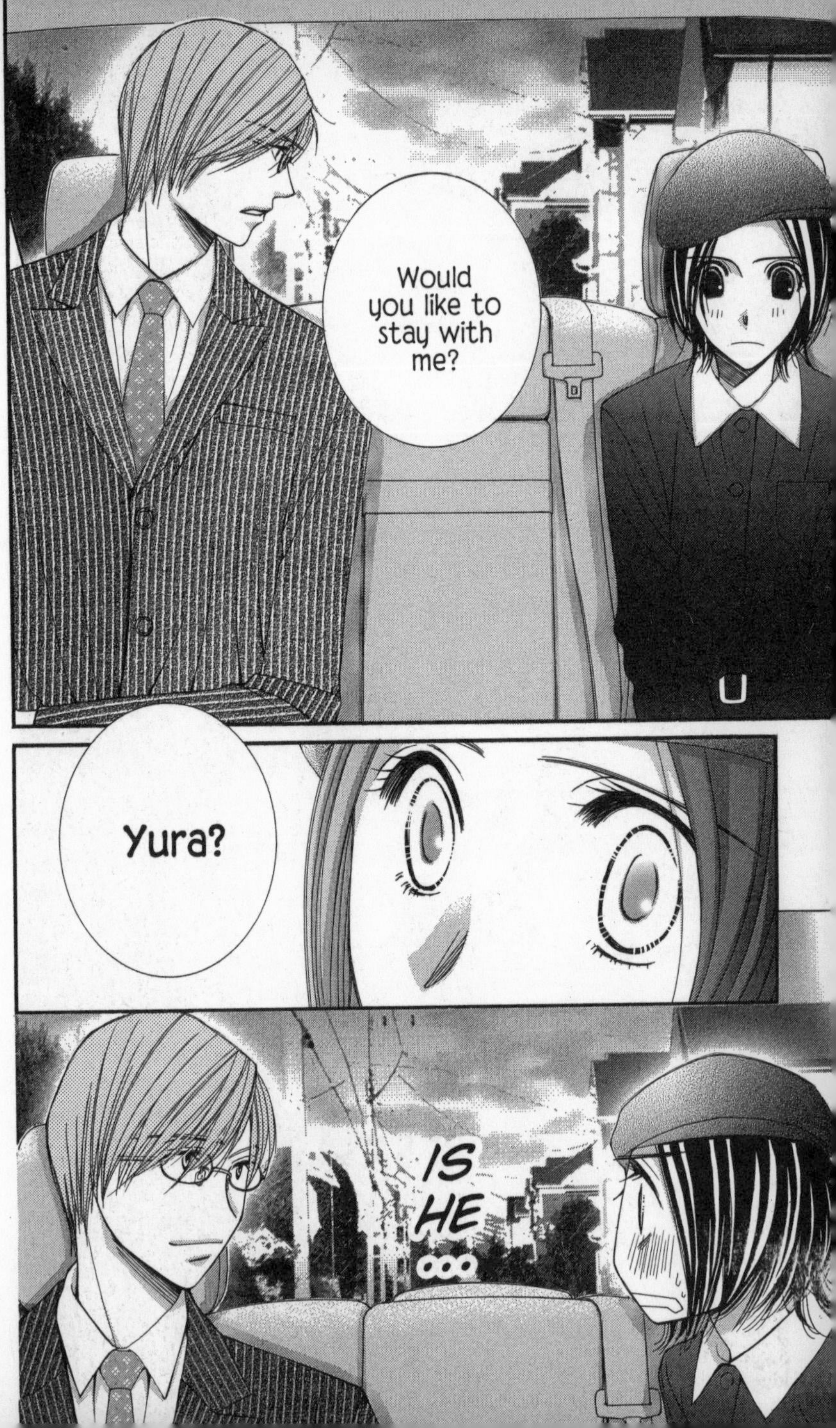
Would you like to stay with me?
Yura?
IS HE ...

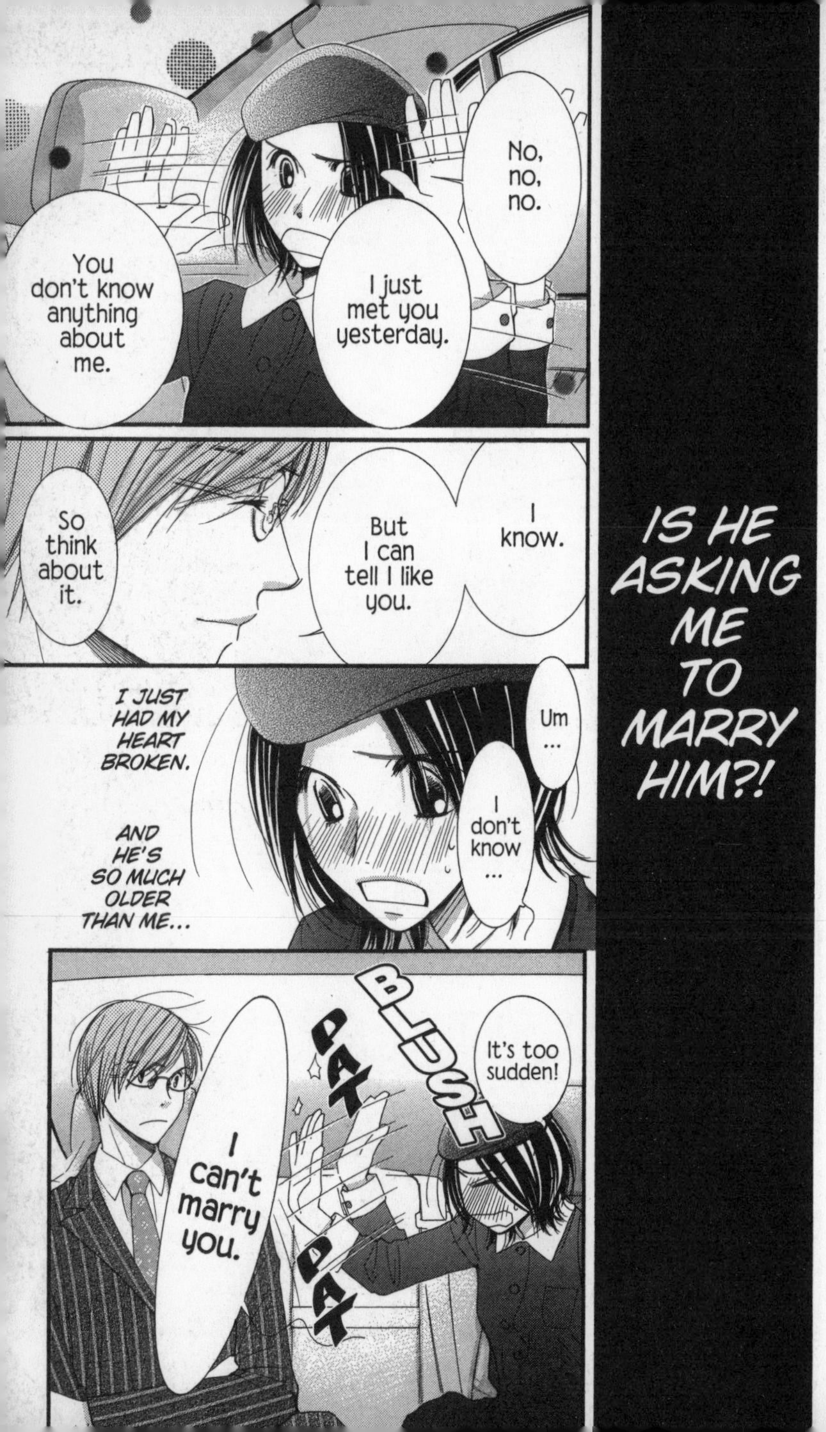
IS HE ASKING ME TO MARRY HIM?!
No, no, no.
I just met you yesterday.
You don't know anything about me.
I know.
But I can tell I like you.
So think about it.
Um...
I don't know...
I JUST HAD MY HEART BROKEN.
AND HE'S SO MUCH OLDER THAN ME...
BLUSH
It's too sudden!
PAT PAT
I can't marry you.

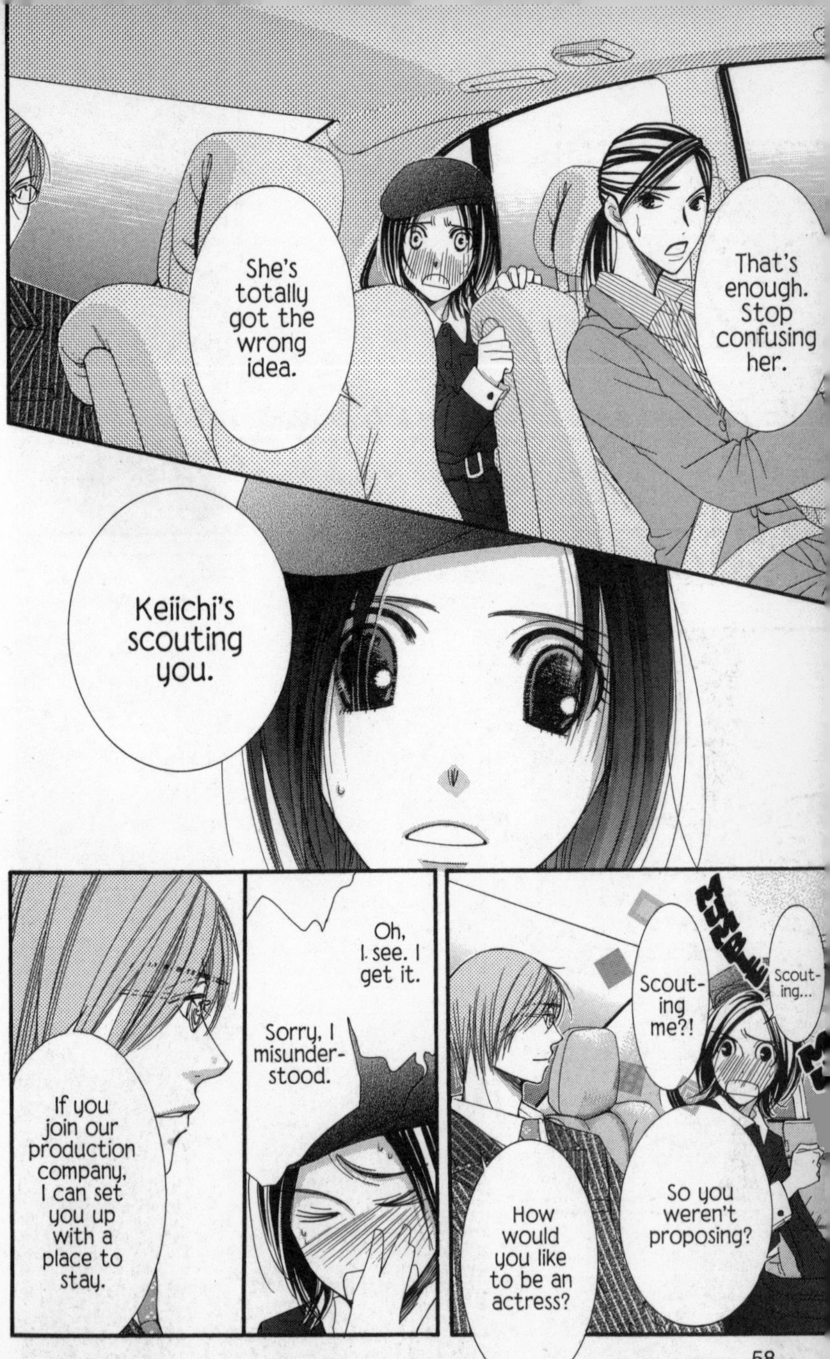
That's enough. Stop confusing her.
She's totally got the wrong idea.
Keiichi's scouting you.
Scout-ing...
Scout-ing me?!
MUMBLE
So you weren't proposing?
How would you like to be an actress?
Oh, I see. I get it.
Sorry, I misunder-stood.
If you join our production company, I can set you up with a place to stay.

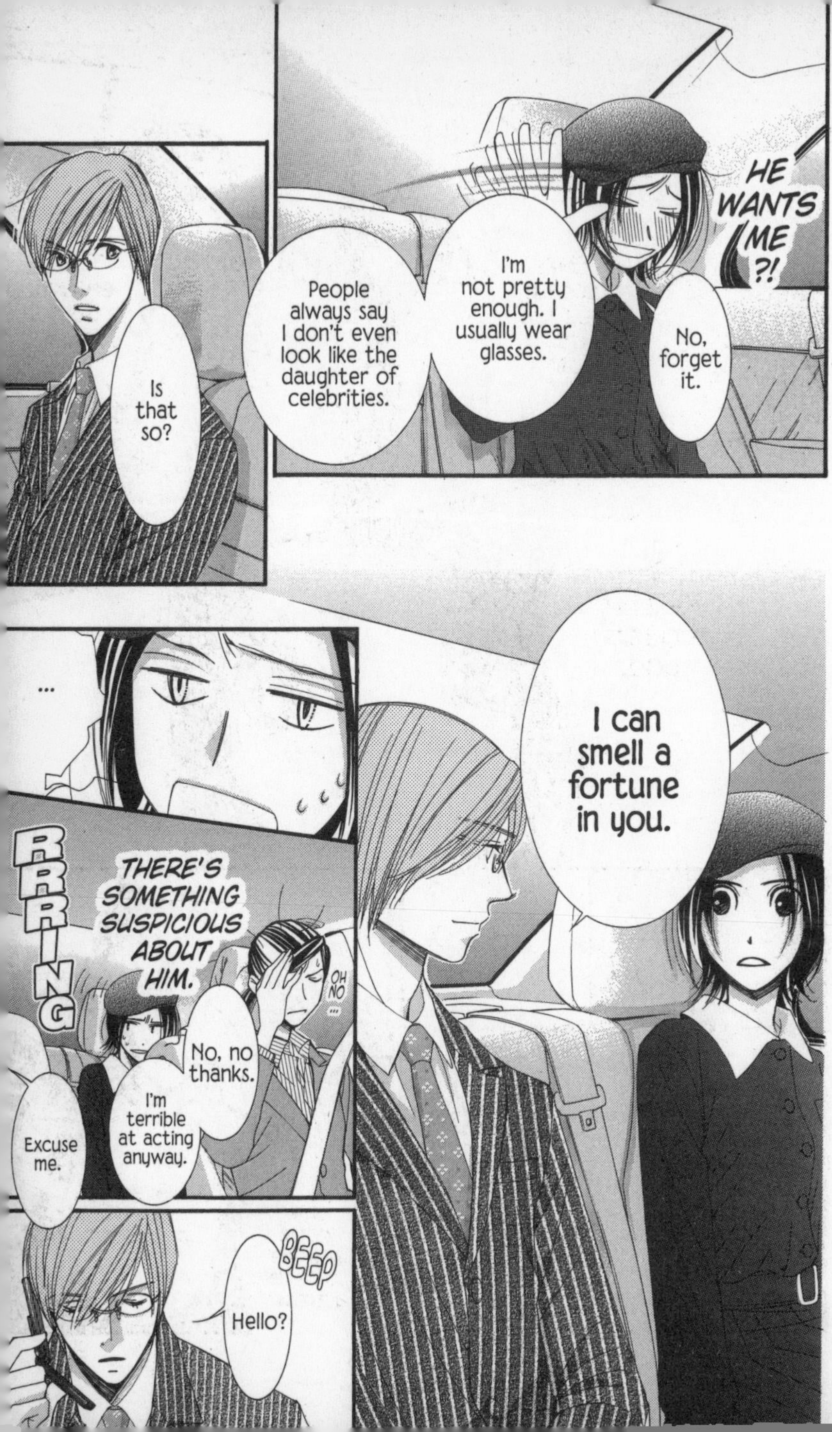
HE WANTS ME?!
No, forget it.
I'm not pretty enough. I usually wear glasses.
People always say I don't even look like the daughter of celebrities.
Is that so?
I can smell a fortune in you.
...
THERE'S SOMETHING SUSPICIOUS ABOUT HIM.
OH NO...
No, no thanks.
I'm terrible at acting anyway.
RRRING
Excuse me.
BEEP
Hello?

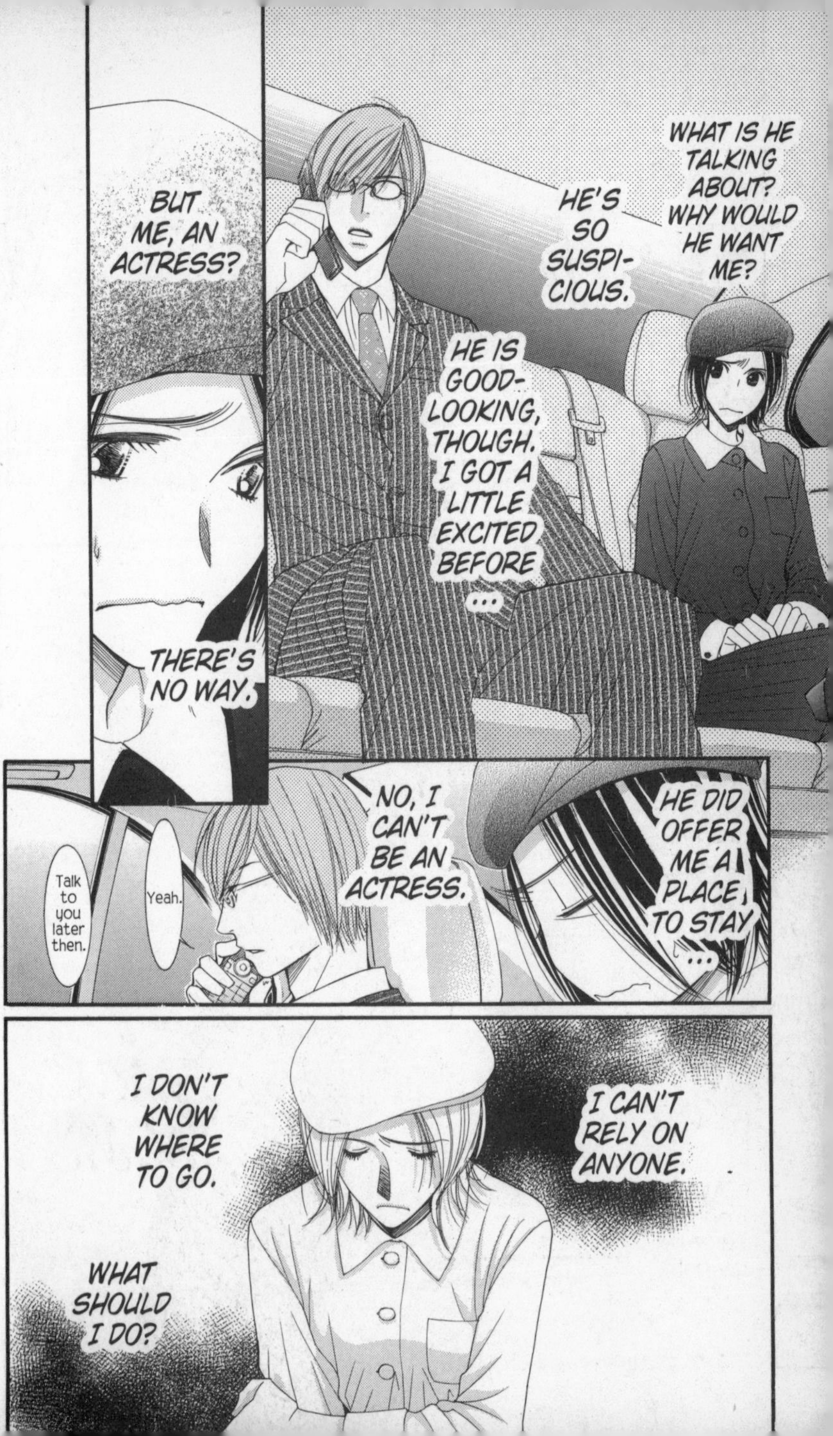
WHAT IS HE TALKING ABOUT? WHY WOULD HE WANT ME?
HE'S SO SUSPICIOUS.
HE IS GOOD-LOOKING, THOUGH. I GOT A LITTLE EXCITED BEFORE...
BUT ME, AN ACTRESS?
THERE'S NO WAY.
HE DID OFFER ME A PLACE TO STAY...
NO, I CAN'T BE AN ACTRESS.
Yeah.
Talk to you later then.
I CAN'T RELY ON ANYONE.
I DON'T KNOW WHERE TO GO.
WHAT SHOULD I DO?

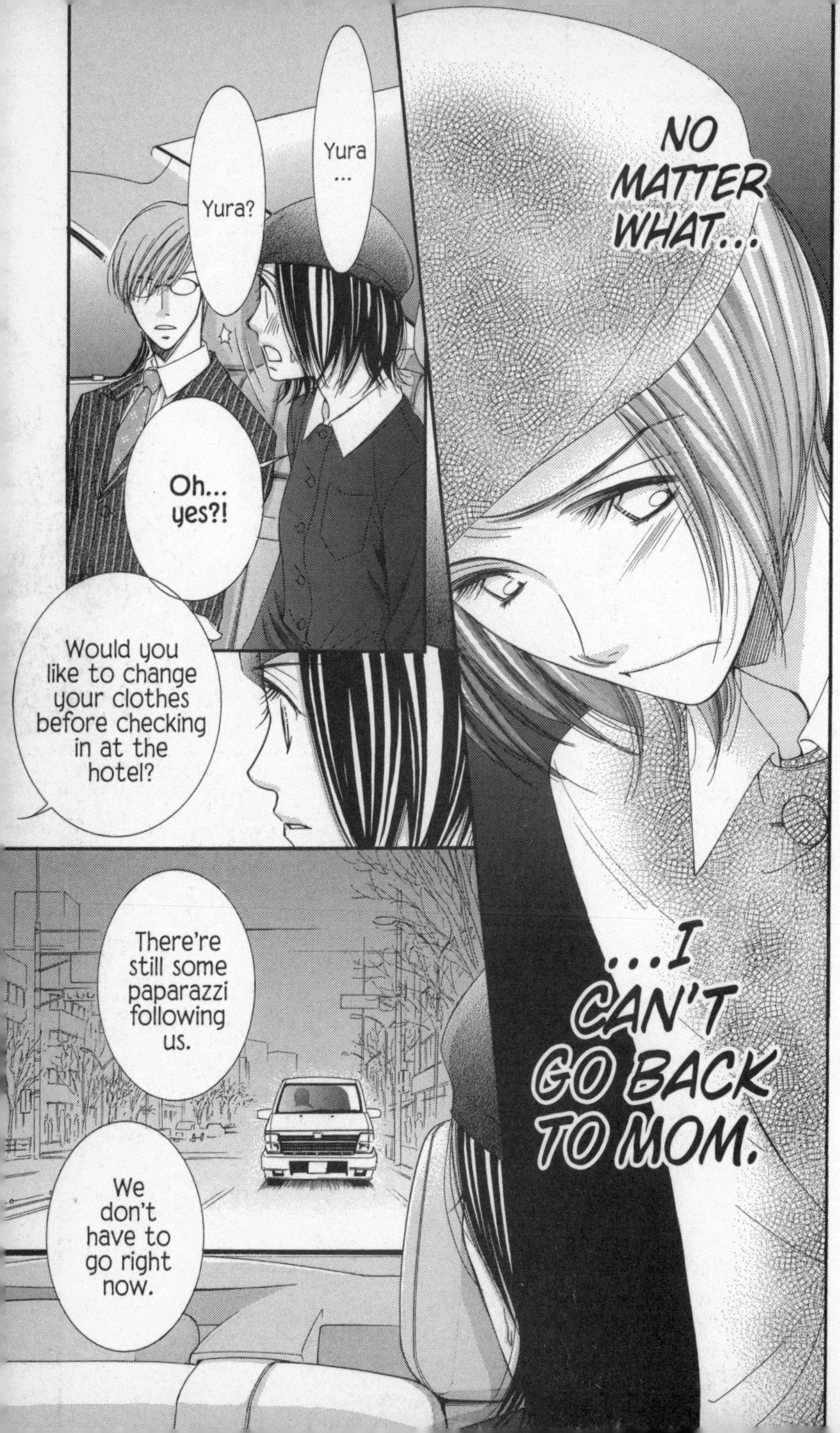
NO MATTER WHAT...
...I CAN'T GO BACK TO MOM.
Yura ...
Yura?
Oh... yes?!
Would you like to change your clothes before checking in at the hotel?
There're still some paparazzi following us.
We don't have to go right now.

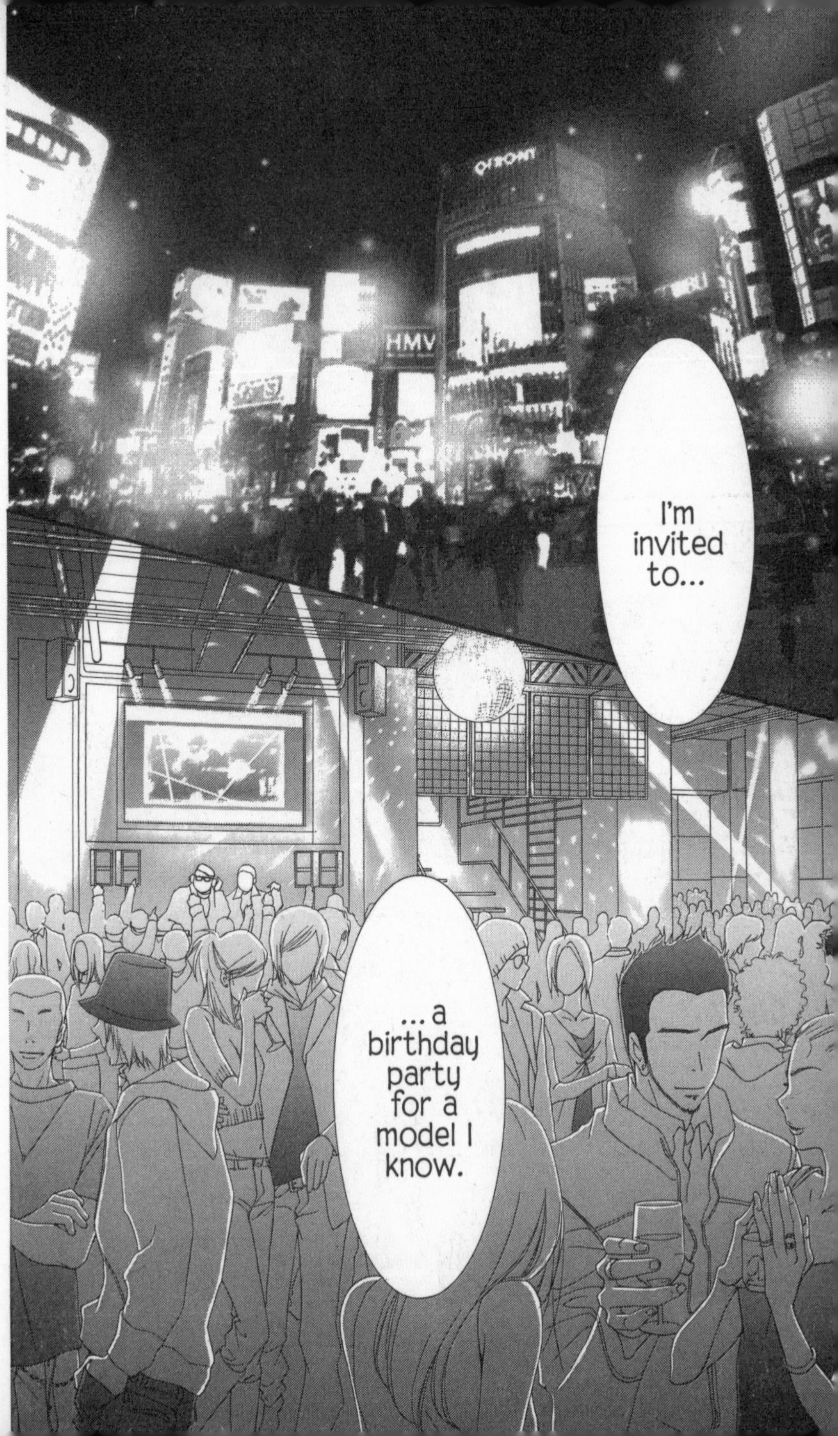
I'm invited to...
... a birthday party for a model I know.

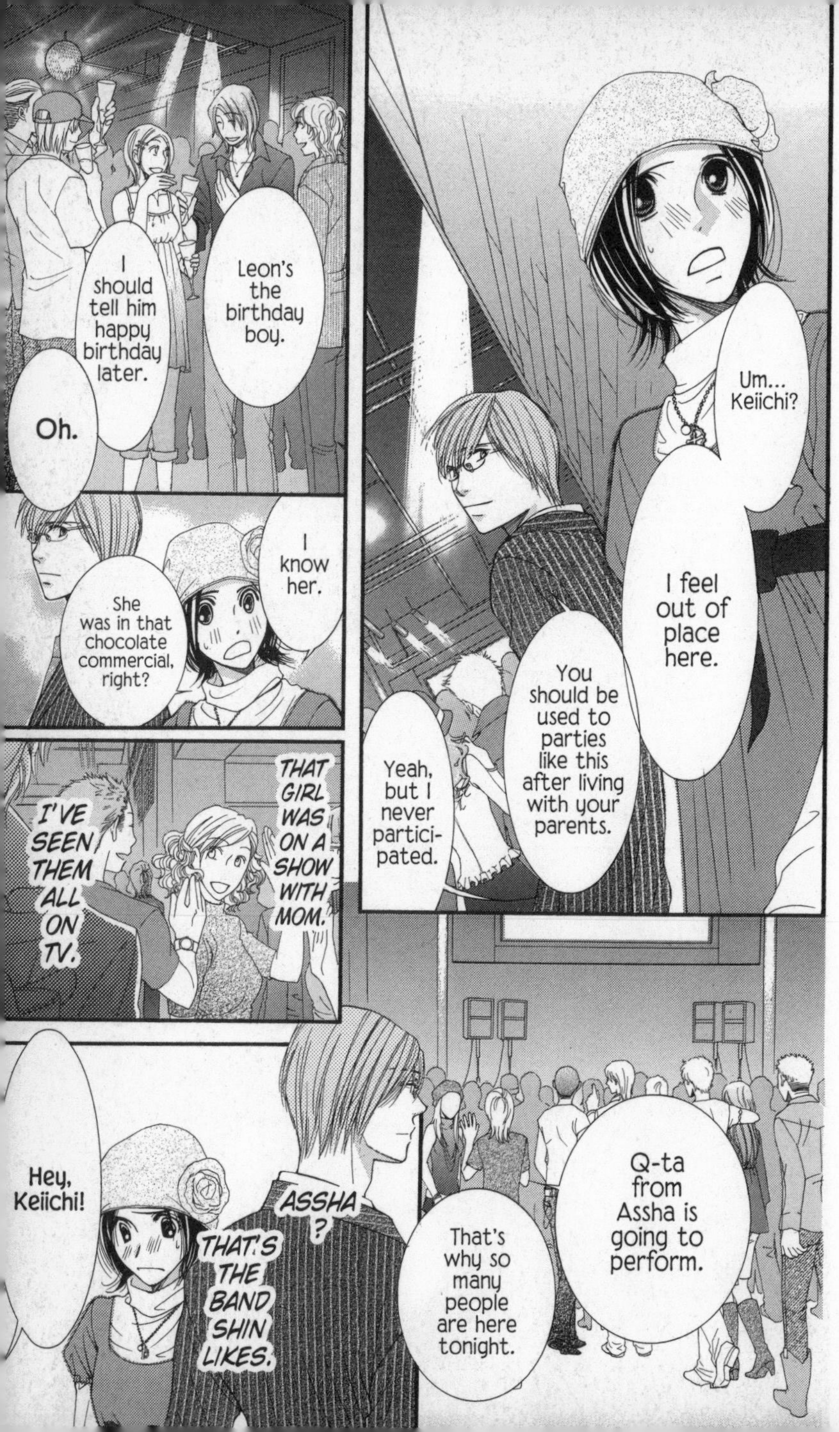
Um... Keiichi?
I feel out of place here.
You should be used to parties like this after living with your parents.
Yeah, but I never partici-pated.
Leon's the birthday boy.
I should tell him happy birthday later.
Oh.
I know her.
She was in that chocolate commercial, right?
THAT GIRL WAS ON A SHOW WITH MOM.
I'VE SEEN THEM ALL ON TV.
Q-ta from Assha is going to perform.
That's why so many people are here tonight.
ASSHA?
THAT'S THE BAND SHIN LIKES.
Hey, Keiichi!

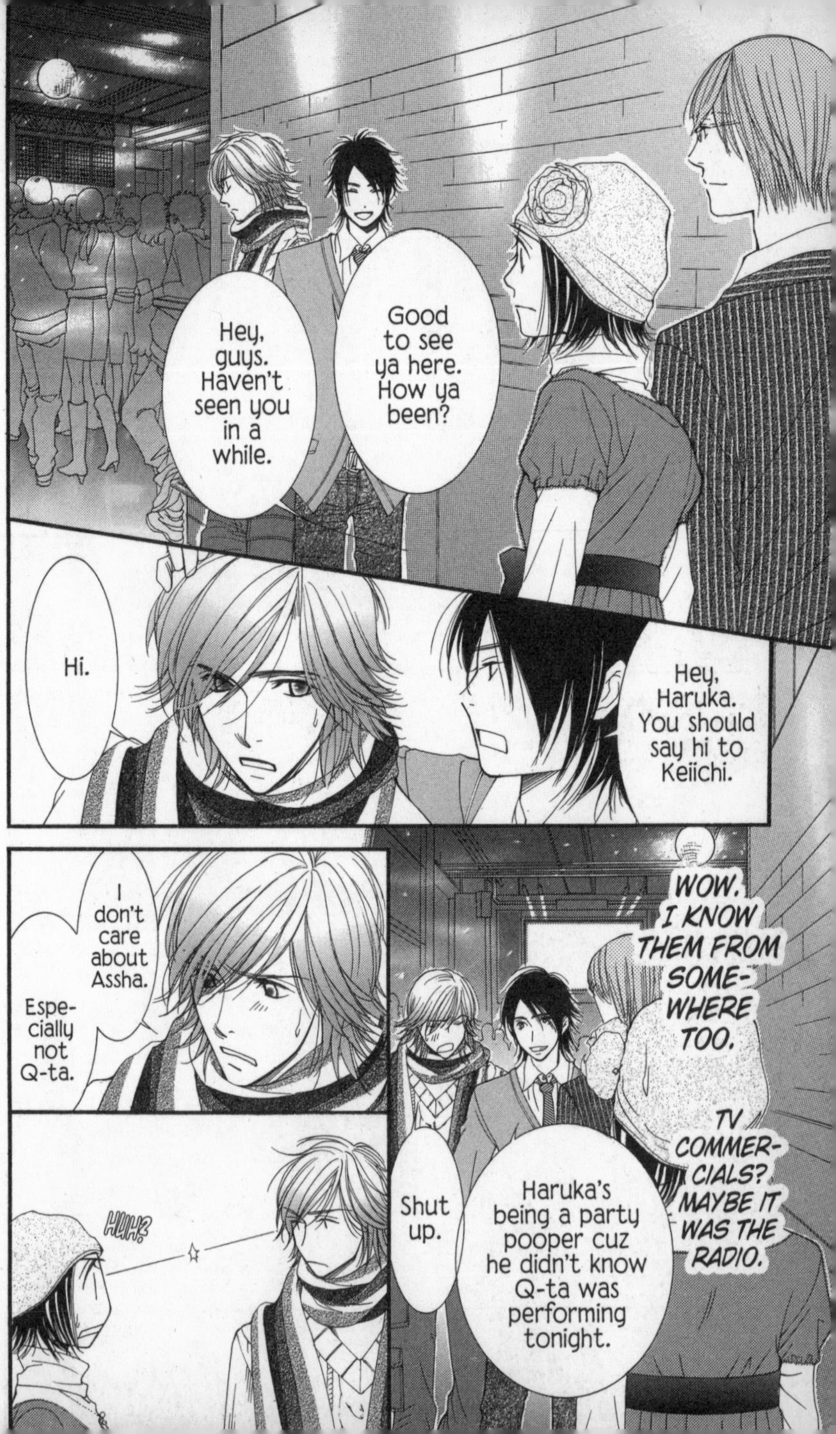
Good to see ya here. How ya been?
Hey, guys. Haven't seen you in a while.
Hey, Haruka. You should say hi to Keiichi.
Hi.
WOW. I KNOW THEM FROM SOMEWHERE TOO.
TV COMMERCIALS? MAYBE IT WAS THE RADIO.
Haruka's being a party pooper cuz he didn't know Q-ta was performing tonight.
Shut up.
I don't care about Assha.
Especially not Q-ta.
HUH?

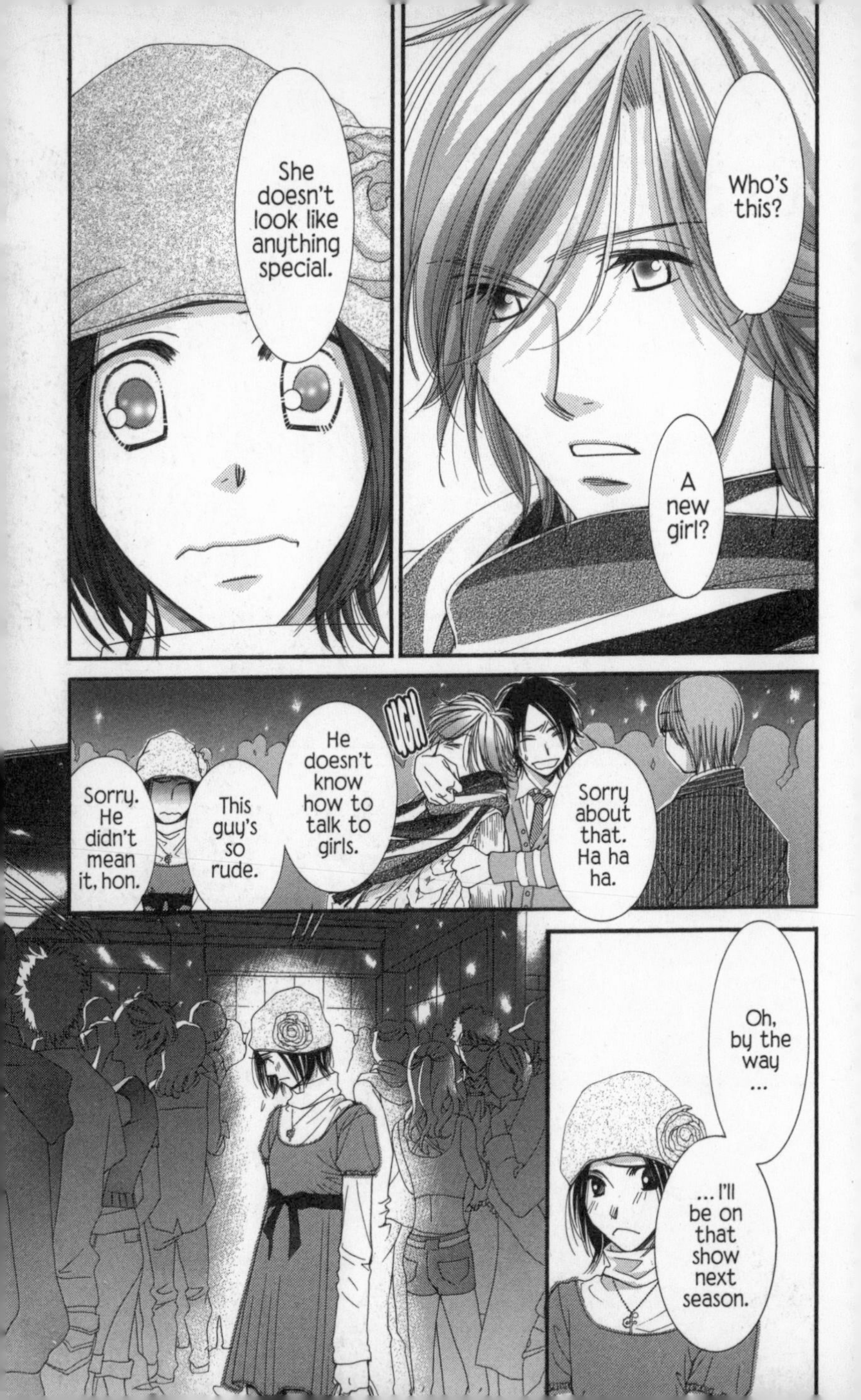
Who's this?
A new girl?
She doesn't look like anything special.
Sorry about that. Ha ha ha.
UGH
He doesn't know how to talk to girls.
This guy's so rude.
Sorry. He didn't mean it, hon.
Oh, by the way ...
... I'll be on that show next season.

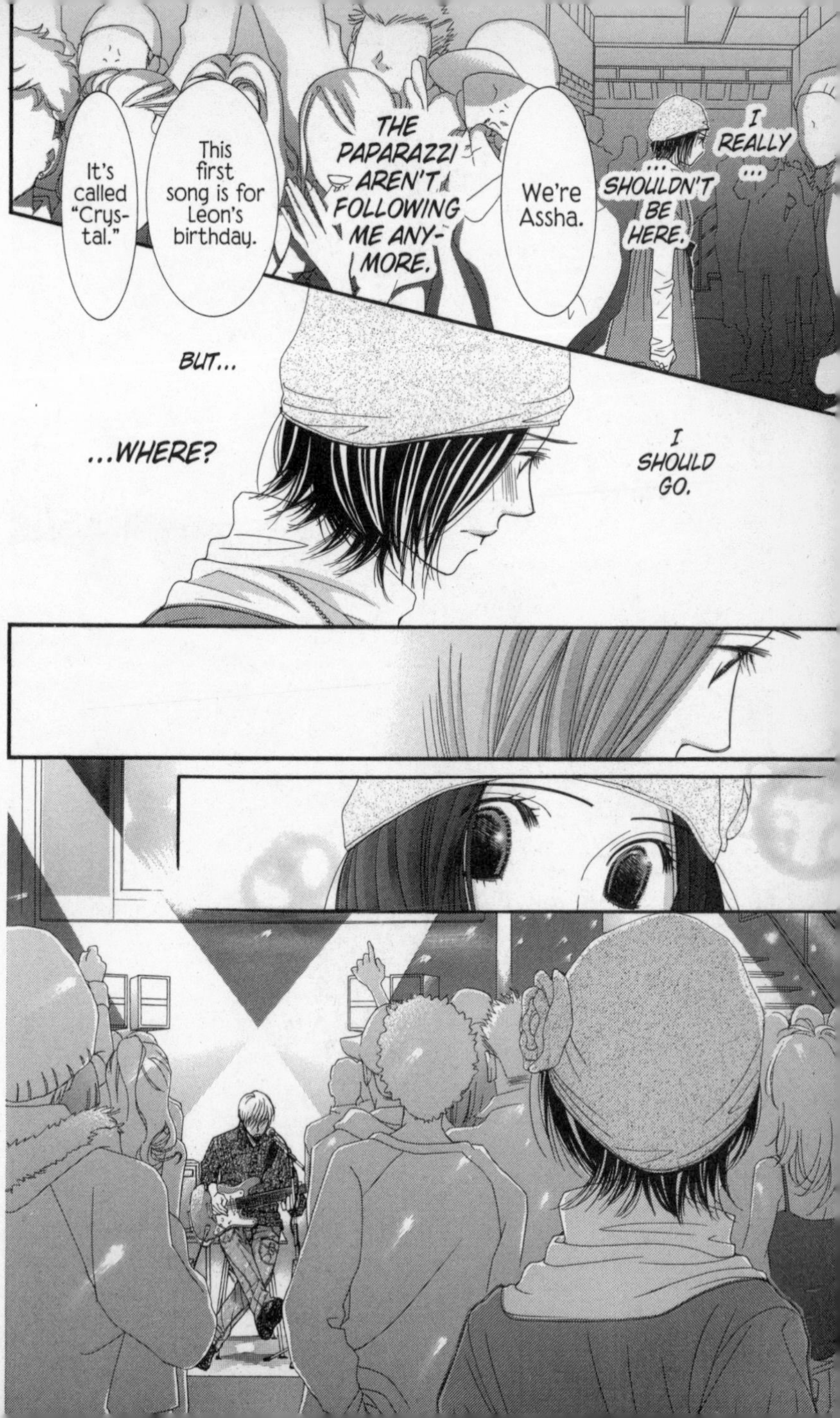
I REALLY... SHOULDN'T BE HERE.
We're Assha.
THE PAPARAZZI AREN'T FOLLOWING ME ANY-MORE.
This first song is for Leon's birthday.
It's called "Crys-tal."
I SHOULD GO.
BUT...
...WHERE?

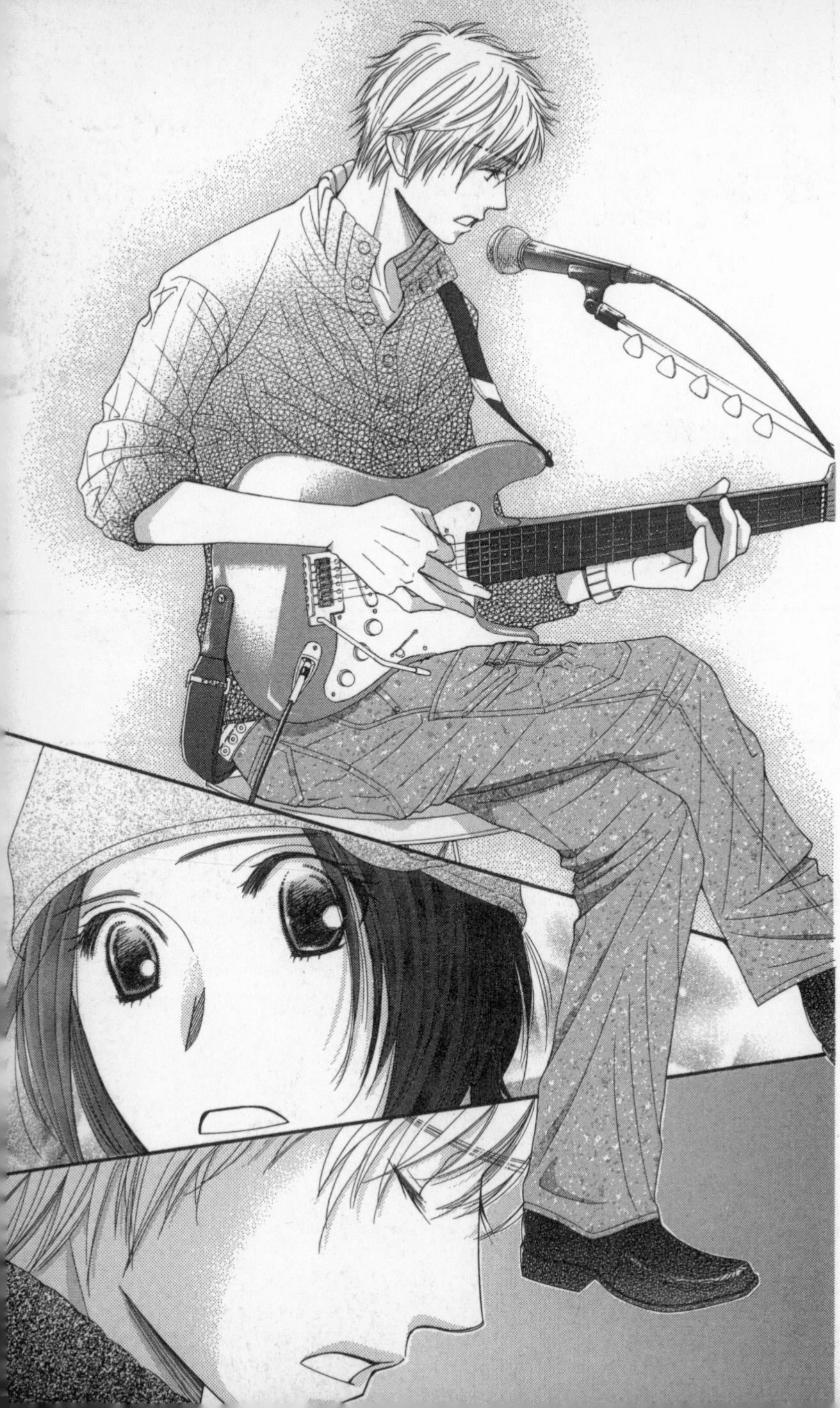

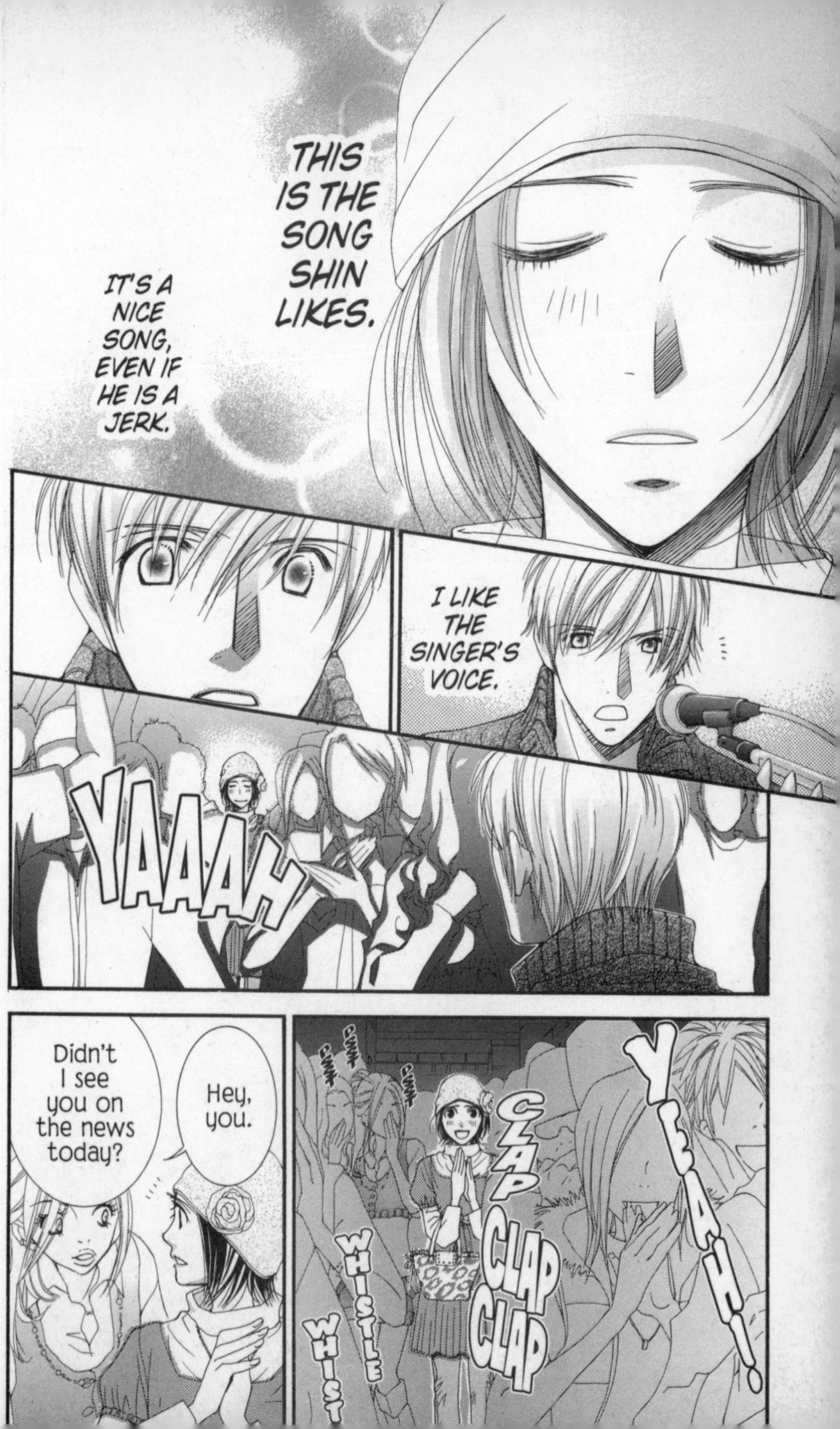
THIS IS THE SONG SHIN LIKES.
IT'S A NICE SONG, EVEN IF HE IS A JERK.
I LIKE THE SINGER'S VOICE.
YAAAH
YEAAH!
CLAP CLAP CLAP CLAP
WHISTLE WHIST
Hey, you.
Didn't I see you on the news today?

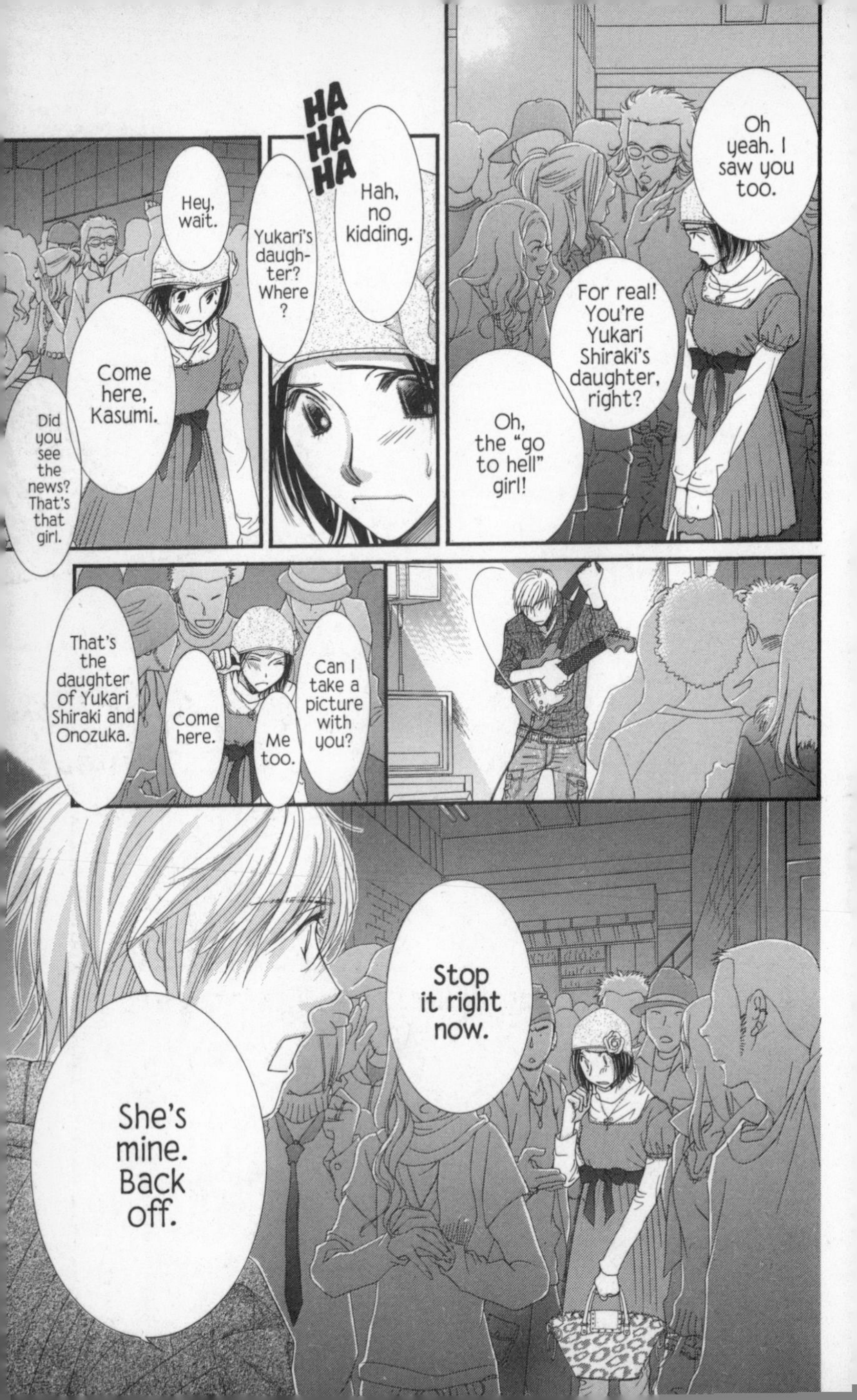
Oh yeah. I saw you too.
For real! You're Yukari Shiraki's daughter, right?
Oh, the "go to hell" girl!
HA HA HA
Hah, no kidding.
Yukari's daughter? Where?
Hey, wait.
Come here, Kasumi.
Did you see the news? That's that girl.
Can I take a picture with you?
Me too.
Come here.
That's the daughter of Yukari Shiraki and Onozuka.
Stop it right now.
She's mine. Back off.

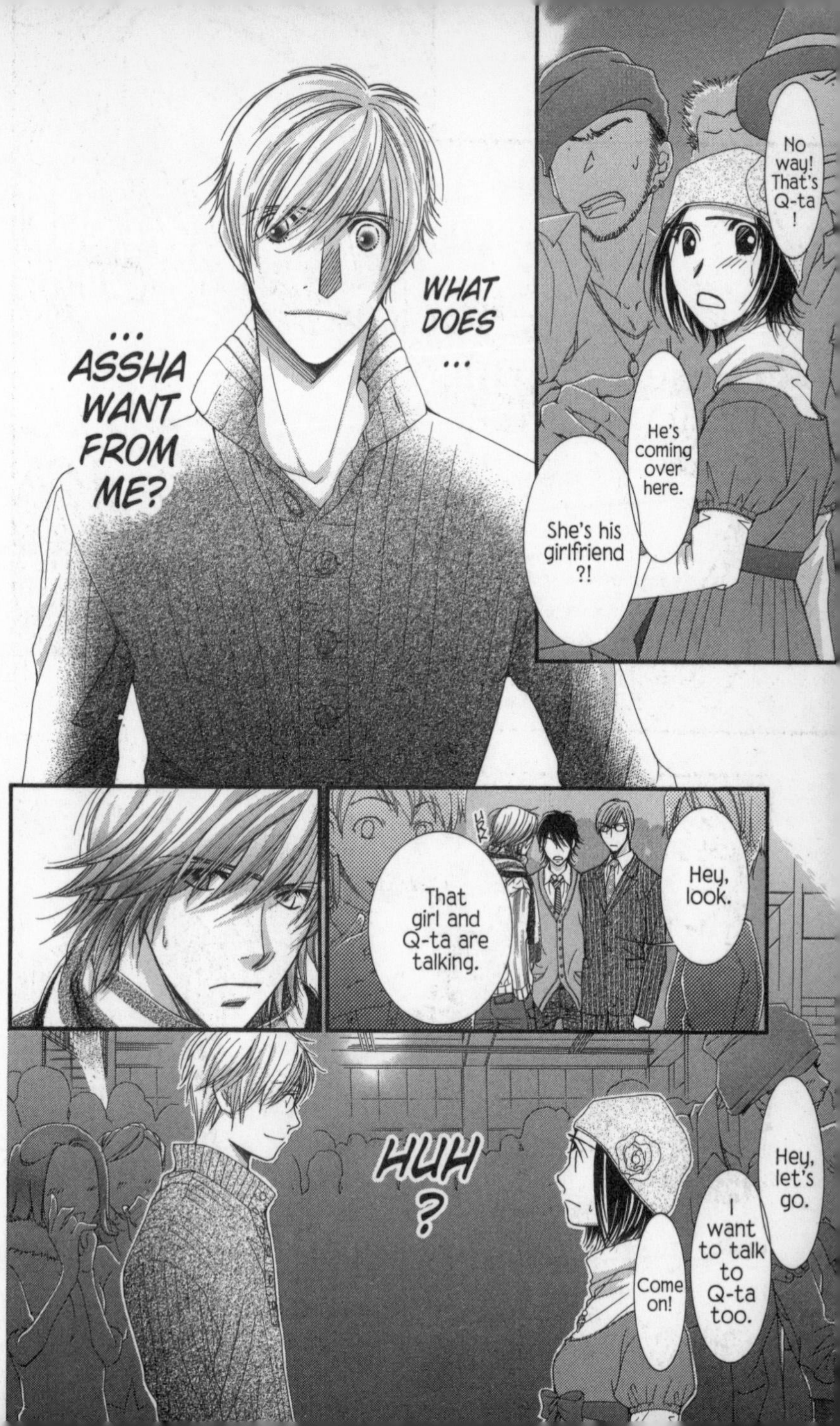
No way! That's Q-ta!
He's coming over here.
She's his girlfriend?!
WHAT DOES...
...ASSHA WANT FROM ME?
Hey, look.
That girl and Q-ta are talking.
Hey, let's go.
I want to talk to Q-ta too.
Come on!
HUH?

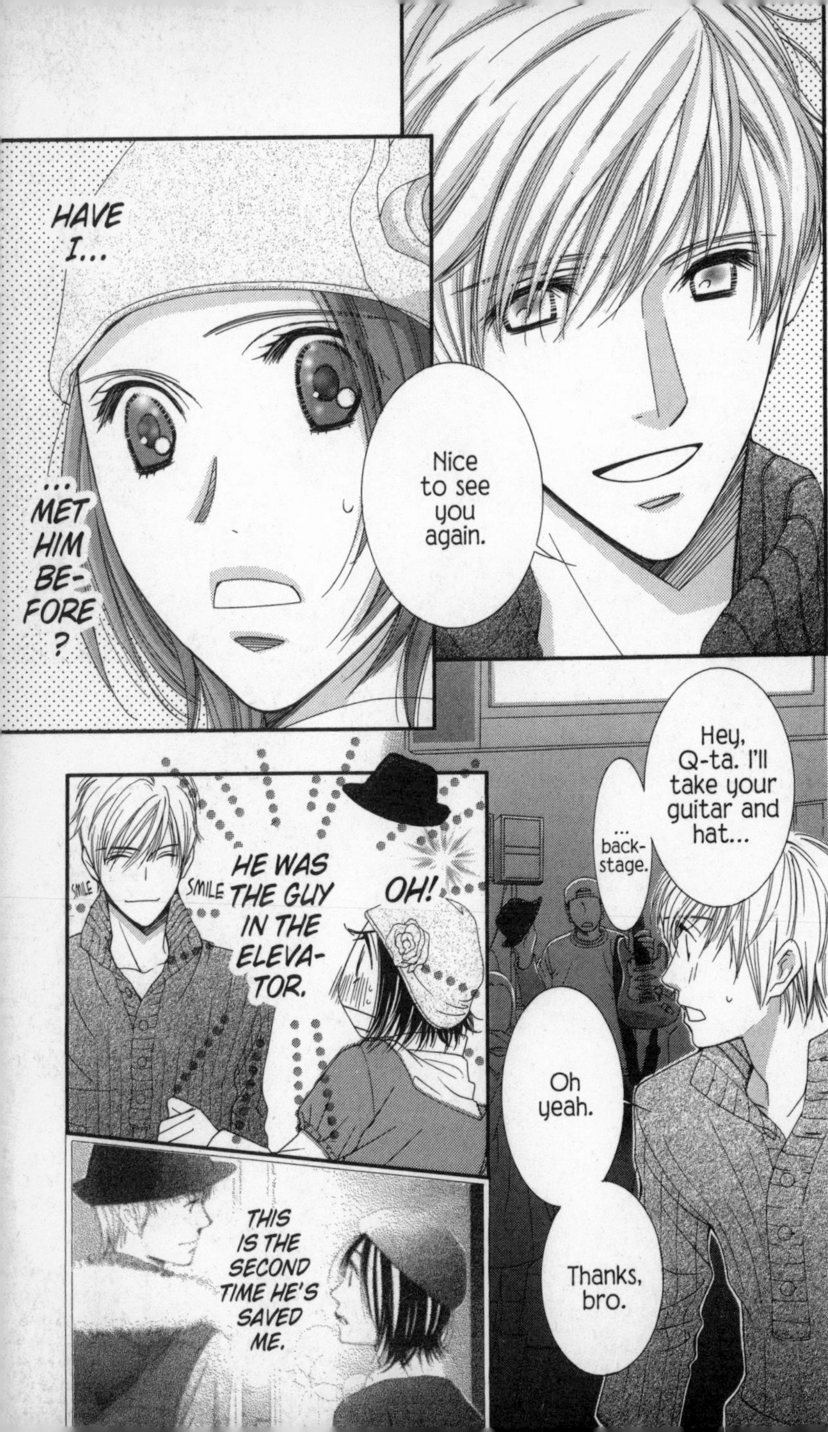
Nice to see you again.
HAVE I...
...MET HIM BEFORE?
Hey, Q-ta. I'll take your guitar and hat...
...backstage.
Oh yeah.
Thanks, bro.
OH!
HE WAS THE GUY IN THE ELEVATOR.
SMILE
SMILE
THIS IS THE SECOND TIME HE'S SAVED ME.

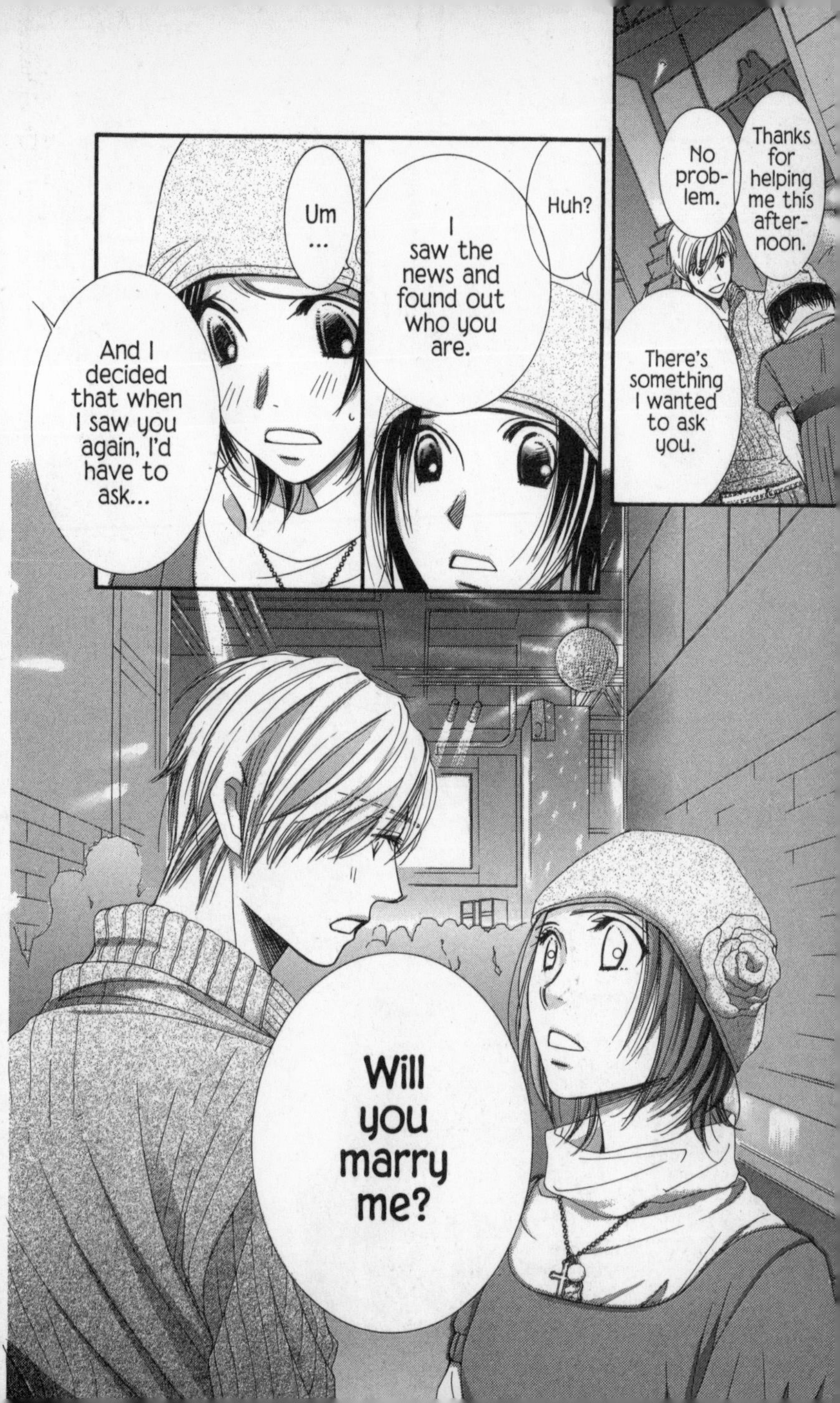
Thanks for helping me this after-noon.
No prob-lem.
There's something I wanted to ask you.
Huh?
I saw the news and found out who you are.
Um ...
And I decided that when I saw you again, I'd have to ask...
Will you marry me?

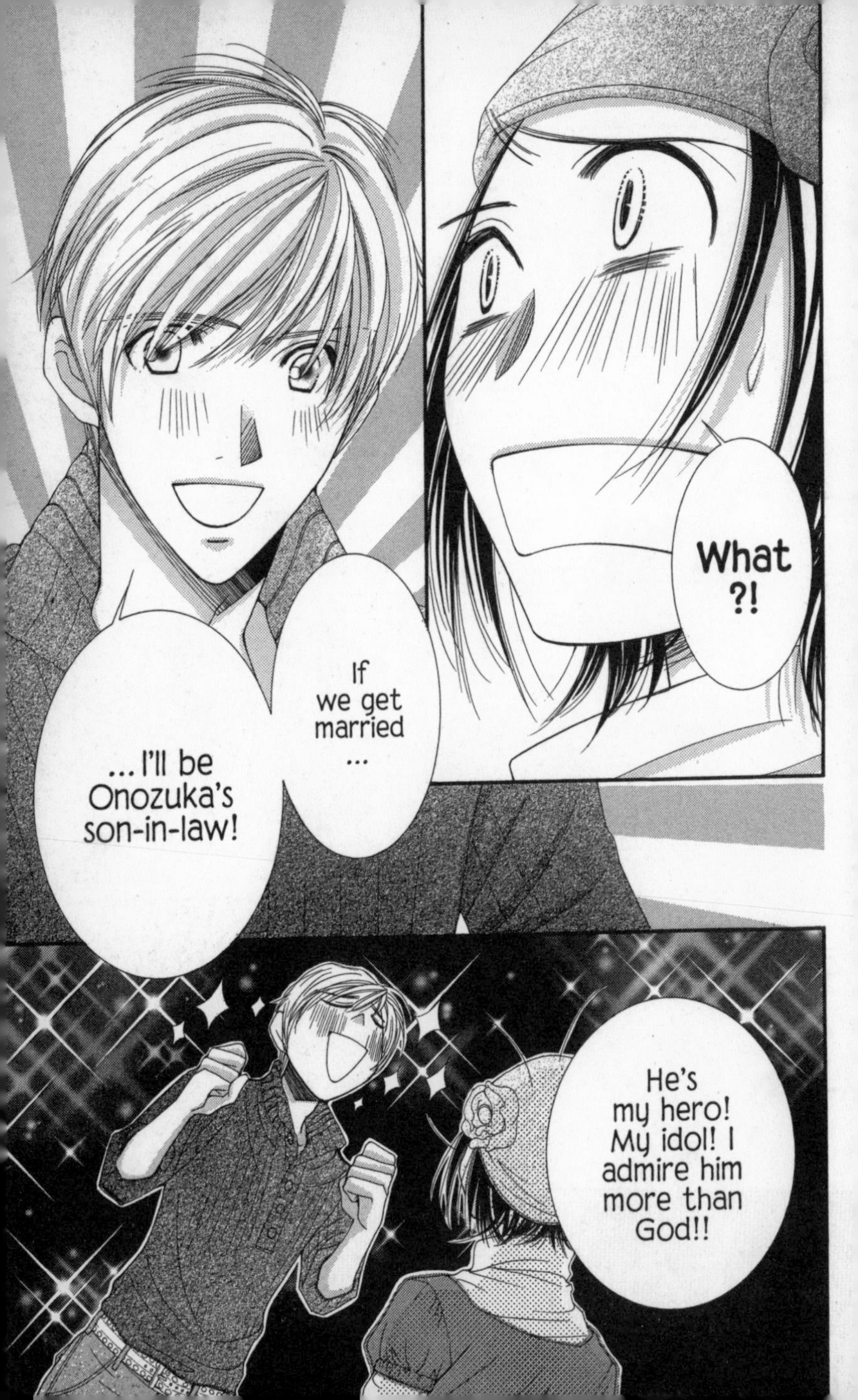
What?!
If we get married ...
... I'll be Onozuka's son-in-law!
He's my hero! My idol! I admire him more than God!!

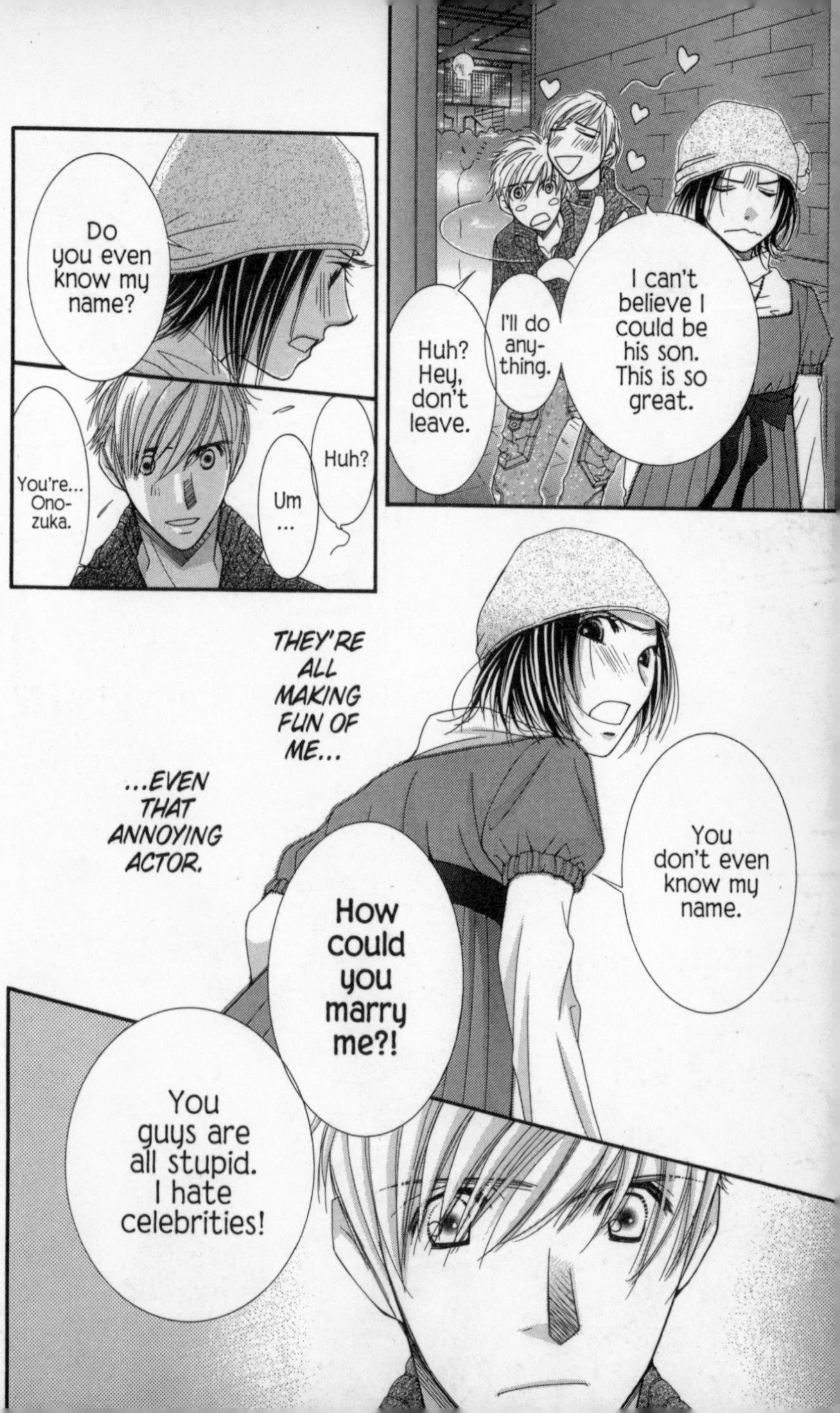
I can't believe I could be his son. This is so great.
I'll do anything.
Huh? Hey, don't leave.
Do you even know my name?
Huh?
Um...
You're... Ono-zuka.
THEY'RE ALL MAKING FUN OF ME...
...EVEN THAT ANNOYING ACTOR.
You don't even know my name.
How could you marry me?!
You guys are all stupid. I hate celebrities!

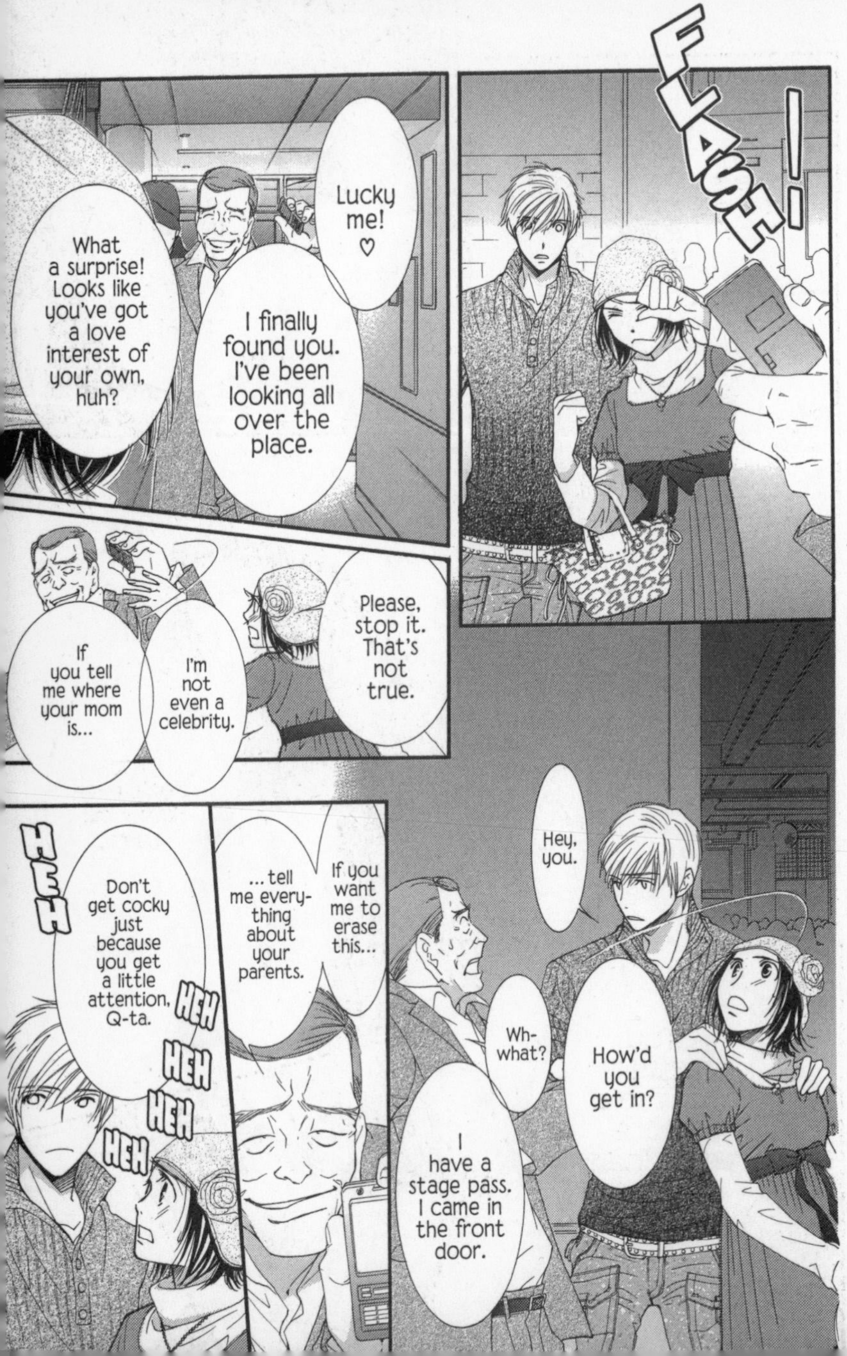
FLASH!!
Lucky me! ♡
I finally found you. I've been looking all over the place.
What a surprise! Looks like you've got a love interest of your own, huh?
Please, stop it. That's not true.
I'm not even a celebrity.
If you tell me where your mom is...
Hey, you.
Wh-what?
How'd you get in?
I have a stage pass. I came in the front door.
If you want me to erase this...
... tell me every-thing about your parents.
Don't get cocky just because you get a little attention, Q-ta.
HEH HEH HEH HEH HEH

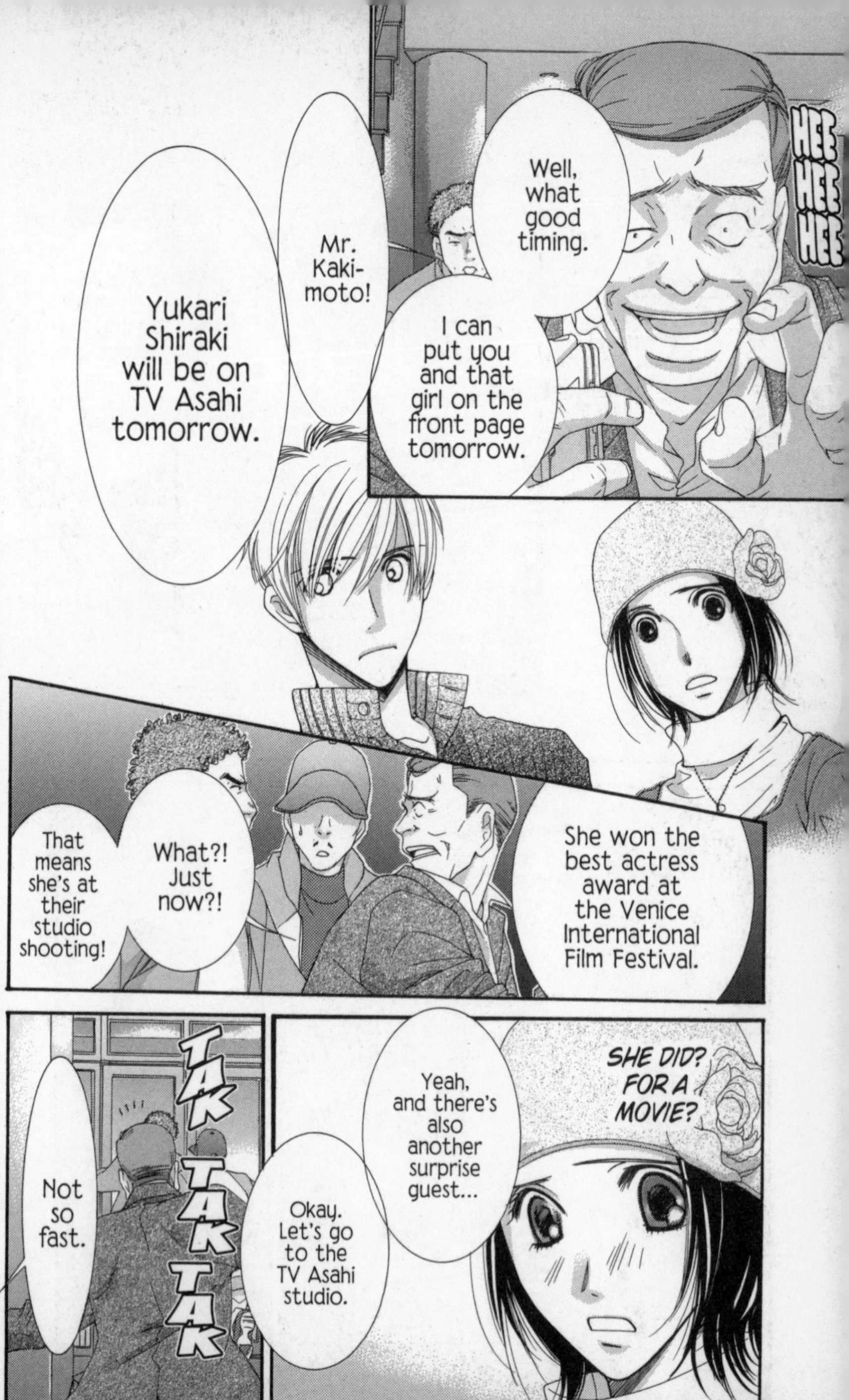
HEE HEE HEE
Well, what good timing.
I can put you and that girl on the front page tomorrow.
Mr. Kaki-moto!
Yukari Shiraki will be on TV Asahi tomorrow.
She won the best actress award at the Venice International Film Festival.
What?! Just now?!
That means she's at their studio shooting!
SHE DID? FOR A MOVIE?
Yeah, and there's also another surprise guest...
Okay. Let's go to the TV Asahi studio.
TAK TAK TAK
Not so fast.

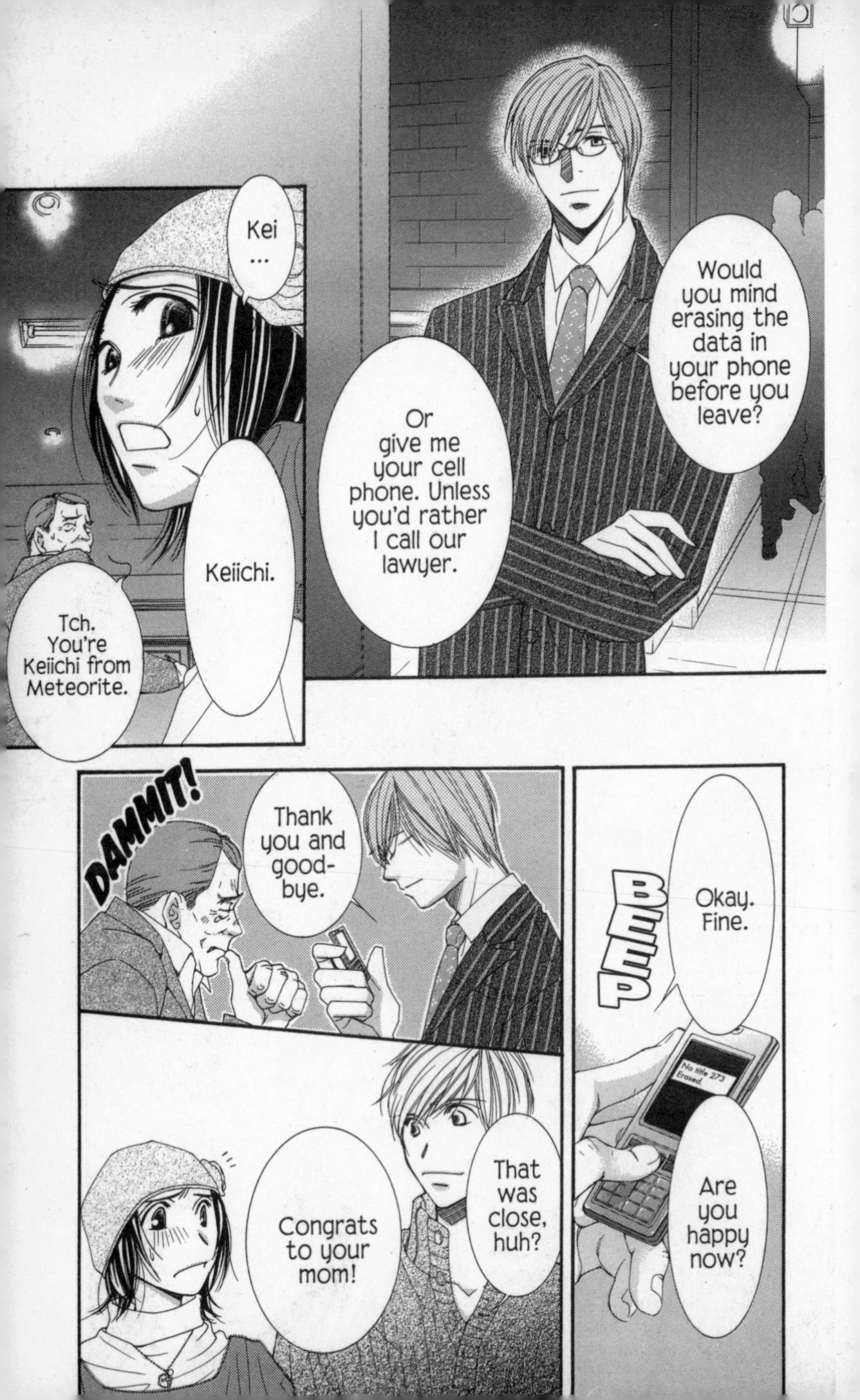
Would you mind erasing the data in your phone before you leave?
Or give me your cell phone. Unless you'd rather I call our lawyer.
Kei ...
Keiichi.
Tch. You're Keiichi from Meteorite.
BEEP
Okay. Fine.
No title 273 Erased.
Are you happy now?
DAMMIT!
Thank you and good-bye.
That was close, huh?
Congrats to your mom!

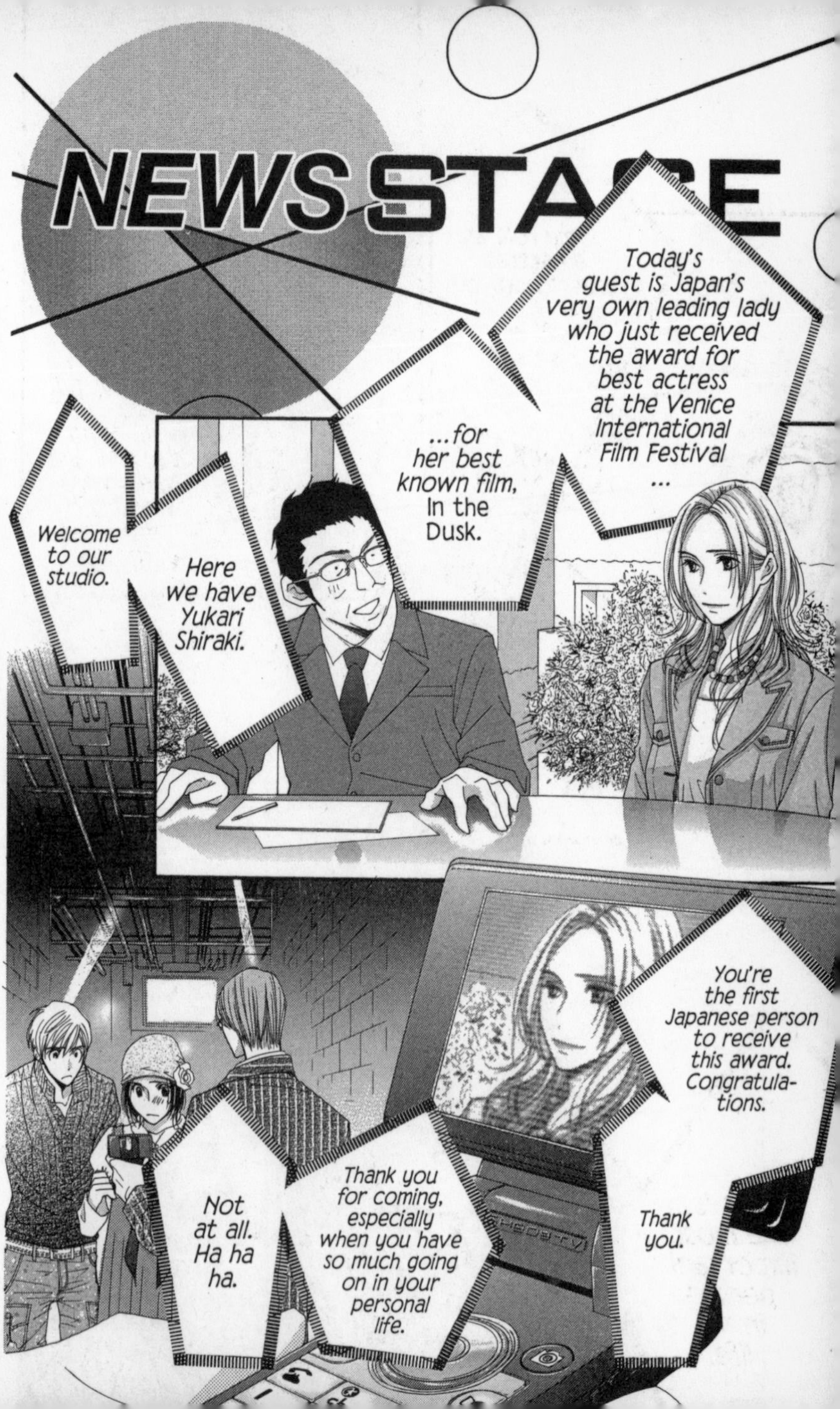
NEWS STAGE
Today's guest is Japan's very own leading lady who just received the award for best actress at the Venice International Film Festival...
...for her best known film, In the Dusk.
Here we have Yukari Shiraki.
Welcome to our studio.
You're the first Japanese person to receive this award. Congratula-tions.
Thank you.
Thank you for coming, especially when you have so much going on in your personal life.
Not at all. Ha ha ha.

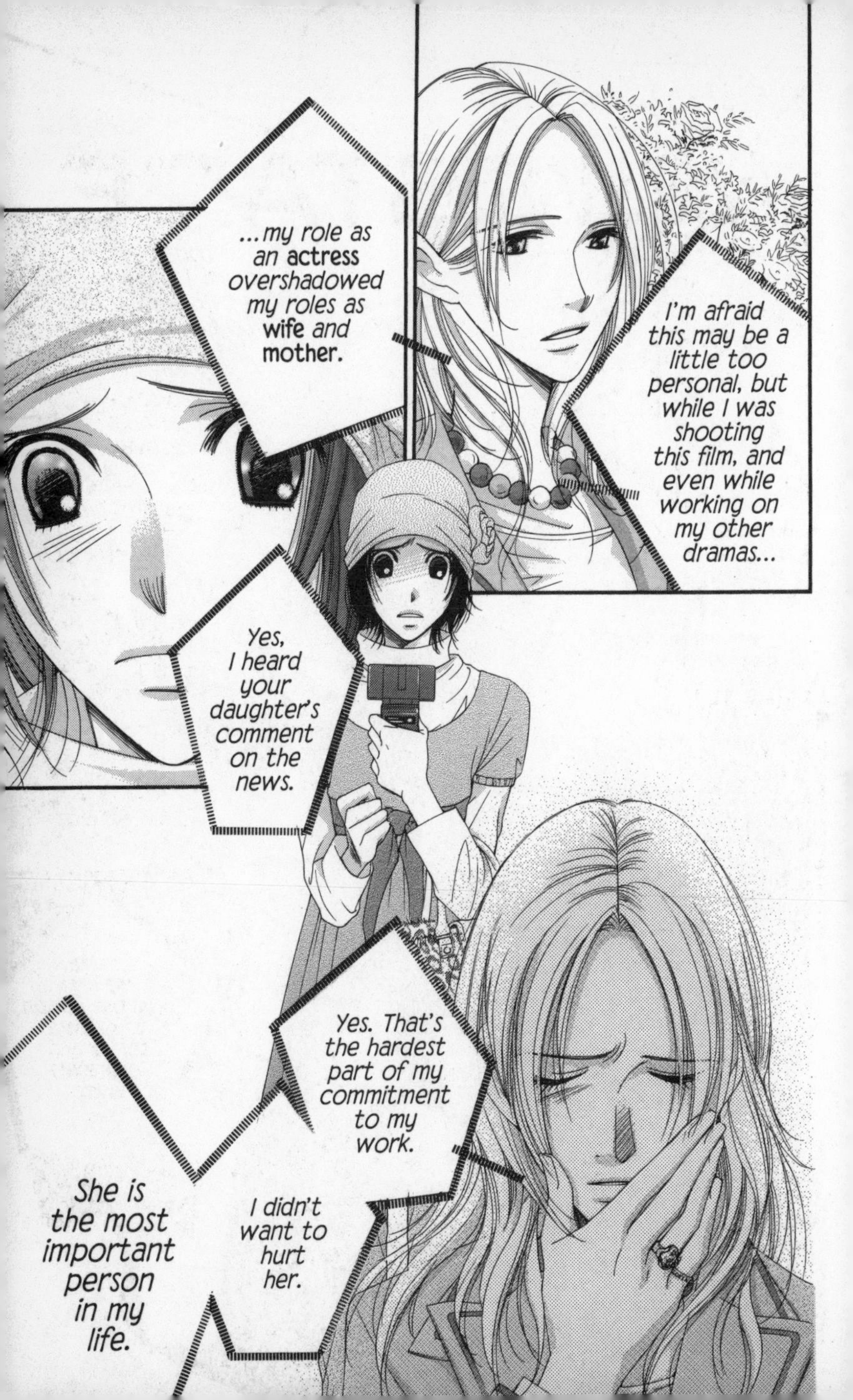
I'm afraid this may be a little too personal, but while I was shooting this film, and even while working on my other dramas...
...my role as an actress overshadowed my roles as wife and mother.
Yes, I heard your daughter's comment on the news.
Yes. That's the hardest part of my commitment to my work.
I didn't want to hurt her.
She is the most important person in my life.

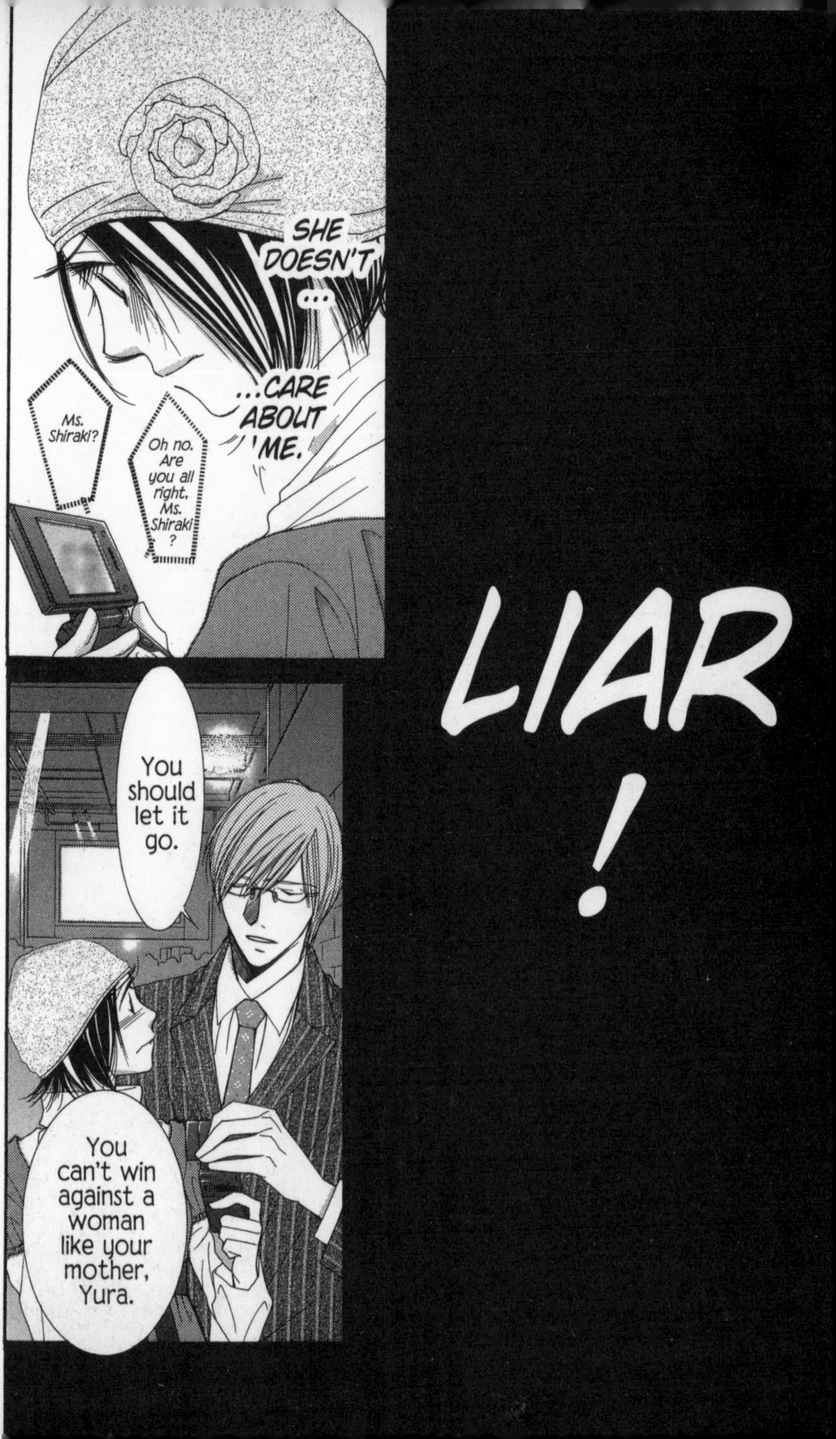
LIAR!
SHE DOESN'T...
...CARE ABOUT ME.
Oh no. Are you all right, Ms. Shiraki?
Ms. Shiraki?
You should let it go.
You can't win against a woman like your mother, Yura.

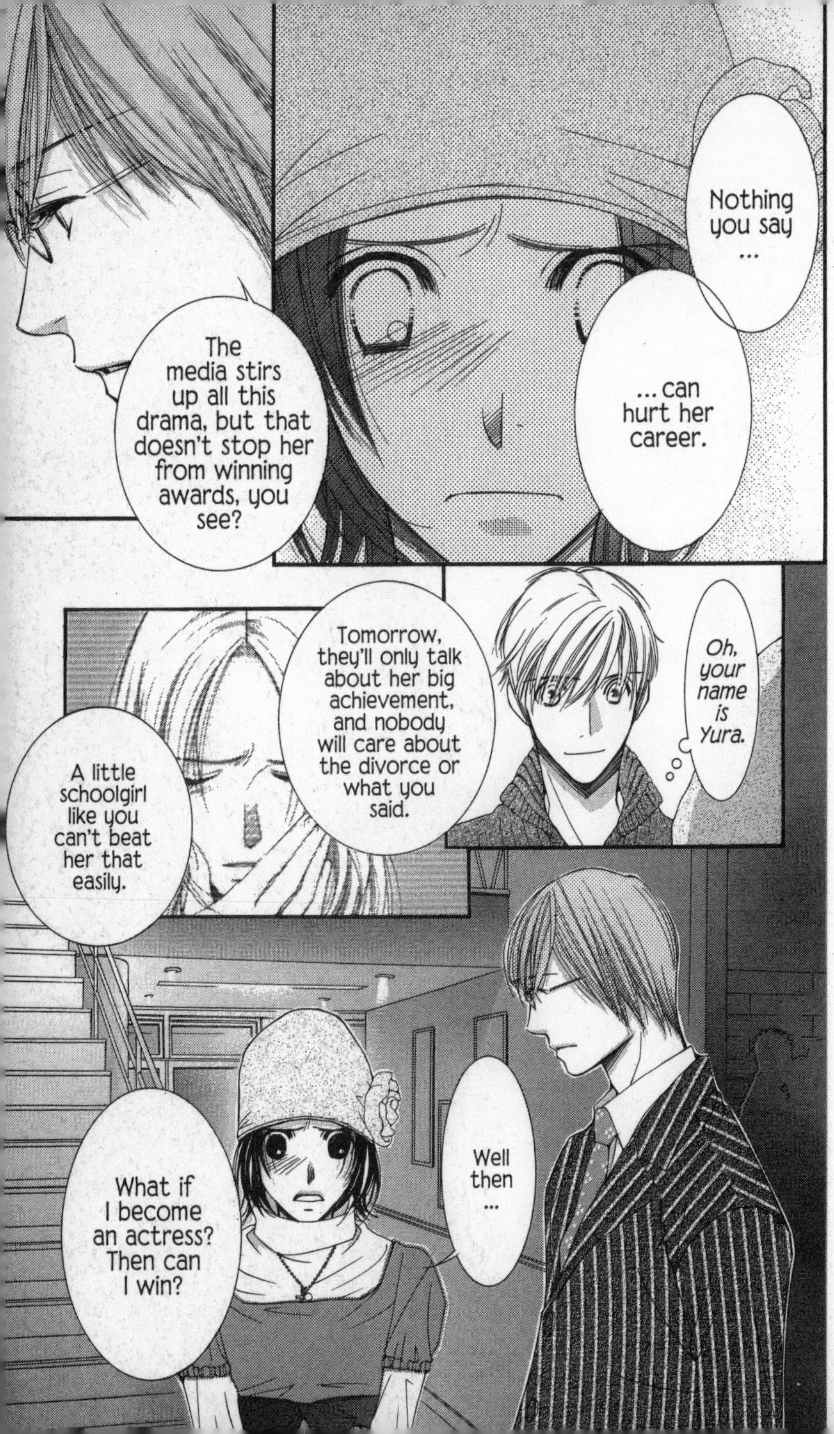
Nothing you say ...
... can hurt her career.
The media stirs up all this drama, but that doesn't stop her from winning awards, you see?
Oh, your name is Yura.
Tomorrow, they'll only talk about her big achievement, and nobody will care about the divorce or what you said.
A little schoolgirl like you can't beat her that easily.
Well then ...
What if I become an actress? Then can I win?

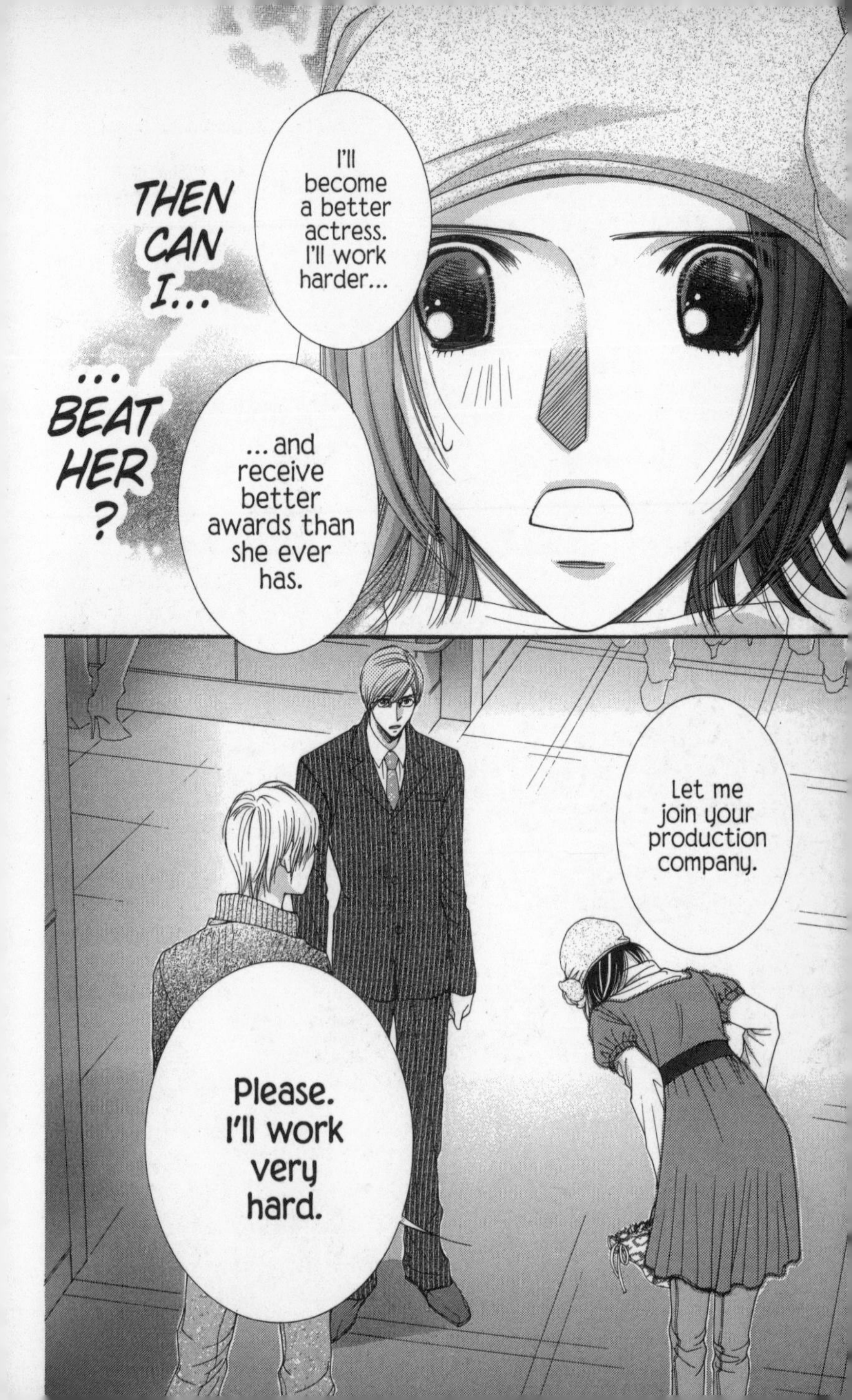
I'll become a better actress. I'll work harder...
...and receive better awards than she ever has.
THEN CAN I...
...BEAT HER?
Let me join your production company.
Please. I'll work very hard.

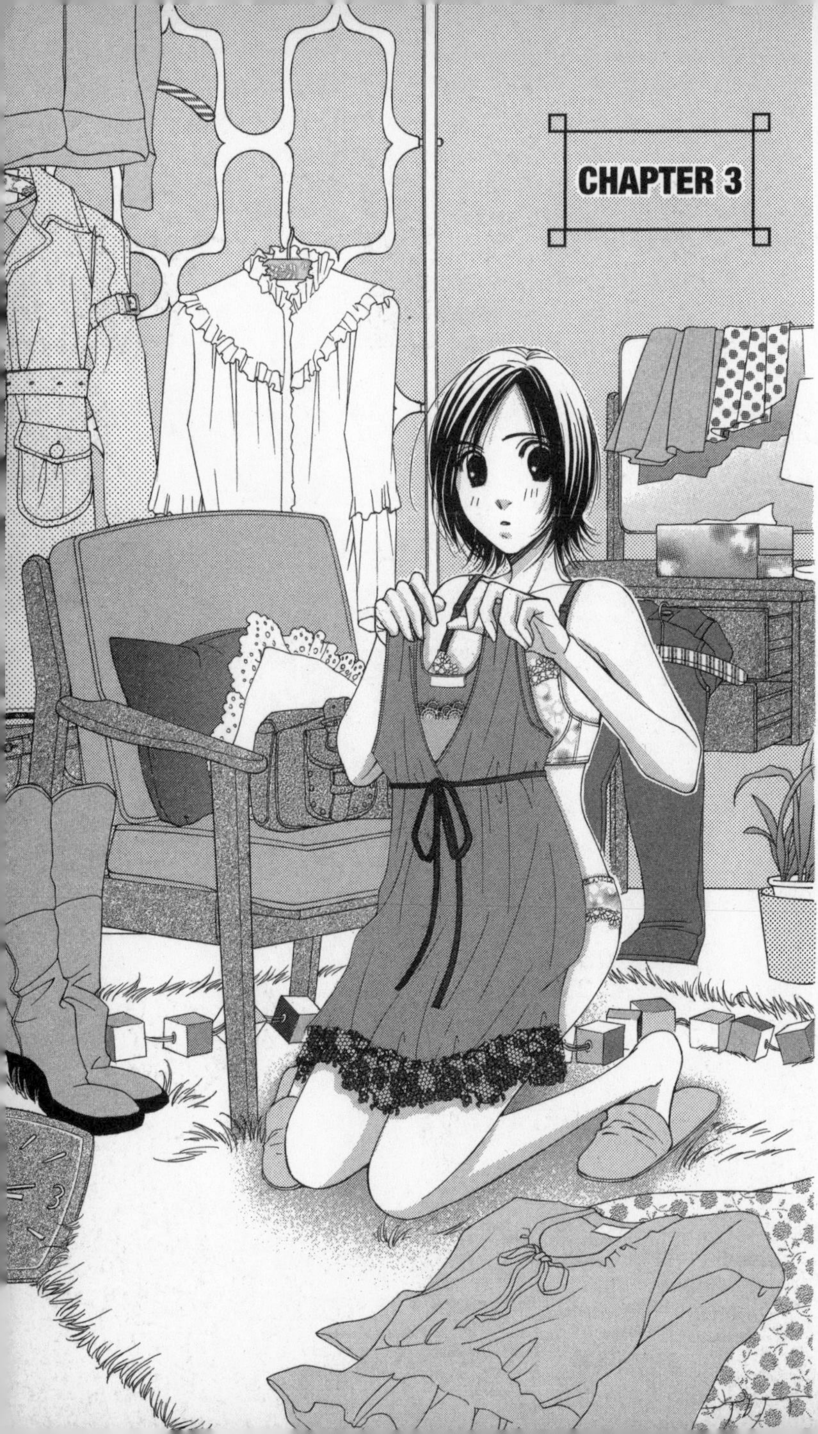
CHAPTER 3

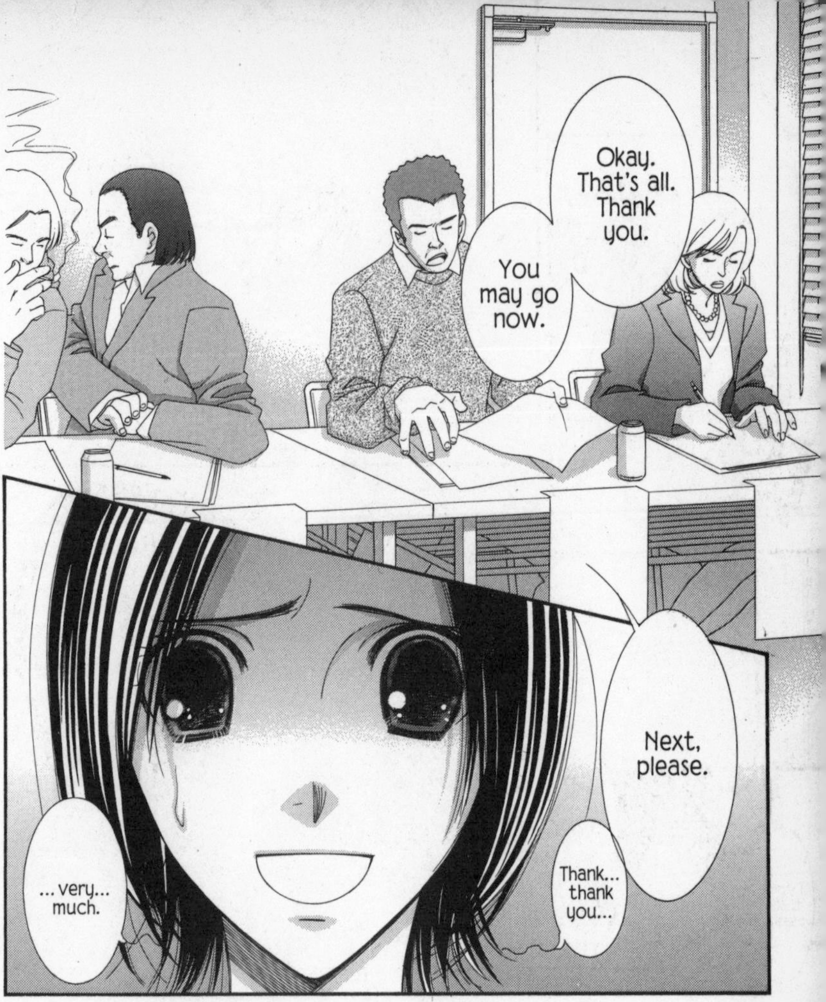
Okay. That's all. Thank you.
You may go now.
Next, please.
Thank... thank you...
...very... much.

Honey Hunt

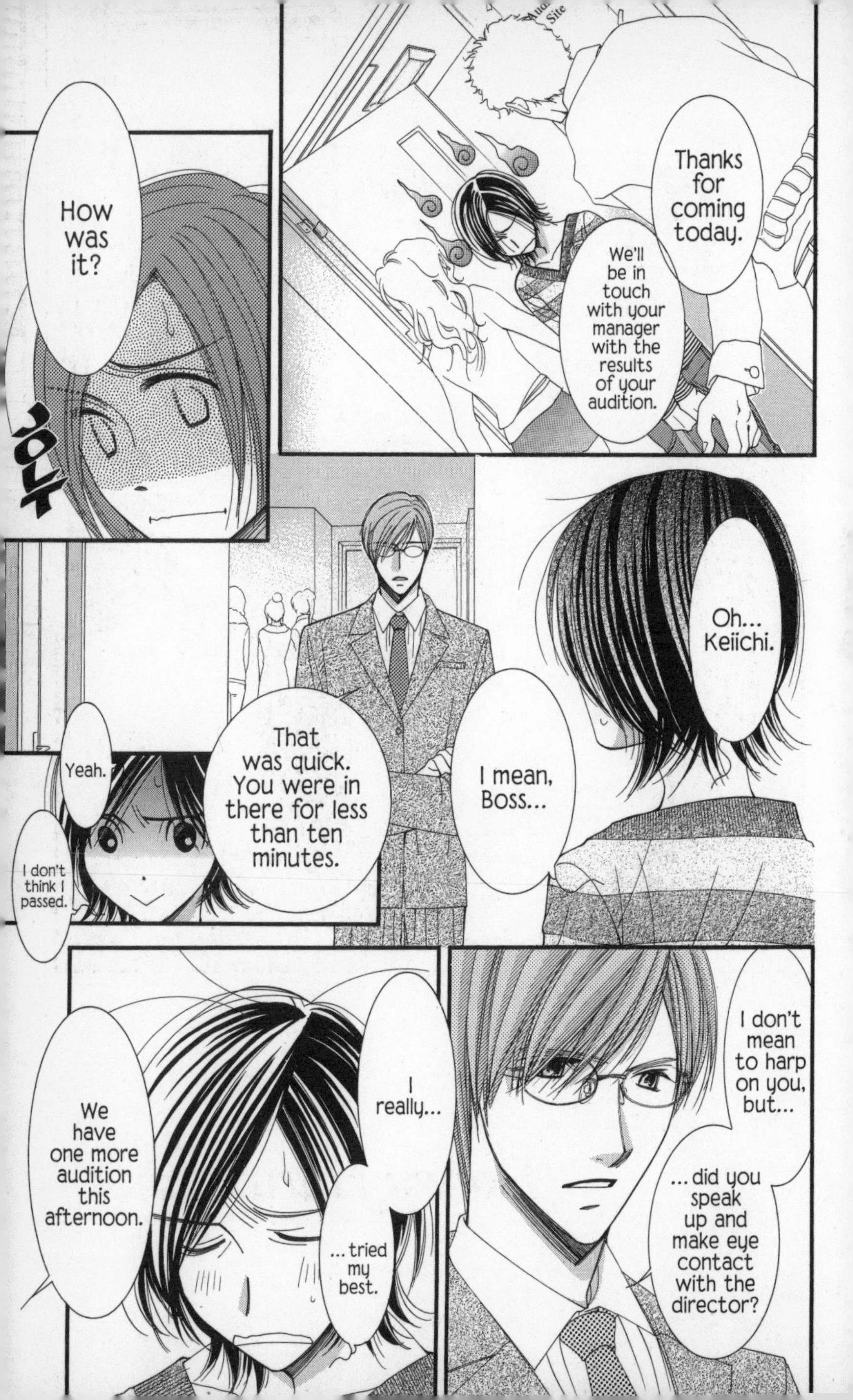
Thanks for coming today.
We'll be in touch with your manager with the results of your audition.
How was it?
JOLT
Oh... Keiichi.
I mean, Boss...
That was quick. You were in there for less than ten minutes.
Yeah.
I don't think I passed.
I don't mean to harp on you, but...
...did you speak up and make eye contact with the director?
I really...
...tried my best.
We have one more audition this afternoon.

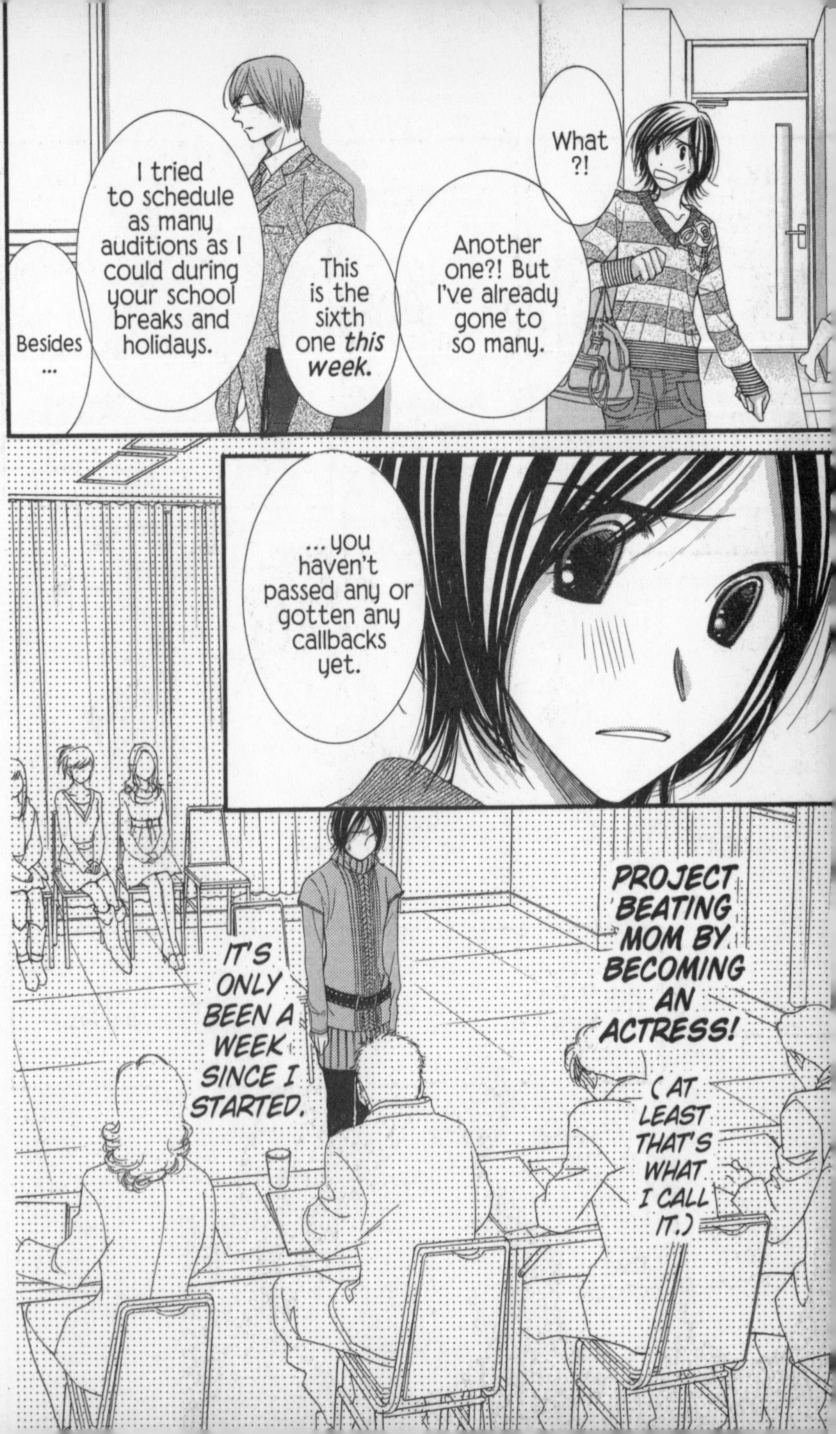
What?!
Another one?! But I've already gone to so many.
This is the sixth one *this week.*
I tried to schedule as many auditions as I could during your school breaks and holidays.
Besides...
...you haven't passed any or gotten any callbacks yet.
PROJECT BEATING MOM BY BECOMING AN ACTRESS!
(AT LEAST THAT'S WHAT I CALL IT.)
IT'S ONLY BEEN A WEEK SINCE I STARTED.

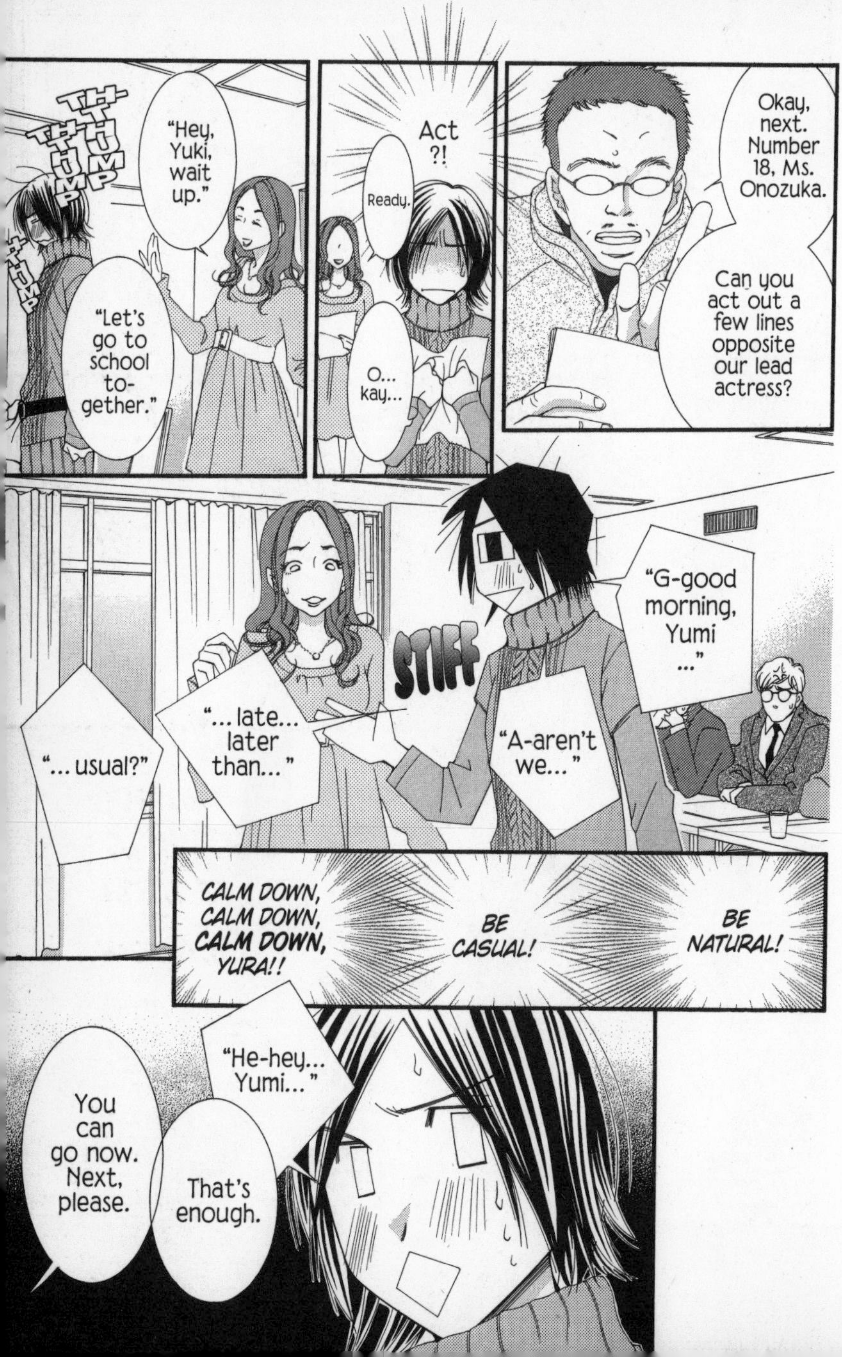
Okay, next. Number 18, Ms. Onozuka.
Can you act out a few lines opposite our lead actress?
Act ?!
Ready.
O... kay...
TH-THUMP
THUMP
"Hey, Yuki, wait up."
THUMP
"Let's go to school to-gether."
"G-good morning, Yumi ..."
STIFF
"A-aren't we..."
"... late... later than..."
"... usual?"
BE NATURAL!
BE CASUAL!
CALM DOWN, CALM DOWN, CALM DOWN, YURA!!
"He-hey... Yumi..."
That's enough.
You can go now. Next, please.

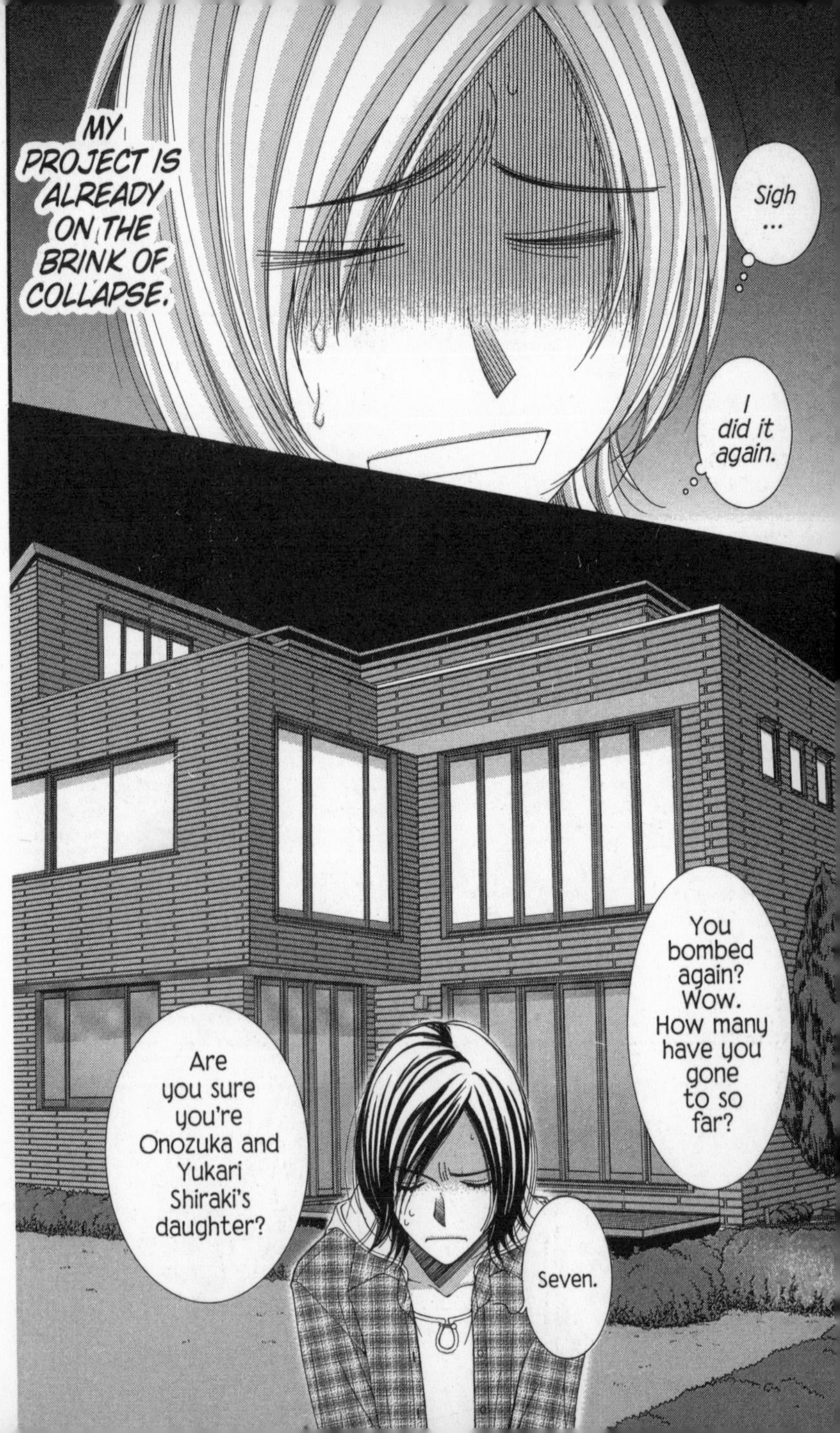
Sigh ...
I did it again.
MY PROJECT IS ALREADY ON THE BRINK OF COLLAPSE.
You bombed again? Wow. How many have you gone to so far?
Seven.
Are you sure you're Onozuka and Yukari Shiraki's daughter?

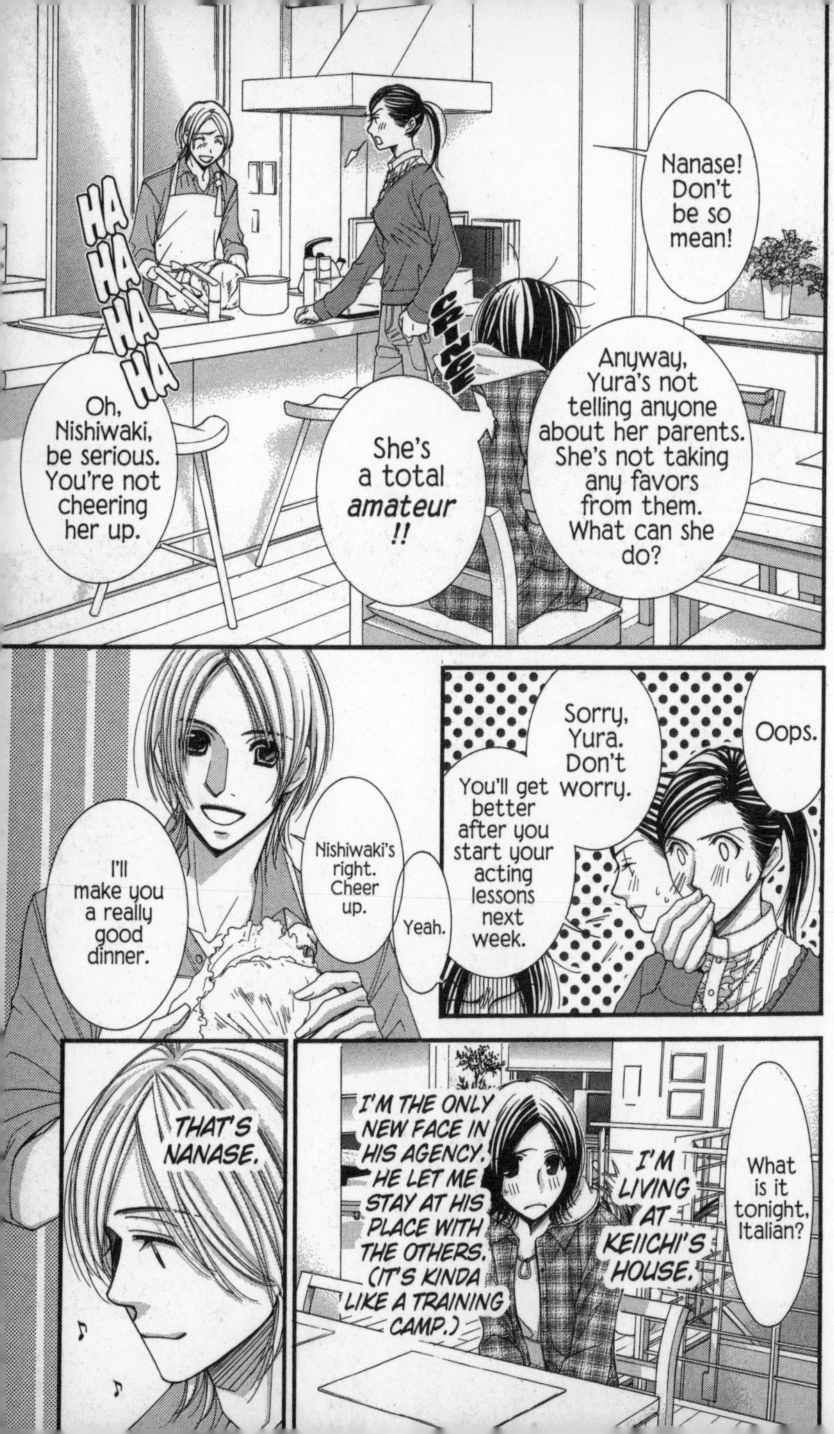
Nanase! Don't be so mean!
Anyway, Yura's not telling anyone about her parents. She's not taking any favors from them. What can she do?
CRINGE
She's a total *amateur* !!
HA HA HA HA HA
Oh, Nishiwaki, be serious. You're not cheering her up.
Oops.
Sorry, Yura. Don't worry.
You'll get better after you start your acting lessons next week.
Nishiwaki's right. Cheer up.
Yeah.
I'll make you a really good dinner.
What is it tonight, Italian?
I'M LIVING AT KEIICHI'S HOUSE.
I'M THE ONLY NEW FACE IN HIS AGENCY. HE LET ME STAY AT HIS PLACE WITH THE OTHERS. (IT'S KINDA LIKE A TRAINING CAMP.)
THAT'S NANASE.

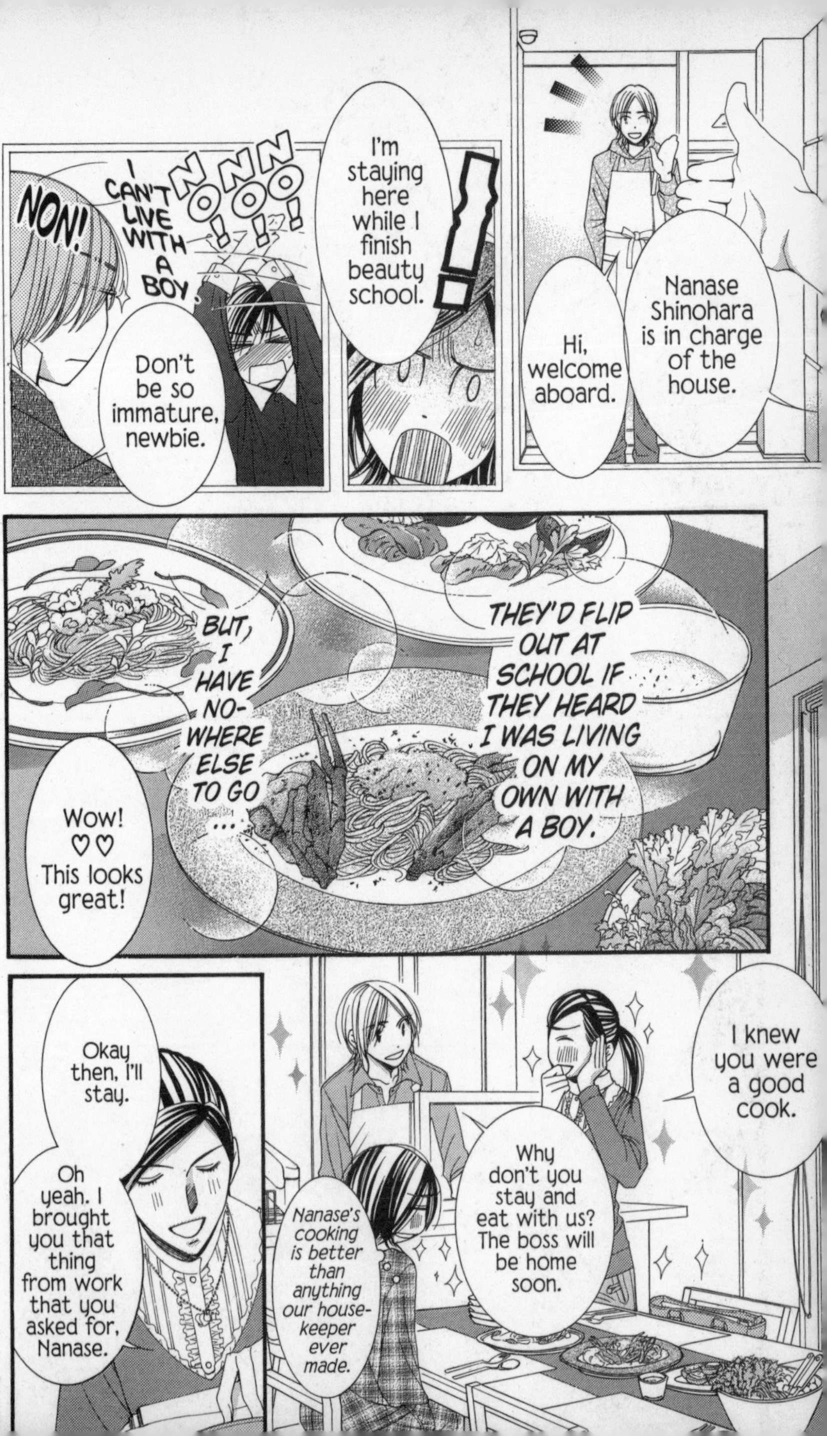
Nanase Shinohara is in charge of the house.
Hi, welcome aboard.
!
I'm staying here while I finish beauty school.
NNNOOO!!
I CAN'T LIVE WITH A BOY.
NON!
Don't be so immature, newbie.
THEY'D FLIP OUT AT SCHOOL IF THEY HEARD I WAS LIVING ON MY OWN WITH A BOY.
BUT, I HAVE NO-WHERE ELSE TO GO...
Wow! ♡♡ This looks great!
I knew you were a good cook.
Why don't you stay and eat with us? The boss will be home soon.
Nanase's cooking is better than anything our house-keeper ever made.
Okay then, I'll stay.
Oh yeah. I brought you that thing from work that you asked for, Nanase.

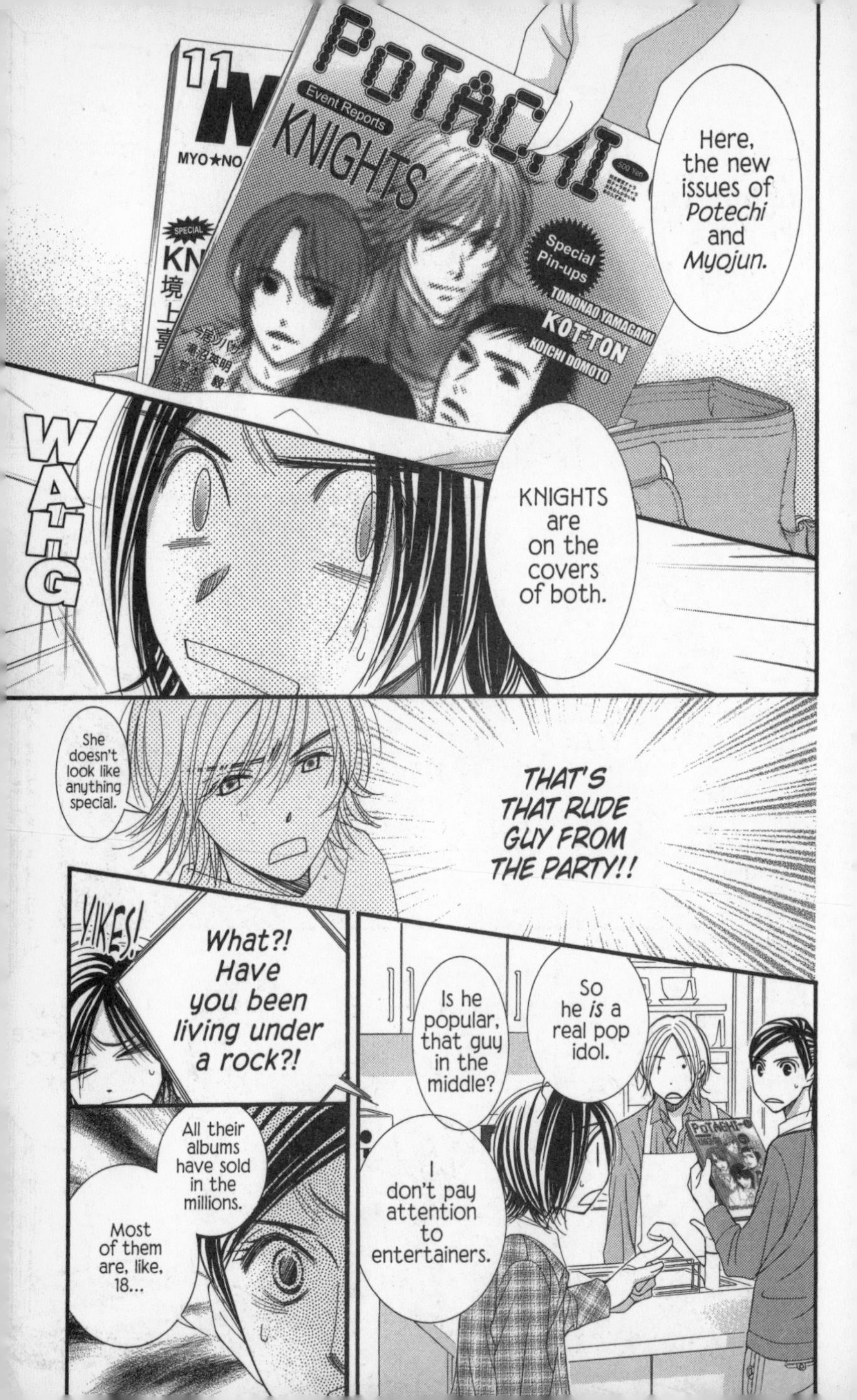
Event Reports
KNIGHTS
Special Pin-ups
TOMONAO YAMAGAMI
KOT-TON
KOICHI DOMOTO
Here, the new issues of *Potechi* and *Myojun.*
KNIGHTS are on the covers of both.
WAHG
THAT'S THAT RUDE GUY FROM THE PARTY!!
She doesn't look like anything special.
So he *is* a real pop idol.
Is he popular, that guy in the middle?
I don't pay attention to entertainers.
YIKES!
What?! Have you been living under a rock?!
All their albums have sold in the millions.
Most of them are, like, 18...

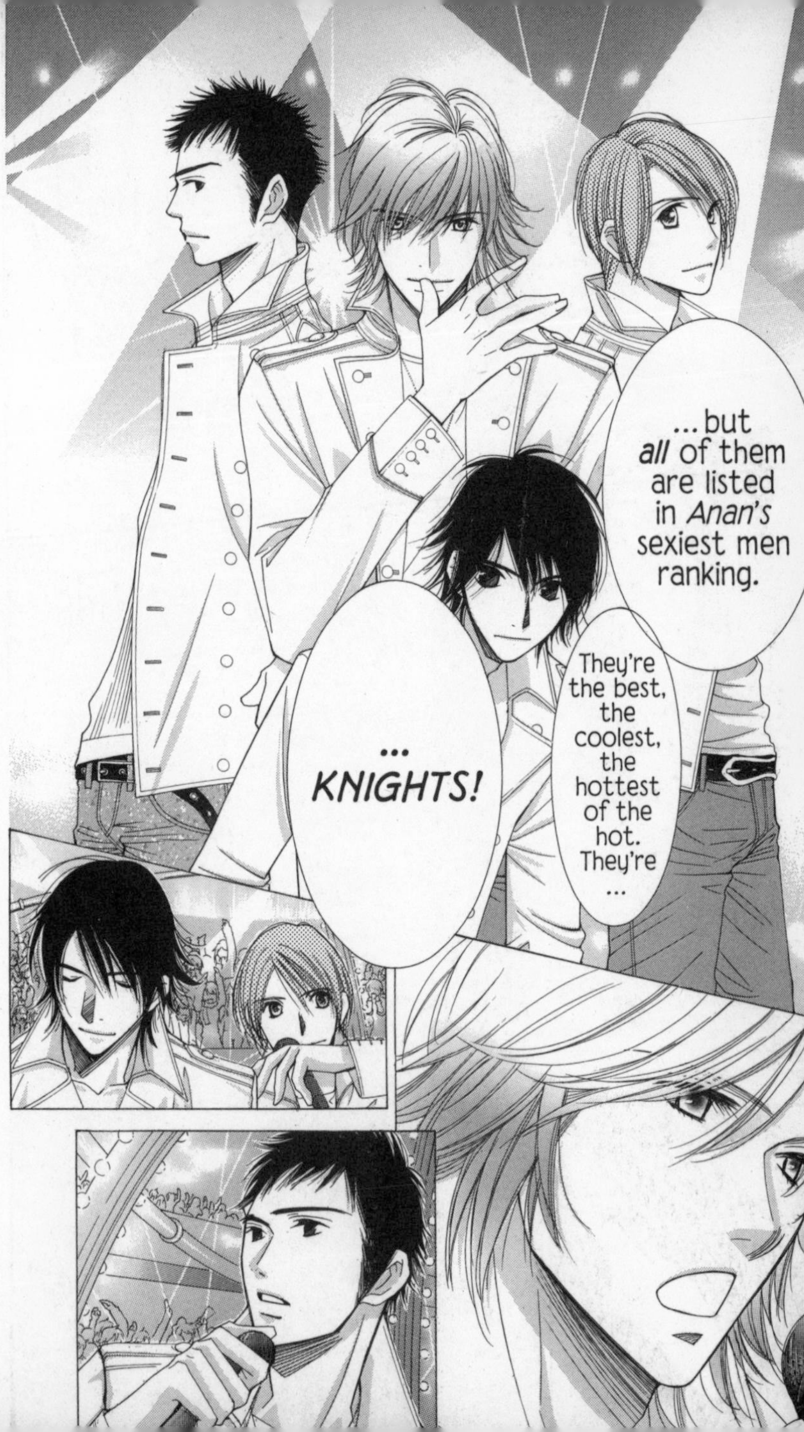
...but *all* of them are listed in *Anan's* sexiest men ranking.
They're the best, the coolest, the hottest of the hot. They're ...
... KNIGHTS!

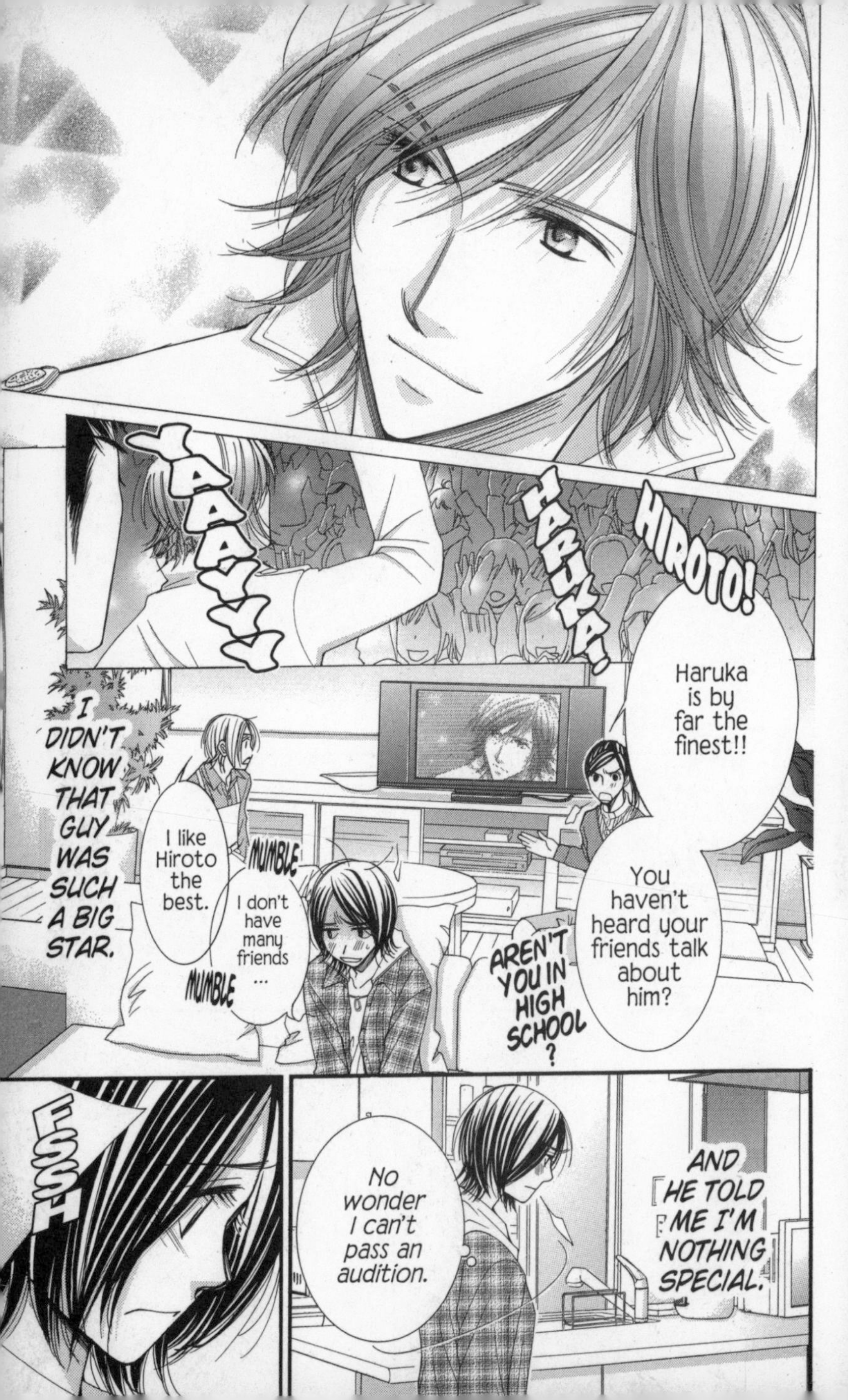
HIROTO!
HARUKA!
YAAAYYY
Haruka is by far the finest!!
You haven't heard your friends talk about him?
AREN'T YOU IN HIGH SCHOOL?
MUMBLE
I don't have many friends ...
MUMBLE
I like Hiroto the best.
I DIDN'T KNOW THAT GUY WAS SUCH A BIG STAR.
AND HE TOLD ME I'M NOTHING SPECIAL.
No wonder I can't pass an audition.
FSSH

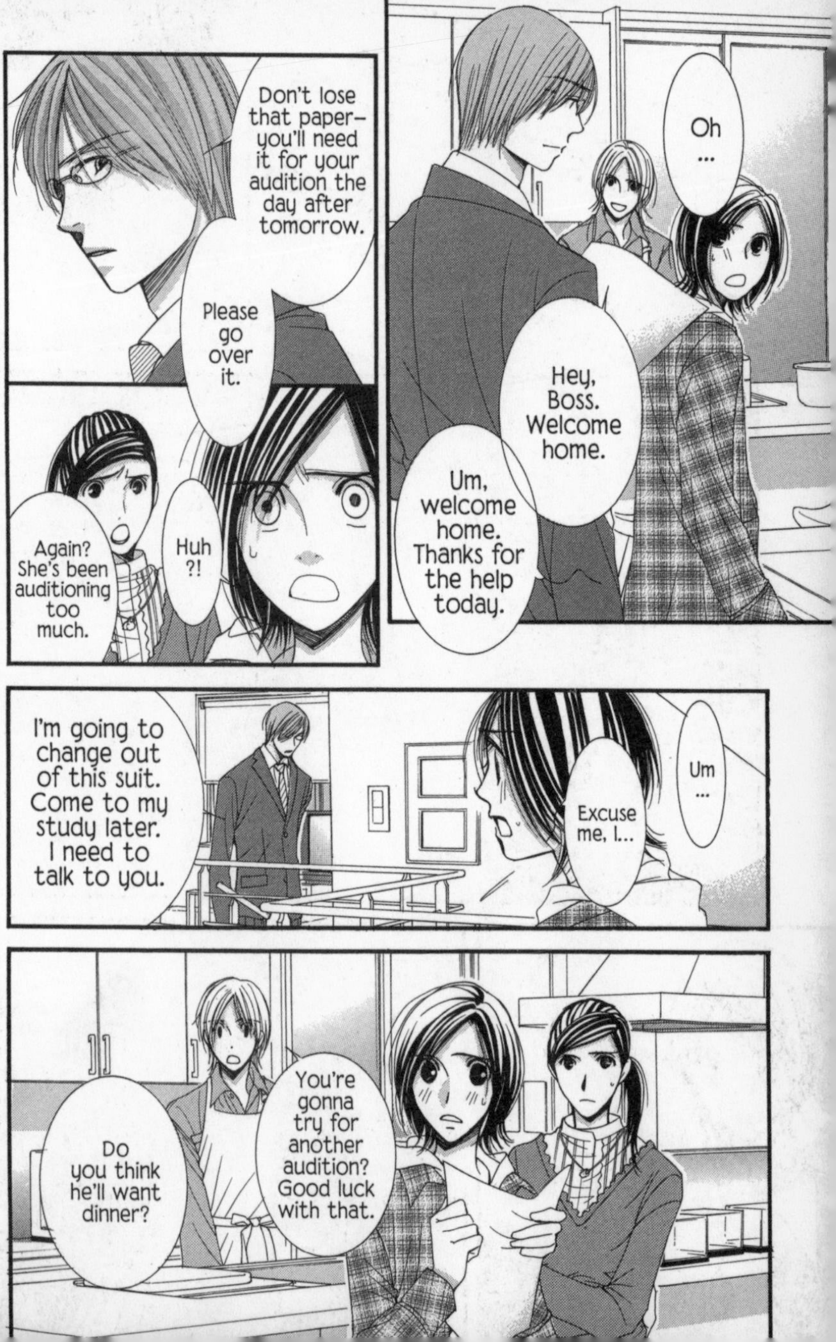
Oh ...
Hey, Boss. Welcome home.
Um, welcome home. Thanks for the help today.
Don't lose that paper—you'll need it for your audition the day after tomorrow.
Please go over it.
Huh ?!
Again? She's been auditioning too much.
Um ...
Excuse me, I...
I'm going to change out of this suit. Come to my study later. I need to talk to you.
You're gonna try for another audition? Good luck with that.
Do you think he'll want dinner?

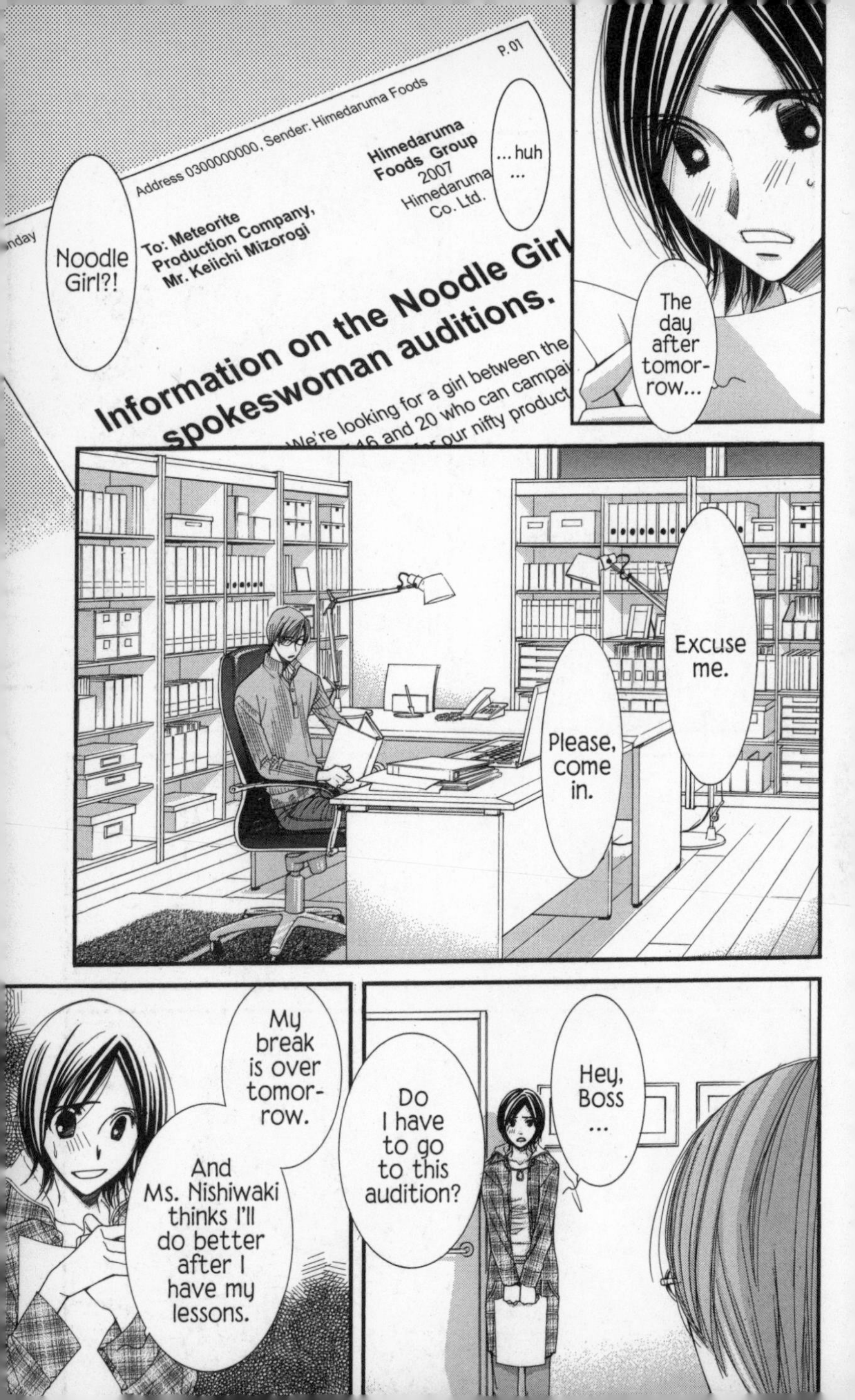
The day after tomorrow...
...huh ...
P.01
Address 0300000000, Sender: Himedaruma Foods
Himedaruma Foods Group 2007 Himedaruma Co. Ltd.
To: Meteorite Production Company, Mr. Keiichi Mizorogi
Information on the Noodle Girl spokeswoman auditions.
We're looking for a girl between the
Noodle Girl?!
Excuse me.
Please, come in.
Hey, Boss ...
Do I have to go to this audition?
My break is over tomorrow.
And Ms. Nishiwaki thinks I'll do better after I have my lessons.

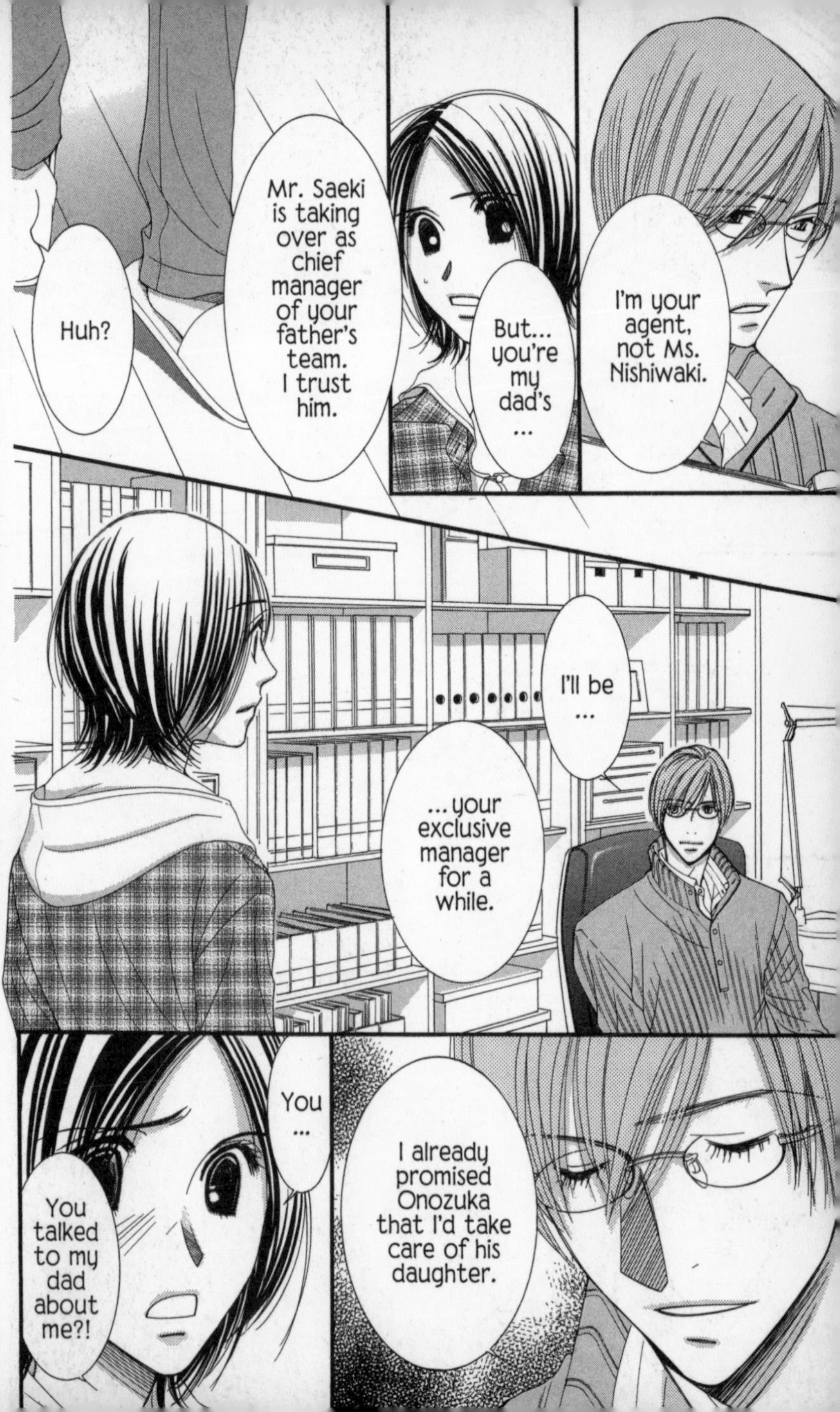
I'm your agent, not Ms. Nishiwaki.
But... you're my dad's ...
Mr. Saeki is taking over as chief manager of your father's team. I trust him.
Huh?
I'll be ...
...your exclusive manager for a while.
I already promised Onozuka that I'd take care of his daughter.
You ...
You talked to my dad about me?!

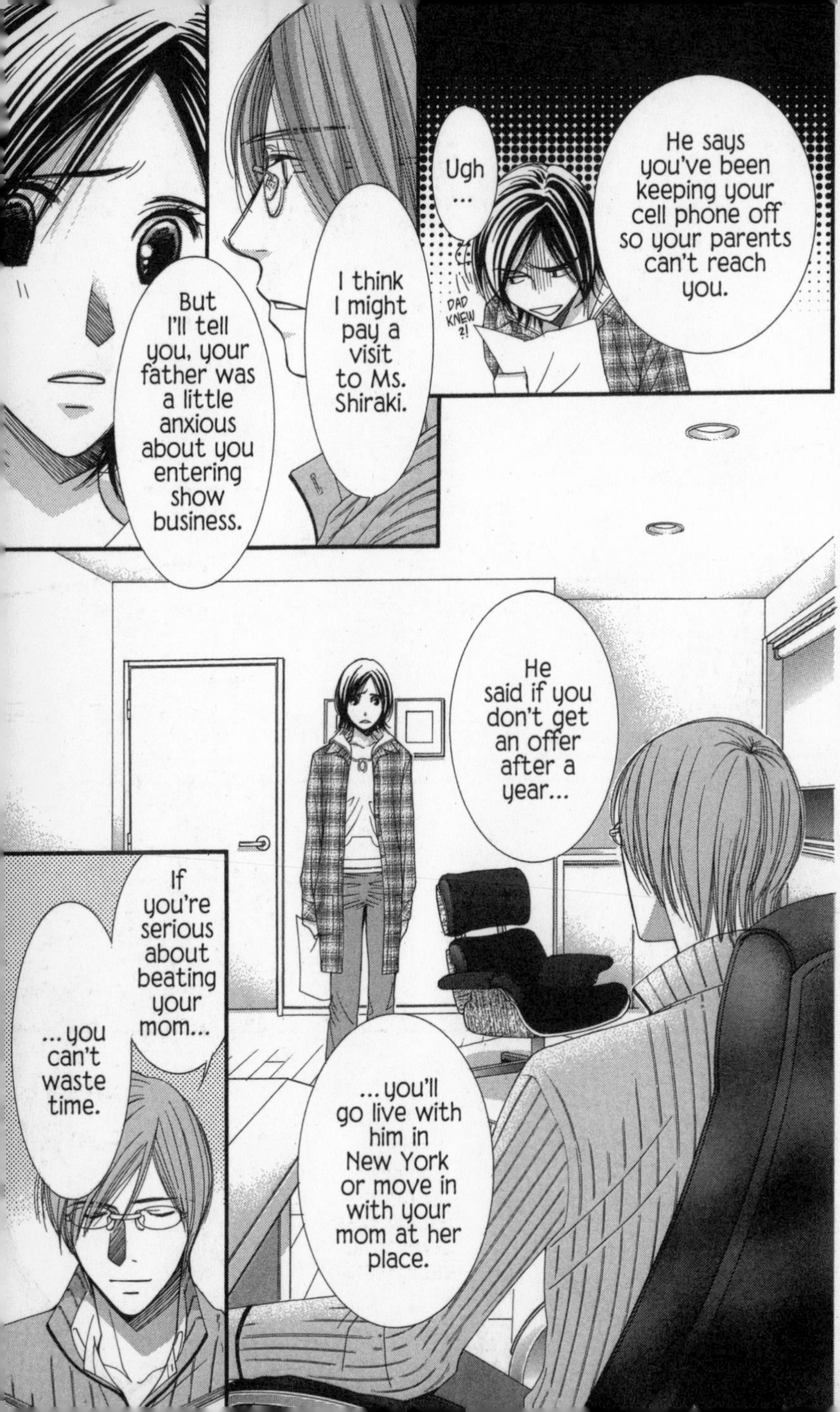
He says you've been keeping your cell phone off so your parents can't reach you.
Ugh...
DAD KNEW?!
I think I might pay a visit to Ms. Shiraki.
But I'll tell you, your father was a little anxious about you entering show business.
He said if you don't get an offer after a year...
...you'll go live with him in New York or move in with your mom at her place.
If you're serious about beating your mom...
...you can't waste time.

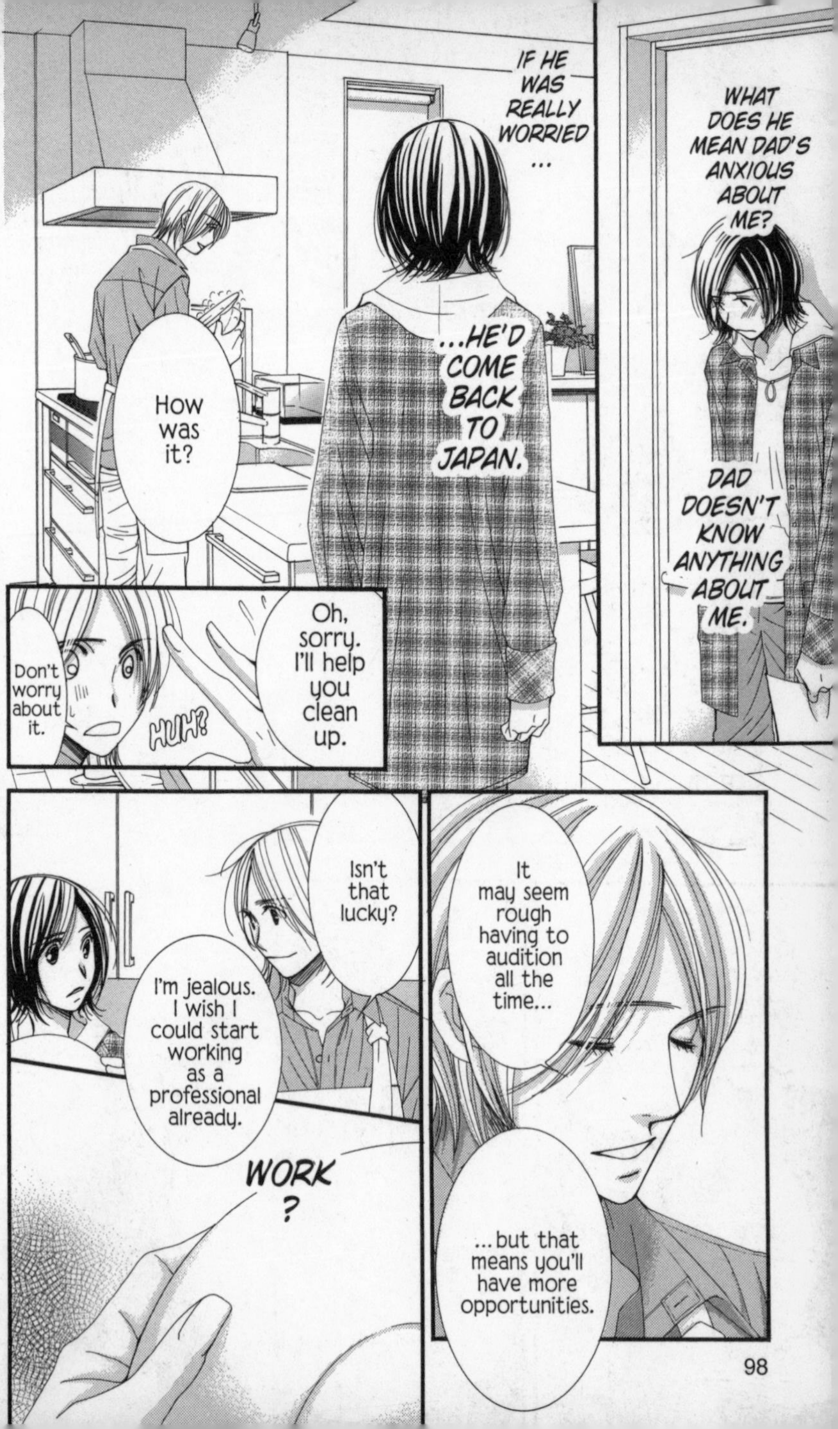
WHAT DOES HE MEAN DAD'S ANXIOUS ABOUT ME?
DAD DOESN'T KNOW ANYTHING ABOUT ME.
IF HE WAS REALLY WORRIED ...
...HE'D COME BACK TO JAPAN.
How was it?
Oh, sorry. I'll help you clean up.
HUH?
Don't worry about it.
It may seem rough having to audition all the time...
...but that means you'll have more opportunities.
Isn't that lucky?
I'm jealous. I wish I could start working as a professional already.
WORK ?

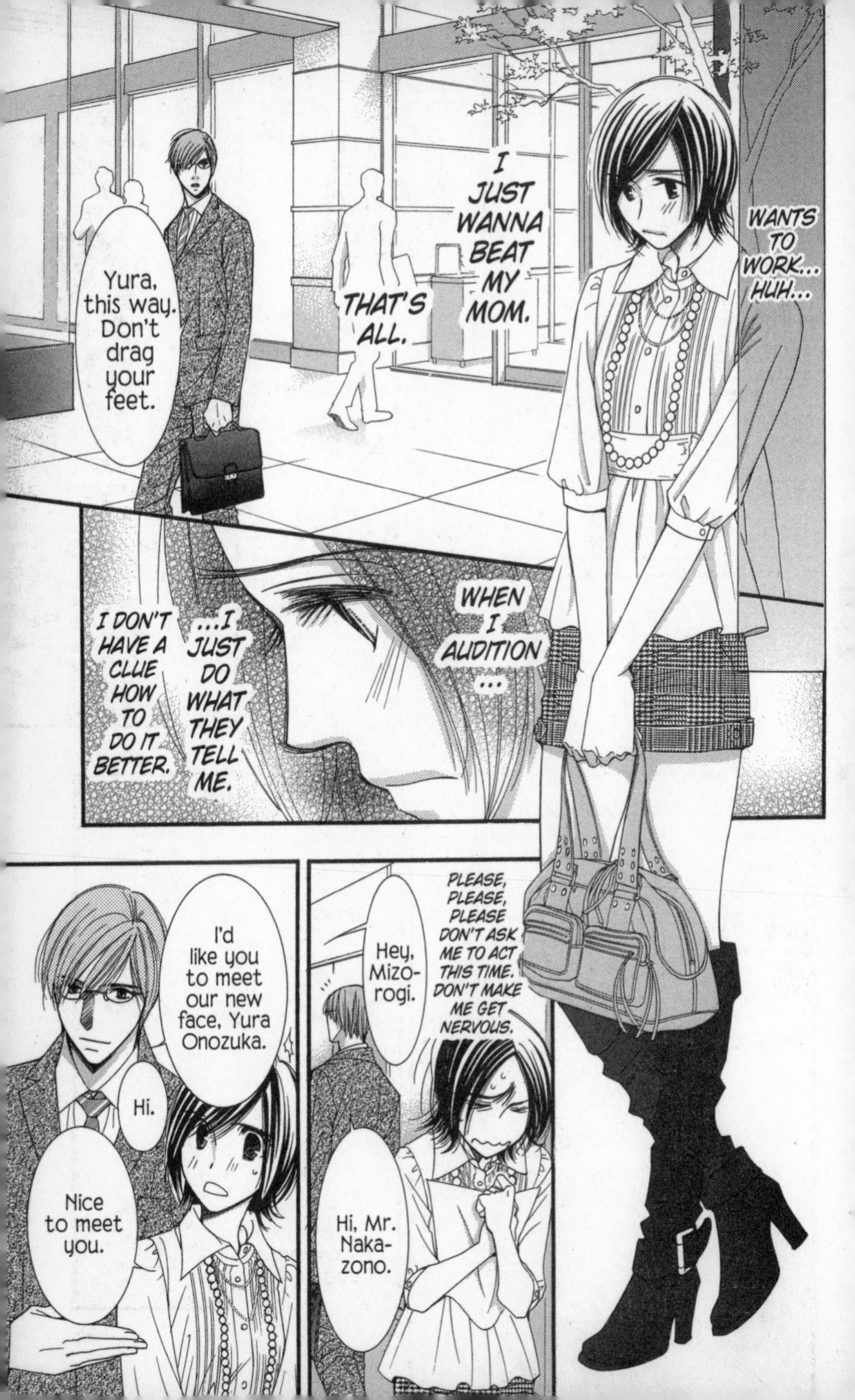

WANTS TO WORK... HUH...
I JUST WANNA BEAT MY MOM.
THAT'S ALL.
Yura, this way. Don't drag your feet.
WHEN I AUDITION...
...I JUST DO WHAT THEY TELL ME.
I DON'T HAVE A CLUE HOW TO DO IT BETTER.
PLEASE, PLEASE, PLEASE DON'T ASK ME TO ACT THIS TIME. DON'T MAKE ME GET NERVOUS.
Hey, Mizorogi.
Hi, Mr. Naka-zono.
I'd like you to meet our new face, Yura Onozuka.
Hi.
Nice to meet you.

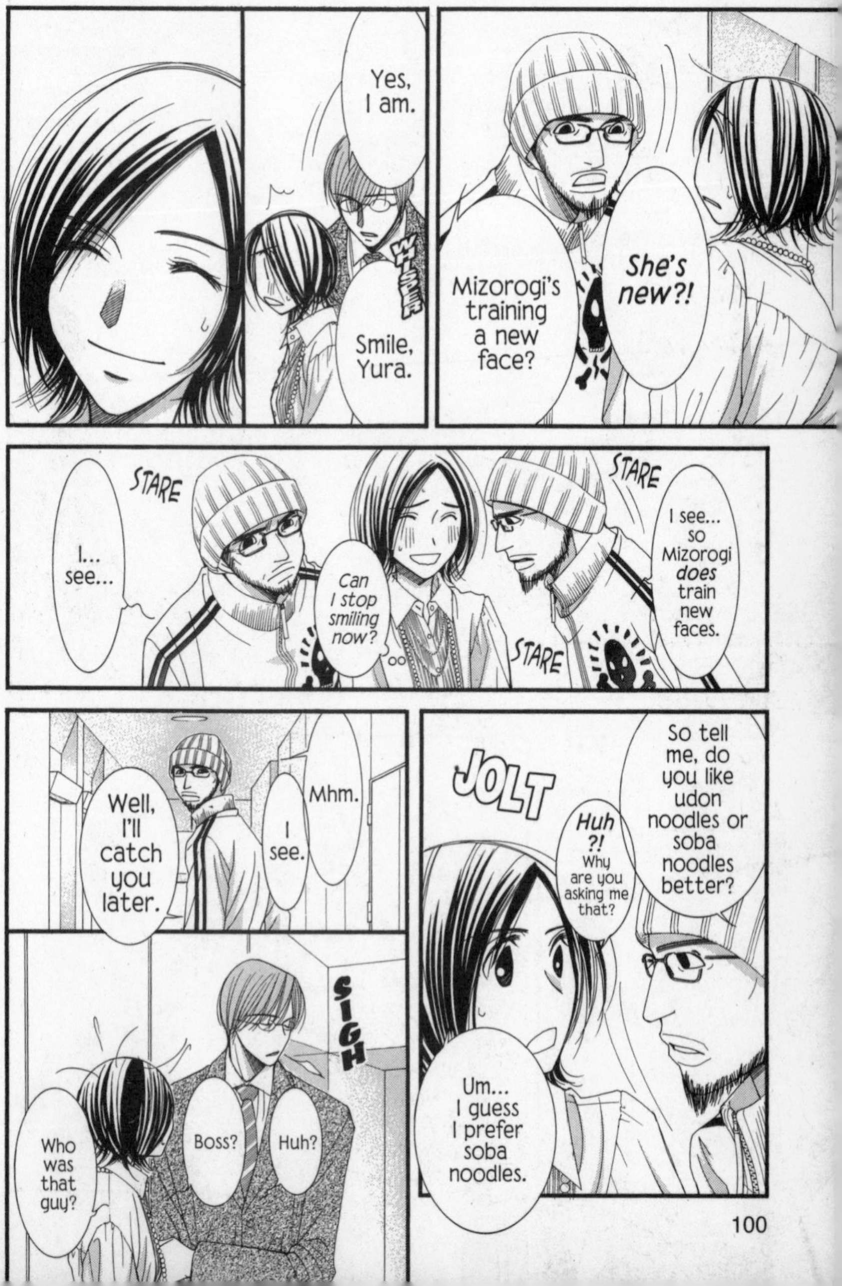
She's new?!
Mizorogi's training a new face?
Yes, I am.
WHISPER
Smile, Yura.
STARE
I see... so Mizorogi *does* train new faces.
STARE
Can I stop smiling now?
STARE
I... see...
So tell me, do you like udon noodles or soba noodles better?
JOLT
Huh ?! Why are you asking me that?
Um... I guess I prefer soba noodles.
Mhm.
I see.
Well, I'll catch you later.
SIGH
Huh?
Boss?
Who was that guy?

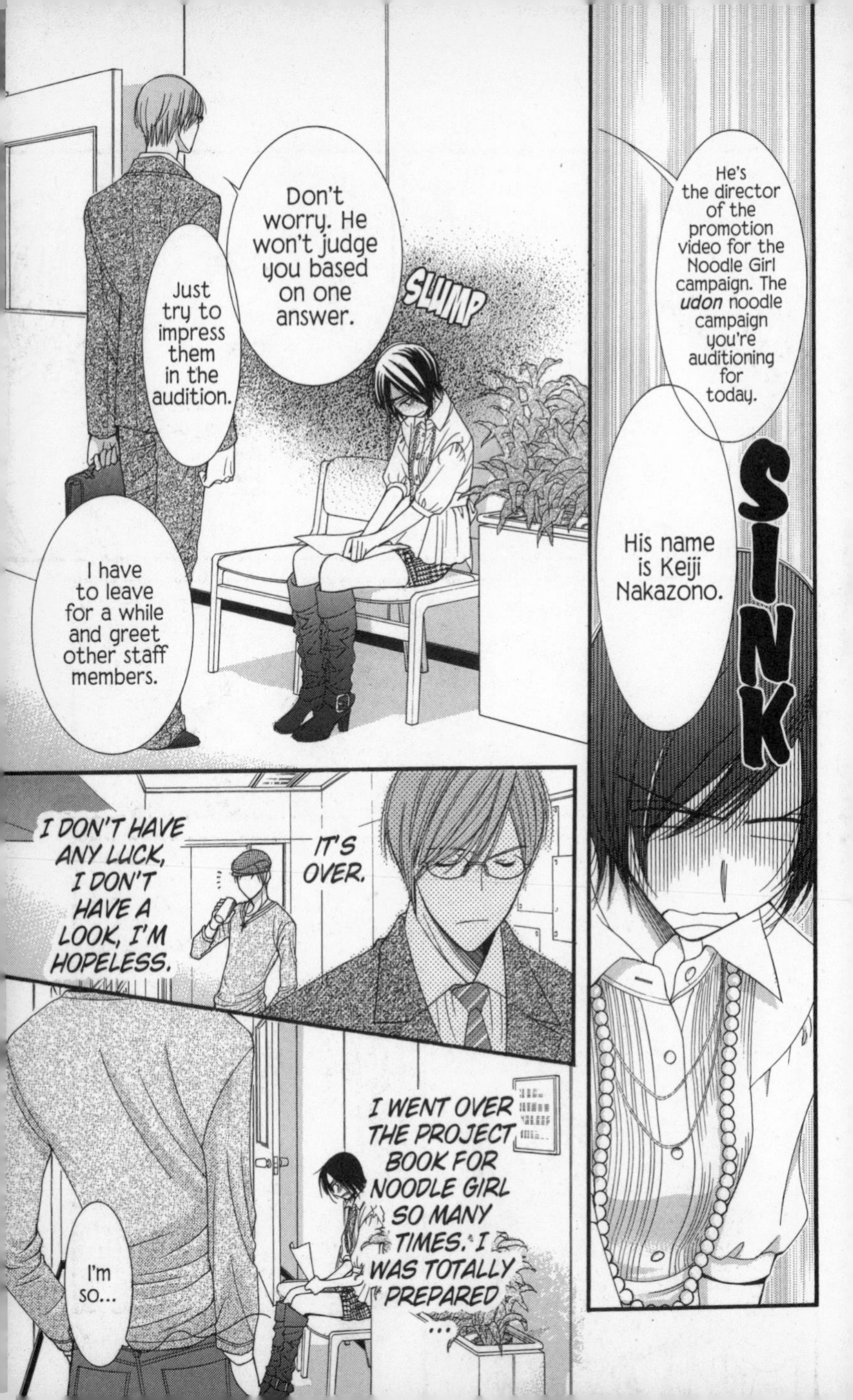
He's the director of the promotion video for the Noodle Girl campaign. The udon noodle campaign you're auditioning for today.
His name is Keiji Nakazono.
SINK
Don't worry. He won't judge you based on one answer.
SLUMP
Just try to impress them in the audition.
I have to leave for a while and greet other staff members.
IT'S OVER.
I DON'T HAVE ANY LUCK, I DON'T HAVE A LOOK, I'M HOPELESS.
I WENT OVER THE PROJECT BOOK FOR NOODLE GIRL SO MANY TIMES. I WAS TOTALLY PREPARED
...
I'm so...

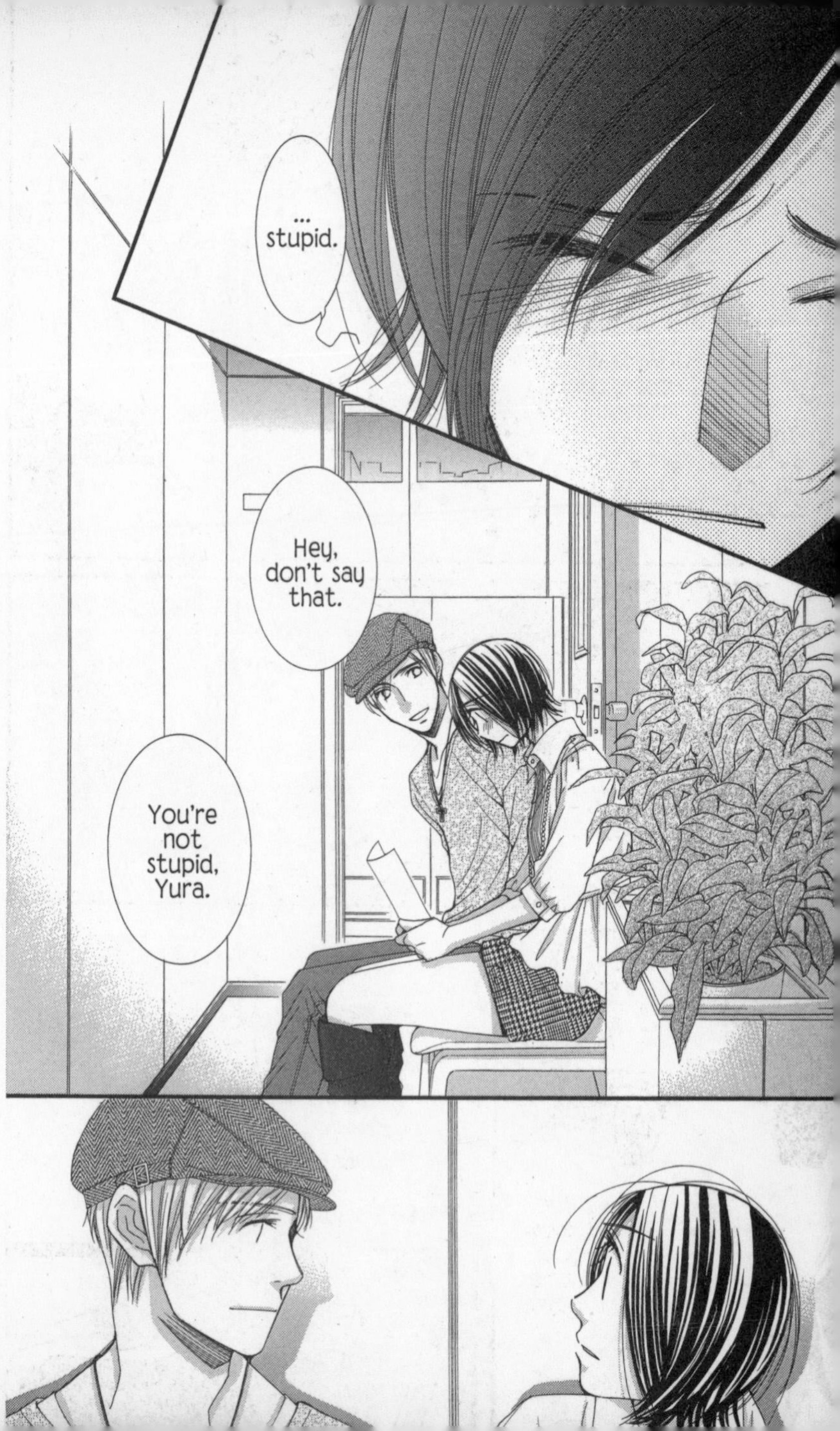
...
stupid.
Hey, don't say that.
You're not stupid, Yura.

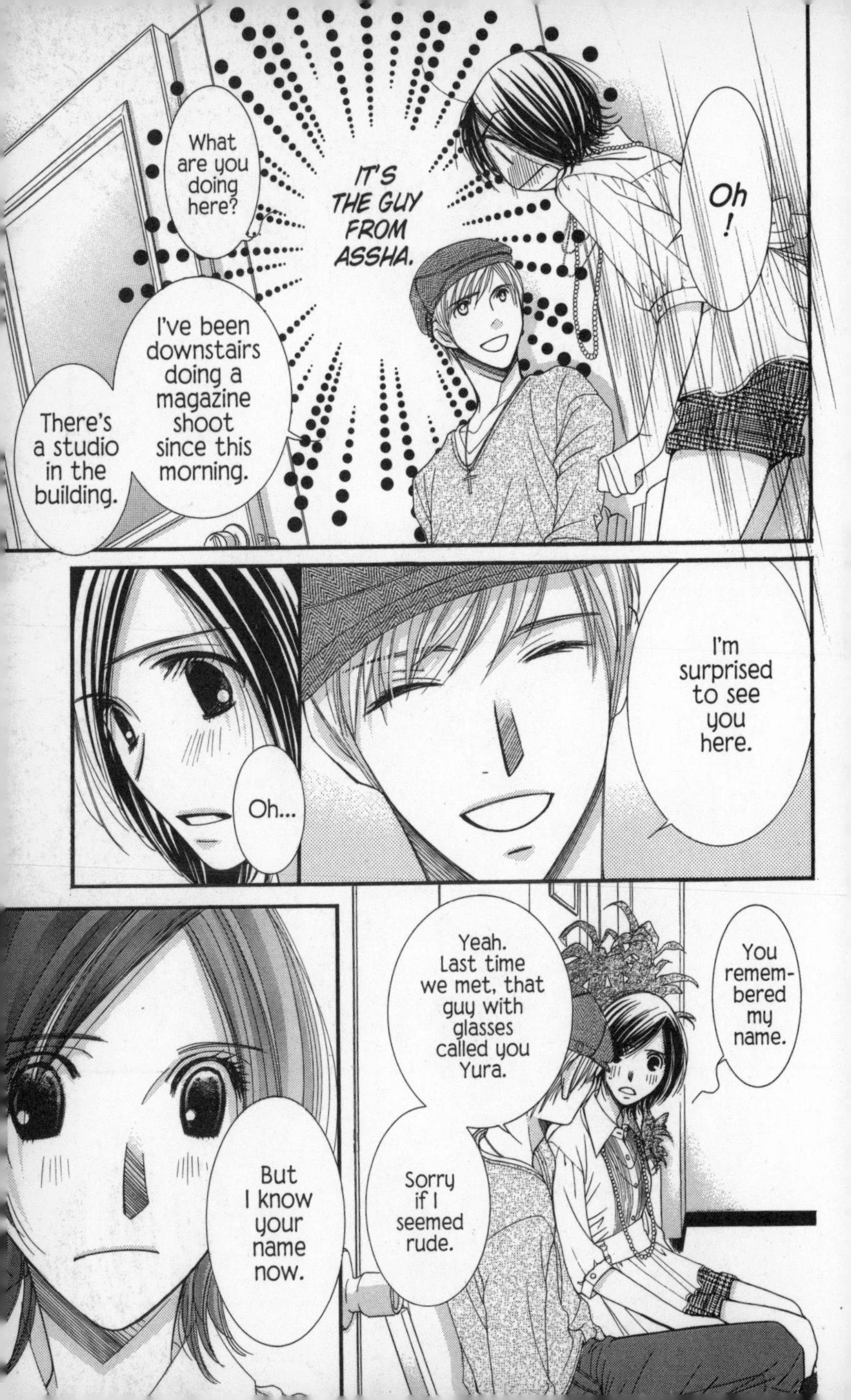
Oh!
IT'S THE GUY FROM ASSHA.
What are you doing here?
I've been downstairs doing a magazine shoot since this morning.
There's a studio in the building.
I'm surprised to see you here.
Oh...
You remem-bered my name.
Yeah. Last time we met, that guy with glasses called you Yura.
Sorry if I seemed rude.
But I know your name now.

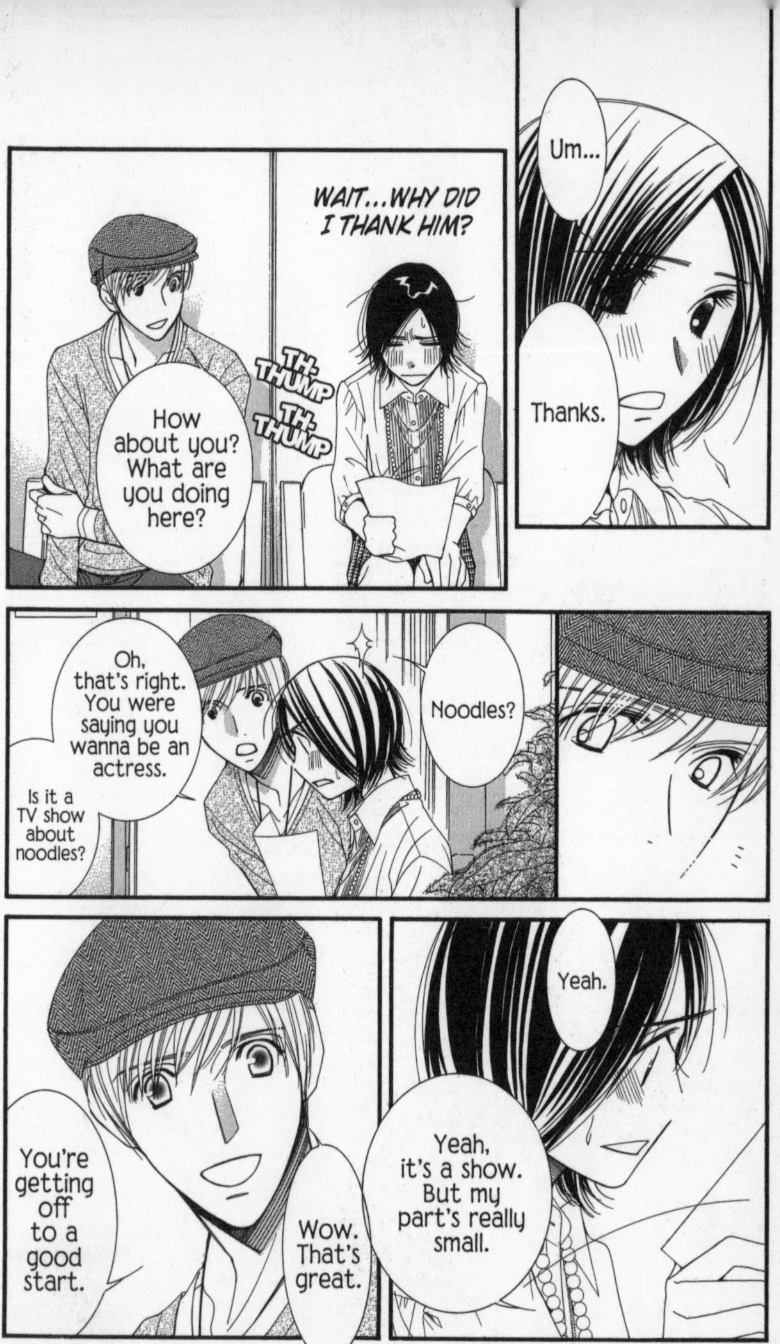
Um...
Thanks.
WAIT...WHY DID I THANK HIM?
TH-THUMP
TH-THUMP
How about you? What are you doing here?
Noodles?
Oh, that's right. You were saying you wanna be an actress.
Is it a TV show about noodles?
Yeah.
Yeah, it's a show. But my part's really small.
Wow. That's great.
You're getting off to a good start.

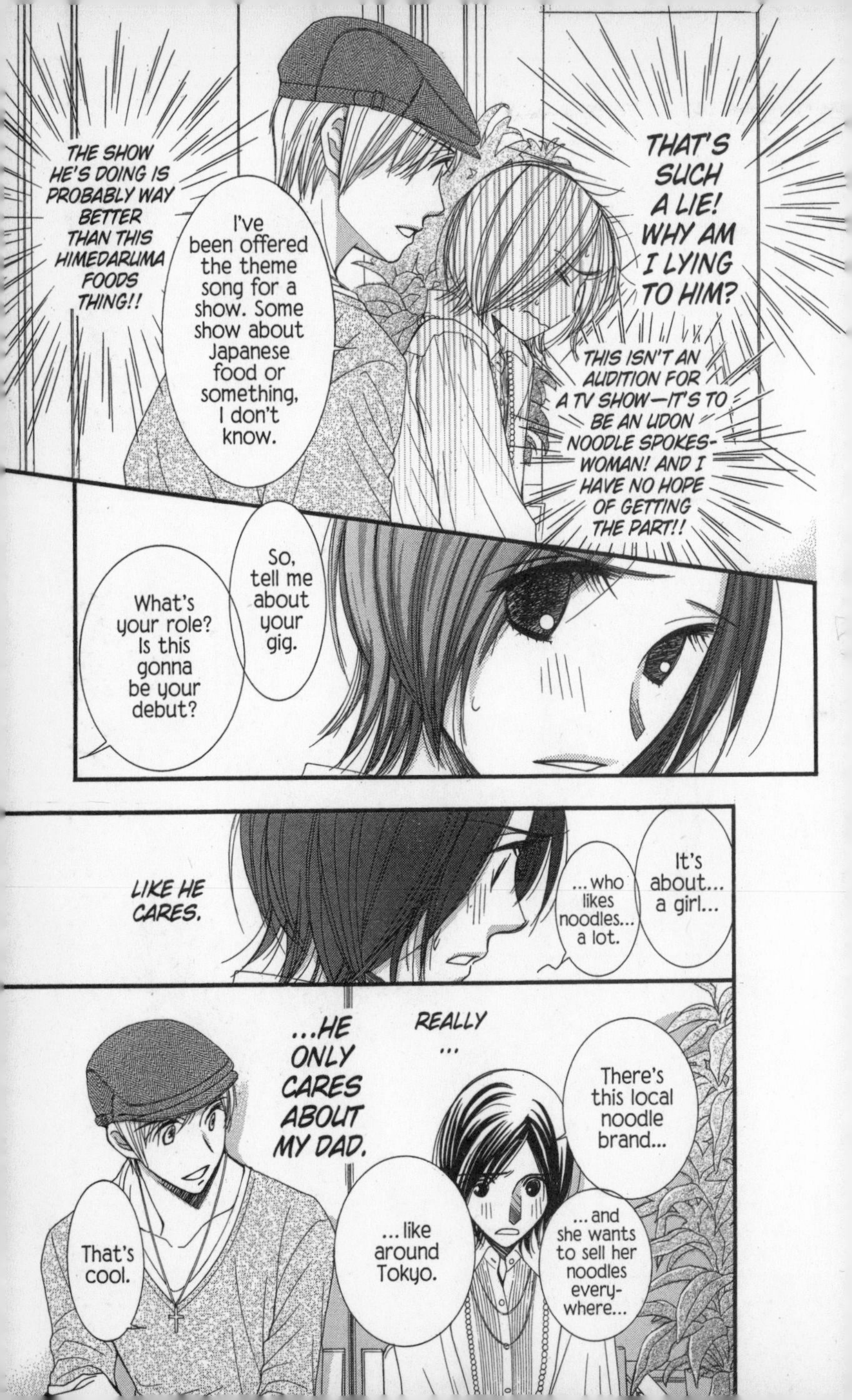
THAT'S SUCH A LIE! WHY AM I LYING TO HIM?
THIS ISN'T AN AUDITION FOR A TV SHOW—IT'S TO BE AN UDON NOODLE SPOKES-WOMAN! AND I HAVE NO HOPE OF GETTING THE PART!!
I've been offered the theme song for a show. Some show about Japanese food or something, I don't know.
THE SHOW HE'S DOING IS PROBABLY WAY BETTER THAN THIS HIMEDARUMA FOODS THING!!
So, tell me about your gig.
What's your role? Is this gonna be your debut?
It's about... a girl...
...who likes noodles... a lot.
LIKE HE CARES.
REALLY...
...HE ONLY CARES ABOUT MY DAD.
There's this local noodle brand...
...and she wants to sell her noodles every-where...
...like around Tokyo.
That's cool.

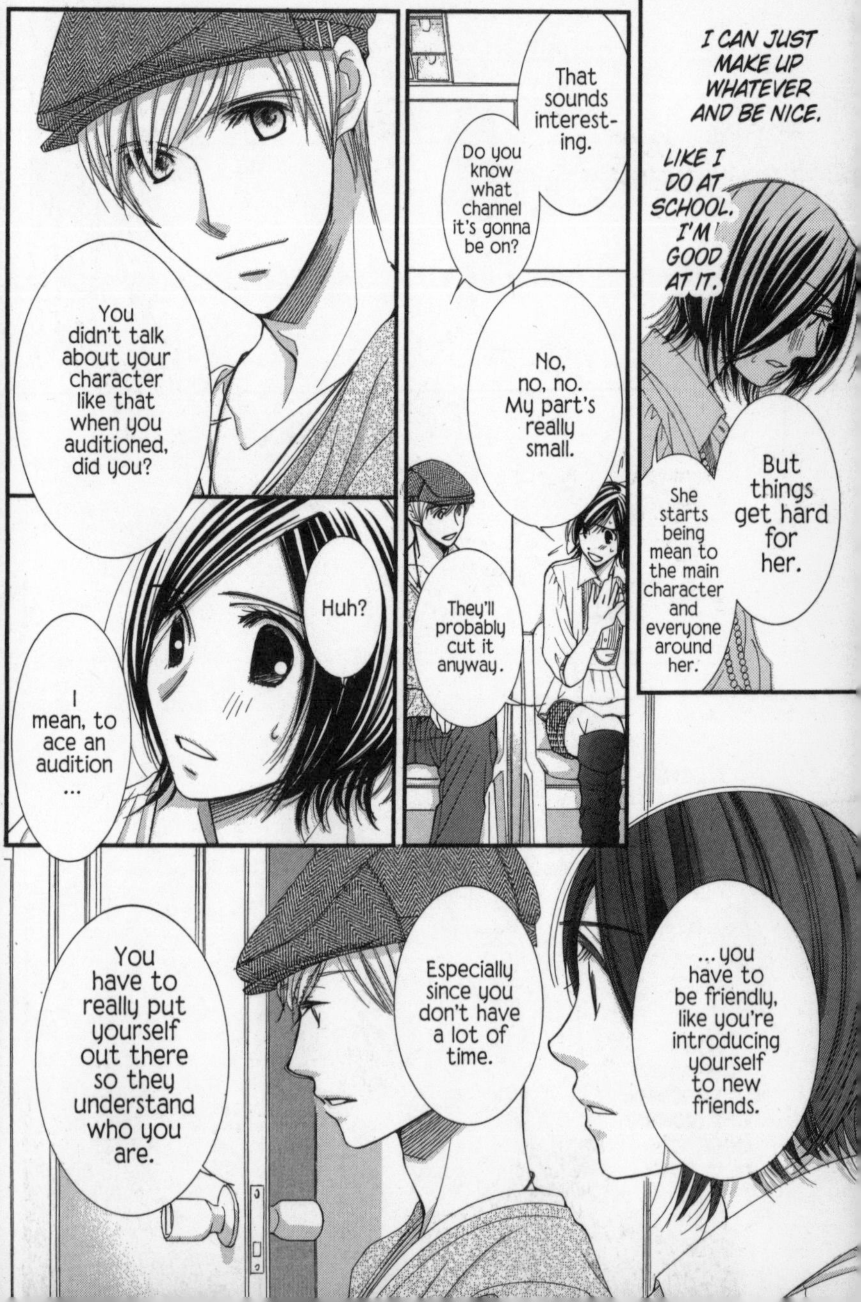
I CAN JUST MAKE UP WHATEVER AND BE NICE.
LIKE I DO AT SCHOOL. I'M GOOD AT IT.
But things get hard for her.
She starts being mean to the main character and everyone around her.
That sounds interesting-ing.
Do you know what channel it's gonna be on?
No, no, no. My part's really small.
They'll probably cut it anyway.
You didn't talk about your character like that when you auditioned, did you?
Huh?
I mean, to ace an audition ...
...you have to be friendly, like you're introducing yourself to new friends.
Especially since you don't have a lot of time.
You have to really put yourself out there so they understand who you are.

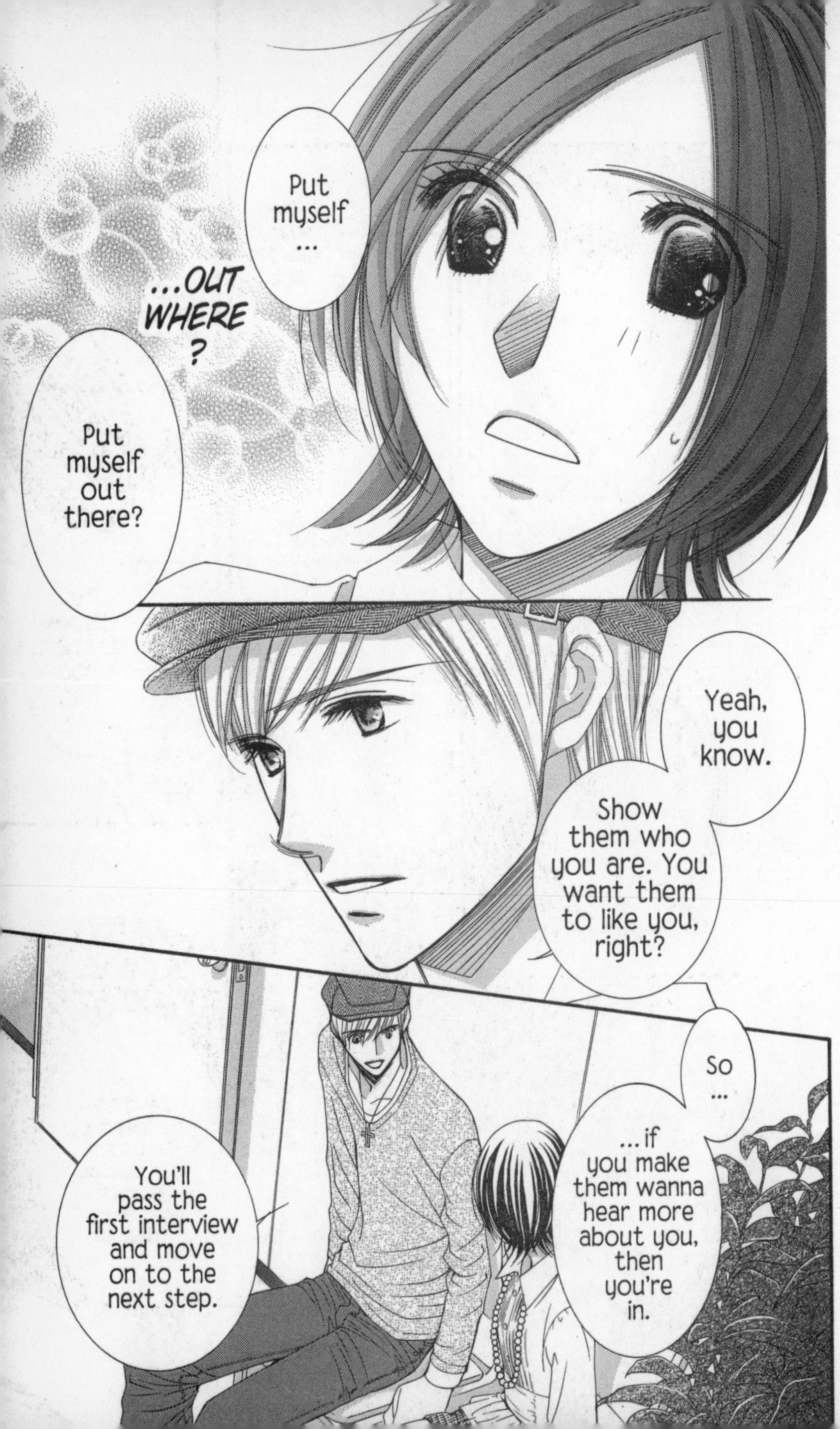
Put myself ...
...OUT WHERE?
Put myself out there?
Yeah, you know.
Show them who you are. You want them to like you, right?
So ...
... if you make them wanna hear more about you, then you're in.
You'll pass the first interview and move on to the next step.

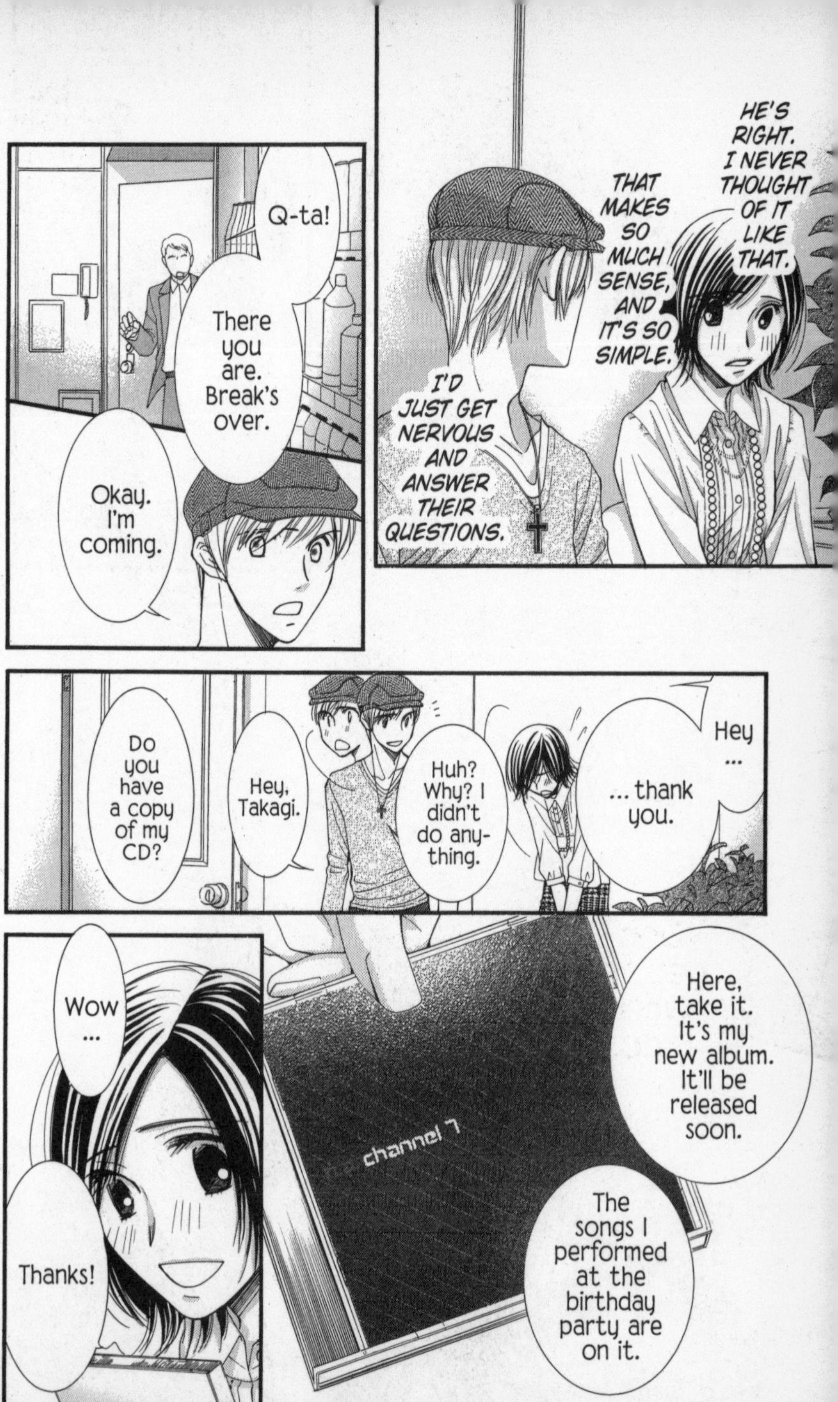
HE'S RIGHT. I NEVER THOUGHT OF IT LIKE THAT.
THAT MAKES SO MUCH SENSE, AND IT'S SO SIMPLE.
I'D JUST GET NERVOUS AND ANSWER THEIR QUESTIONS.
Q-ta!
There you are. Break's over.
Okay. I'm coming.
Hey ...
... thank you.
Huh? Why? I didn't do any-thing.
Hey, Takagi.
Do you have a copy of my CD?
Here, take it. It's my new album. It'll be released soon.
The songs I performed at the birthday party are on it.
channel 7
Wow ...
Thanks!

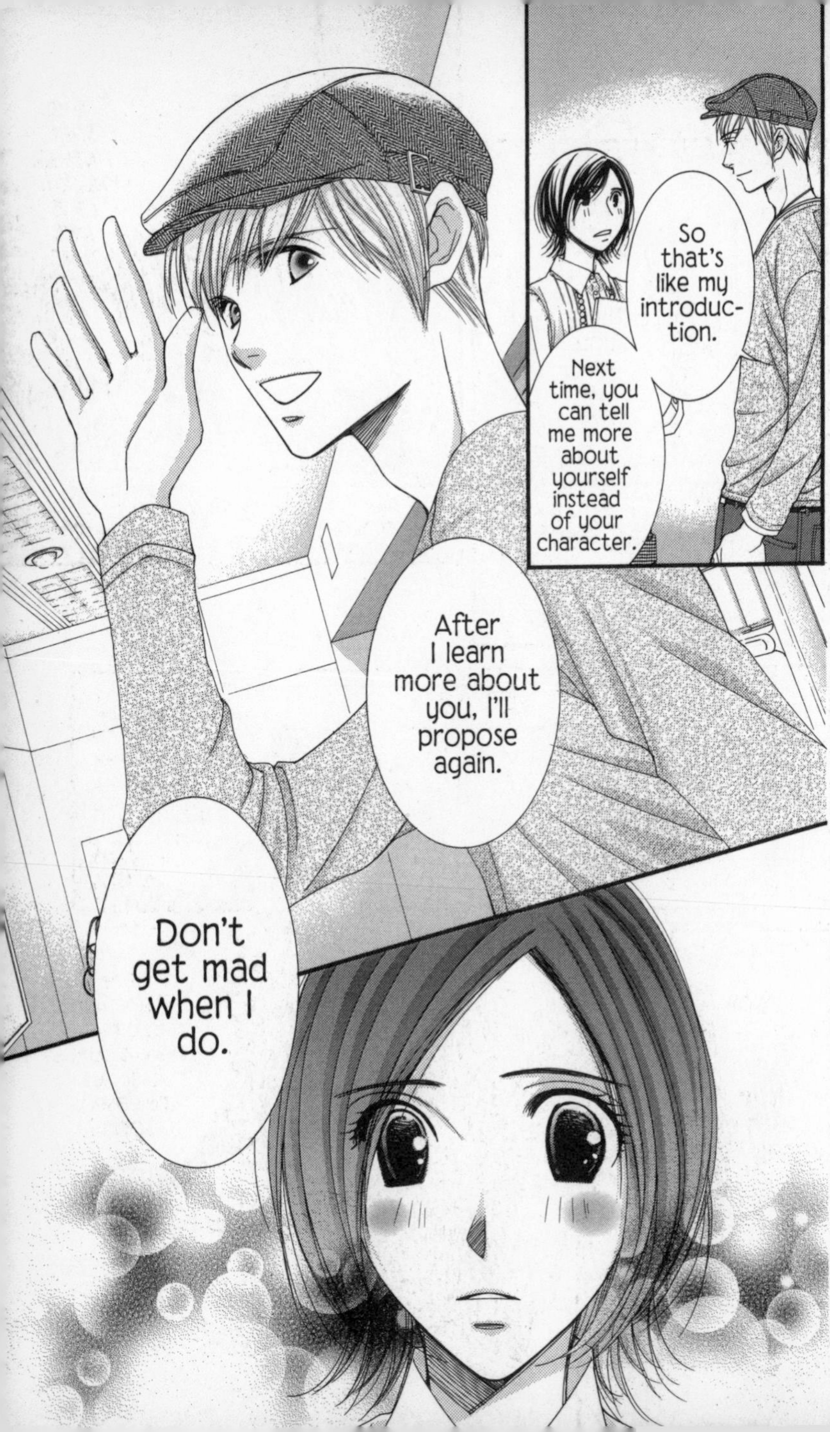
So that's like my introduc-tion.
Next time, you can tell me more about yourself instead of your character.
After I learn more about you, I'll propose again.
Don't get mad when I do.

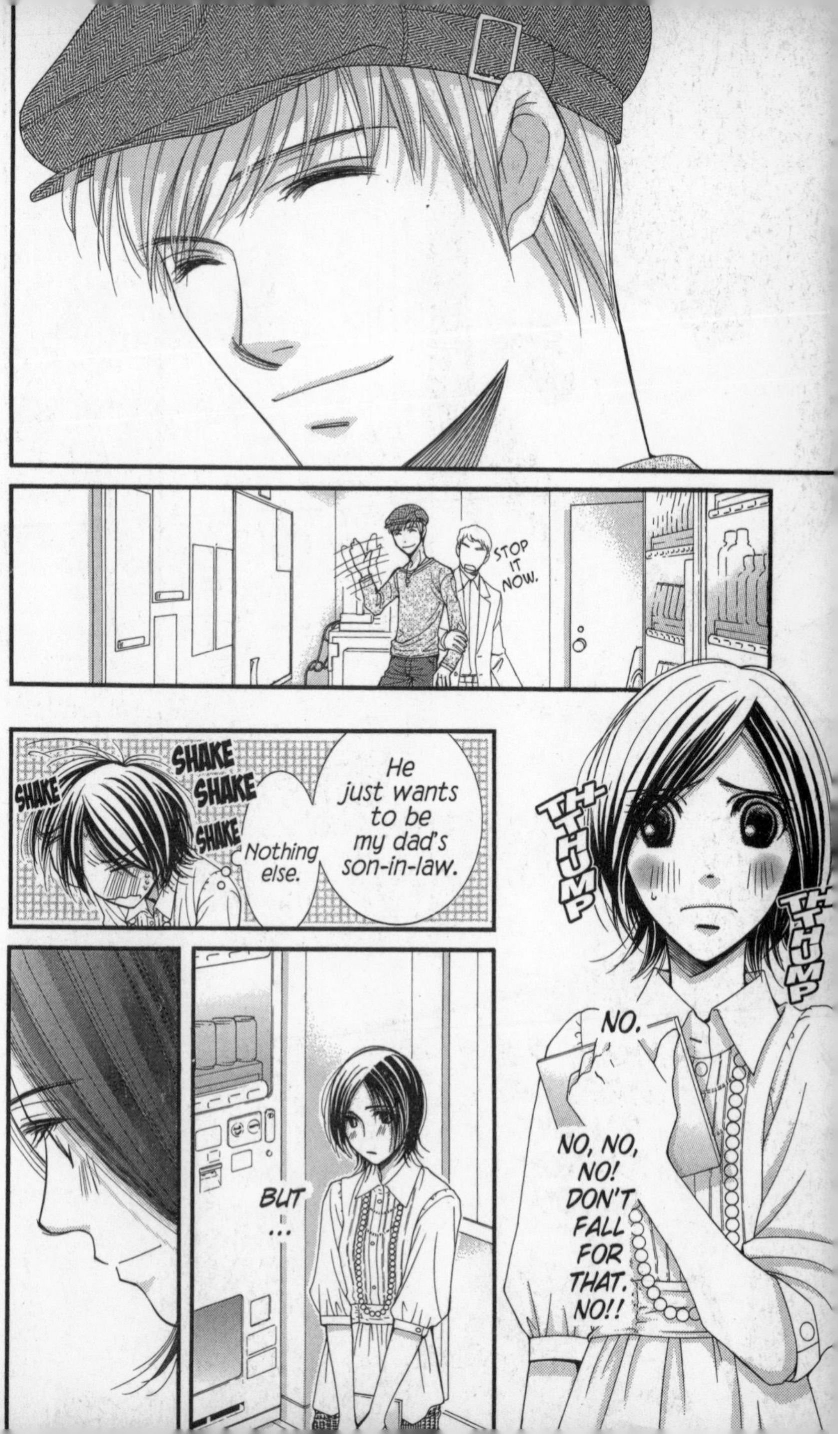
STOP IT NOW.
TH-THUMP
TH-THUMP
NO.
NO, NO, NO! DON'T FALL FOR THAT. NO!!
He just wants to be my dad's son-in-law.
Nothing else.
SHAKE SHAKE SHAKE SHAKE
BUT ...

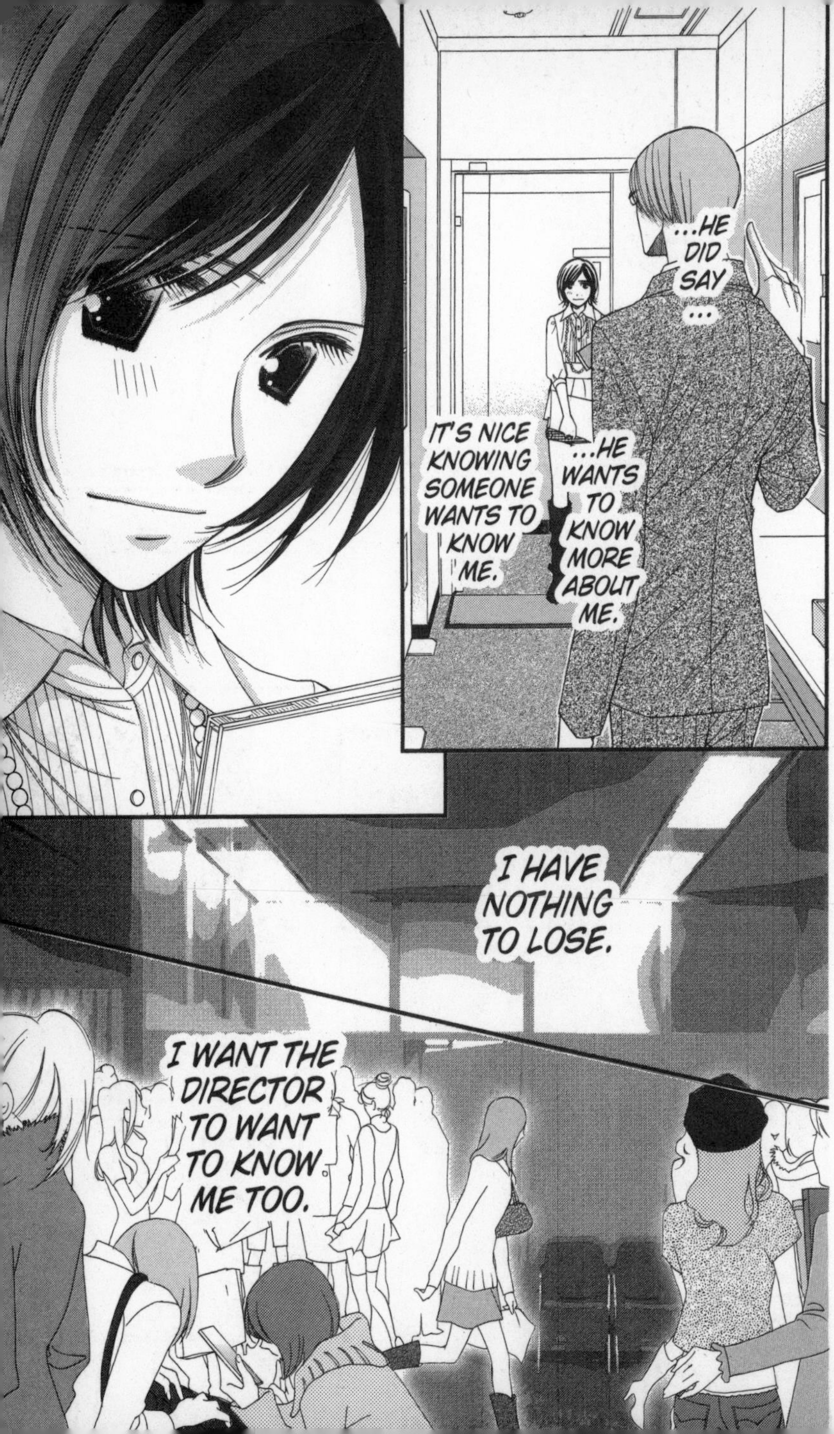
...HE DID SAY...
...HE WANTS TO KNOW MORE ABOUT ME.
IT'S NICE KNOWING SOMEONE WANTS TO KNOW ME.
I HAVE NOTHING TO LOSE.
I WANT THE DIRECTOR TO WANT TO KNOW ME TOO.

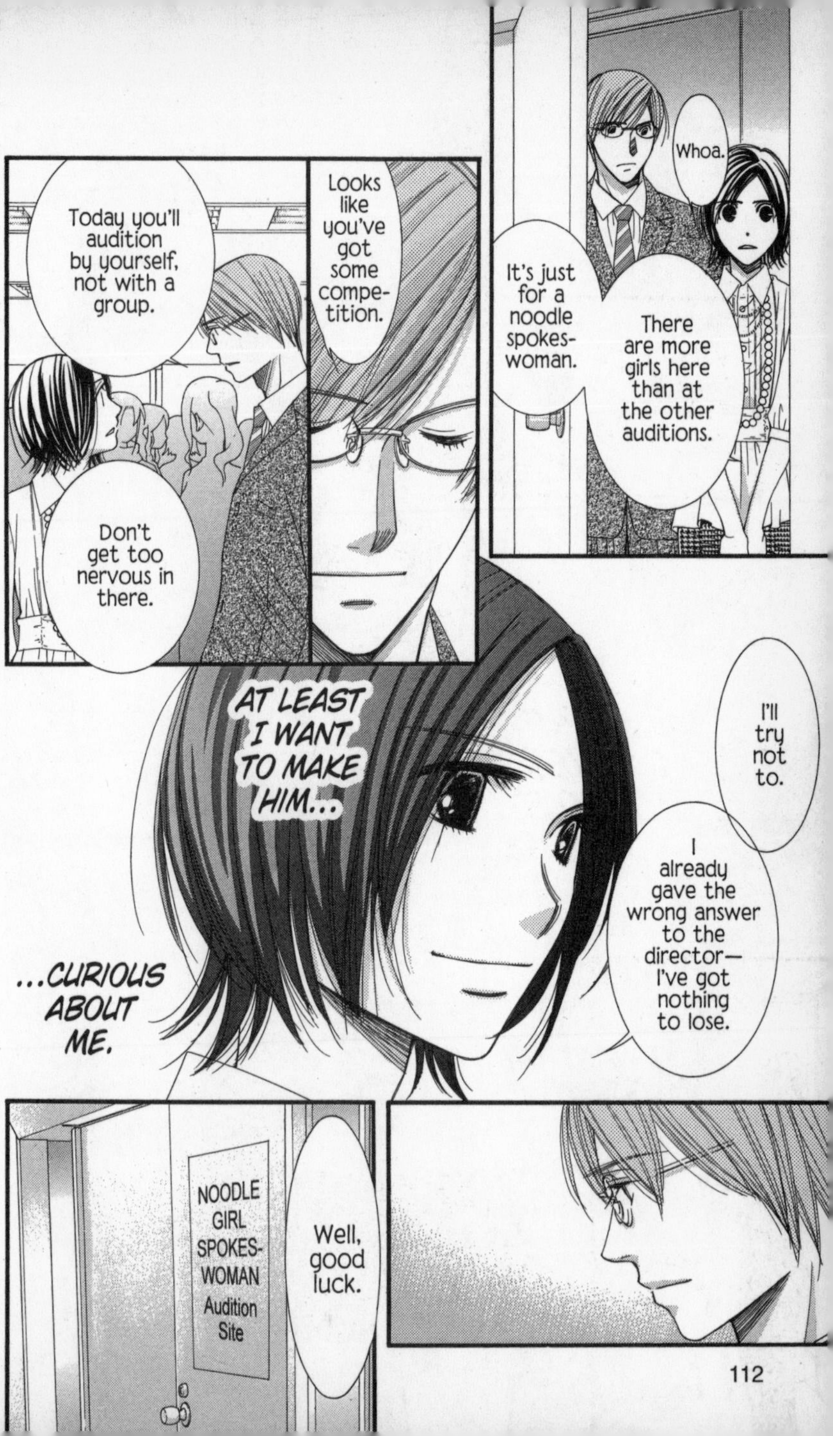
Whoa.
There are more girls here than at the other auditions.
It's just for a noodle spokes-woman.
Looks like you've got some compe-tition.
Today you'll audition by yourself, not with a group.
Don't get too nervous in there.
I'll try not to.
I already gave the wrong answer to the director— I've got nothing to lose.
AT LEAST I WANT TO MAKE HIM...
...CURIOUS ABOUT ME.
NOODLE GIRL SPOKES-WOMAN Audition Site
Well, good luck.

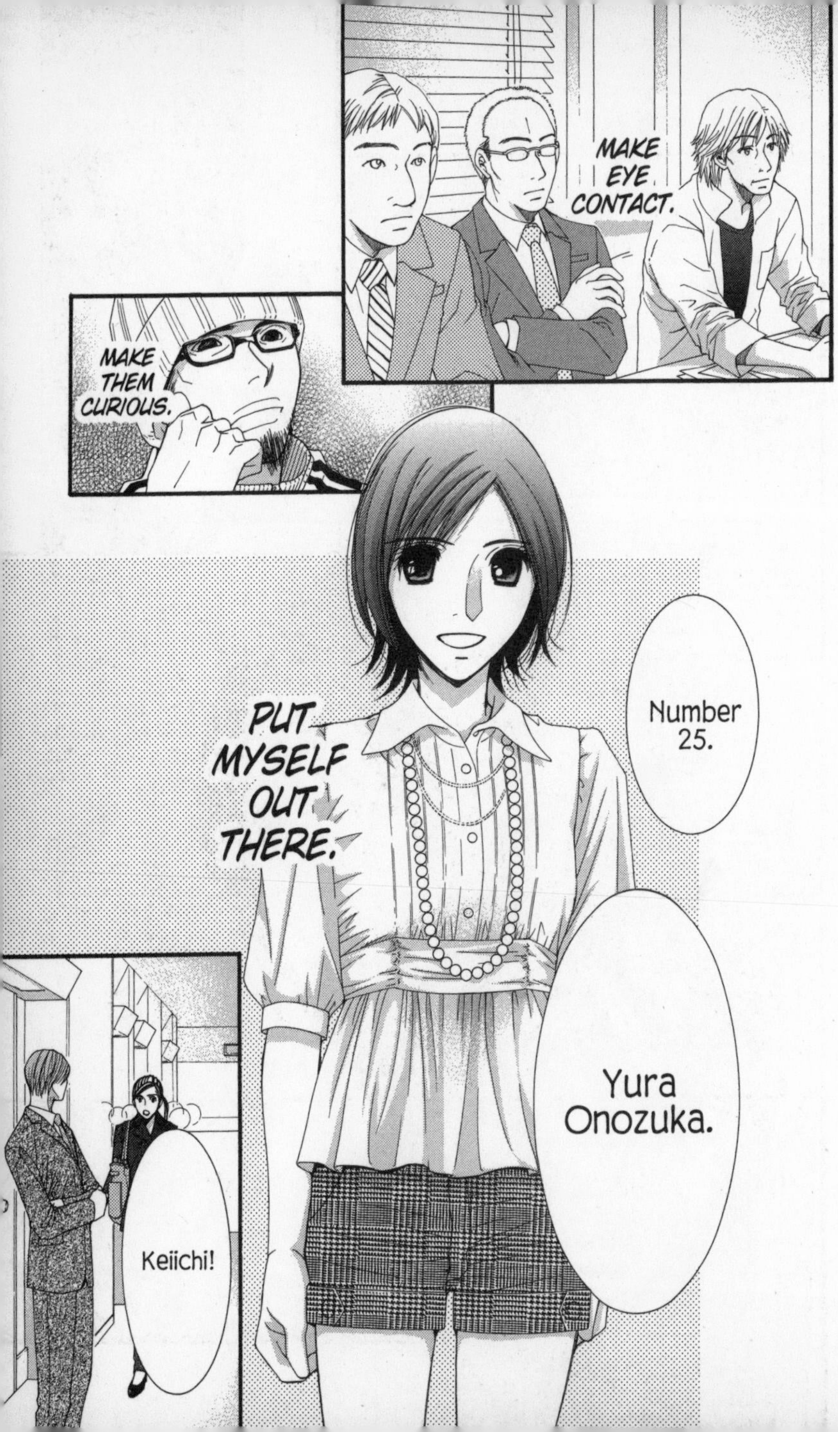
MAKE EYE CONTACT.
MAKE THEM CURIOUS.
Number 25.
Yura Onozuka.
PUT MYSELF OUT THERE.
Keiichi!

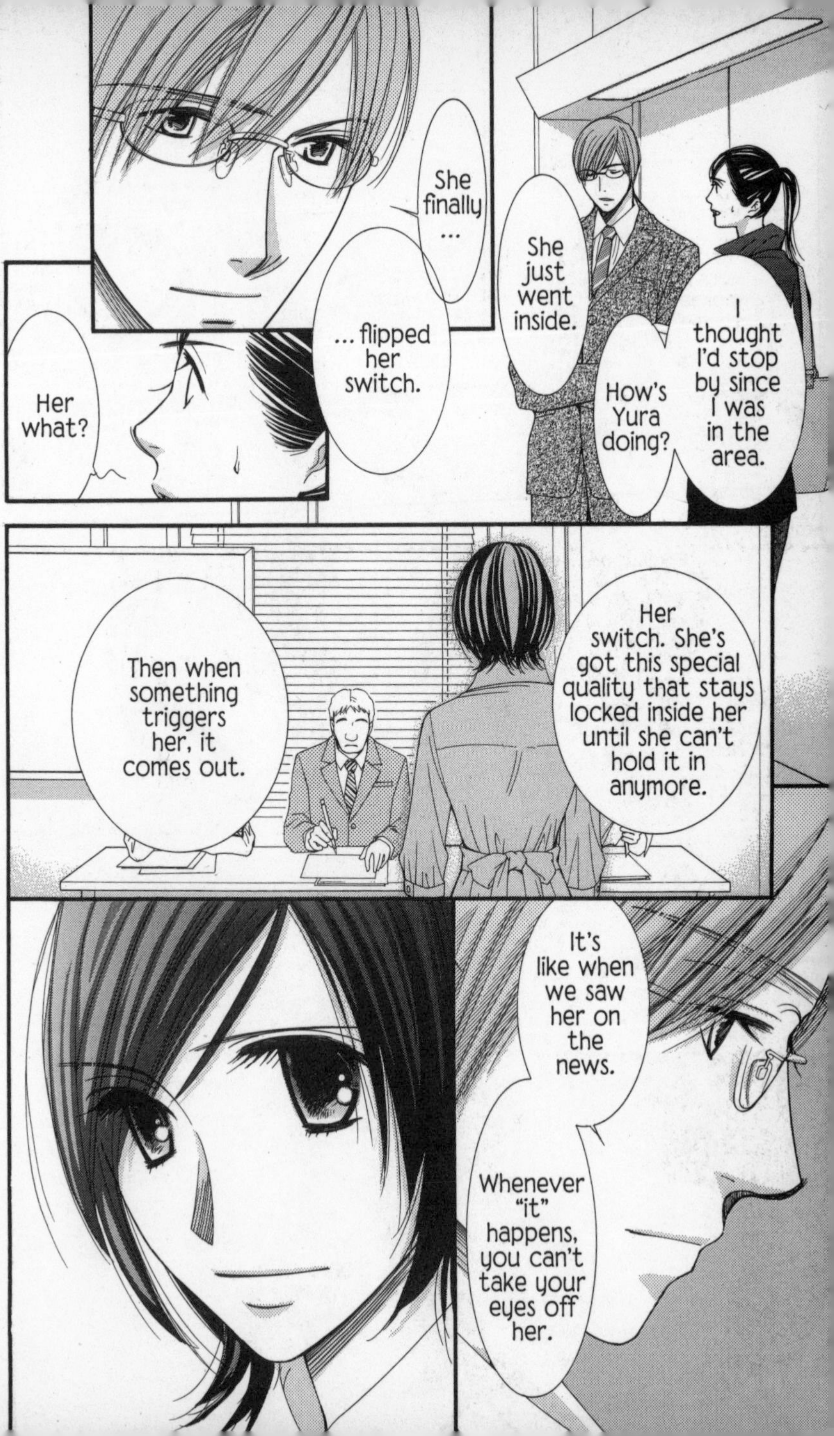
I thought I'd stop by since I was in the area.
How's Yura doing?
She just went inside.
She finally...
... flipped her switch.
Her what?
Her switch. She's got this special quality that stays locked inside her until she can't hold it in anymore.
Then when something triggers her, it comes out.
It's like when we saw her on the news.
Whenever "it" happens, you can't take your eyes off her.

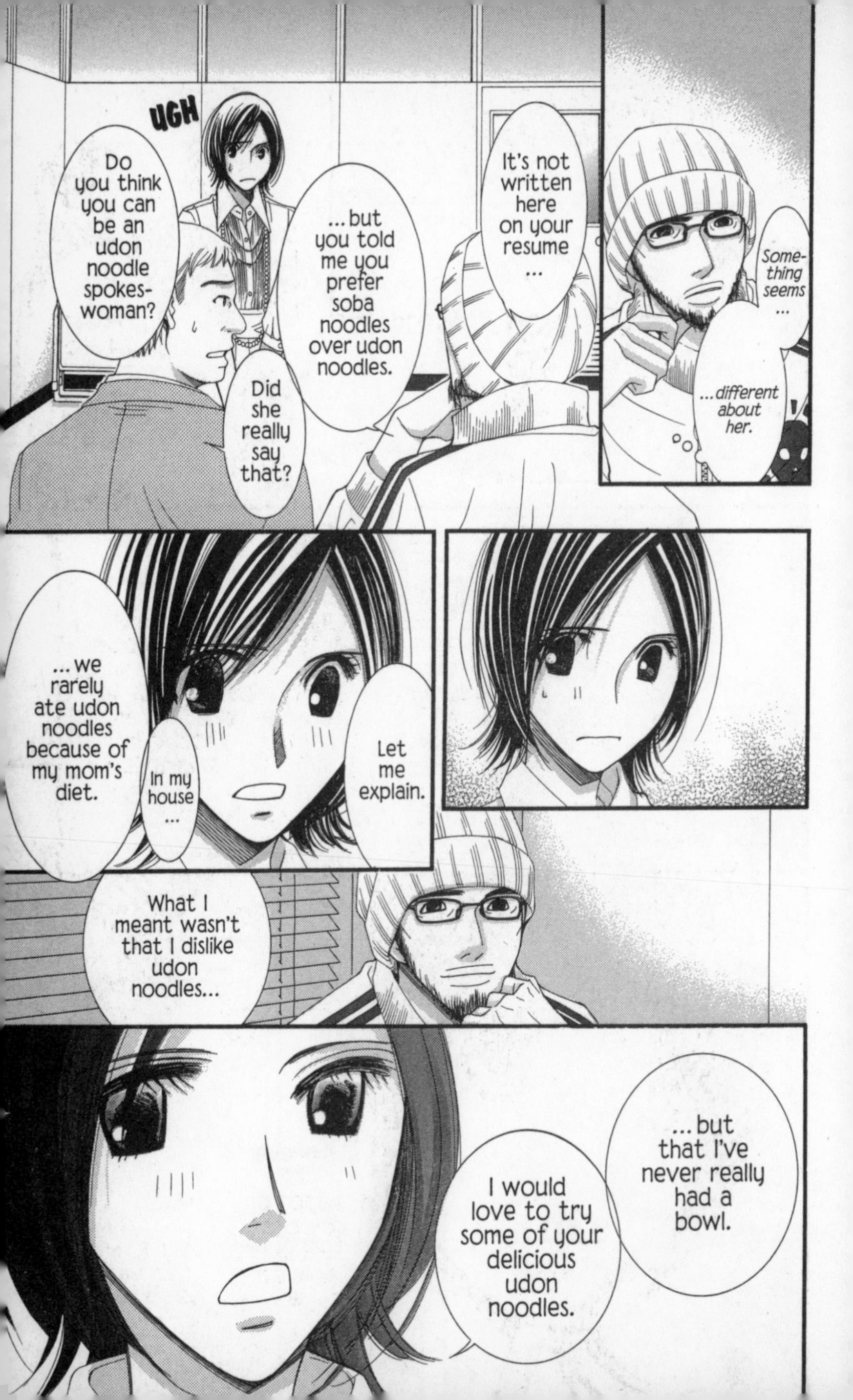
Something seems ...
...different about her.
It's not written here on your resume ...
...but you told me you prefer soba noodles over udon noodles.
UGH
Do you think you can be an udon noodle spokeswoman?
Did she really say that?
Let me explain.
In my house ...
...we rarely ate udon noodles because of my mom's diet.
What I meant wasn't that I dislike udon noodles...
...but that I've never really had a bowl.
I would love to try some of your delicious udon noodles.

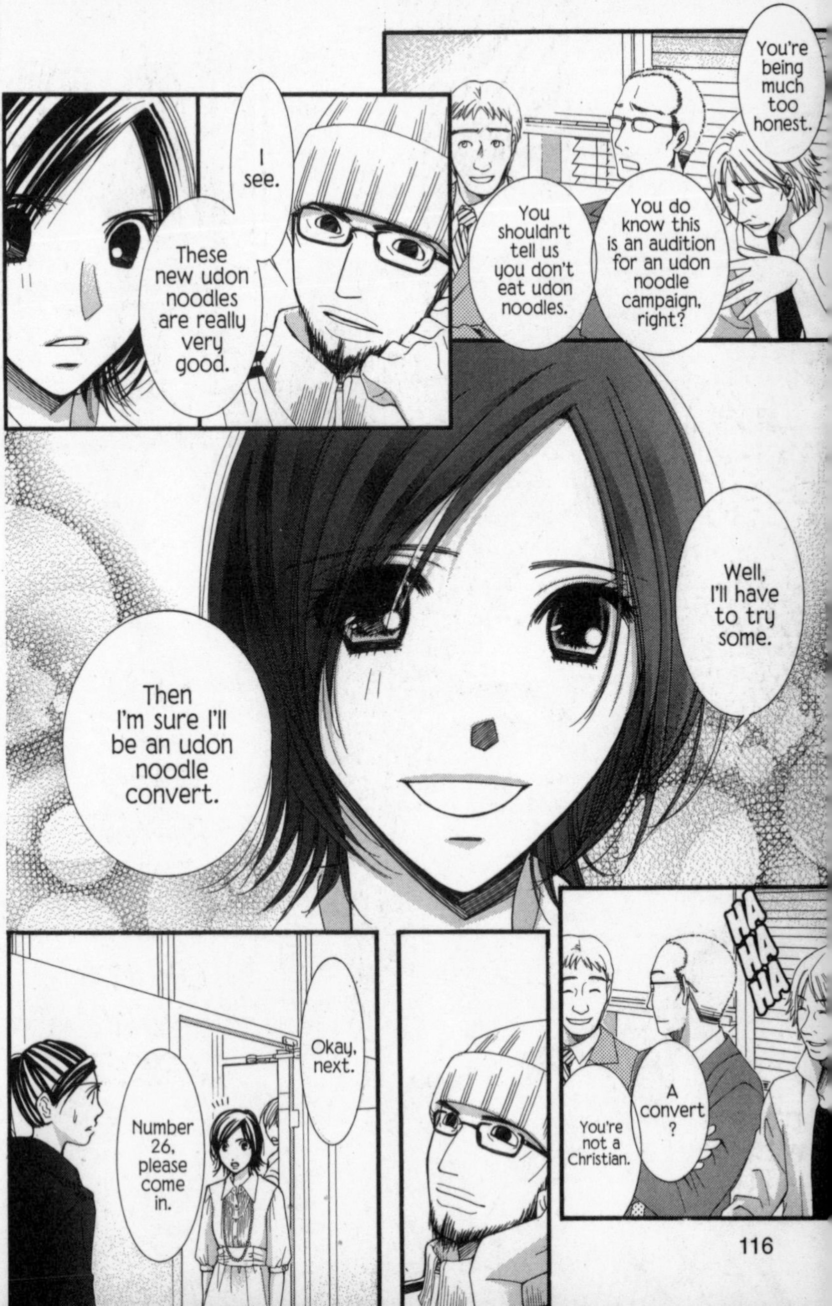

You're being much too honest.
You do know this is an audition for an udon noodle campaign, right?
You shouldn't tell us you don't eat udon noodles.
I see.
These new udon noodles are really very good.
Well, I'll have to try some.
Then I'm sure I'll be an udon noodle convert.
HA HA HA
A convert?
You're not a Christian.
Okay, next.
Number 26, please come in.

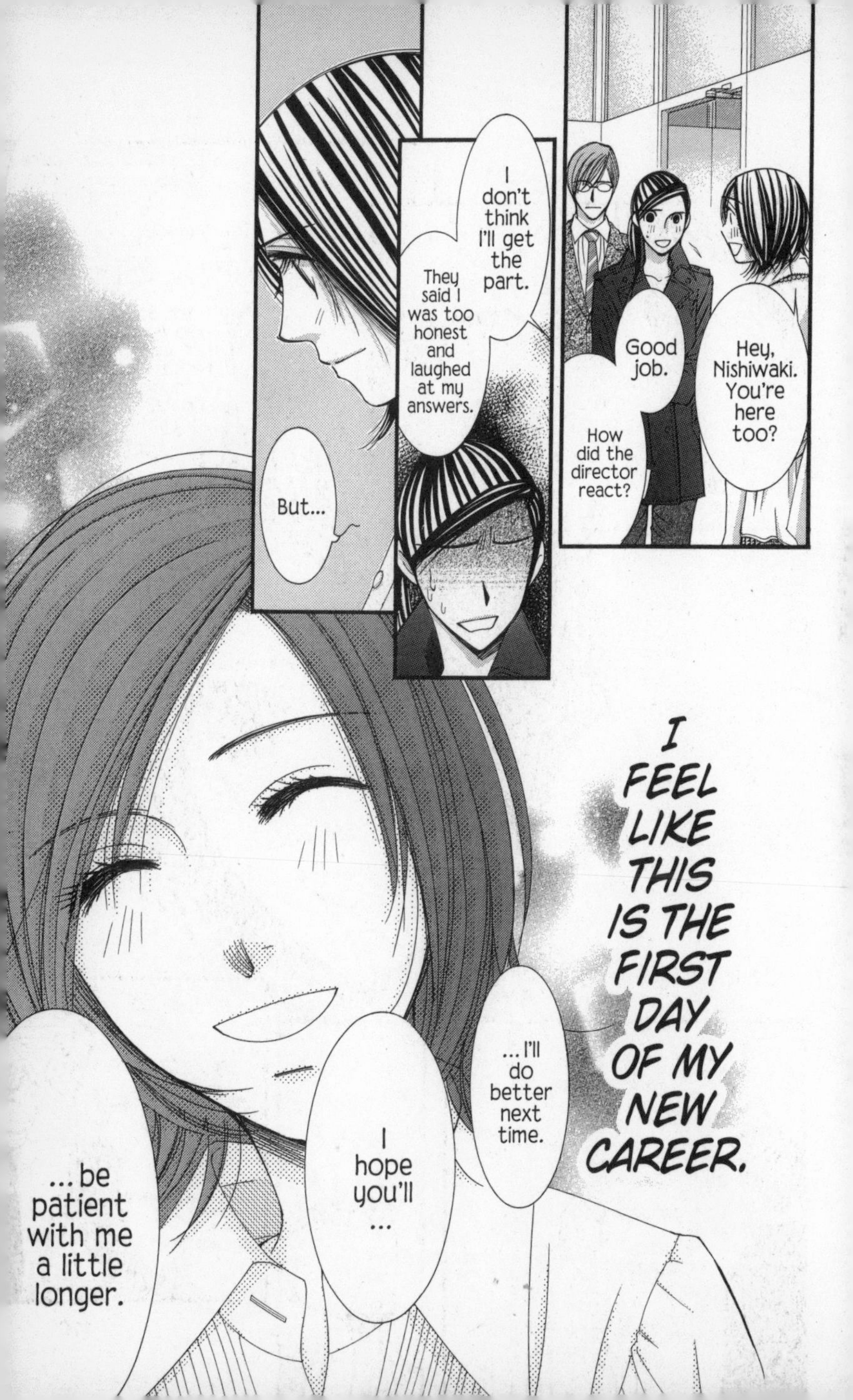
Hey, Nishiwaki. You're here too?
Good job.
How did the director react?
I don't think I'll get the part.
They said I was too honest and laughed at my answers.
But...
I FEEL LIKE THIS IS THE FIRST DAY OF MY NEW CAREER.
...I'll do better next time.
I hope you'll ...
...be patient with me a little longer.

Q-ta Minamitani
19 years old
Blood type B

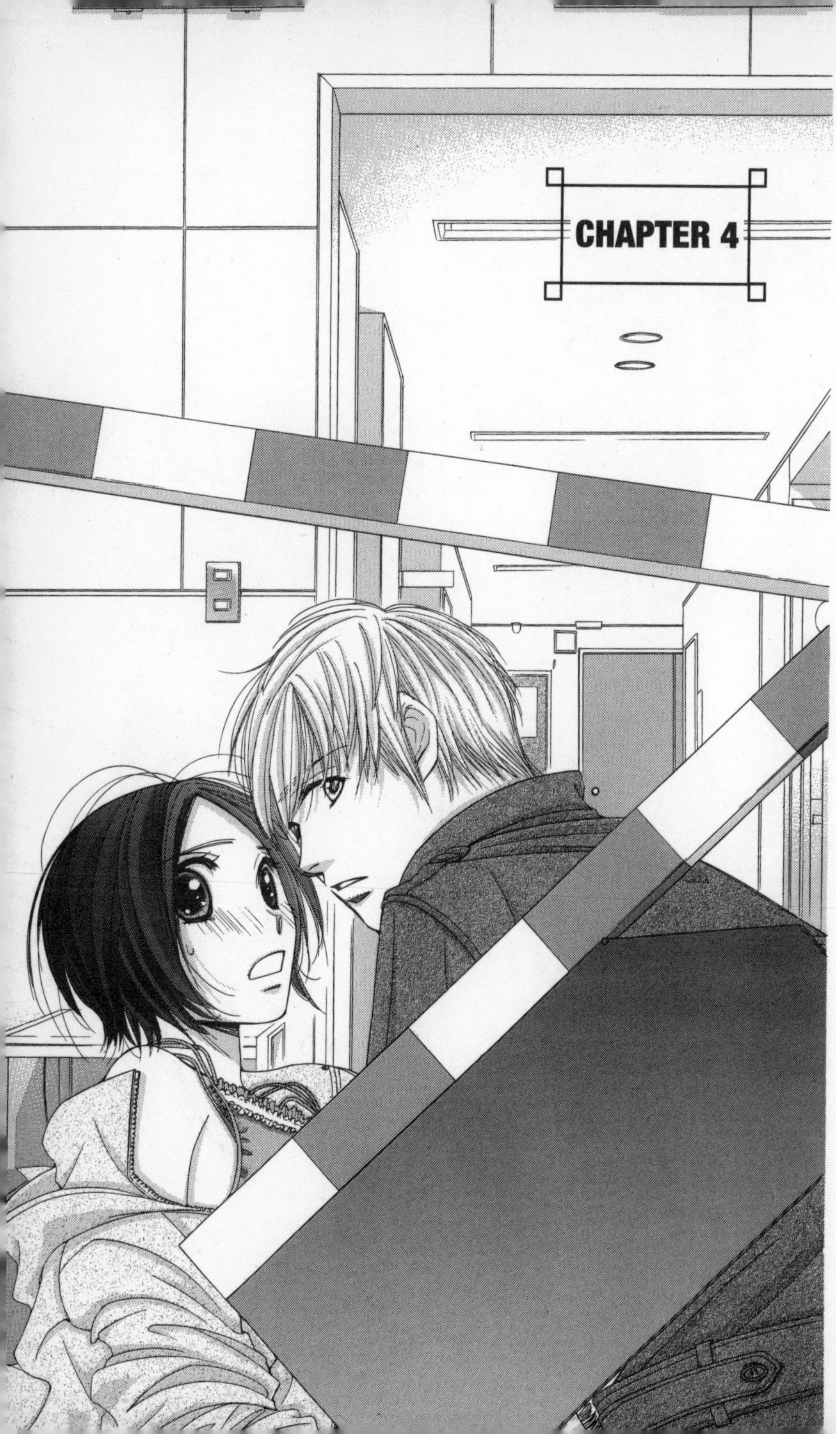
CHAPTER 4

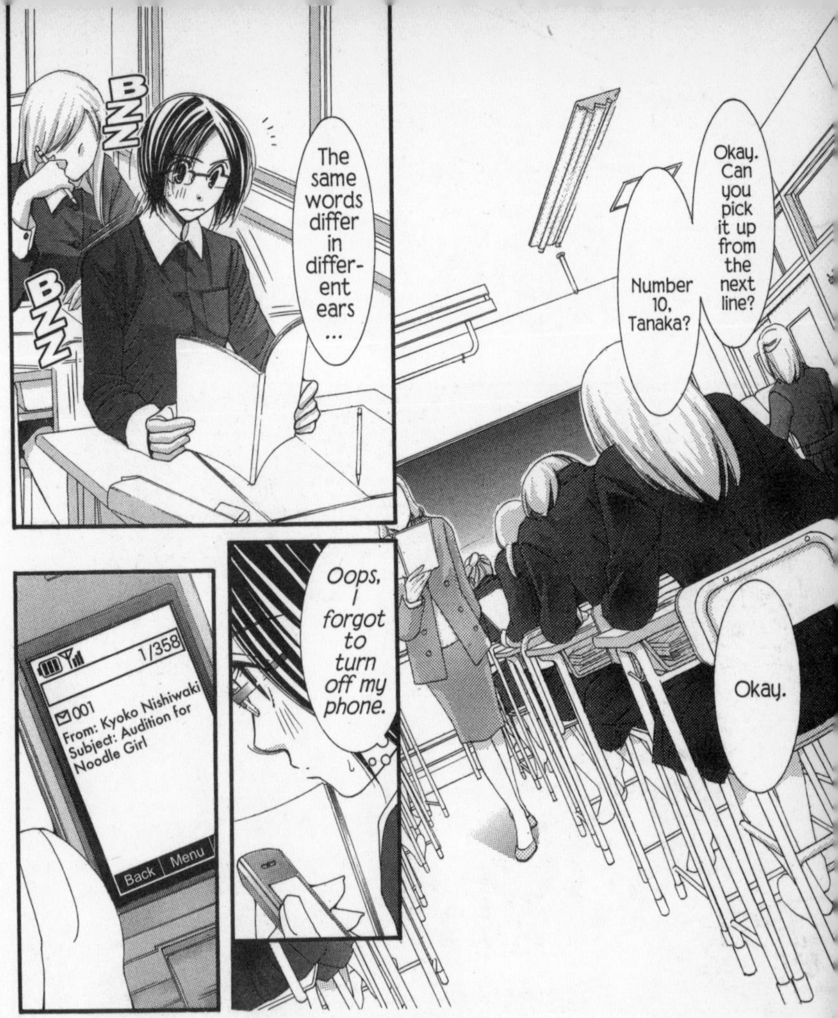
Okay. Can you pick it up from the next line?
Number 10, Tanaka?
Okay.
The same words differ in different ears...
BZZ
BZZ
Oops, I forgot to turn off my phone.
1/358
001
From: Kyoko Nishiwaki
Subject: Audition for Noodle Girl
Back
Menu

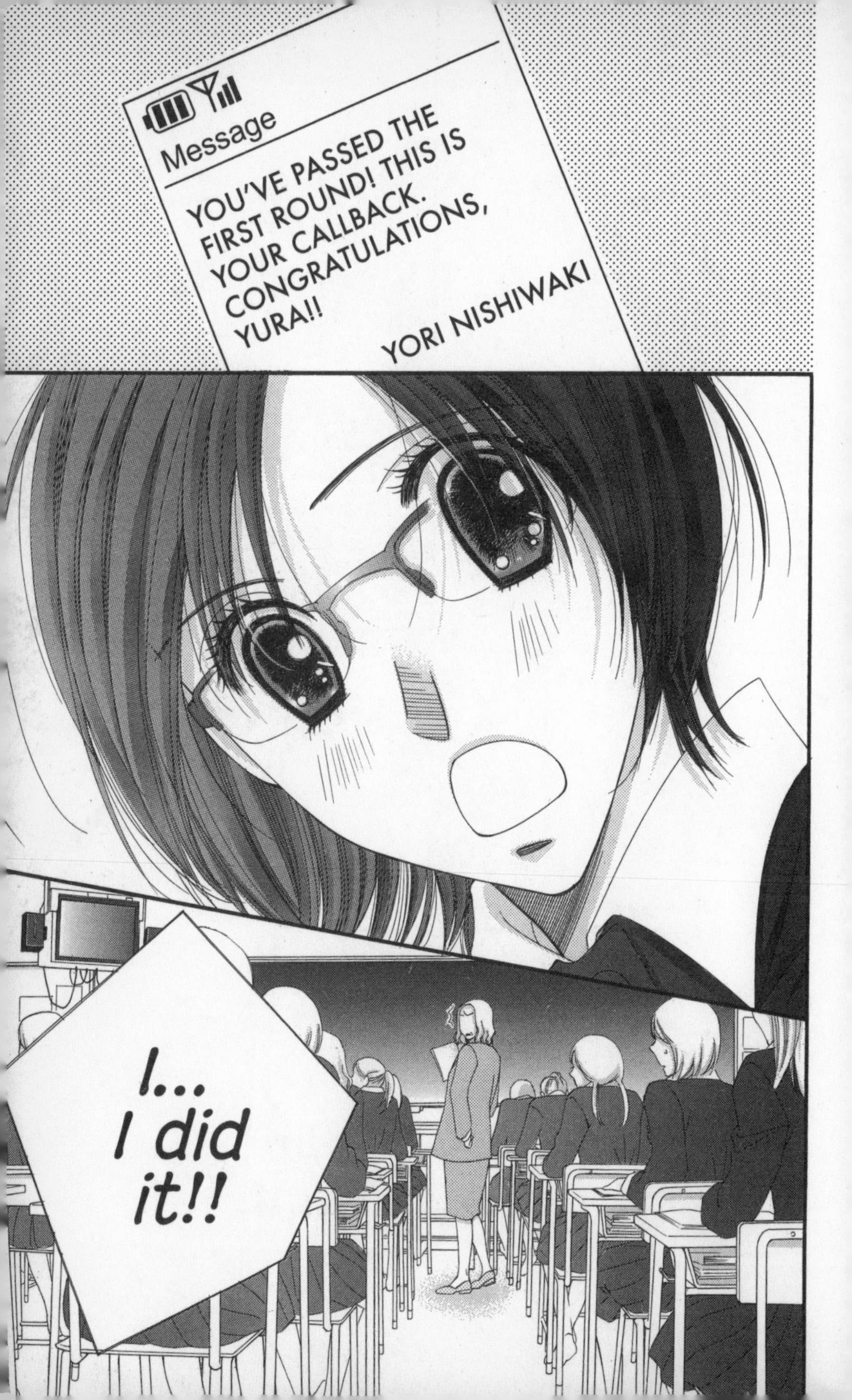
Message
YOU'VE PASSED THE FIRST ROUND! THIS IS YOUR CALLBACK. CONGRATULATIONS, YURA!!
YORI NISHIWAKI
I... I did it!!

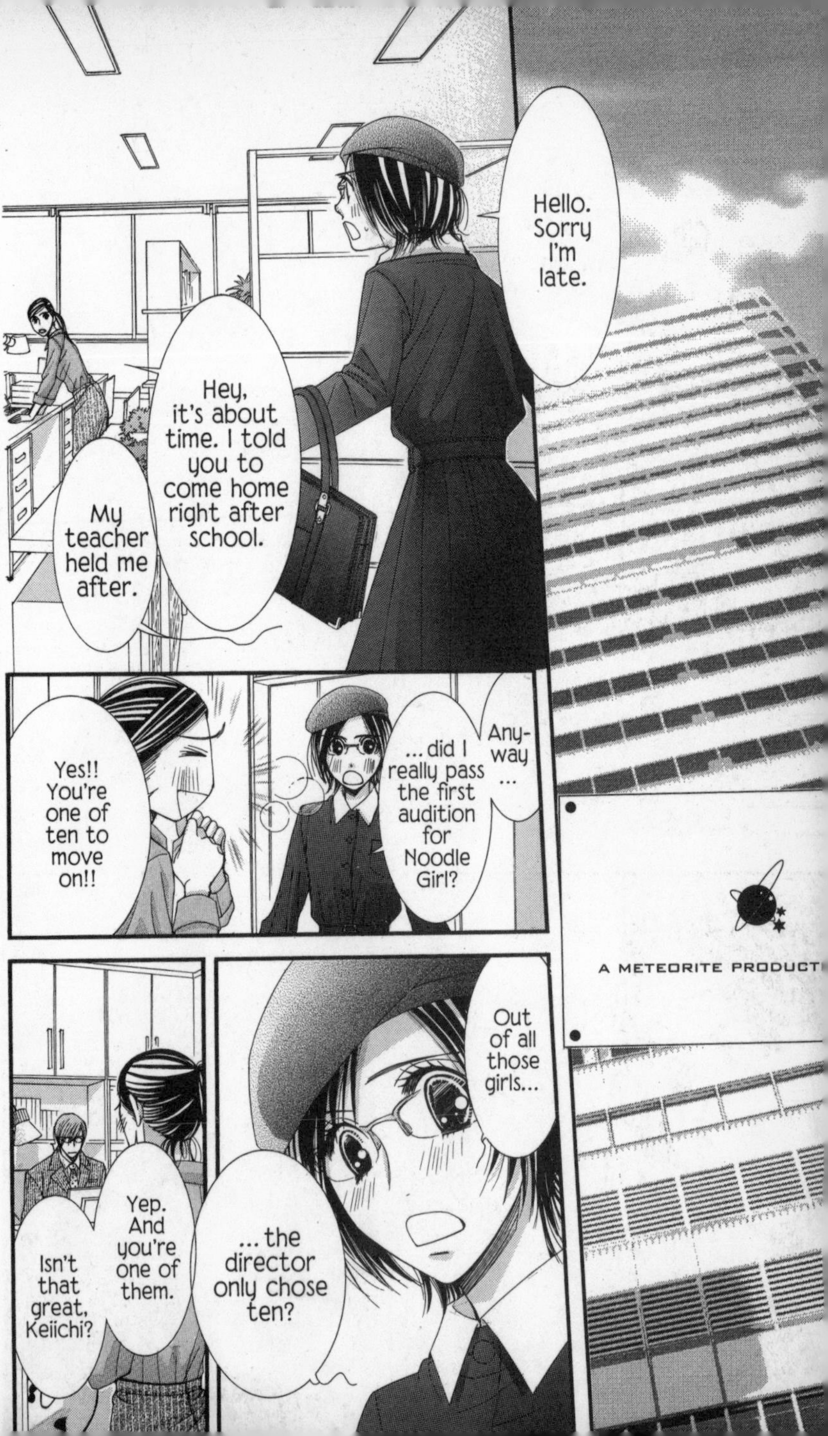
A METEORITE PRODUCT
Hello. Sorry I'm late.
Hey, it's about time. I told you to come home right after school.
My teacher held me after.
Any-way...
...did I really pass the first audition for Noodle Girl?
Yes!! You're one of ten to move on!!
Out of all those girls...
...the director only chose ten?
Yep. And you're one of them.
Isn't that great, Keiichi?

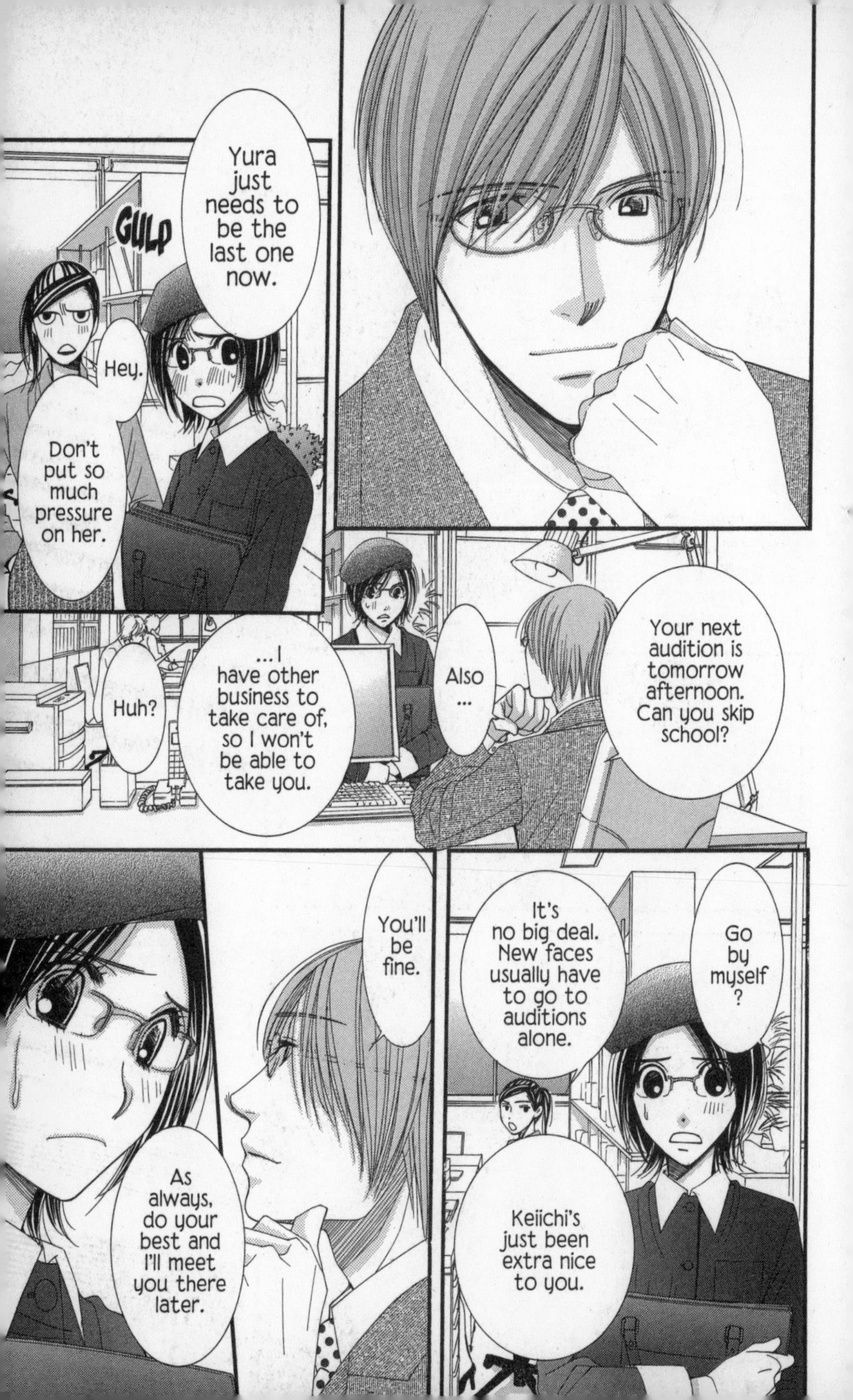
Yura just needs to be the last one now.
GULP
Hey.
Don't put so much pressure on her.
Your next audition is tomorrow afternoon. Can you skip school?
Also ...
...I have other business to take care of, so I won't be able to take you.
Huh?
Go by myself?
It's no big deal. New faces usually have to go to auditions alone.
Keiichi's just been extra nice to you.
You'll be fine.
As always, do your best and I'll meet you there later.

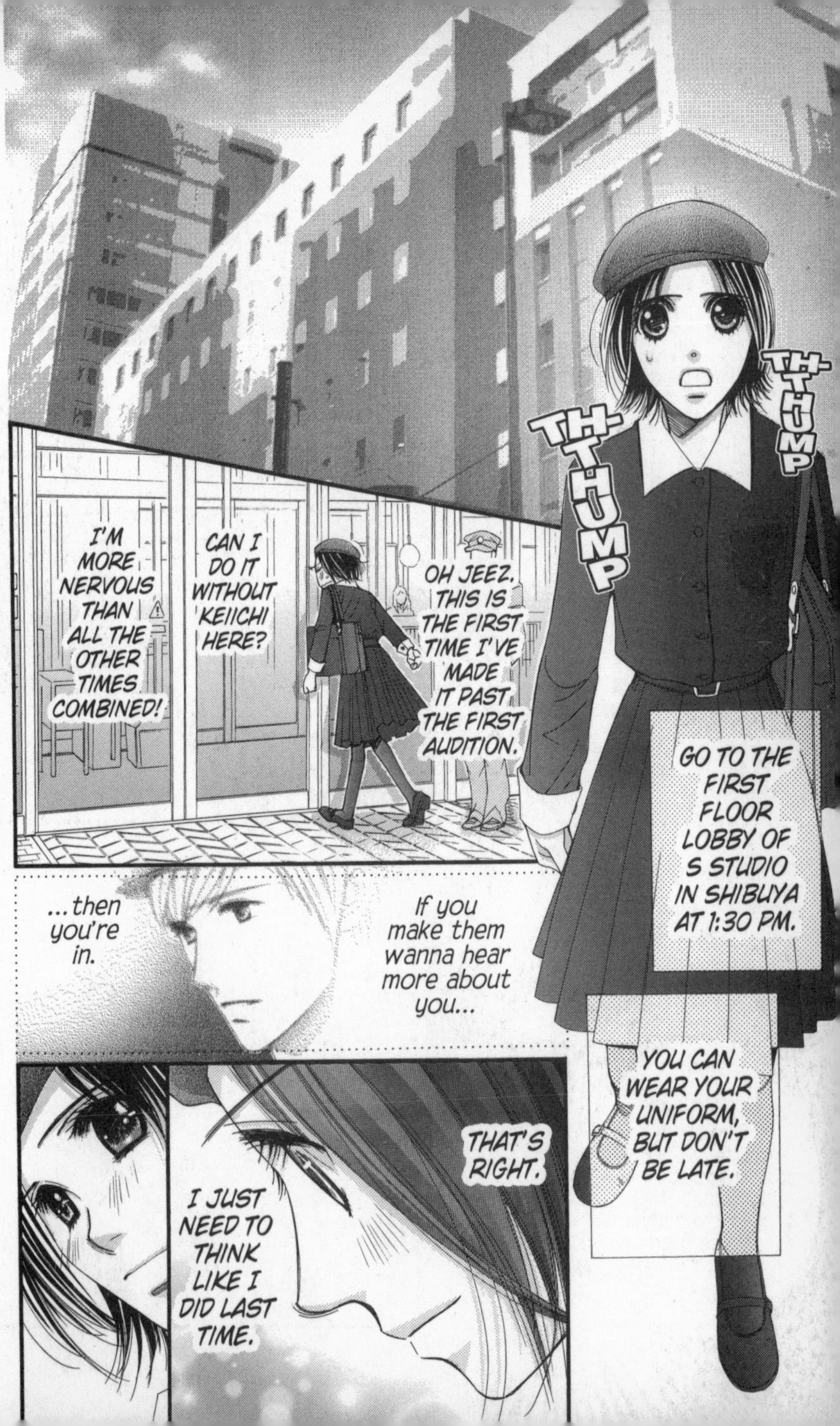
TH-THUMP
TH-THUMP
GO TO THE FIRST FLOOR LOBBY OF S STUDIO IN SHIBUYA AT 1:30 PM.
YOU CAN WEAR YOUR UNIFORM, BUT DON'T BE LATE.
OH JEEZ. THIS IS THE FIRST TIME I'VE MADE IT PAST THE FIRST AUDITION.
CAN I DO IT WITHOUT KEIICHI HERE?
I'M MORE NERVOUS THAN ALL THE OTHER TIMES COMBINED!
If you make them wanna hear more about you...
...then you're in.
THAT'S RIGHT.
I JUST NEED TO THINK LIKE I DID LAST TIME.

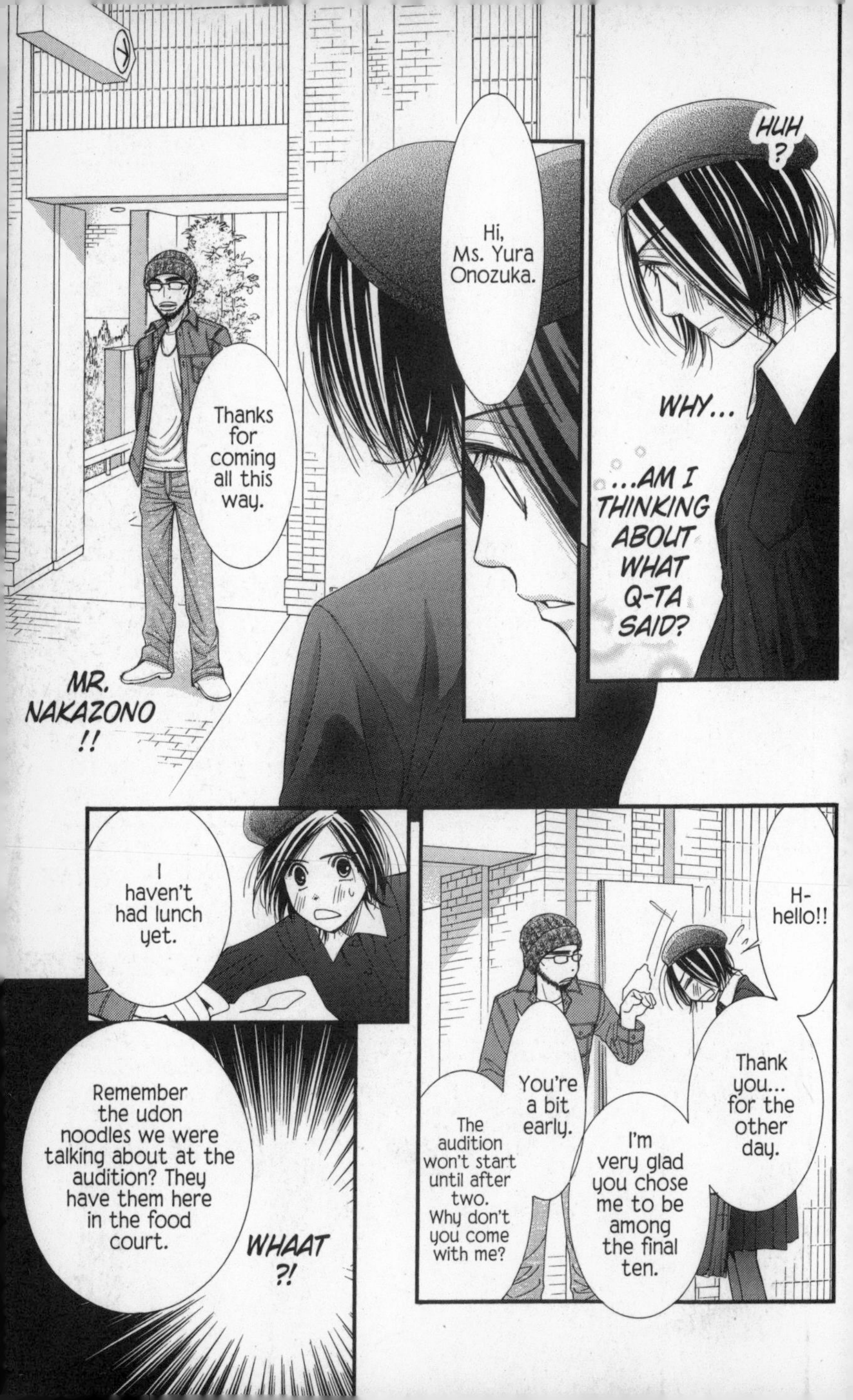
HUH?
WHY...
...AM I THINKING ABOUT WHAT Q-TA SAID?
Hi, Ms. Yura Onozuka.
Thanks for coming all this way.
MR. NAKAZONO!!
H-hello!!
Thank you... for the other day.
I'm very glad you chose me to be among the final ten.
You're a bit early.
The audition won't start until after two. Why don't you come with me?
I haven't had lunch yet.
Remember the udon noodles we were talking about at the audition? They have them here in the food court.
WHAAT?!

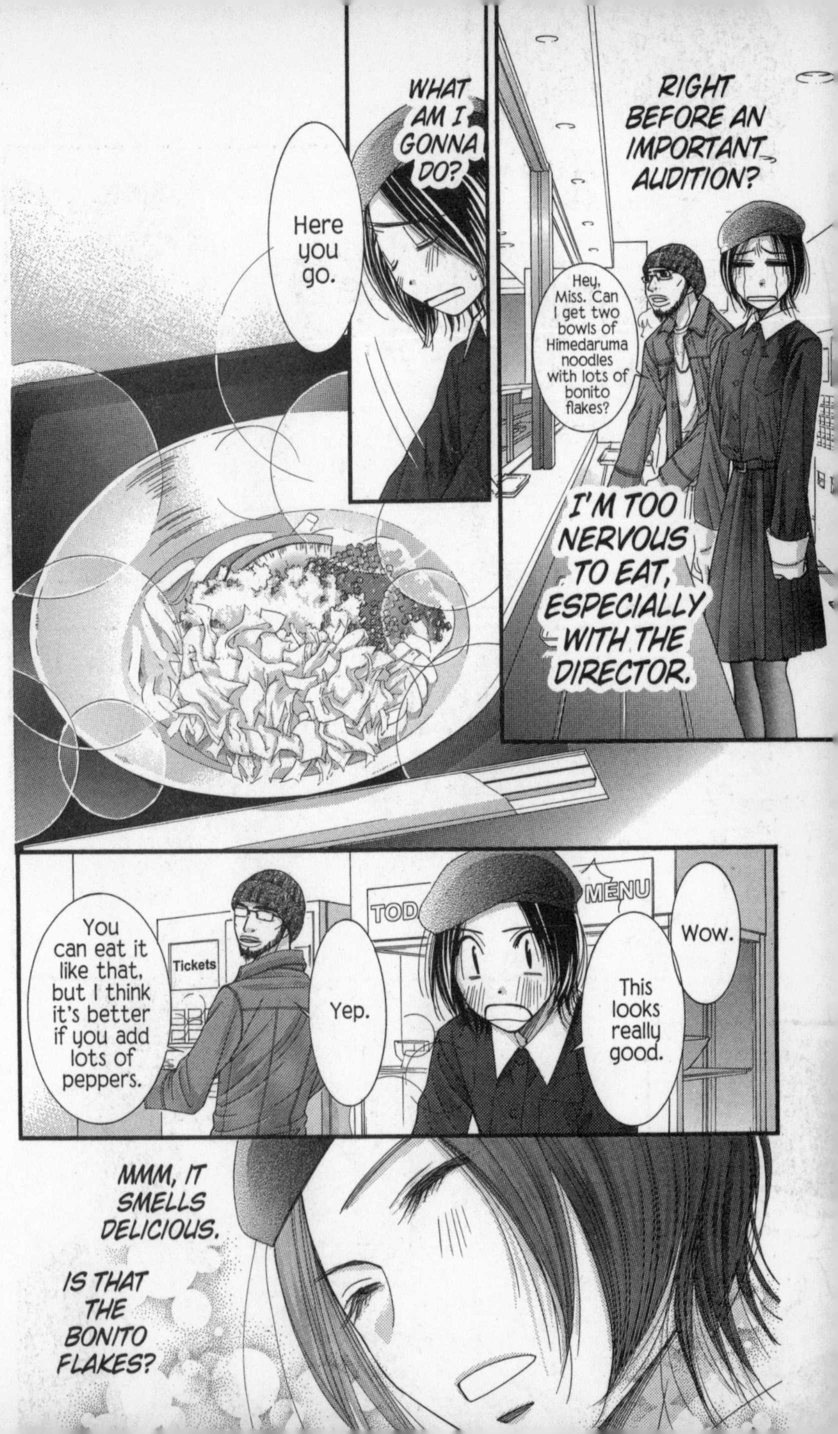
RIGHT BEFORE AN IMPORTANT AUDITION?
Hey, Miss. Can I get two bowls of Himedaruma noodles with lots of bonito flakes?
I'M TOO NERVOUS TO EAT, ESPECIALLY WITH THE DIRECTOR.
WHAT AM I GONNA DO?
Here you go.
MENU
TOD
Wow.
This looks really good.
Yep.
Tickets
You can eat it like that, but I think it's better if you add lots of peppers.
MMM, IT SMELLS DELICIOUS.
IS THAT THE BONITO FLAKES?

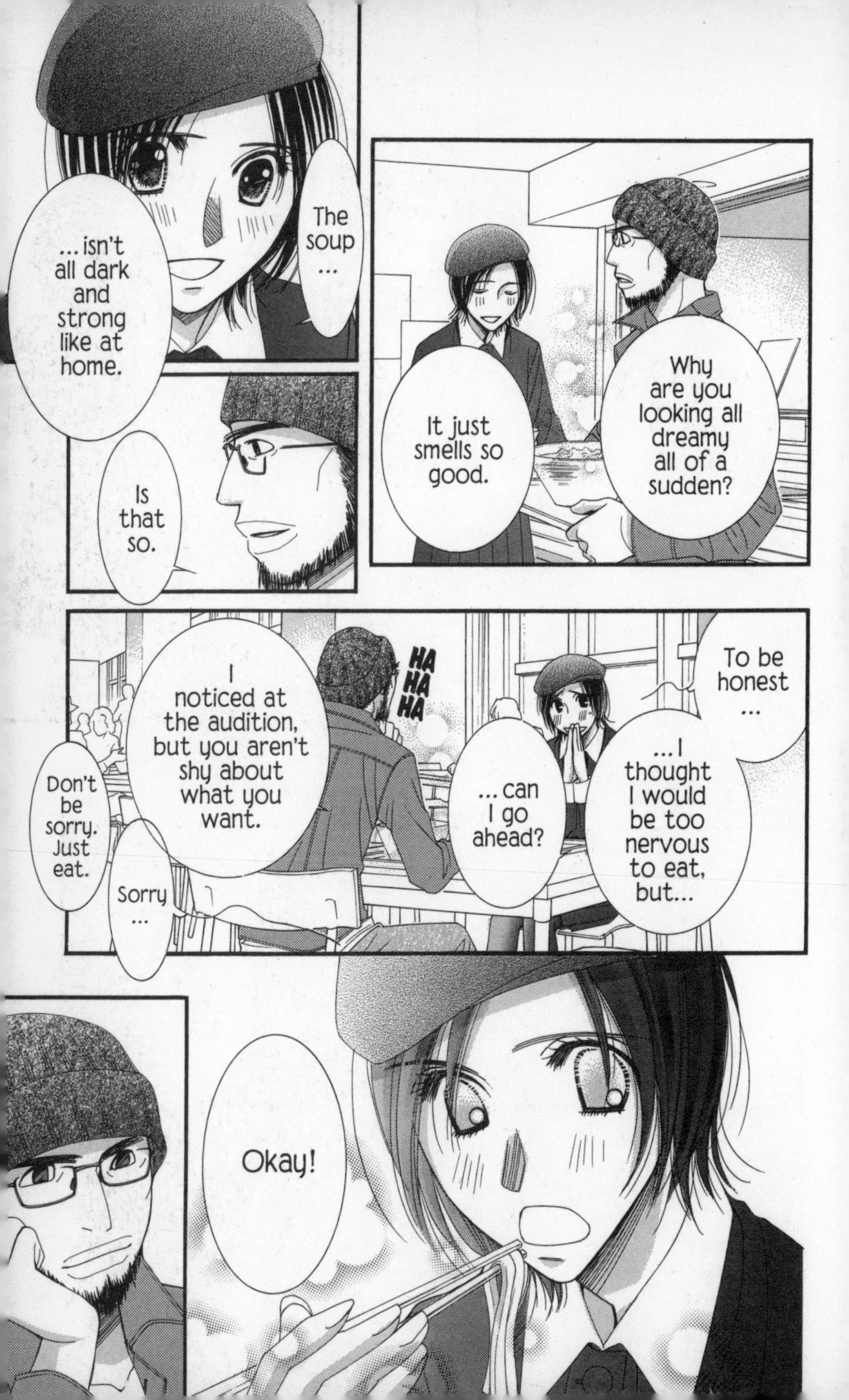
Why are you looking all dreamy all of a sudden?
It just smells so good.
The soup...
...isn't all dark and strong like at home.
Is that so.
To be honest...
...I thought I would be too nervous to eat, but...
...can I go ahead?
HA HA HA
I noticed at the audition, but you aren't shy about what you want.
Sorry...
Don't be sorry. Just eat.
Okay!

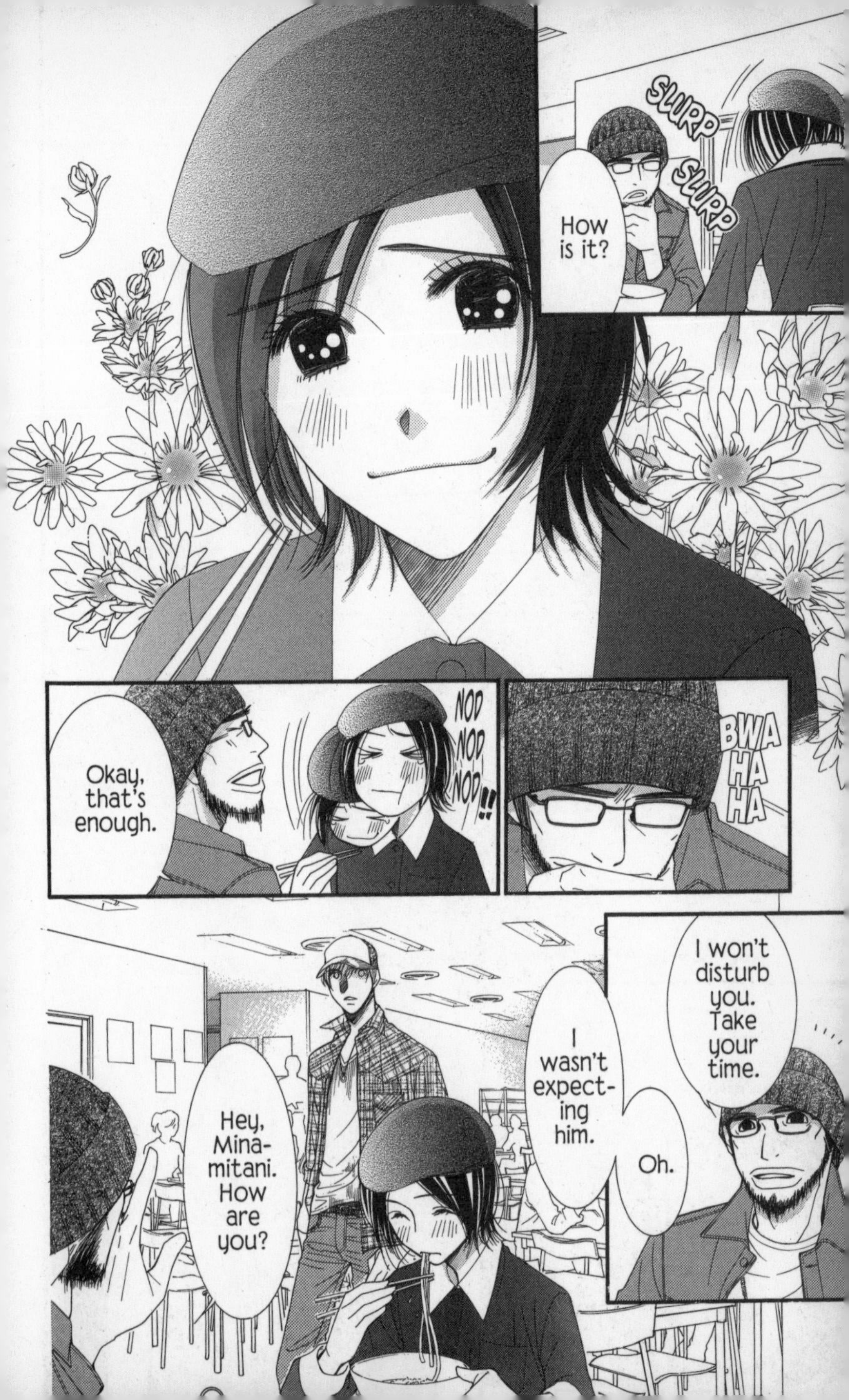
SLURP
SLURP
How is it?
BWA HA HA
NOD NOD NOD!!
Okay, that's enough.
I won't disturb you. Take your time.
Oh.
I wasn't expecting him.
Hey, Minamitani. How are you?

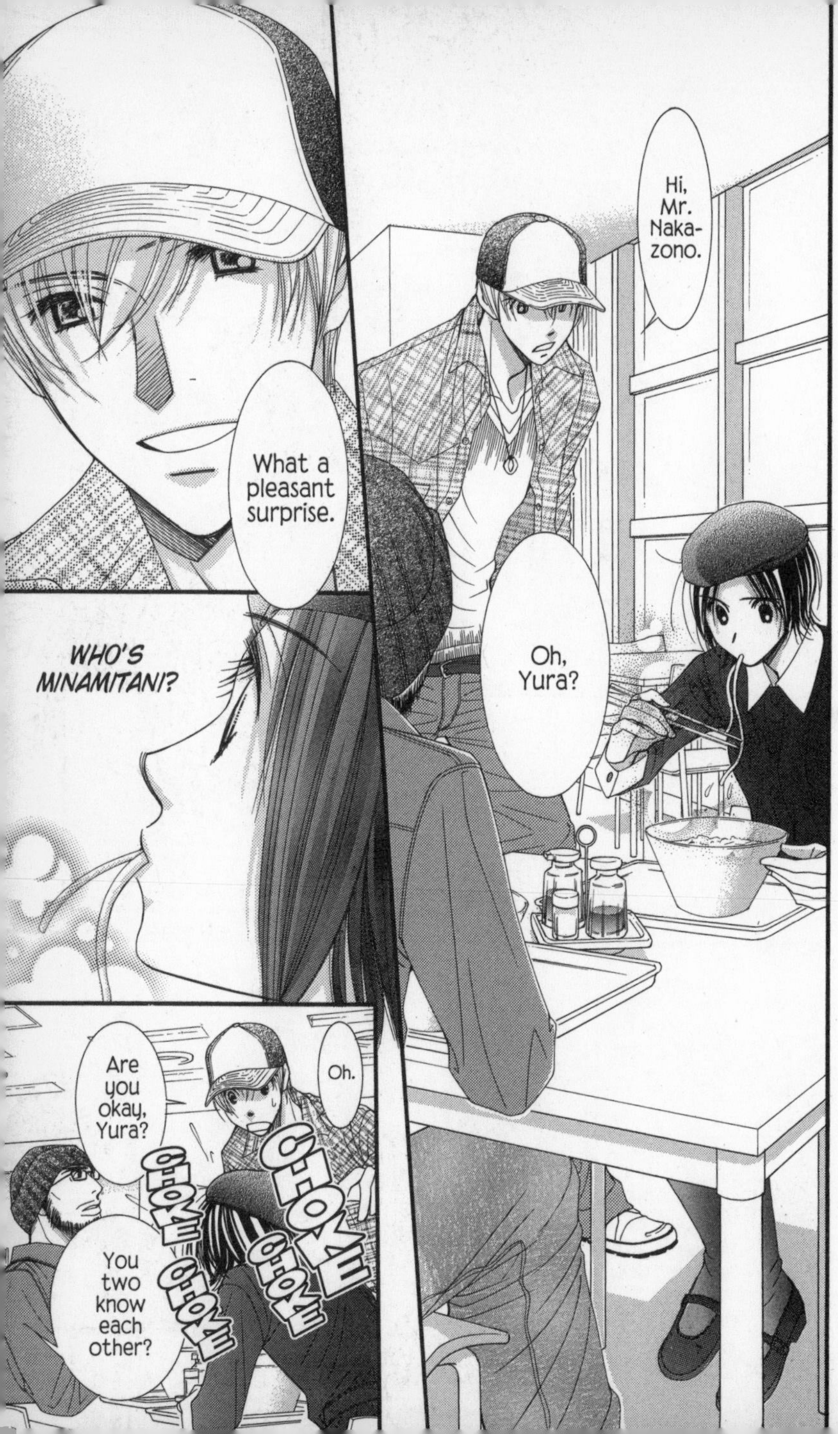
Hi, Mr. Naka-zono.
Oh, Yura?
What a pleasant surprise.
WHO'S MINAMITANI?
Oh.
Are you okay, Yura?
CHOKE CHOKE
CHOKE CHOKE
You two know each other?

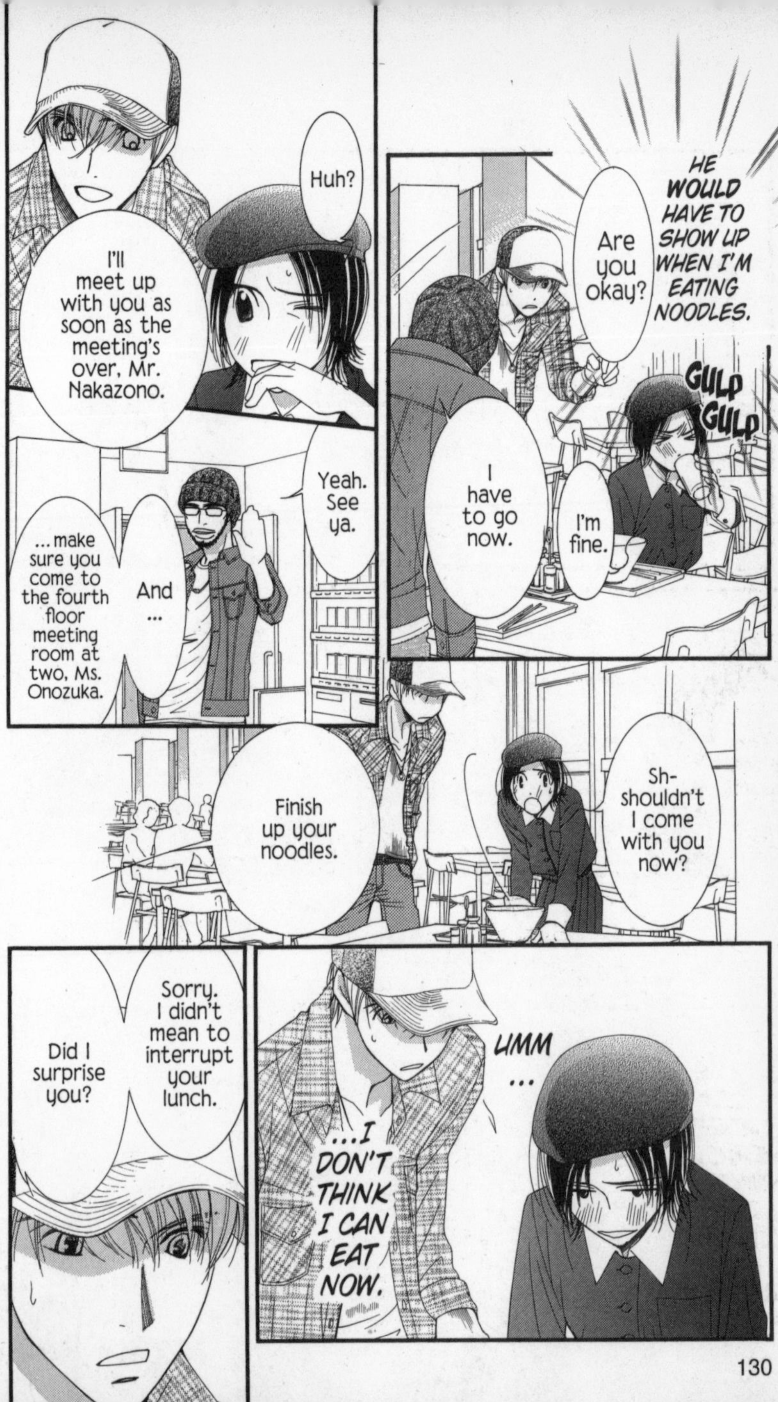
HE WOULD HAVE TO SHOW UP WHEN I'M EATING NOODLES.
Are you okay?
GULP GULP
I'm fine.
I have to go now.
Huh?
I'll meet up with you as soon as the meeting's over, Mr. Nakazono.
Yeah. See ya.
And ...
... make sure you come to the fourth floor meeting room at two, Ms. Onozuka.
Sh-shouldn't I come with you now?
Finish up your noodles.
UMM ...
...I DON'T THINK I CAN EAT NOW.
Sorry. I didn't mean to interrupt your lunch.
Did I surprise you?

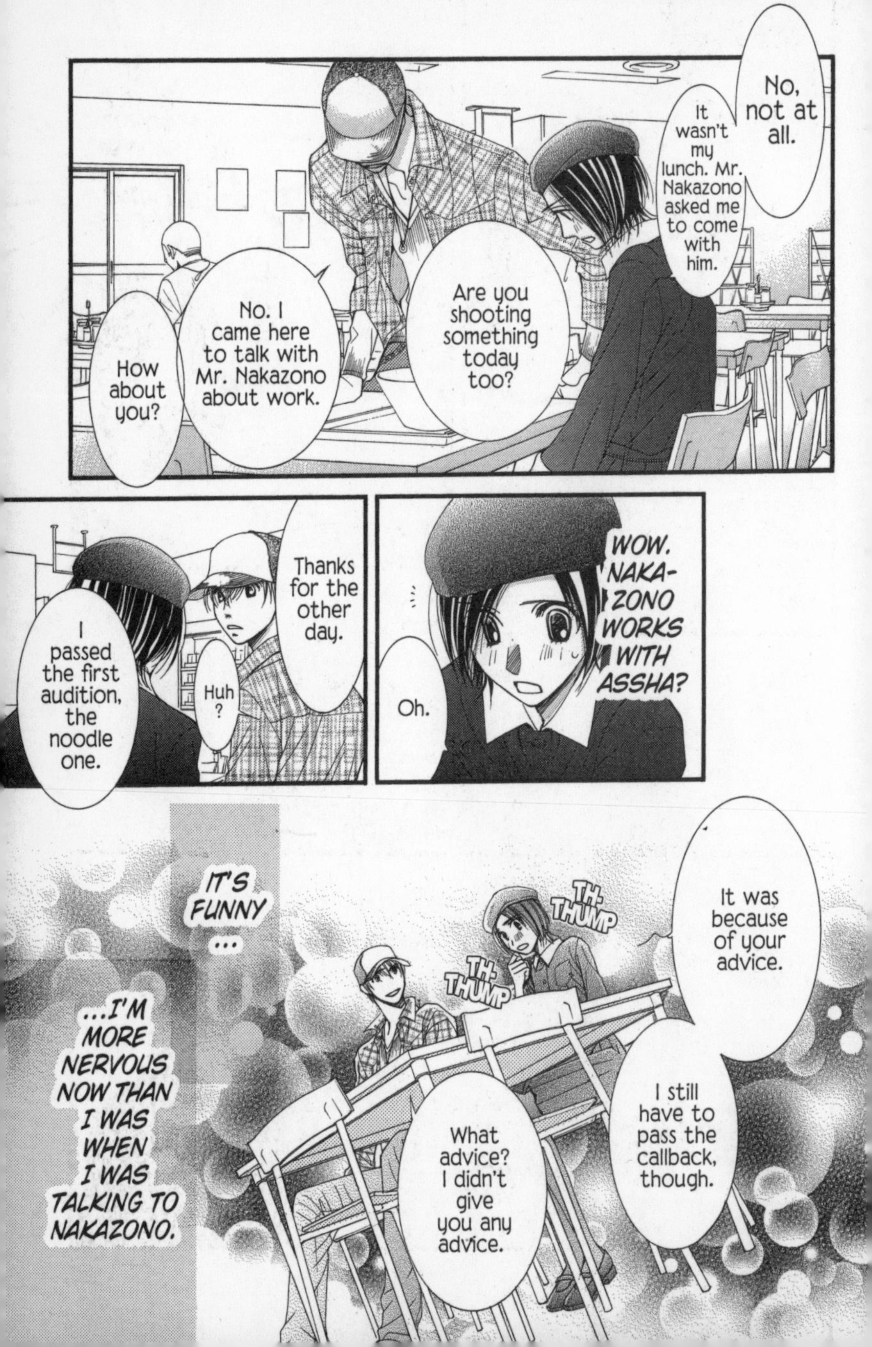
No, not at all.
It wasn't my lunch. Mr. Nakazono asked me to come with him.
Are you shooting something today too?
No. I came here to talk with Mr. Nakazono about work.
How about you?
WOW. NAKAZONO WORKS WITH ASSHA?
Oh.
Thanks for the other day.
Huh?
I passed the first audition, the noodle one.
It was because of your advice.
TH-THUMP
TH-THUMP
I still have to pass the callback, though.
What advice? I didn't give you any advice.
IT'S FUNNY...
...I'M MORE NERVOUS NOW THAN I WAS WHEN I WAS TALKING TO NAKAZONO.

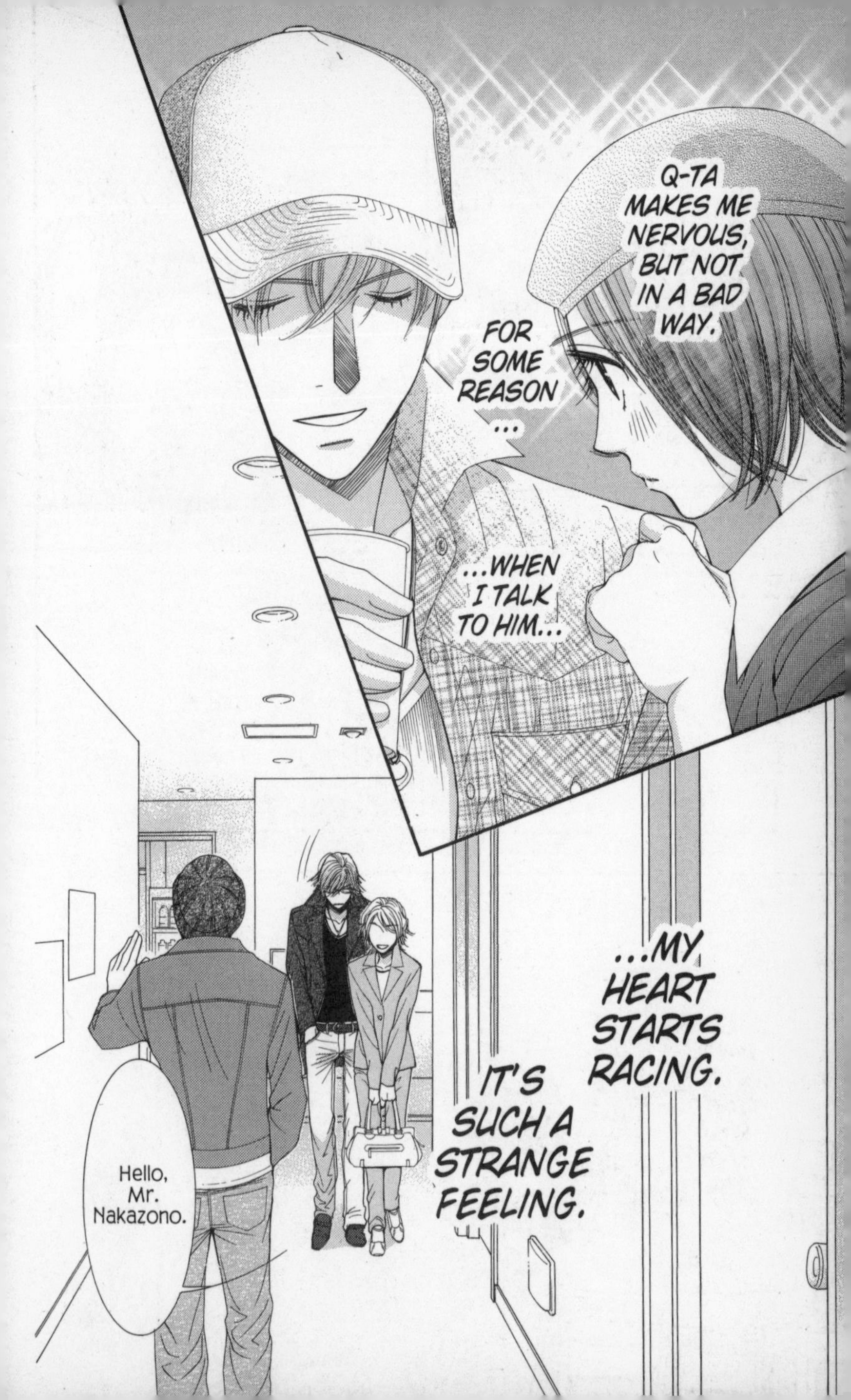

Q-TA MAKES ME NERVOUS, BUT NOT IN A BAD WAY.
FOR SOME REASON...
...WHEN I TALK TO HIM...
...MY HEART STARTS RACING.
IT'S SUCH A STRANGE FEELING.
Hello, Mr. Nakazono.

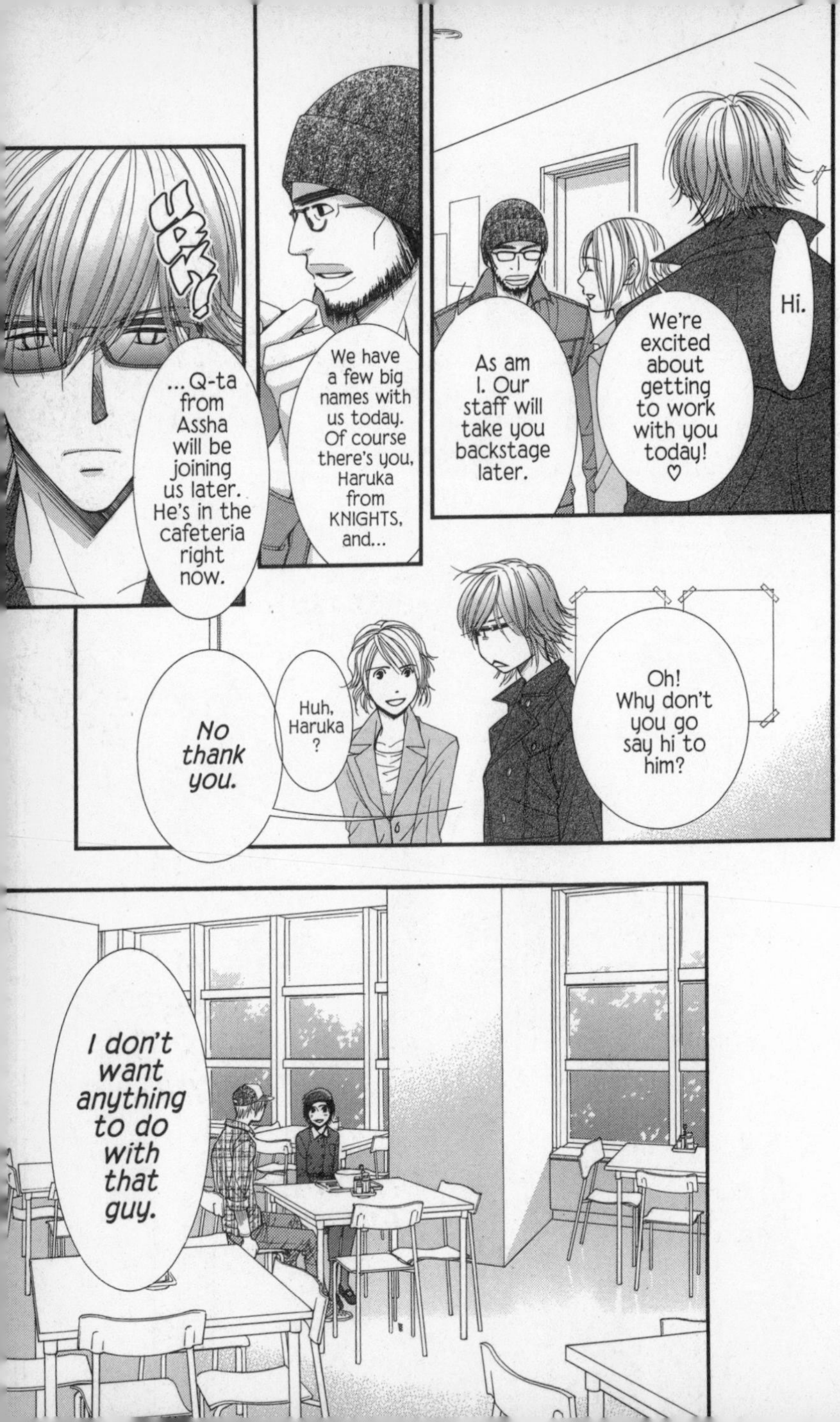
Hi.
We're excited about getting to work with you today! ♡
As am I. Our staff will take you backstage later.
We have a few big names with us today. Of course there's you, Haruka from KNIGHTS, and...
SOK!
...Q-ta from Assha will be joining us later. He's in the cafeteria right now.
Oh! Why don't you go say hi to him?
Huh, Haruka?
No thank you.
I don't want anything to do with that guy.

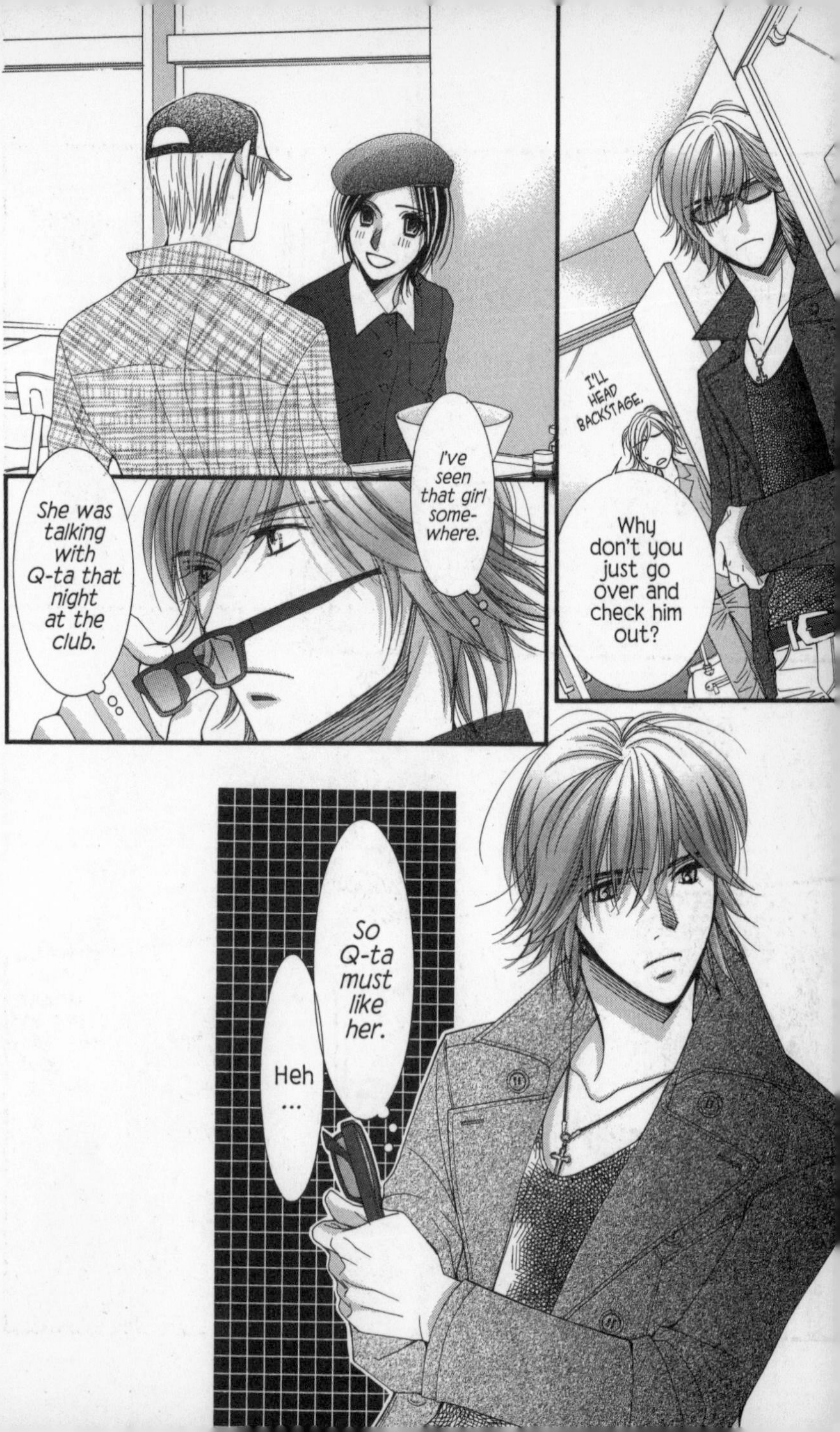
I'LL HEAD BACKSTAGE.
Why don't you just go over and check him out?
I've seen that girl somewhere.
She was talking with Q-ta that night at the club.
So Q-ta must like her.
Heh ...

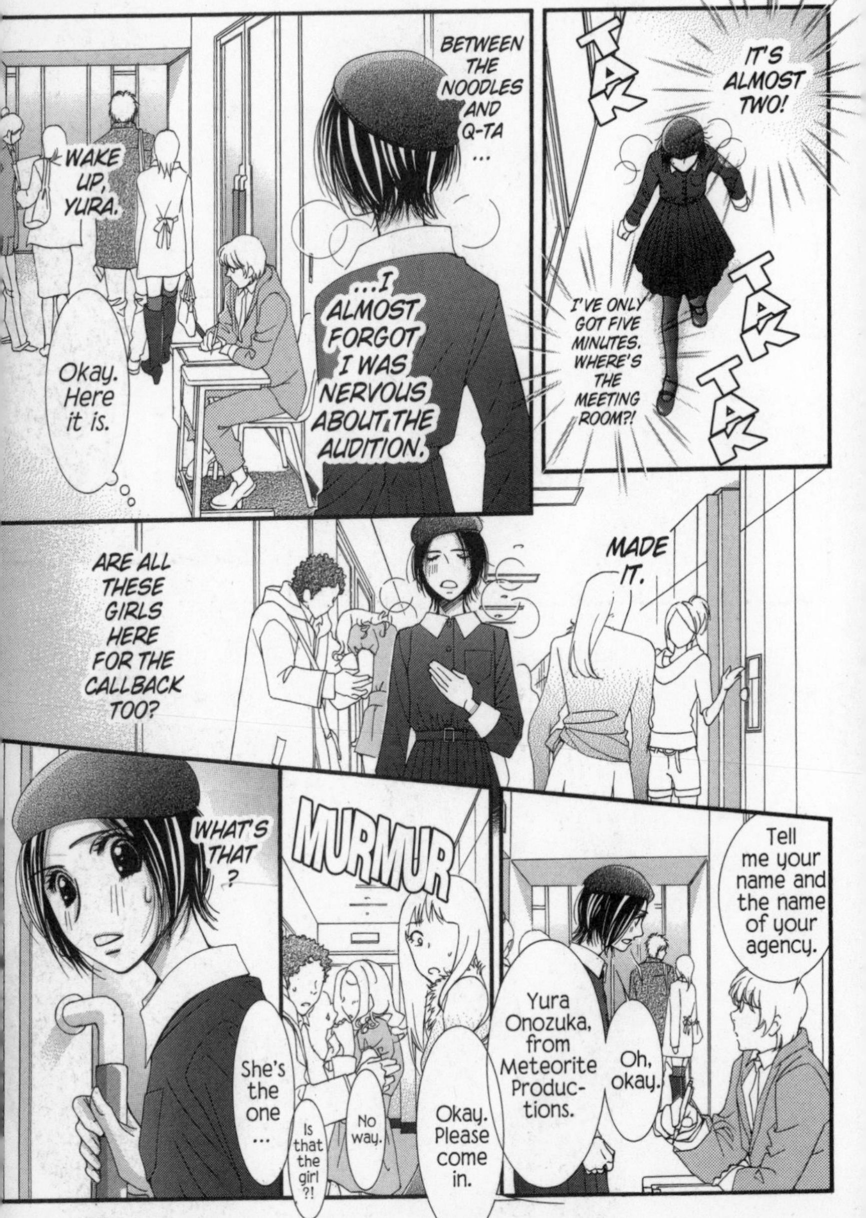
TAK
IT'S ALMOST TWO!
TAK TAK
I'VE ONLY GOT FIVE MINUTES. WHERE'S THE MEETING ROOM?!
BETWEEN THE NOODLES AND Q-TA ...
...I ALMOST FORGOT I WAS NERVOUS ABOUT THE AUDITION.
WAKE UP, YURA.
Okay. Here it is.
MADE IT.
ARE ALL THESE GIRLS HERE FOR THE CALLBACK TOO?
Tell me your name and the name of your agency.
Oh, okay.
Yura Onozuka, from Meteorite Productions.
Okay. Please come in.
MURMUR
She's the one ...
No way.
Is that the girl?!
WHAT'S THAT ?

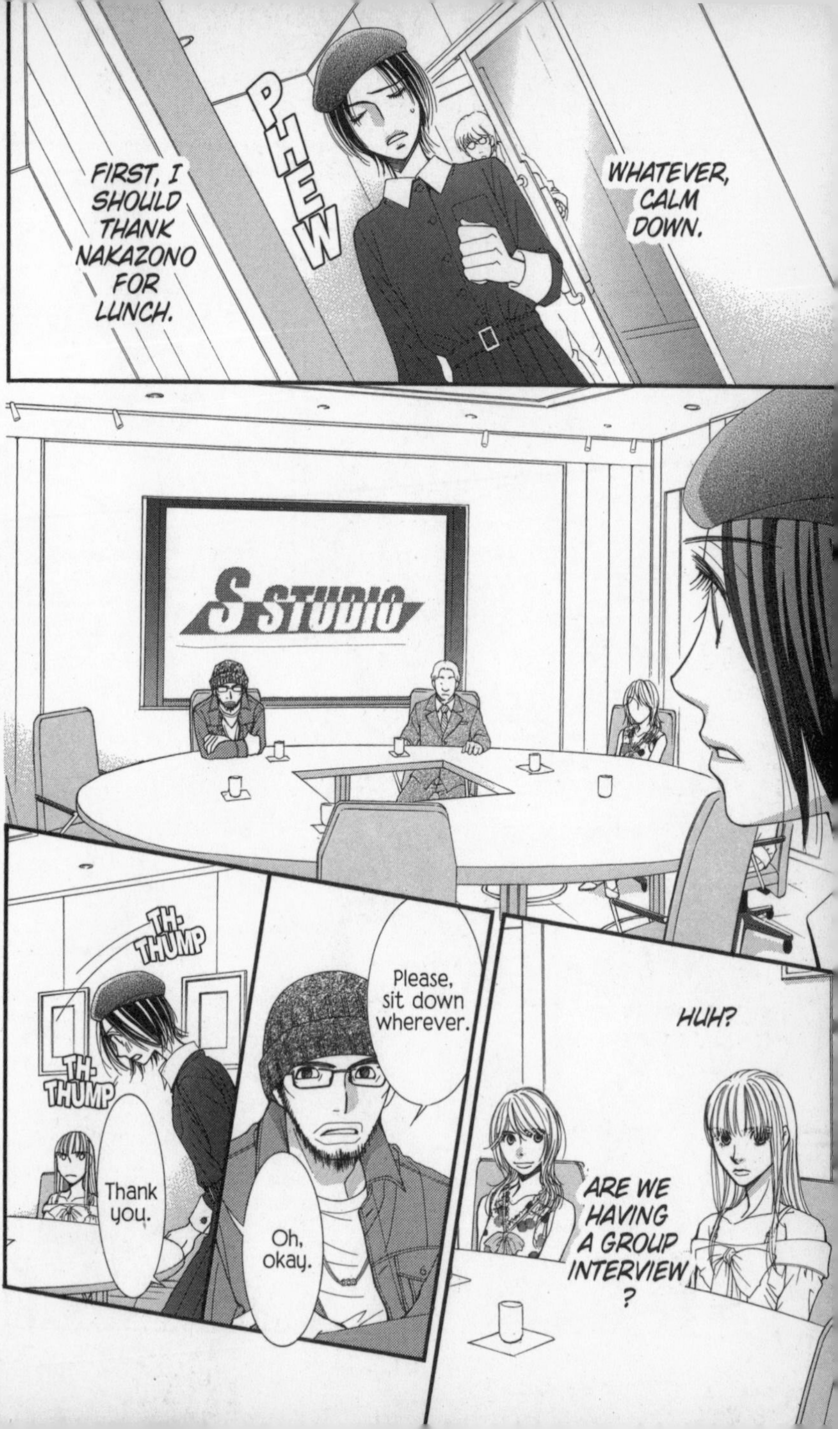
WHATEVER, CALM DOWN.
PHEW
FIRST, I SHOULD THANK NAKAZONO FOR LUNCH.
S STUDIO
HUH?
ARE WE HAVING A GROUP INTERVIEW?
Please, sit down wherever.
TH-THUMP
TH-THUMP
Thank you.
Oh, okay.

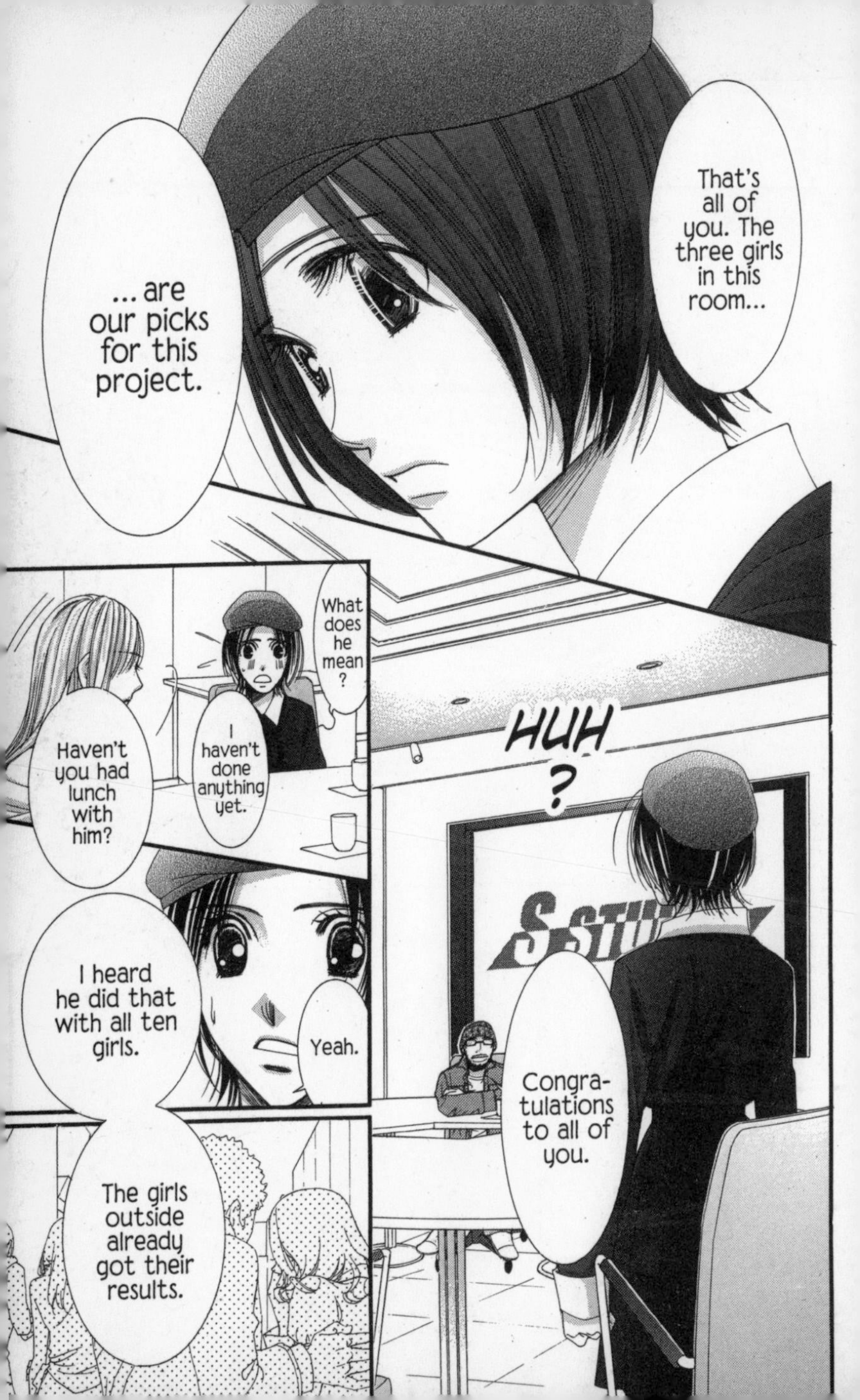
That's all of you. The three girls in this room...
...are our picks for this project.
HUH?
Congratulations to all of you.
What does he mean?
I haven't done anything yet.
Haven't you had lunch with him?
Yeah.
I heard he did that with all ten girls.
The girls outside already got their results.

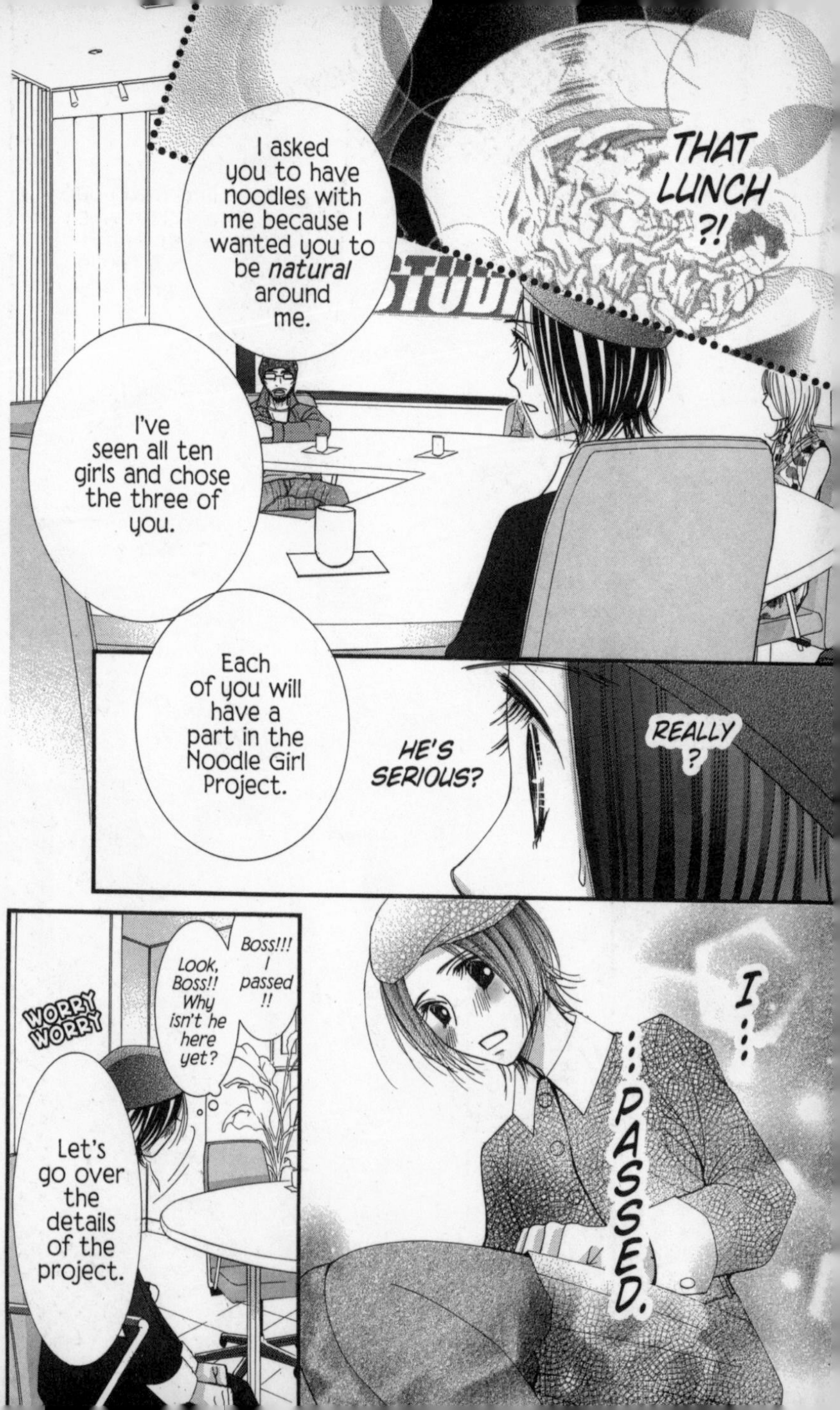
THAT LUNCH?!
I asked you to have noodles with me because I wanted you to be *natural* around me.
I've seen all ten girls and chose the three of you.
Each of you will have a part in the Noodle Girl Project.
REALLY?
HE'S SERIOUS?
I... ...PASSED.
Boss!!! I passed!!
Look, Boss!! Why isn't he here yet?
WORRY WORRY
Let's go over the details of the project.

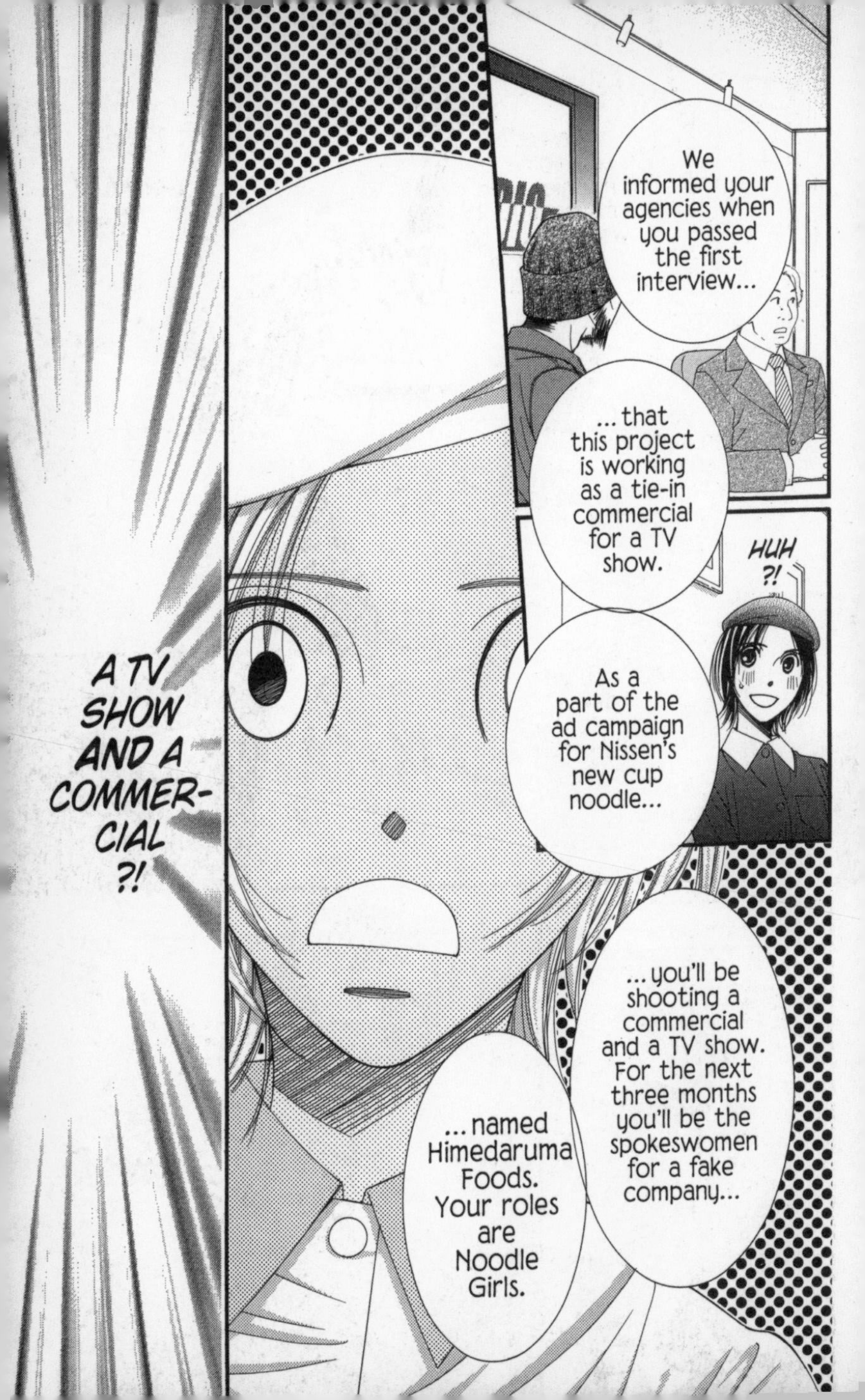
We informed your agencies when you passed the first interview...
...that this project is working as a tie-in commercial for a TV show.
HUH ?!
As a part of the ad campaign for Nissen's new cup noodle...
...you'll be shooting a commercial and a TV show. For the next three months you'll be the spokeswomen for a fake company...
...named Himedaruma Foods. Your roles are Noodle Girls.
A TV SHOW AND A COMMER-CIAL ?!

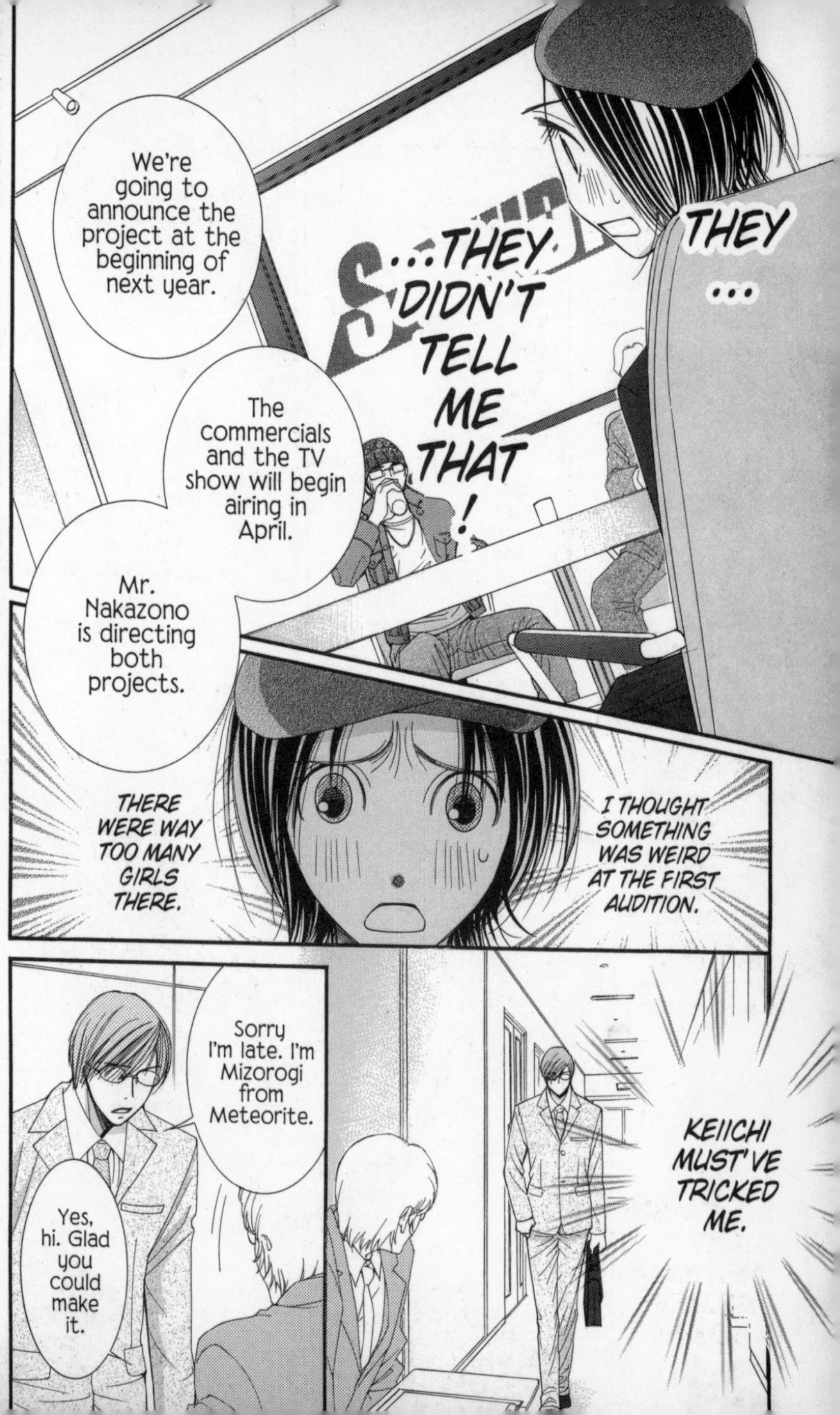
THEY ...
...THEY DIDN'T TELL ME THAT!
We're going to announce the project at the beginning of next year.
The commercials and the TV show will begin airing in April.
Mr. Nakazono is directing both projects.
I THOUGHT SOMETHING WAS WEIRD AT THE FIRST AUDITION.
THERE WERE WAY TOO MANY GIRLS THERE.
KEIICHI MUST'VE TRICKED ME.
Sorry I'm late. I'm Mizorogi from Meteorite.
Yes, hi. Glad you could make it.

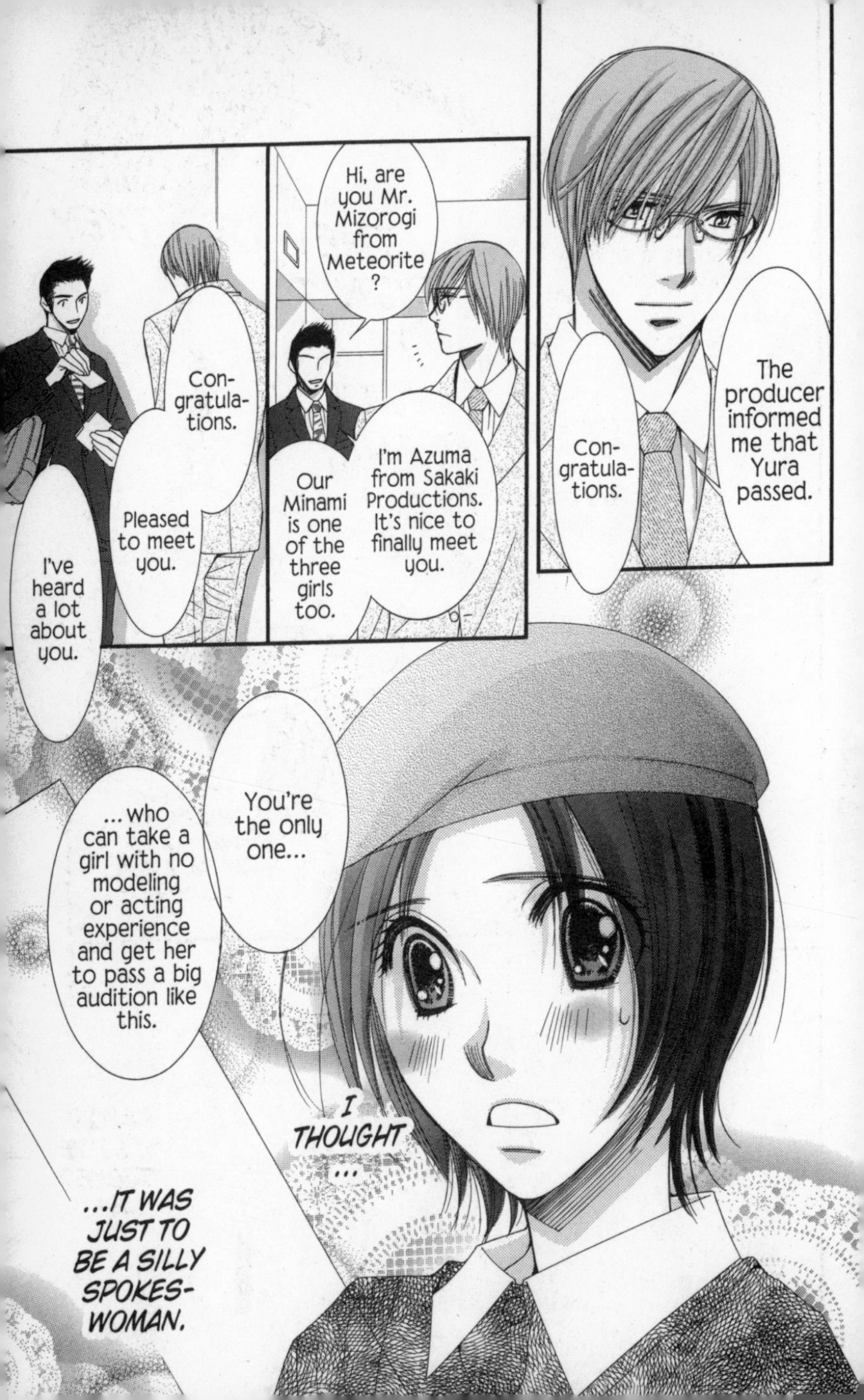
The producer informed me that Yura passed.
Congratulations.
Hi, are you Mr. Mizorogi from Meteorite?
...
I'm Azuma from Sakaki Productions. It's nice to finally meet you.
Our Minami is one of the three girls too.
Congratulations.
Pleased to meet you.
I've heard a lot about you.
You're the only one...
...who can take a girl with no modeling or acting experience and get her to pass a big audition like this.
I THOUGHT...
...IT WAS JUST TO BE A SILLY SPOKESWOMAN.

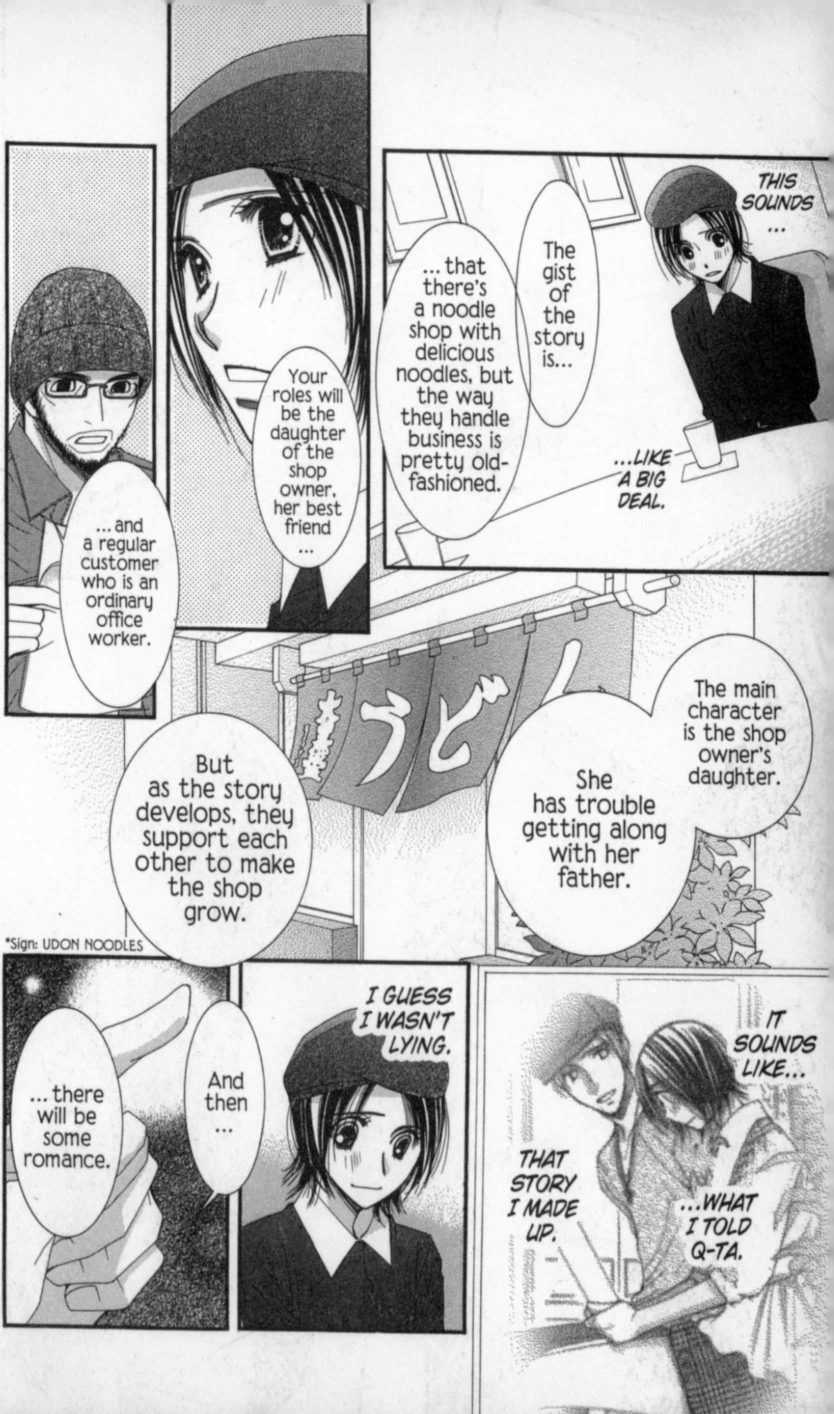
THIS SOUNDS ...
The gist of the story is...
... that there's a noodle shop with delicious noodles, but the way they handle business is pretty old-fashioned.
...LIKE A BIG DEAL.
Your roles will be the daughter of the shop owner, her best friend ...
... and a regular customer who is an ordinary office worker.
The main character is the shop owner's daughter.
She has trouble getting along with her father.
But as the story develops, they support each other to make the shop grow.
*Sign: UDON NOODLES
IT SOUNDS LIKE...
...WHAT I TOLD Q-TA.
THAT STORY I MADE UP.
I GUESS I WASN'T LYING.
And then ...
... there will be some romance.

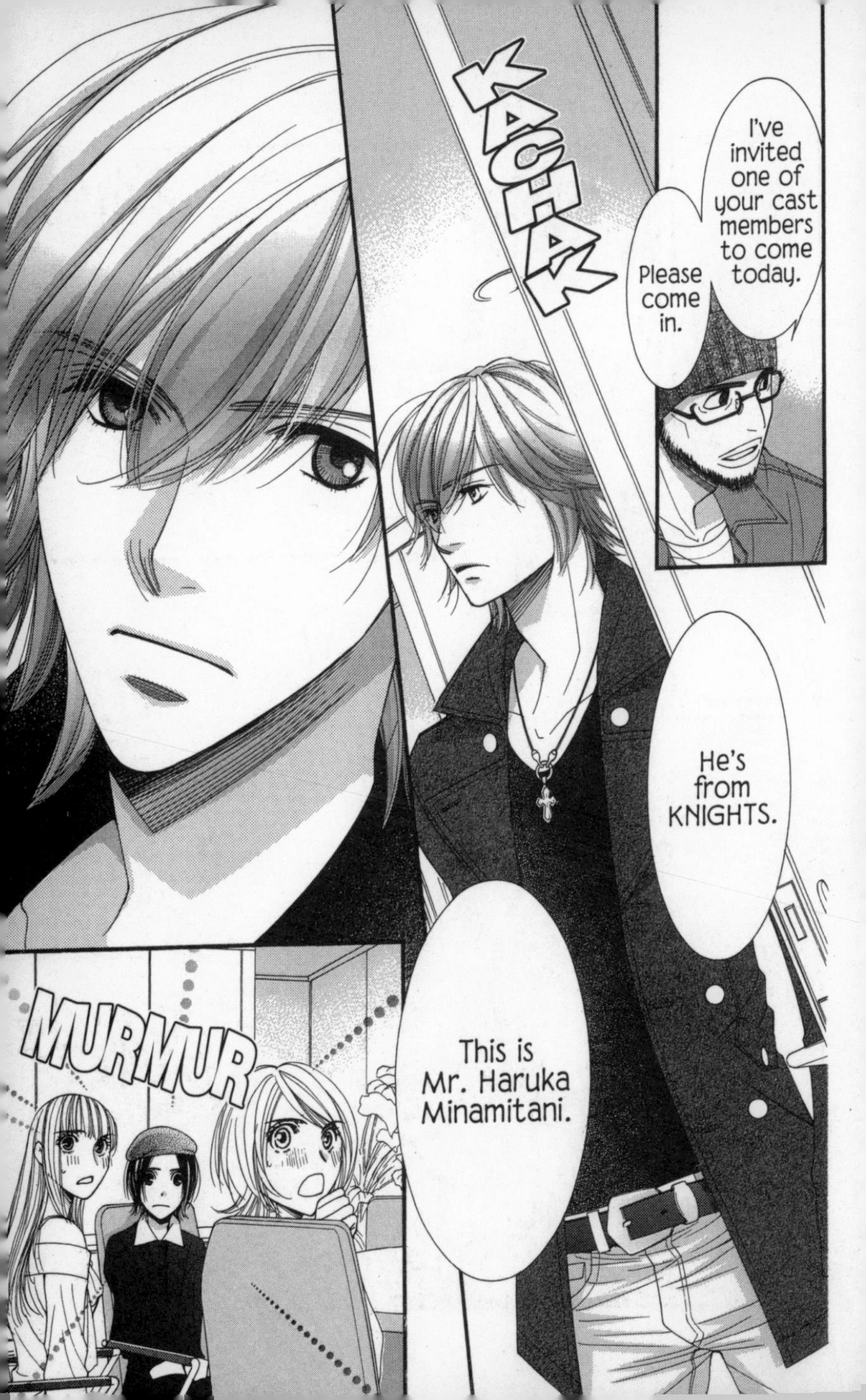
I've invited one of your cast members to come today.
Please come in.
KACHAK
He's from KNIGHTS.
This is Mr. Haruka Minamitani.
MURMUR

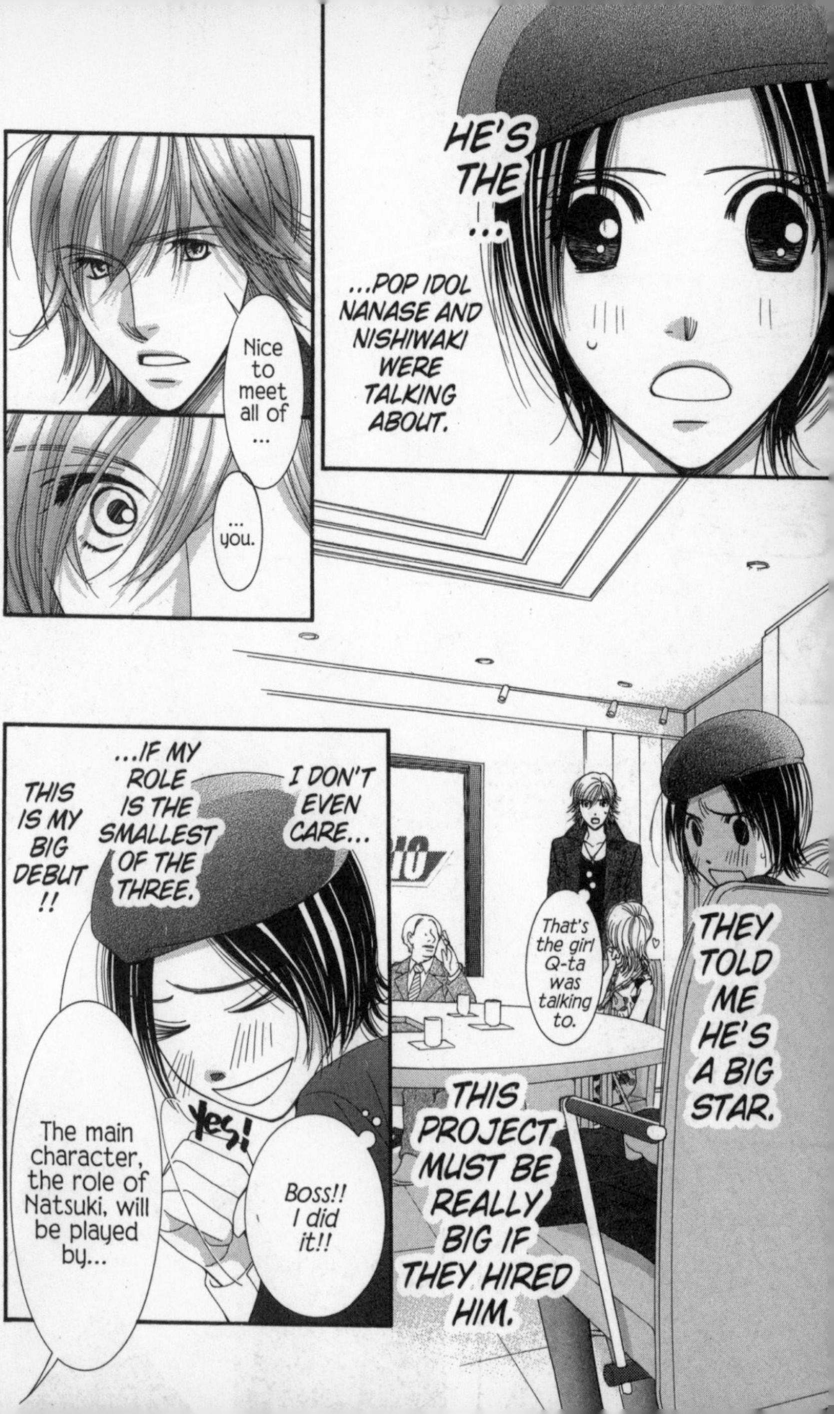
HE'S THE ...
...POP IDOL NANASE AND NISHIWAKI WERE TALKING ABOUT.
Nice to meet all of ...
... you.
THEY TOLD ME HE'S A BIG STAR.
That's the girl Q-ta was talking to.
THIS PROJECT MUST BE REALLY BIG IF THEY HIRED HIM.
I DON'T EVEN CARE...
...IF MY ROLE IS THE SMALLEST OF THE THREE.
THIS IS MY BIG DEBUT !!
Yes!
Boss!! I did it!!
The main character, the role of Natsuki, will be played by...

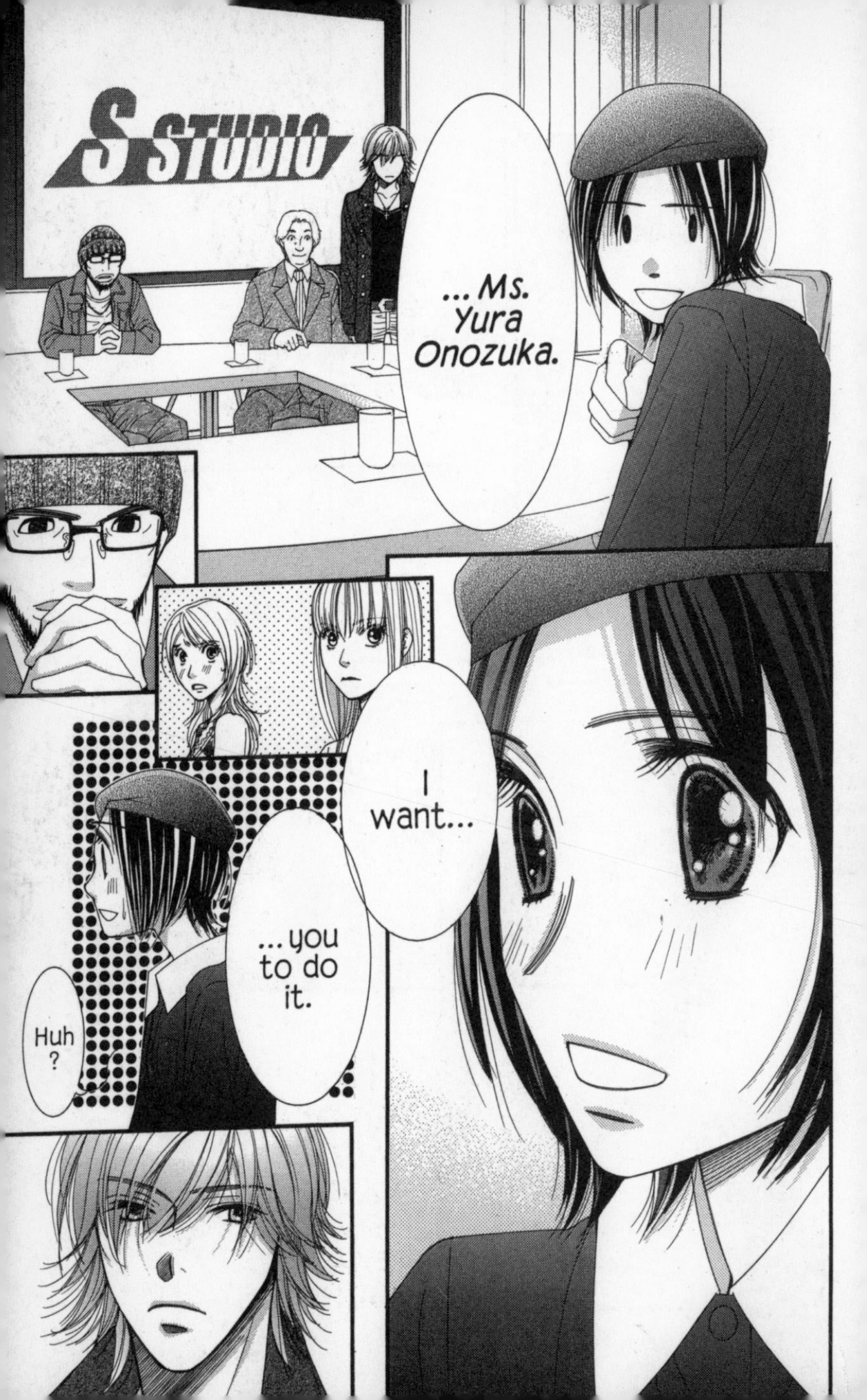
...Ms. Yura Onozuka.
S STUDIO
I want...
...you to do it.
Huh?

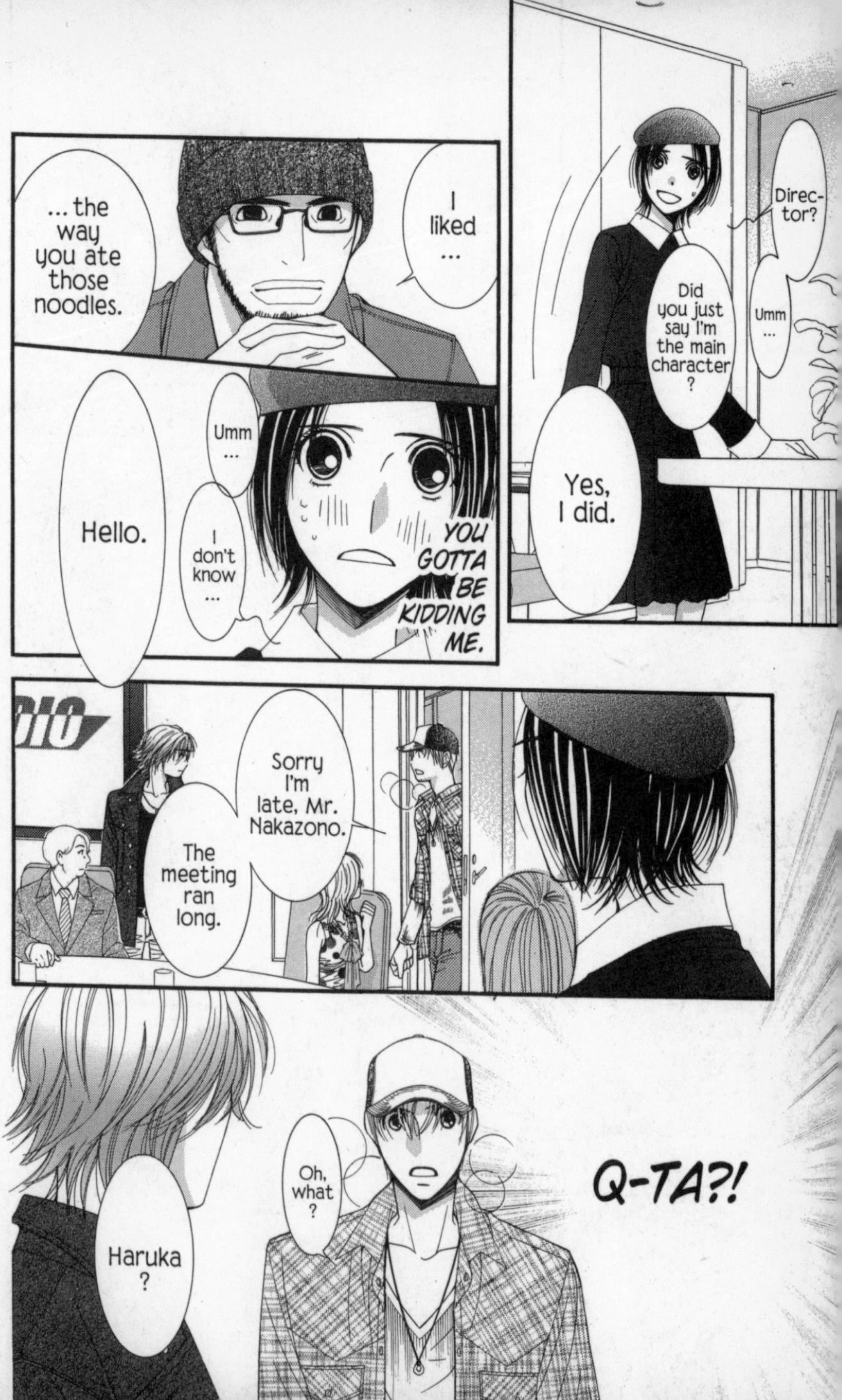
Direc-
tor?
Umm
...
Did you just say I'm the main character?
Yes, I did.
I liked
...
... the way you ate those noodles.
Umm
...
I don't know
...
YOU GOTTA BE KIDDING ME.
Hello.
Sorry I'm late, Mr. Nakazono.
The meeting ran long.
Q-TA?!
Oh, what?
Haruka?

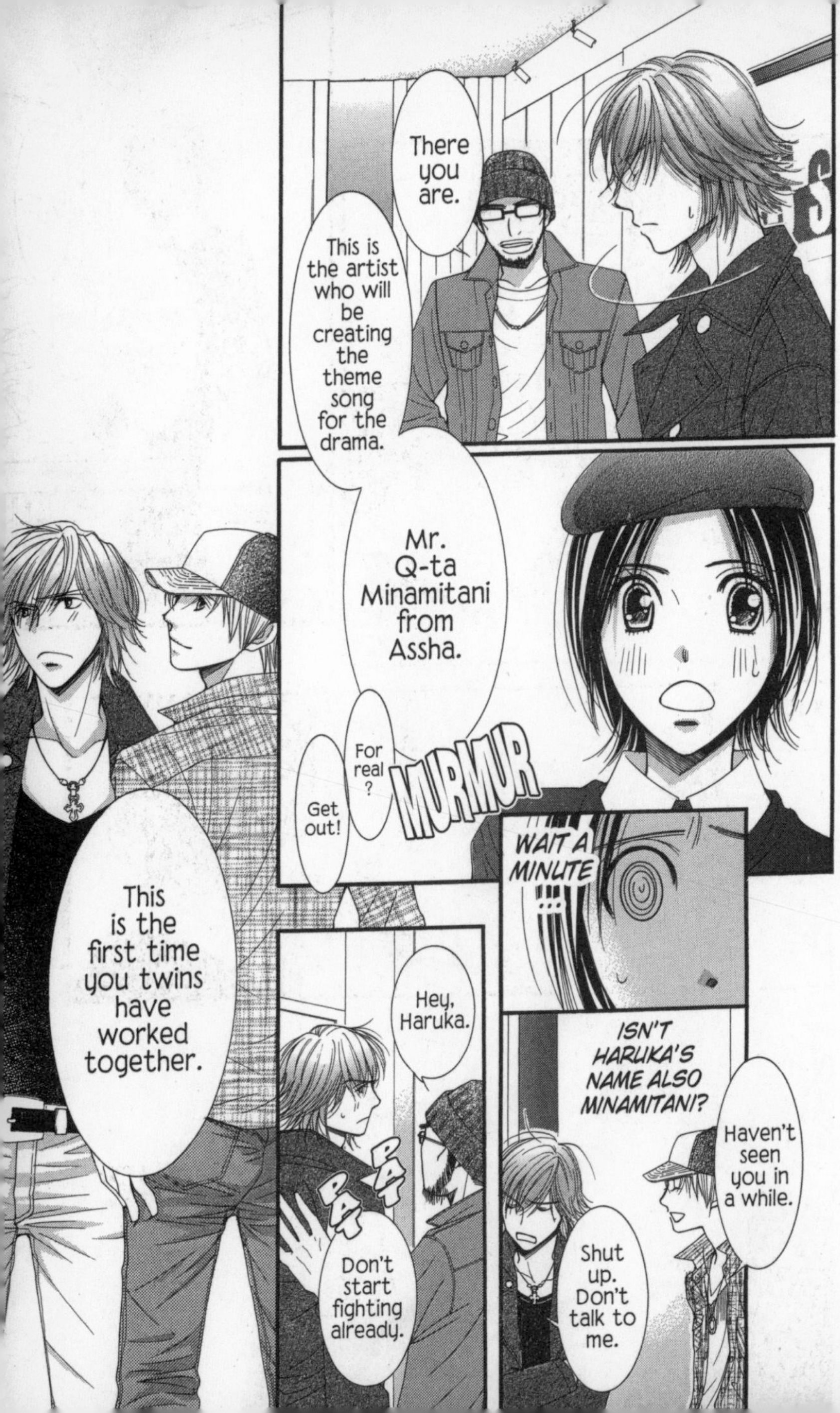
There you are.
This is the artist who will be creating the theme song for the drama.
Mr. Q-ta Minamitani from Assha.
For real?
Get out!
MURMUR
WAIT A MINUTE!!...
This is the first time you twins have worked together.
ISN'T HARUKA'S NAME ALSO MINAMITANI?
Haven't seen you in a while.
Shut up. Don't talk to me.
Hey, Haruka.
PAT PAT
Don't start fighting already.

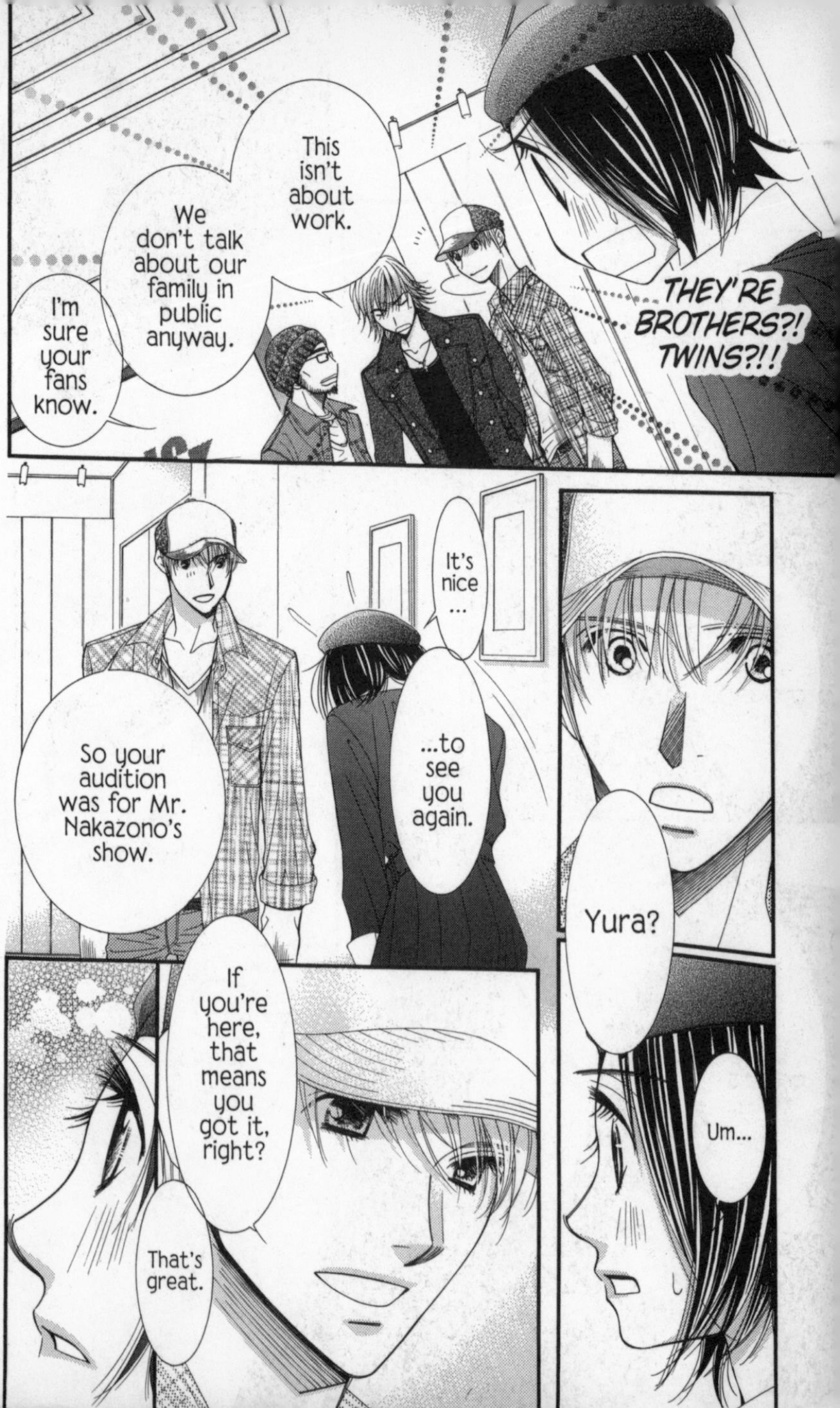
THEY'RE BROTHERS?! TWINS?!!
This isn't about work.
We don't talk about our family in public anyway.
I'm sure your fans know.
Yura?
It's nice ...
...to see you again.
So your audition was for Mr. Nakazono's show.
Um...
If you're here, that means you got it, right?
That's great.

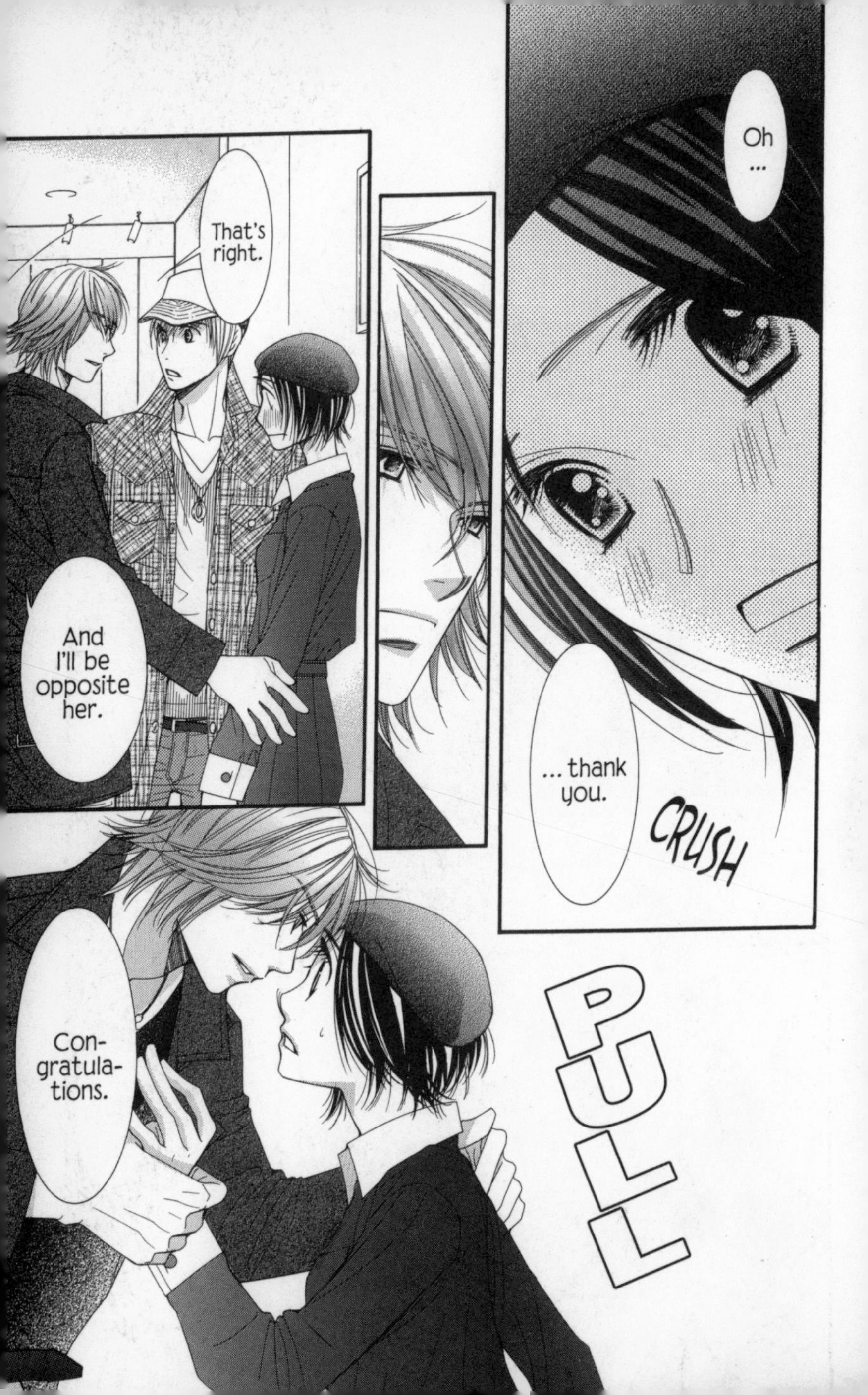
Oh ...
... thank you.
CRUSH
That's right.
And I'll be opposite her.
Con-gratula-tions.
PULL

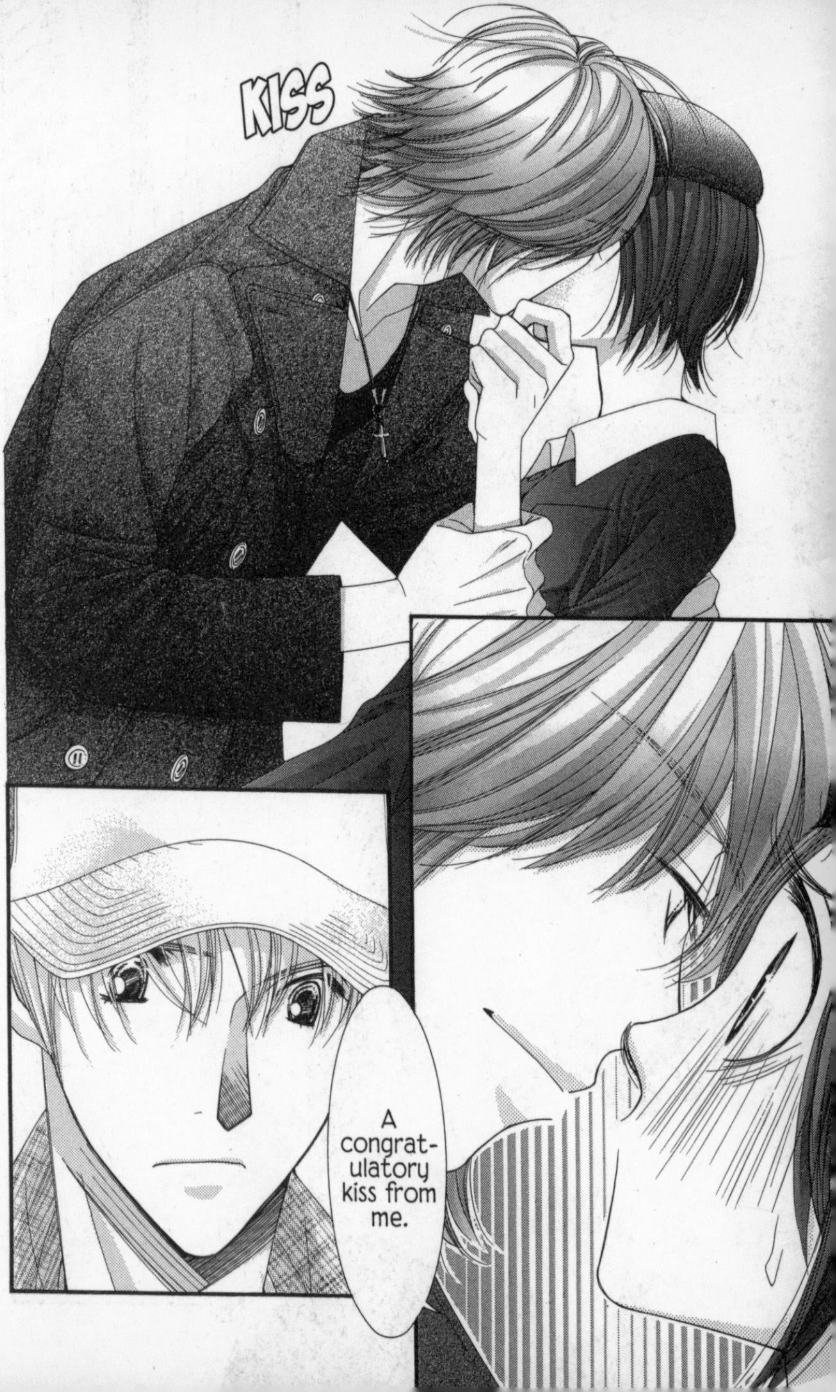
KISS
A congratulatory kiss from me.

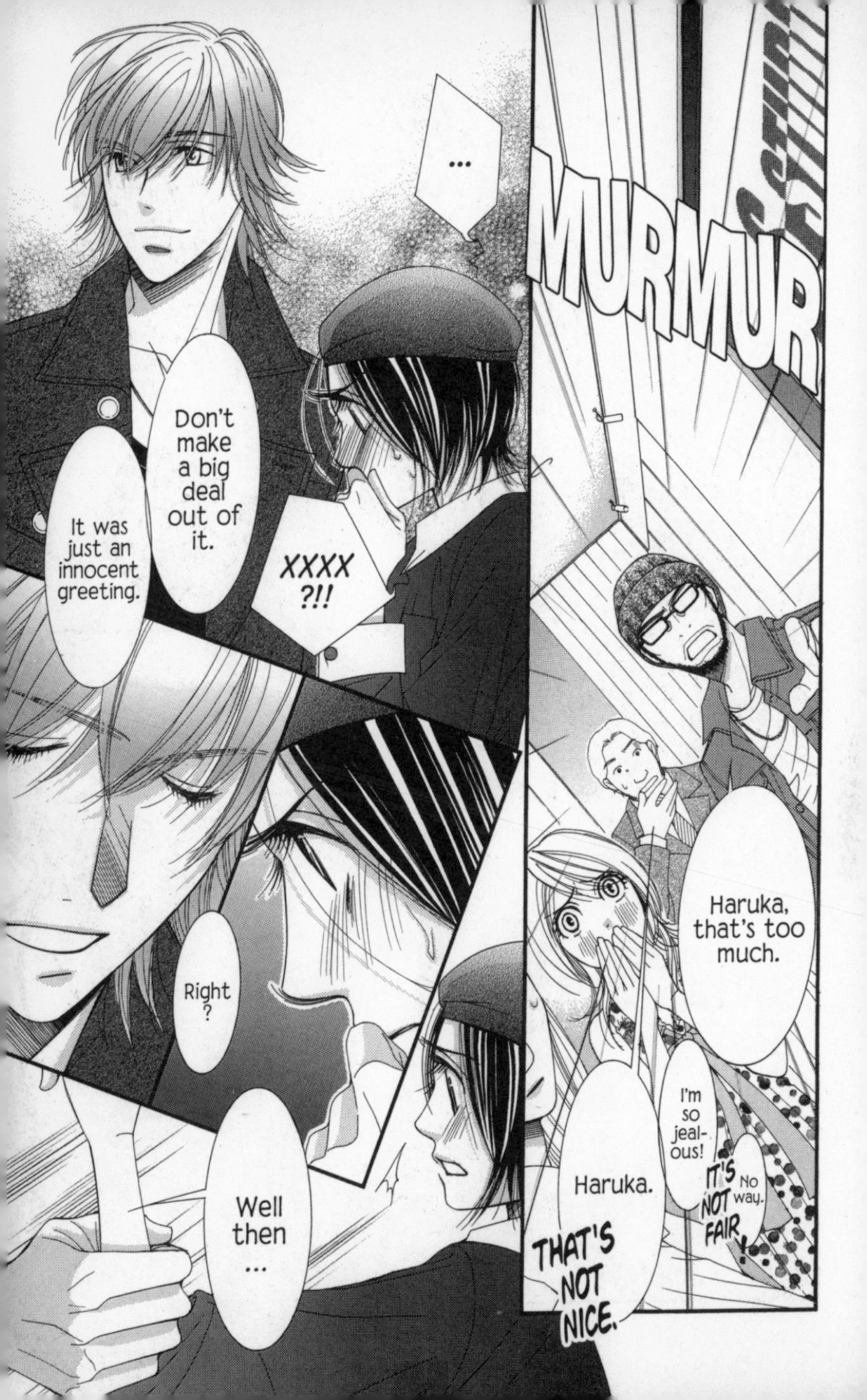
MURMUR
Haruka, that's too much.
No way.
I'm so jeal-ous!
IT'S NOT FAIR!
Haruka.
THAT'S NOT NICE.
...
XXXX ?!!
Don't make a big deal out of it.
It was just an innocent greeting.
Right?
Well then ...

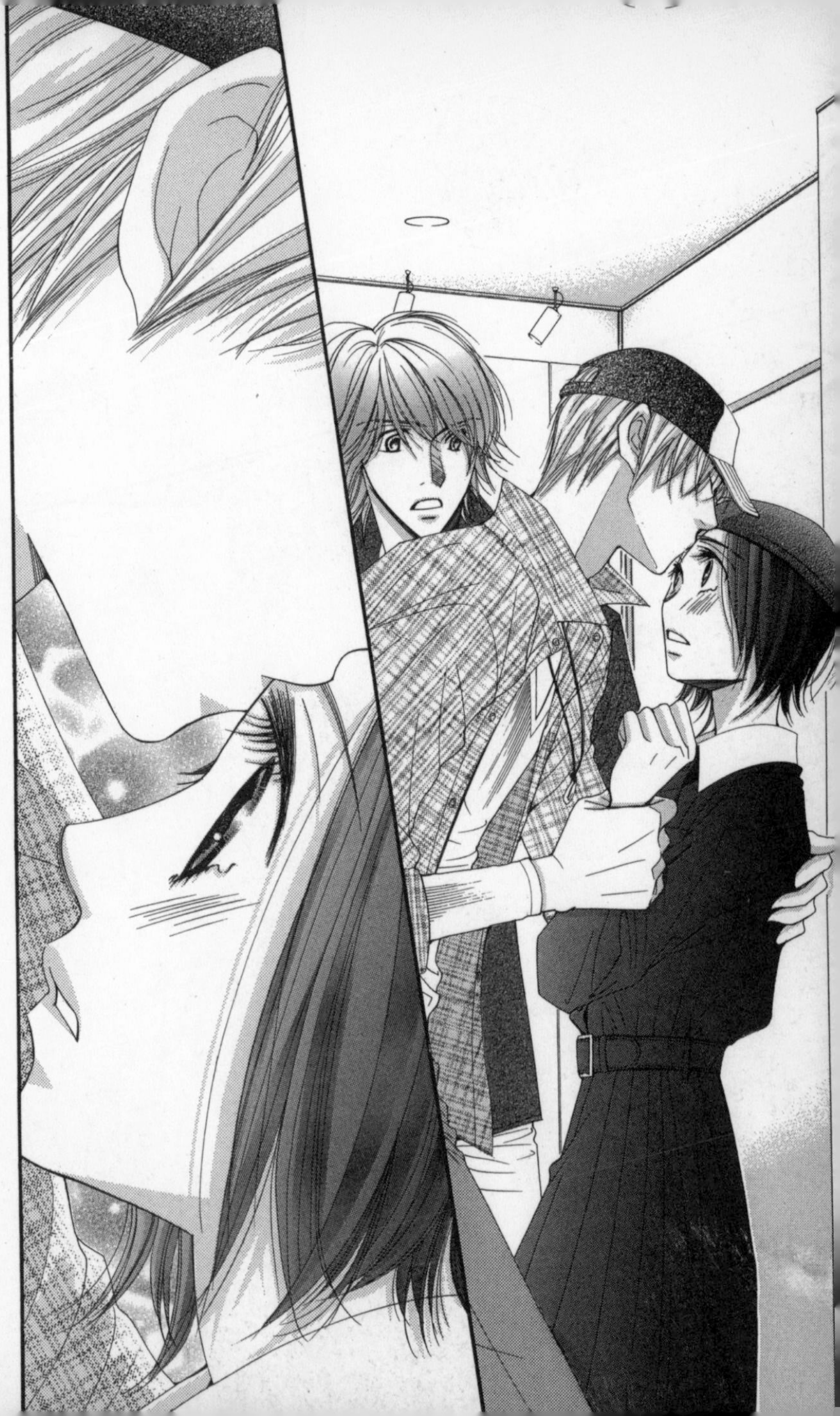

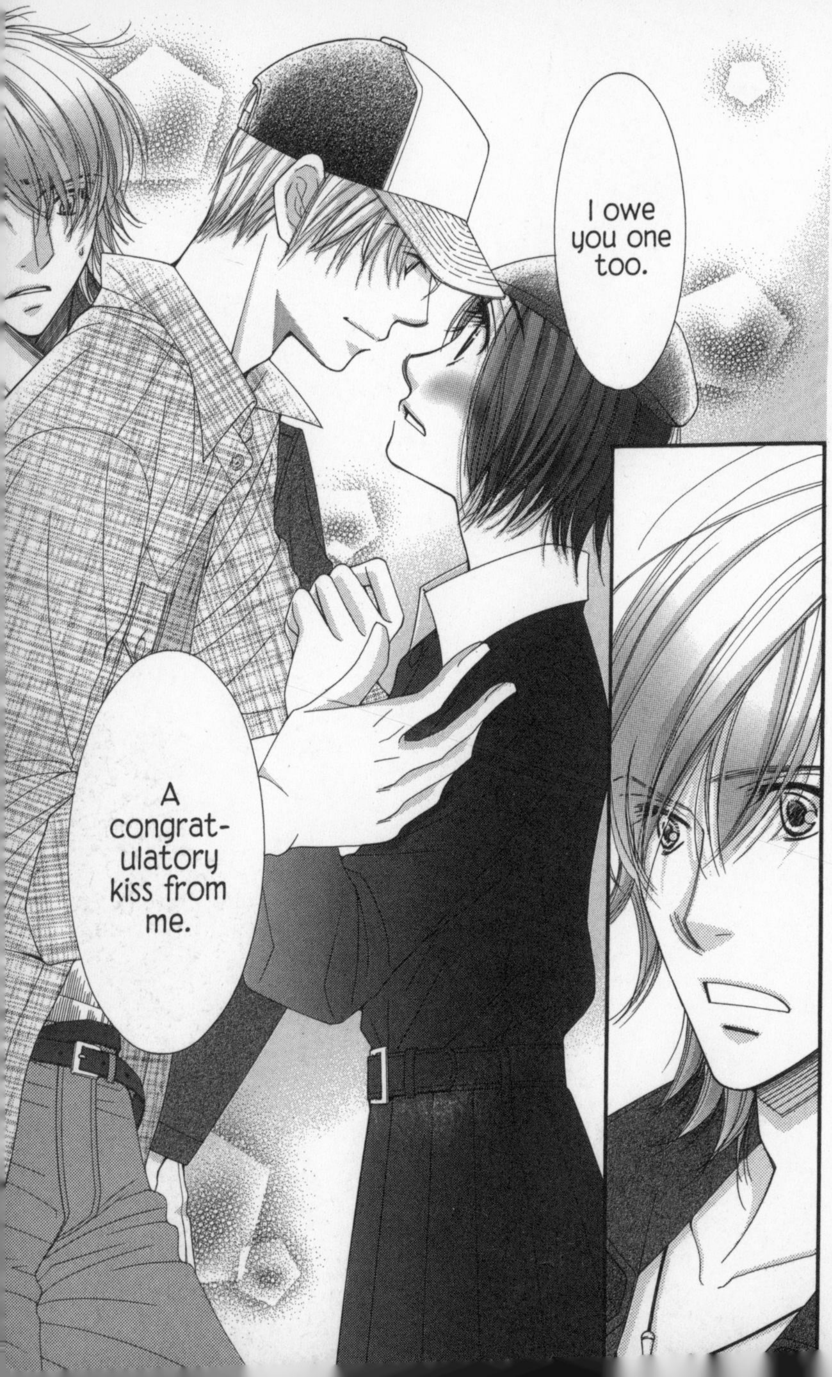
I owe you one too.
A congrat-ulatory kiss from me.

Haruka Minamitani
19 years old
Blood type B

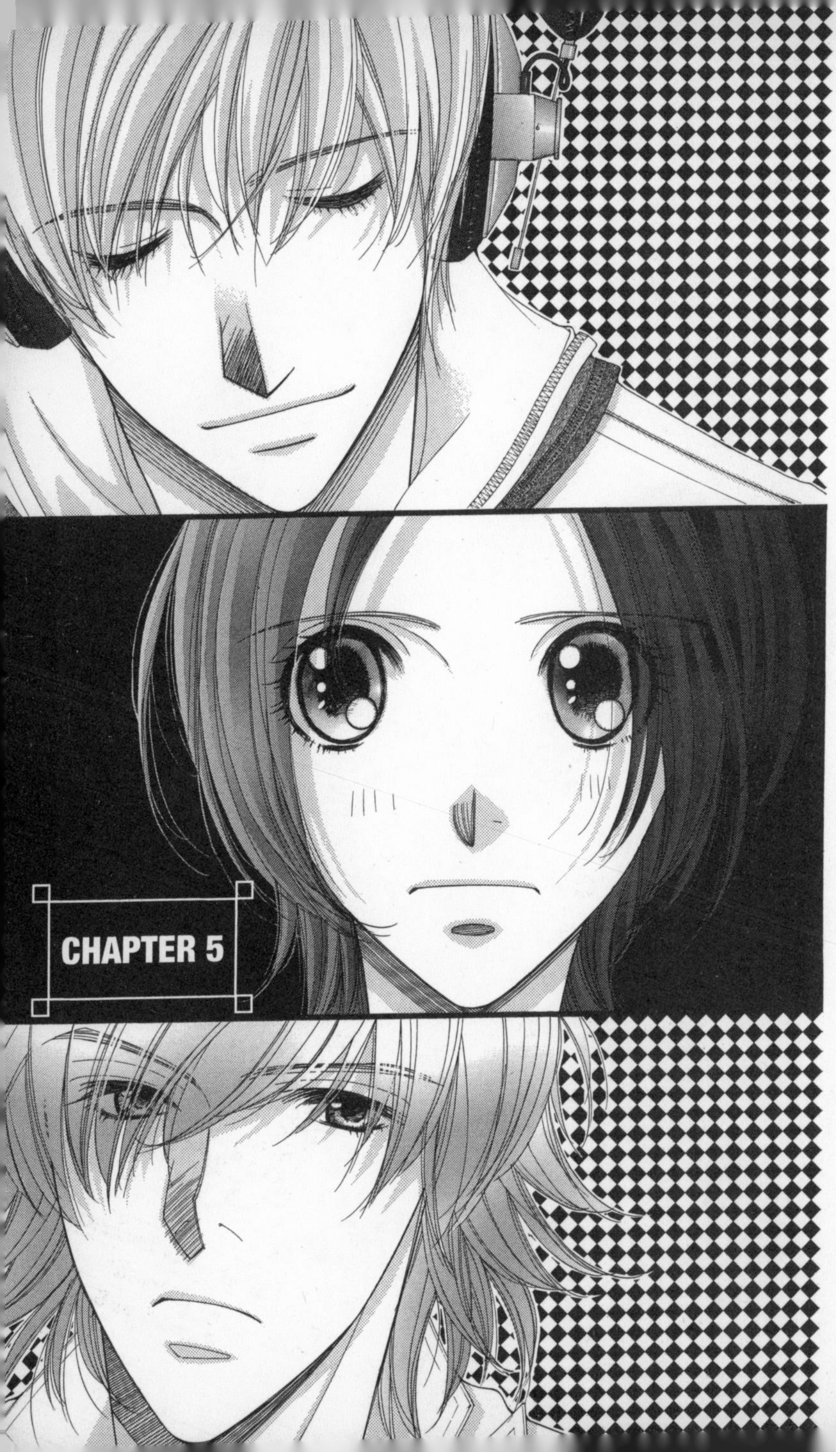
CHAPTER 5

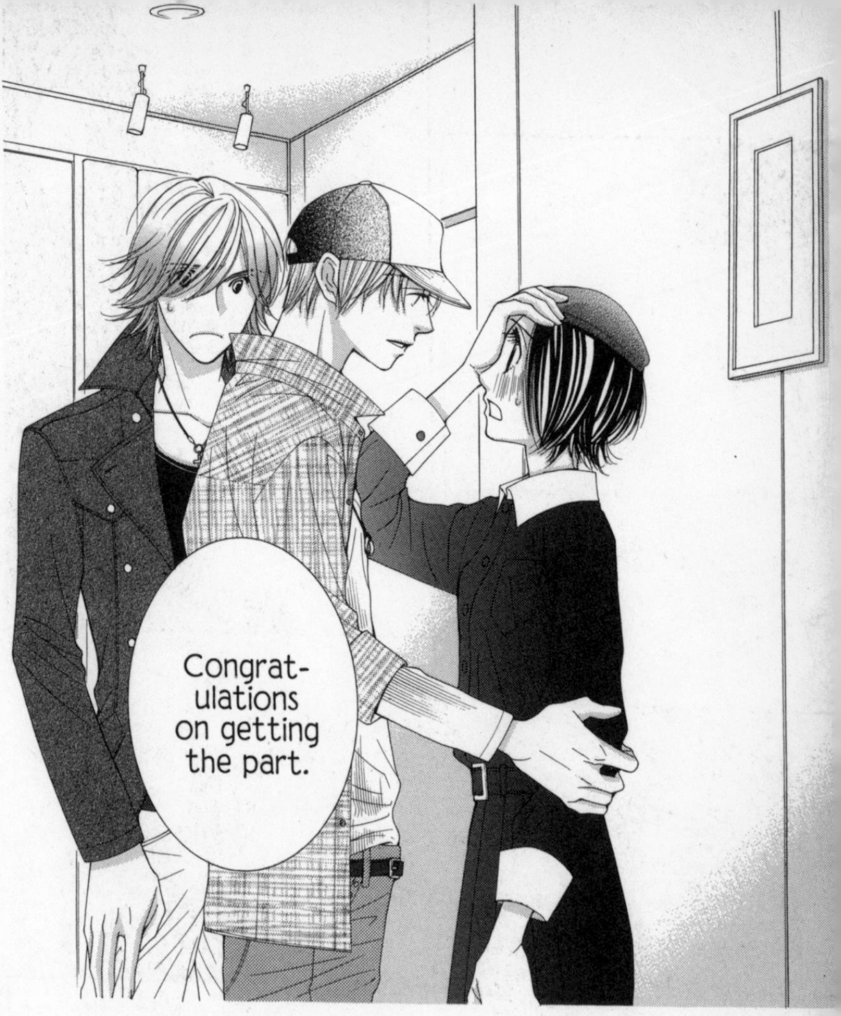
Congratulations on getting the part.

Honey Hunt

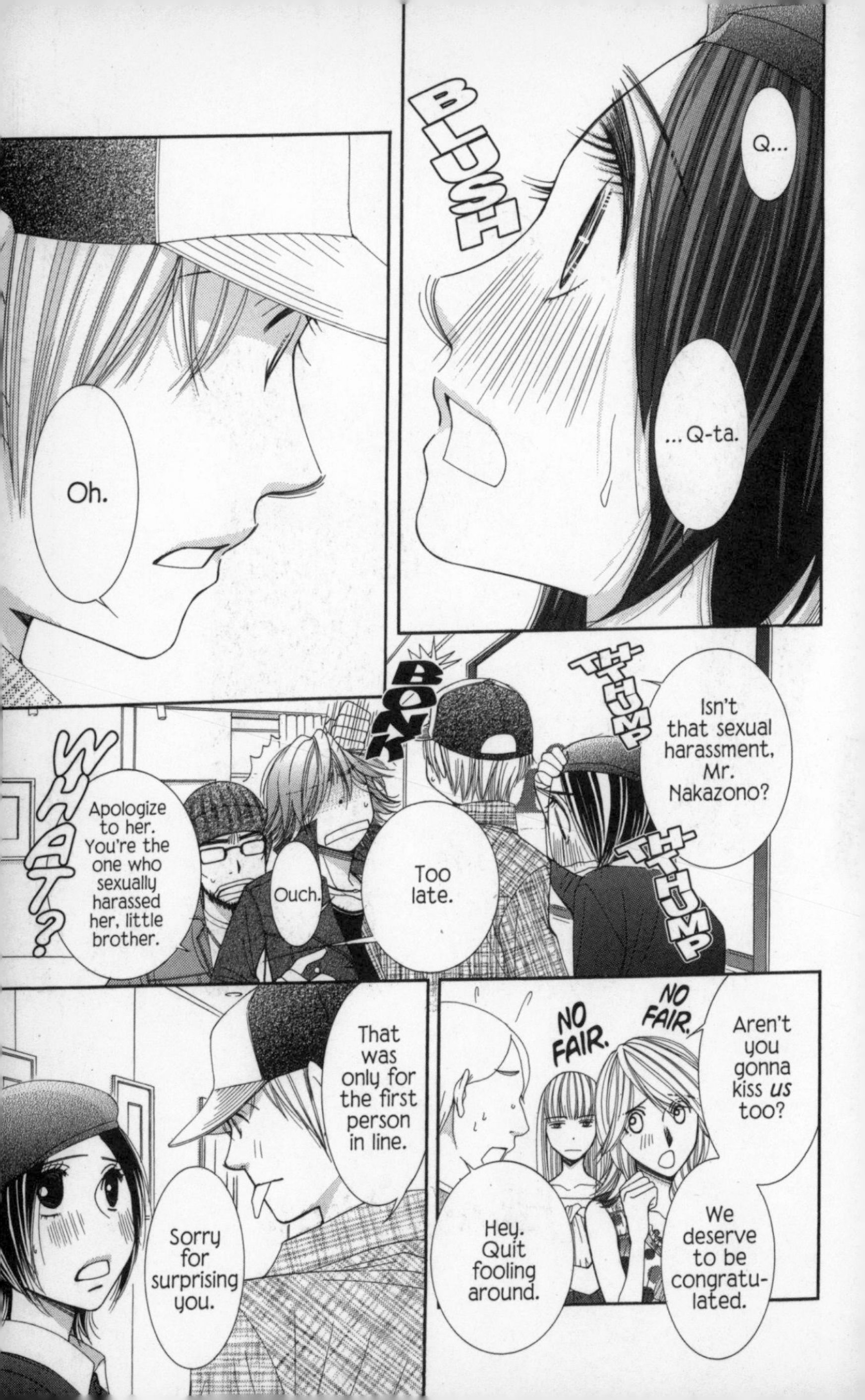
BLUSH
Q...
...Q-ta.
Oh.
TH-THUMP
Isn't that sexual harassment, Mr. Nakazono?
TH-THUMP
BONK
Too late.
Ouch.
Apologize to her. You're the one who sexually harassed her, little brother.
WHAT?
NO FAIR.
NO FAIR.
Aren't you gonna kiss *us* too?
We deserve to be congratulated.
Hey. Quit fooling around.
That was only for the first person in line.
Sorry for surprising you.

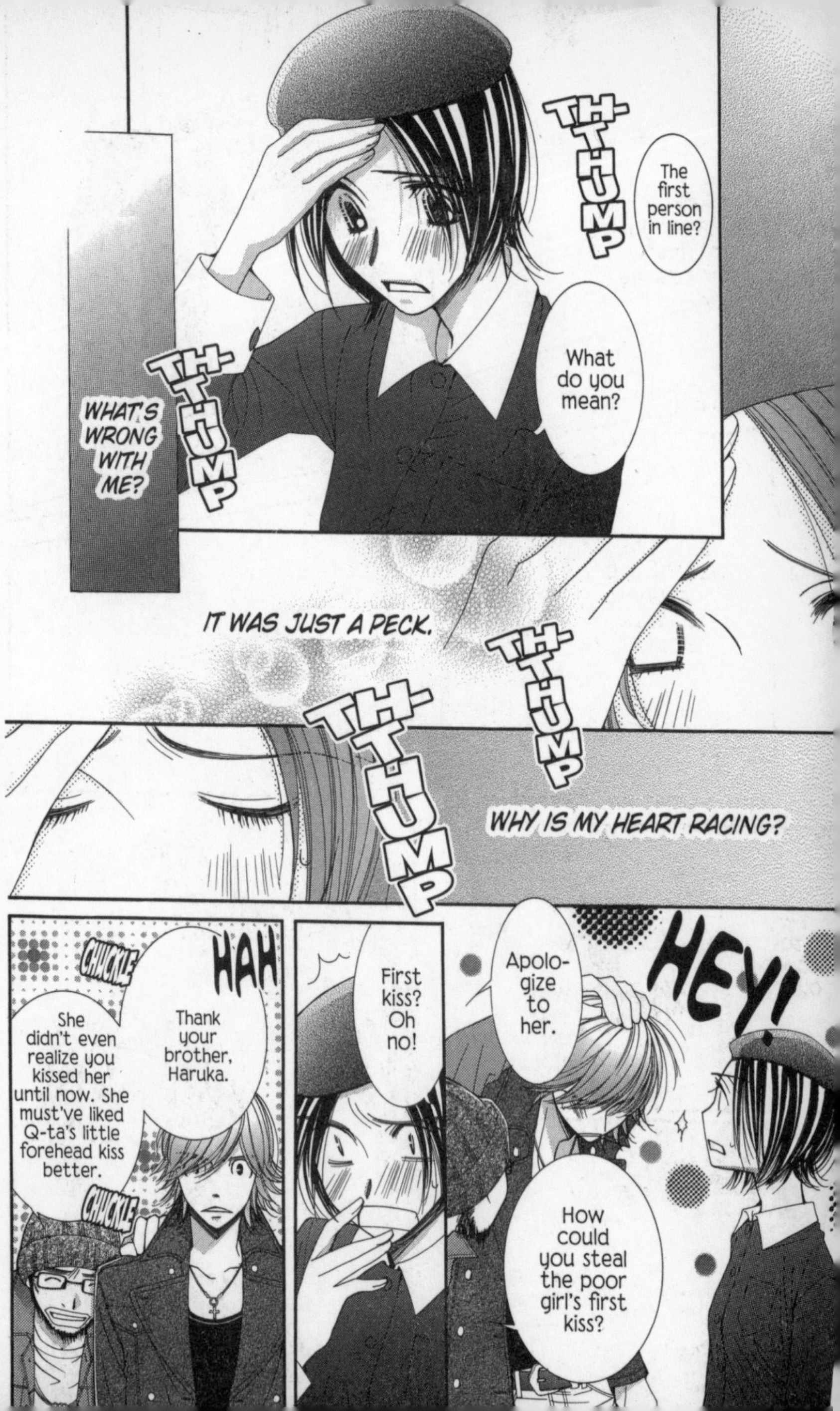
TH-THUMP
The first person in line?
What do you mean?
TH-THUMP
WHAT'S WRONG WITH ME?
IT WAS JUST A PECK.
TH-THUMP
TH-THUMP
WHY IS MY HEART RACING?
HEY!
Apologize to her.
How could you steal the poor girl's first kiss?
First kiss? Oh no!
HAH
Thank your brother, Haruka.
CHUCKLE
She didn't even realize you kissed her until now. She must've liked Q-ta's little forehead kiss better.
CHUCKLE

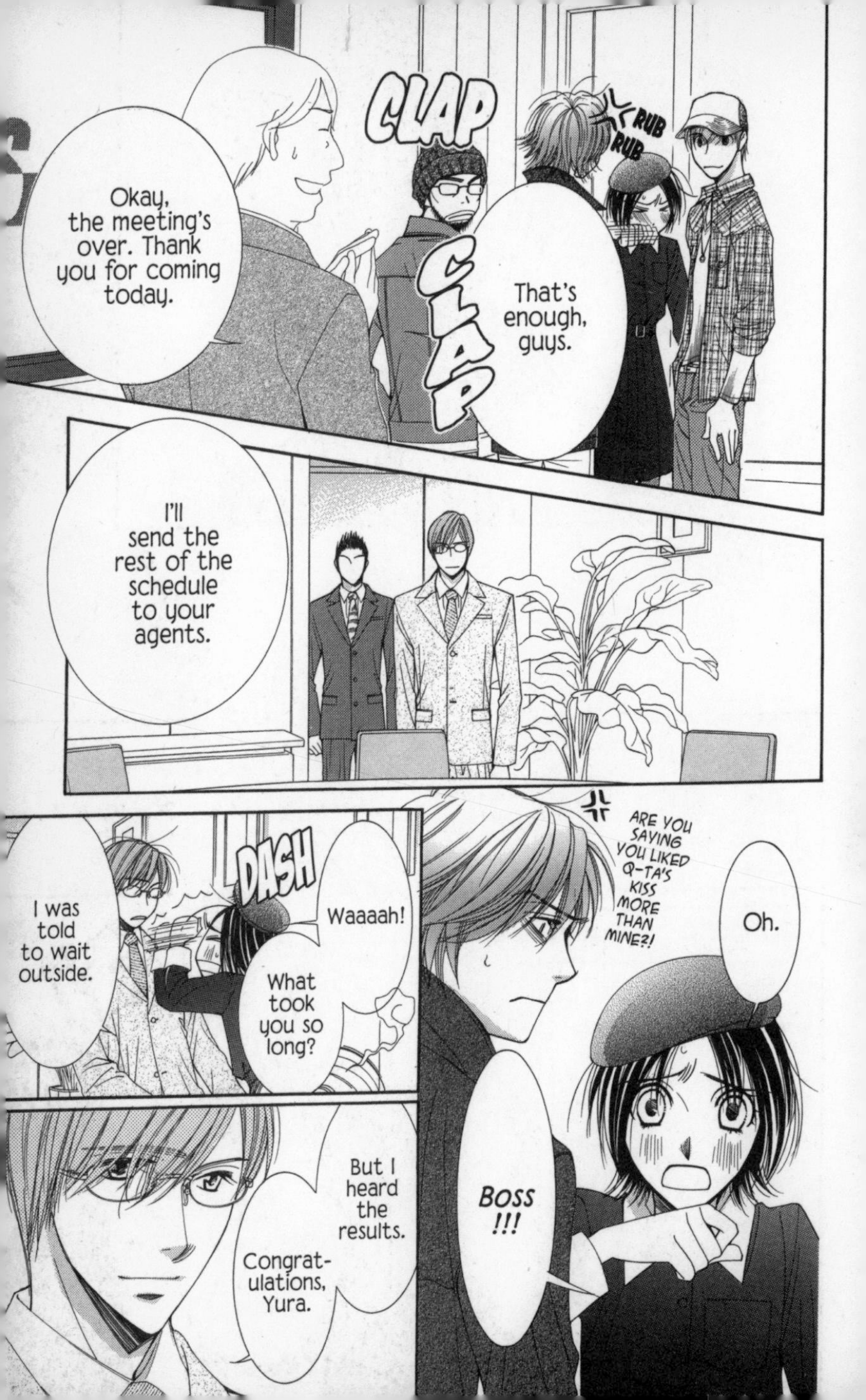
RUB RUB
CLAP
That's enough, guys.
CLAP
Okay, the meeting's over. Thank you for coming today.
I'll send the rest of the schedule to your agents.
ARE YOU SAYING YOU LIKED Q-TA'S KISS MORE THAN MINE?!
Oh.
BOSS !!!
DASH
Waaaah!
What took you so long?
I was told to wait outside.
But I heard the results.
Congratulations, Yura.

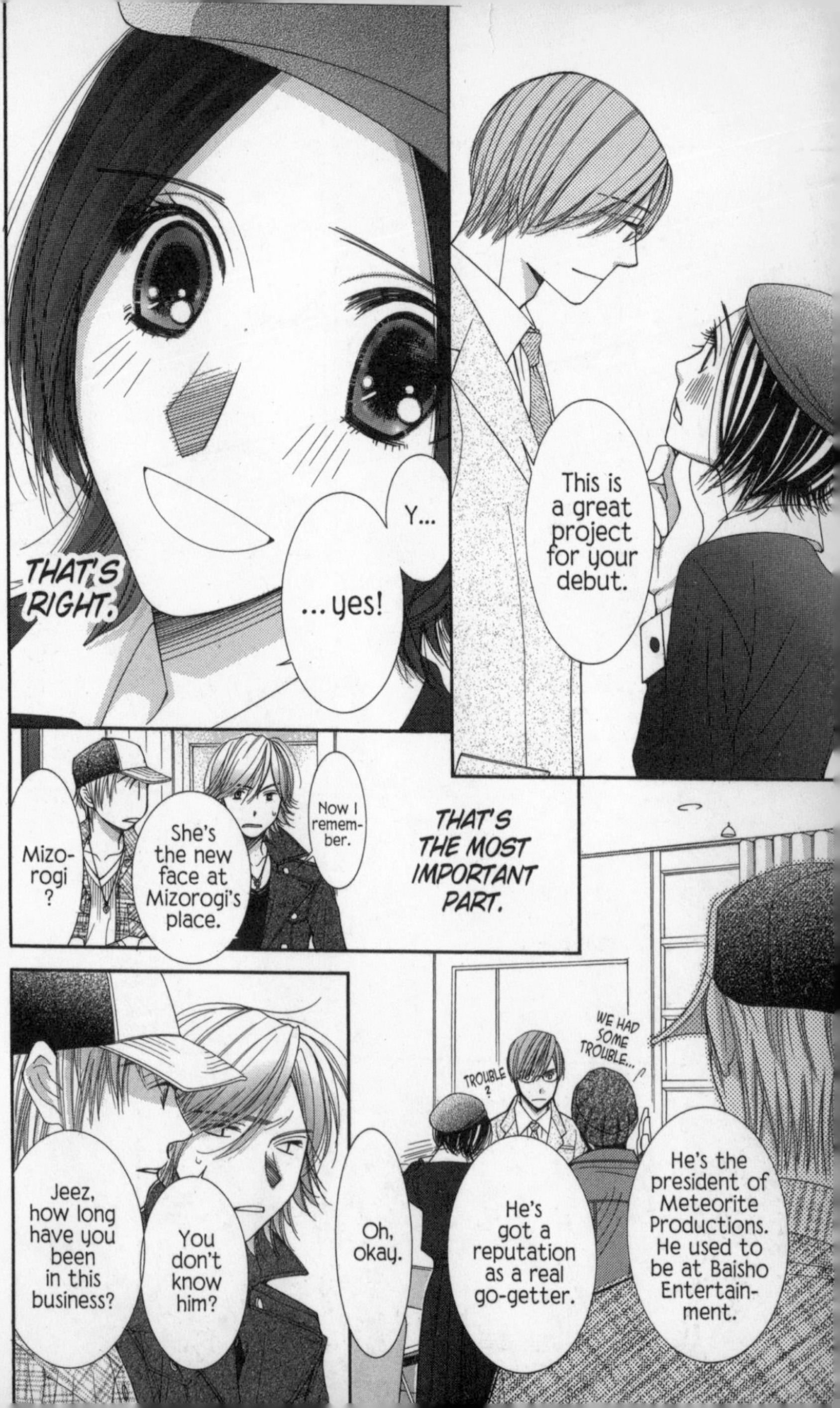

This is a great project for your debut.
Y...
...yes!
THAT'S RIGHT.
THAT'S THE MOST IMPORTANT PART.
Now I remember.
She's the new face at Mizorogi's place.
Mizorogi?
WE HAD SOME TROUBLE...
TROUBLE?
He's the president of Meteorite Productions. He used to be at Baisho Entertainment.
He's got a reputation as a real go-getter.
Oh, okay.
You don't know him?
Jeez, how long have you been in this business?

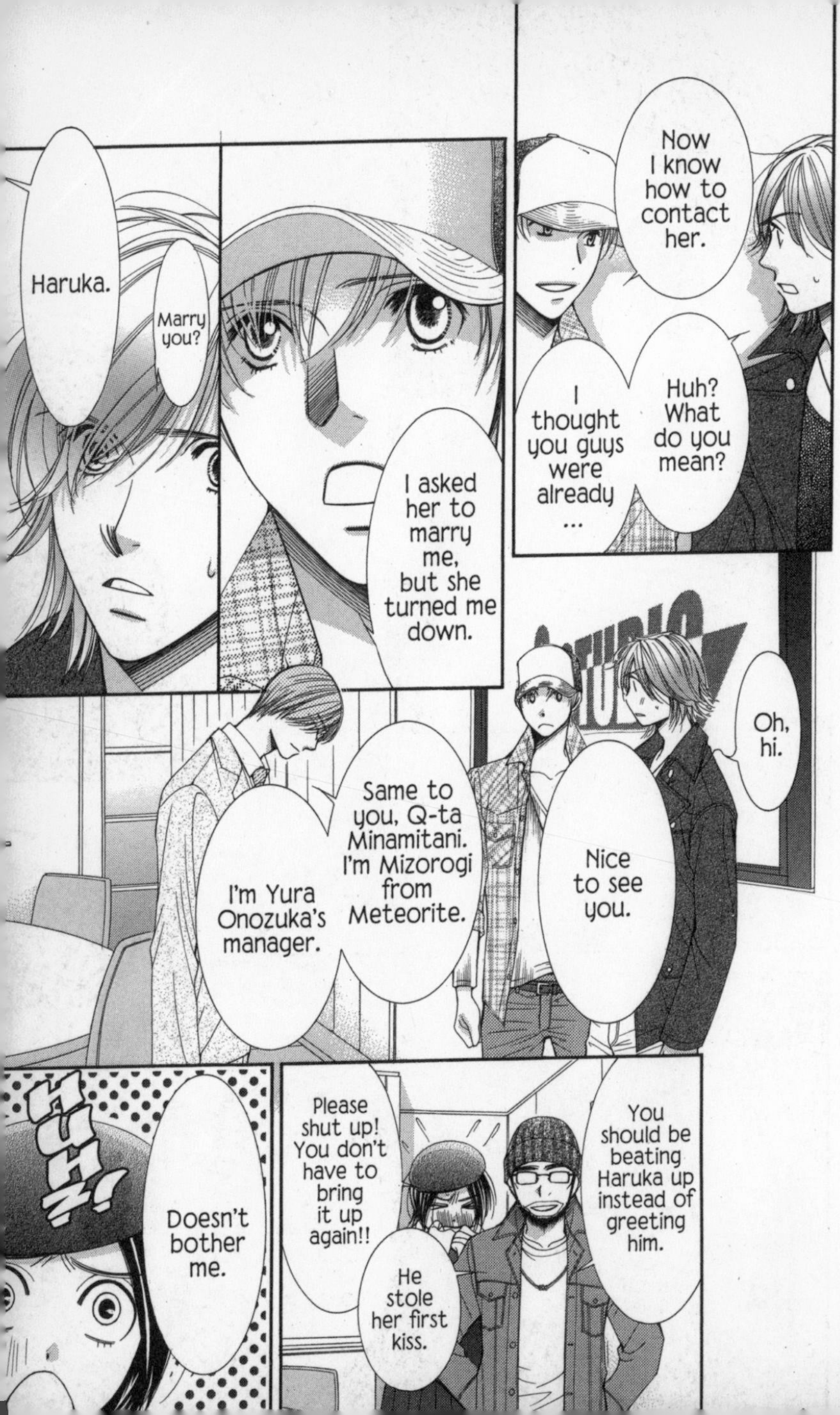
Now I know how to contact her.
Huh? What do you mean?
I thought you guys were already ...
I asked her to marry me, but she turned me down.
Marry you?
Haruka.
Oh, hi.
Nice to see you.
Same to you, Q-ta Minamitani. I'm Mizorogi from Meteorite.
I'm Yura Onozuka's manager.
You should be beating Haruka up instead of greeting him.
Please shut up! You don't have to bring it up again!!
He stole her first kiss.
HUH?!
Doesn't bother me.

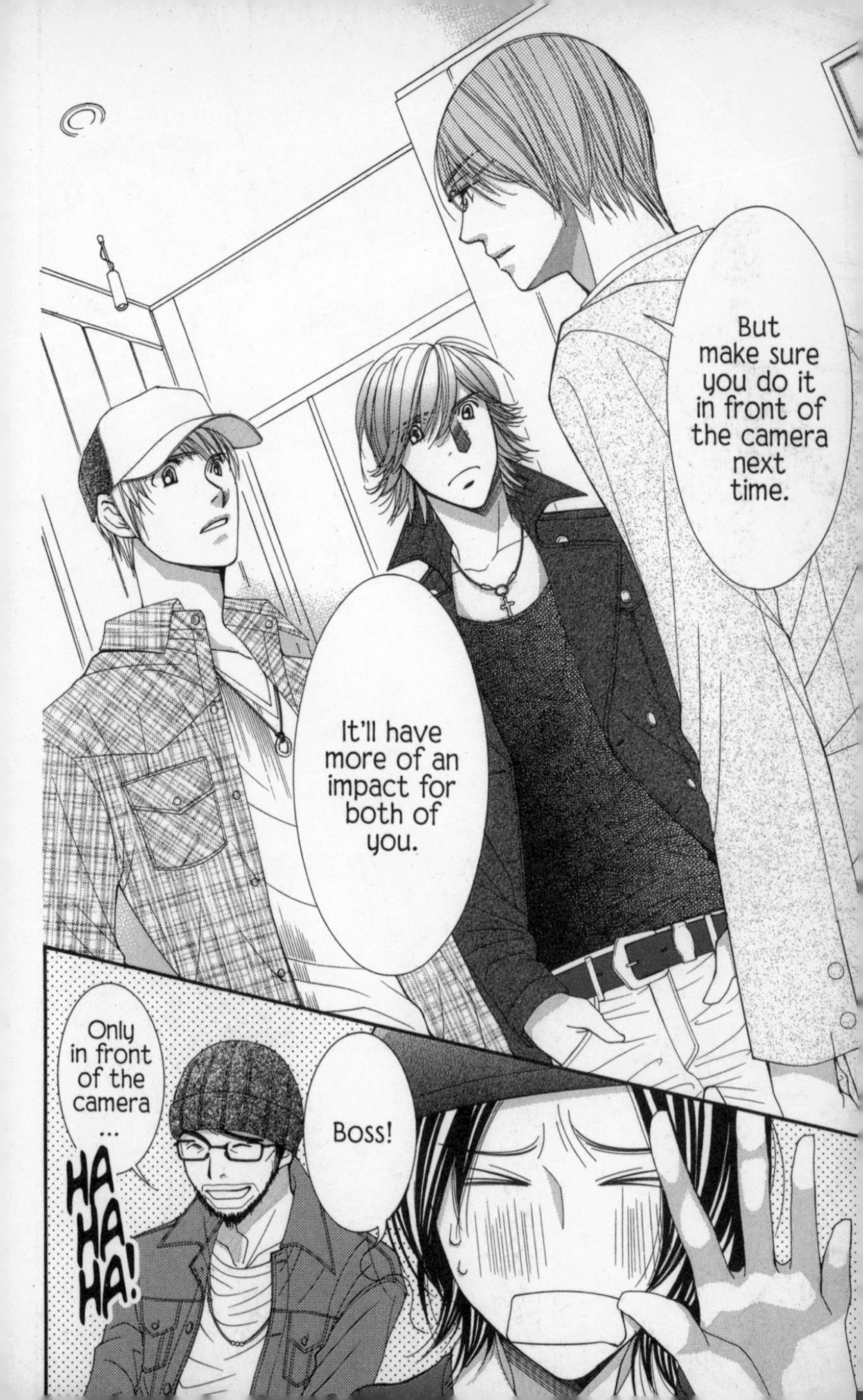
But make sure you do it in front of the camera next time.
It'll have more of an impact for both of you.
Boss!
Only in front of the camera ...
HA HA HA!

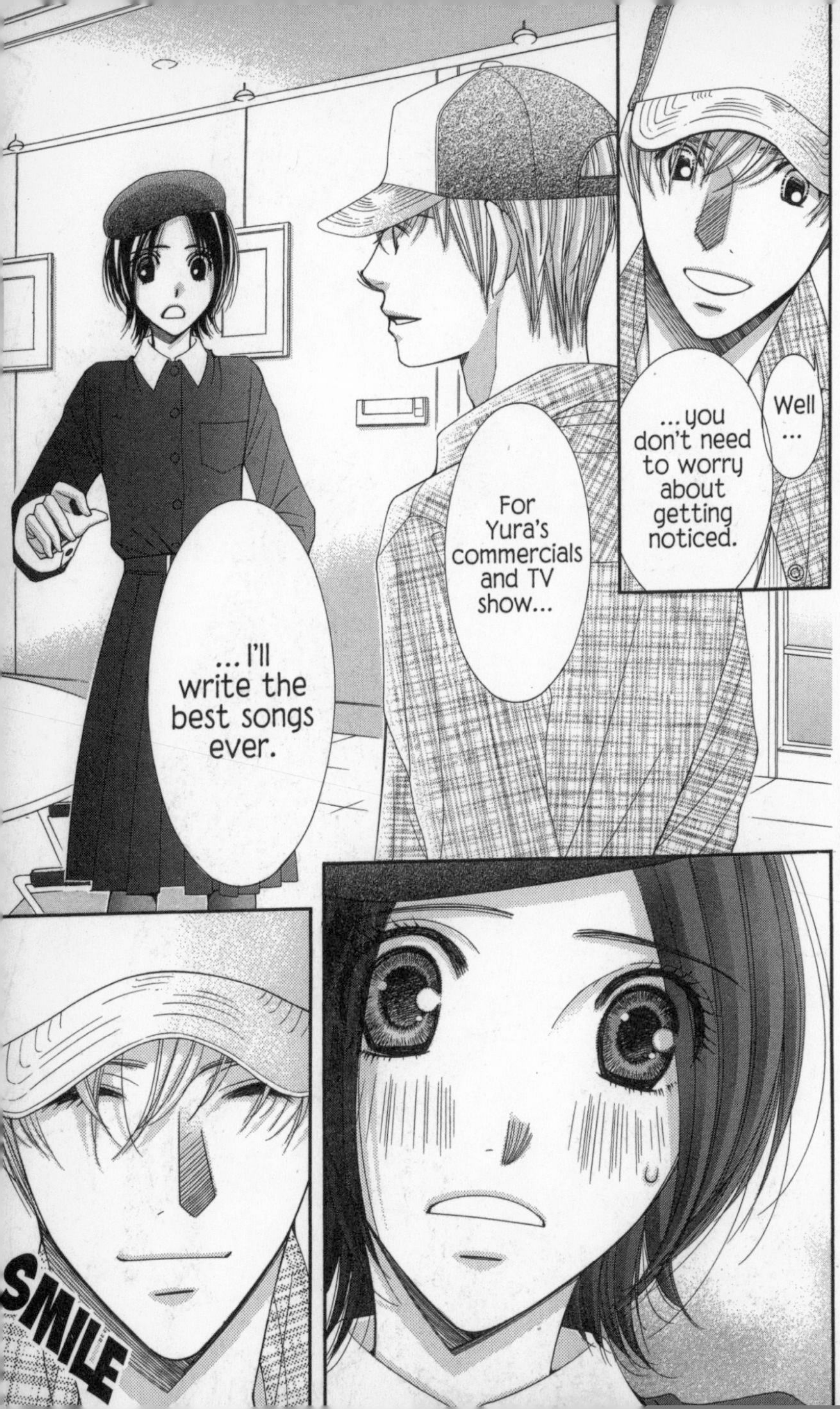
Well ...
... you don't need to worry about getting noticed.
For Yura's commercials and TV show...
... I'll write the best songs ever.
SMILE

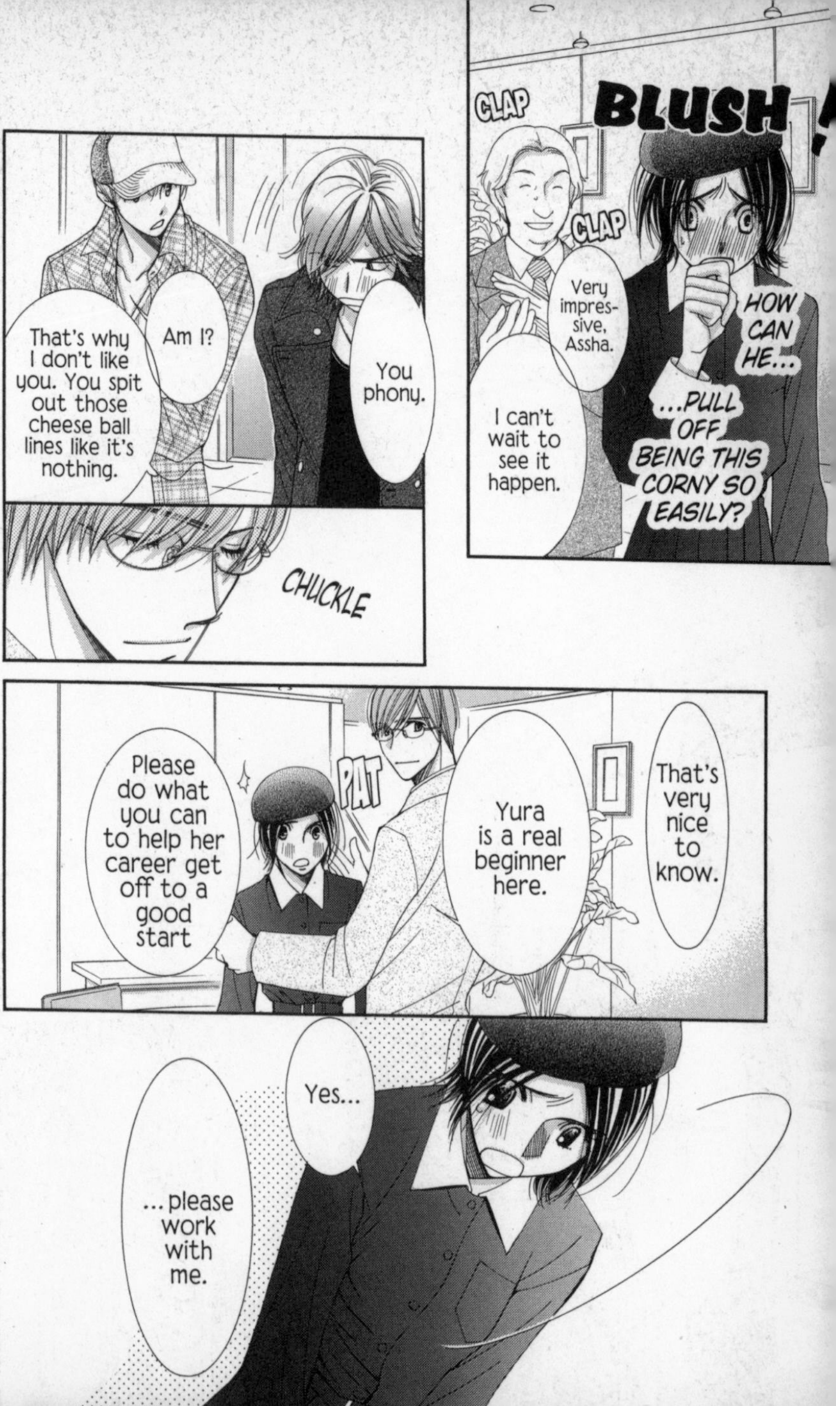
BLUSH!
CLAP
CLAP
Very impressive, Assha.
HOW CAN HE...
...PULL OFF BEING THIS CORNY SO EASILY?
I can't wait to see it happen.
You phony.
Am I?
That's why I don't like you. You spit out those cheese ball lines like it's nothing.
CHUCKLE
That's very nice to know.
Yura is a real beginner here.
PAT
Please do what you can to help her career get off to a good start
Yes...
...please work with me.

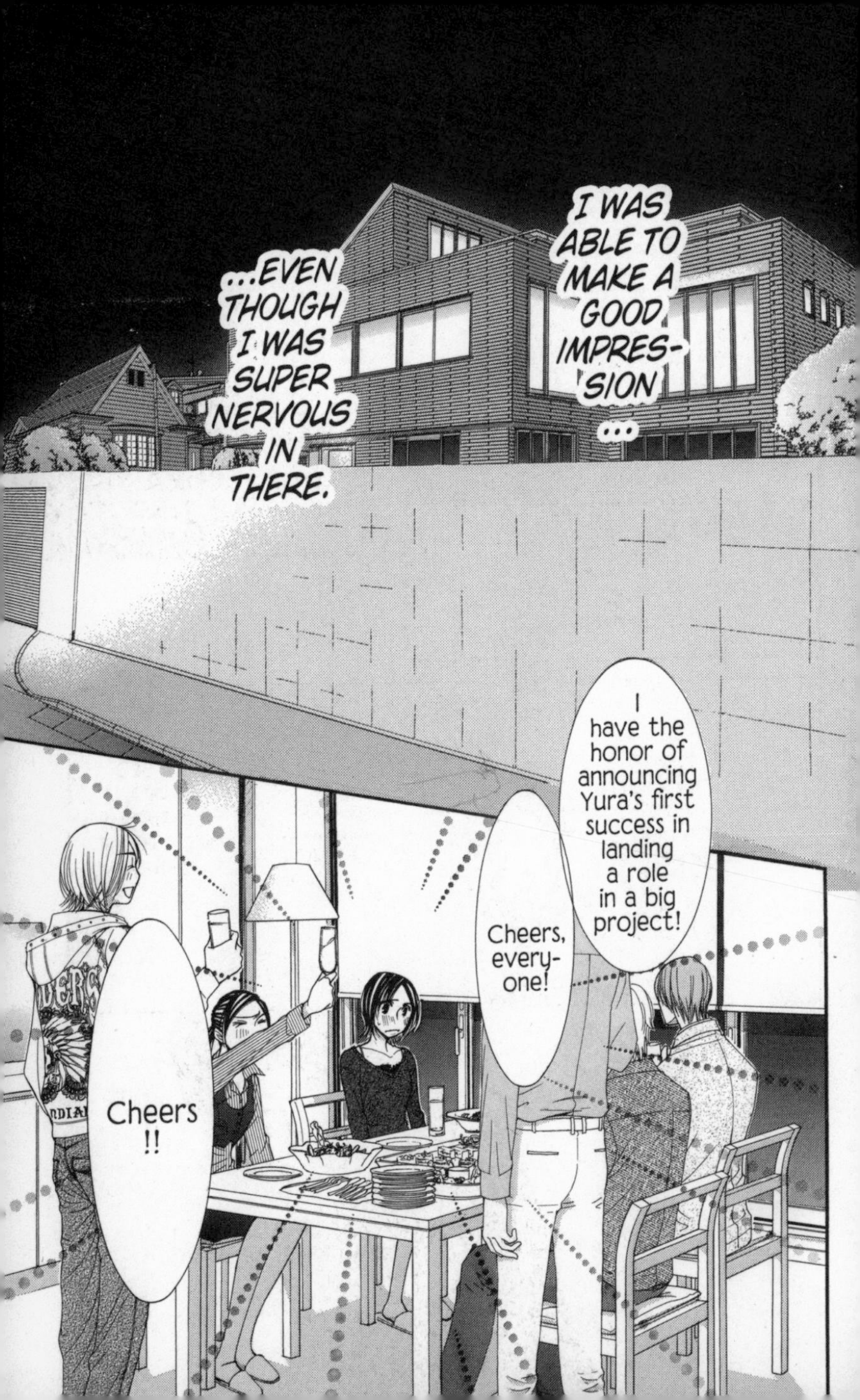
I WAS ABLE TO MAKE A GOOD IMPRESSION...
...EVEN THOUGH I WAS SUPER NERVOUS IN THERE.
I have the honor of announcing Yura's first success in landing a role in a big project!
Cheers, everyone!
Cheers!!

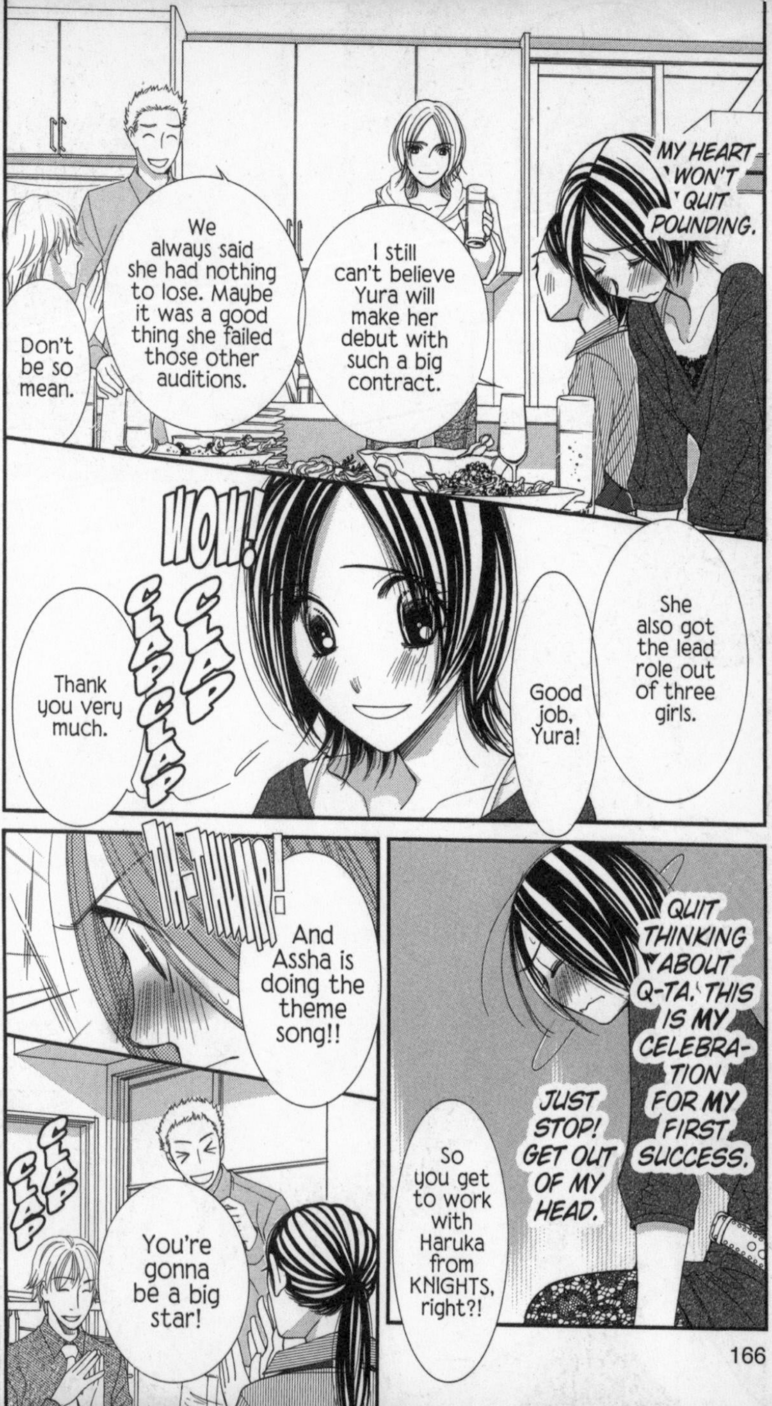
MY HEART WON'T QUIT POUNDING.
I still can't believe Yura will make her debut with such a big contract.
We always said she had nothing to lose. Maybe it was a good thing she failed those other auditions.
Don't be so mean.
She also got the lead role out of three girls.
Good job, Yura!
WOW!
CLAP CLAP CLAP CLAP
Thank you very much.
QUIT THINKING ABOUT Q-TA. THIS IS MY CELEBRATION FOR MY FIRST SUCCESS.
JUST STOP! GET OUT OF MY HEAD.
So you get to work with Haruka from KNIGHTS, right?!
TH-THUMP!
And Assha is doing the theme song!!
CLAP CLAP
You're gonna be a big star!

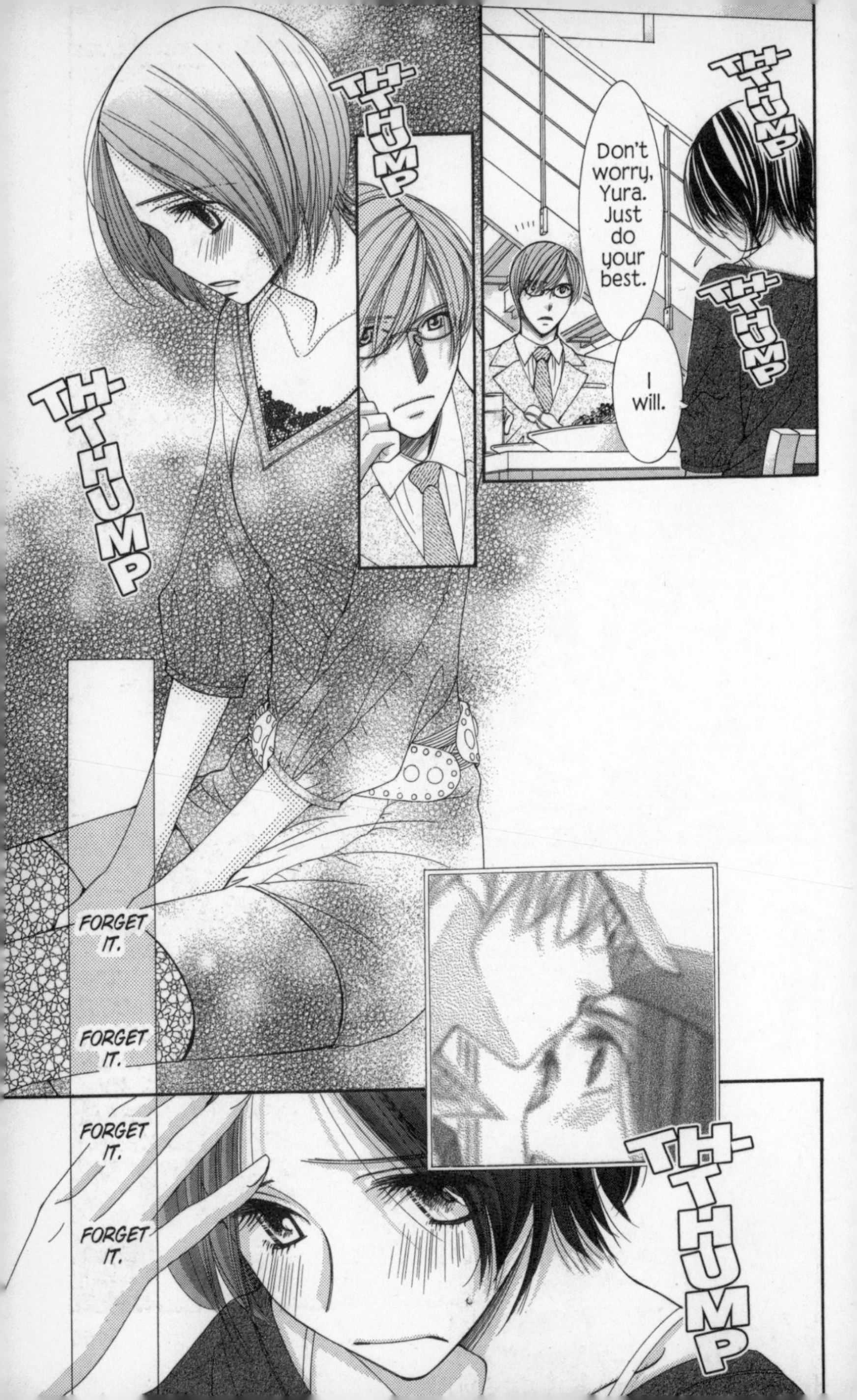
TH-THUMP
Don't worry, Yura. Just do your best.
I will.
TH-THUMP
TH-THUMP
TH-THUMP
FORGET IT.
FORGET IT.
TH-THUMP
FORGET IT.
FORGET IT.

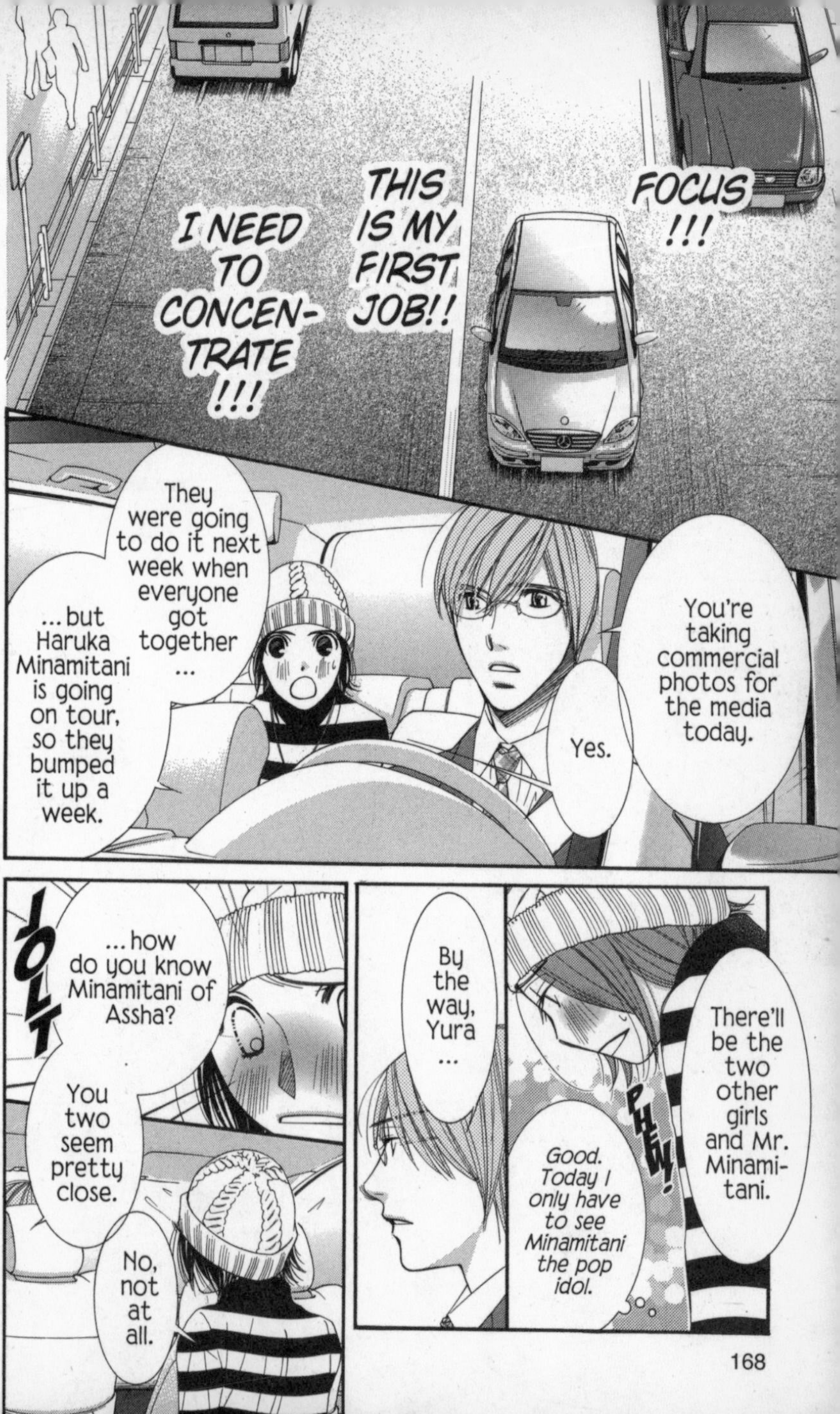
FOCUS!!!
THIS IS MY FIRST JOB!!
I NEED TO CONCENTRATE!!!
You're taking commercial photos for the media today.
Yes.
They were going to do it next week when everyone got together...
...but Haruka Minamitani is going on tour, so they bumped it up a week.
There'll be the two other girls and Mr. Minami-tani.
PHEW!
Good. Today I only have to see Minamitani the pop idol.
By the way, Yura...
...how do you know Minamitani of Assha?
JOLT
You two seem pretty close.
No, not at all.

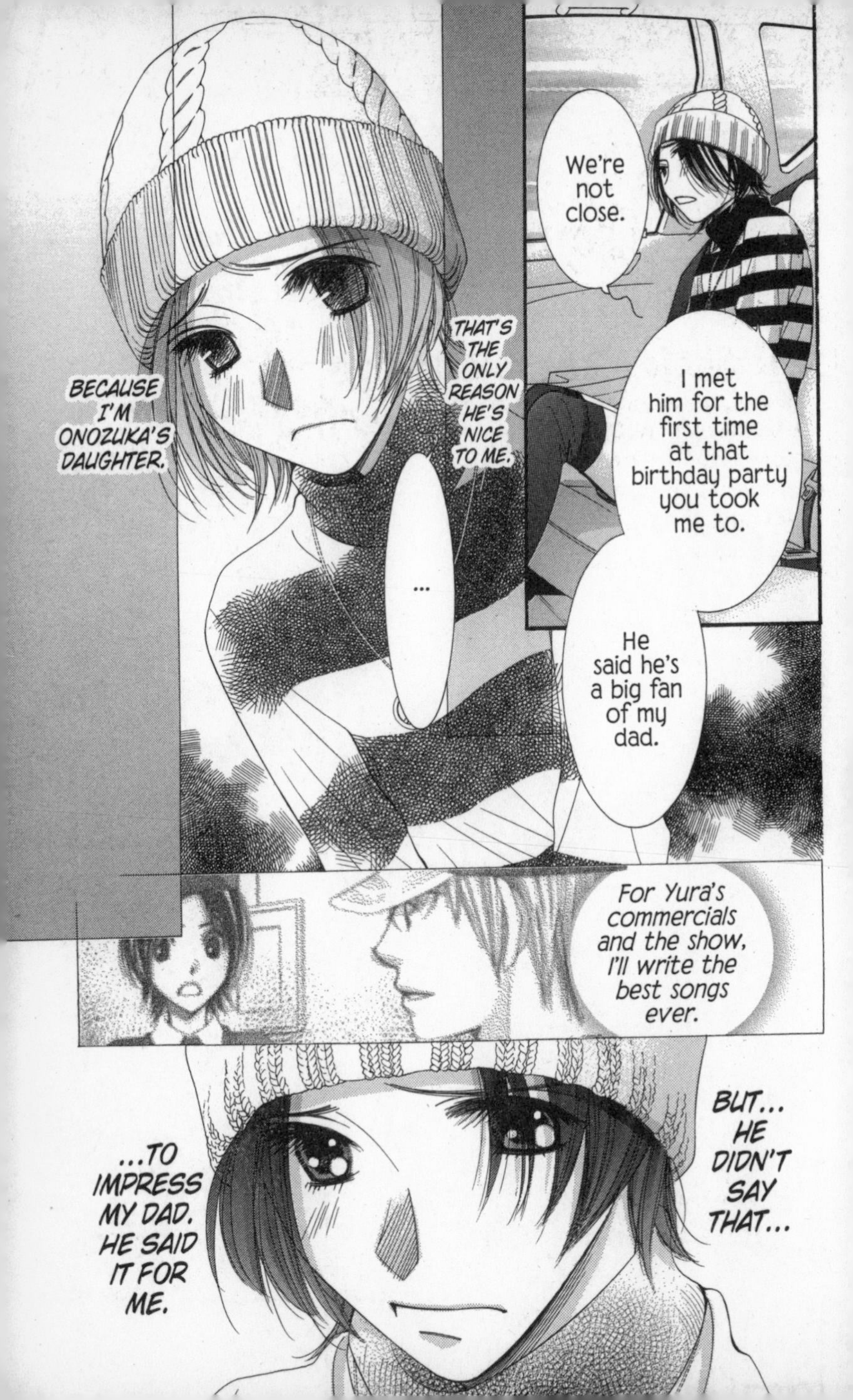

We're not close.
I met him for the first time at that birthday party you took me to.
He said he's a big fan of my dad.
...
THAT'S THE ONLY REASON HE'S NICE TO ME.
BECAUSE I'M ONOZUKA'S DAUGHTER.
For Yura's commercials and the show, I'll write the best songs ever.
BUT... HE DIDN'T SAY THAT...
...TO IMPRESS MY DAD. HE SAID IT FOR ME.

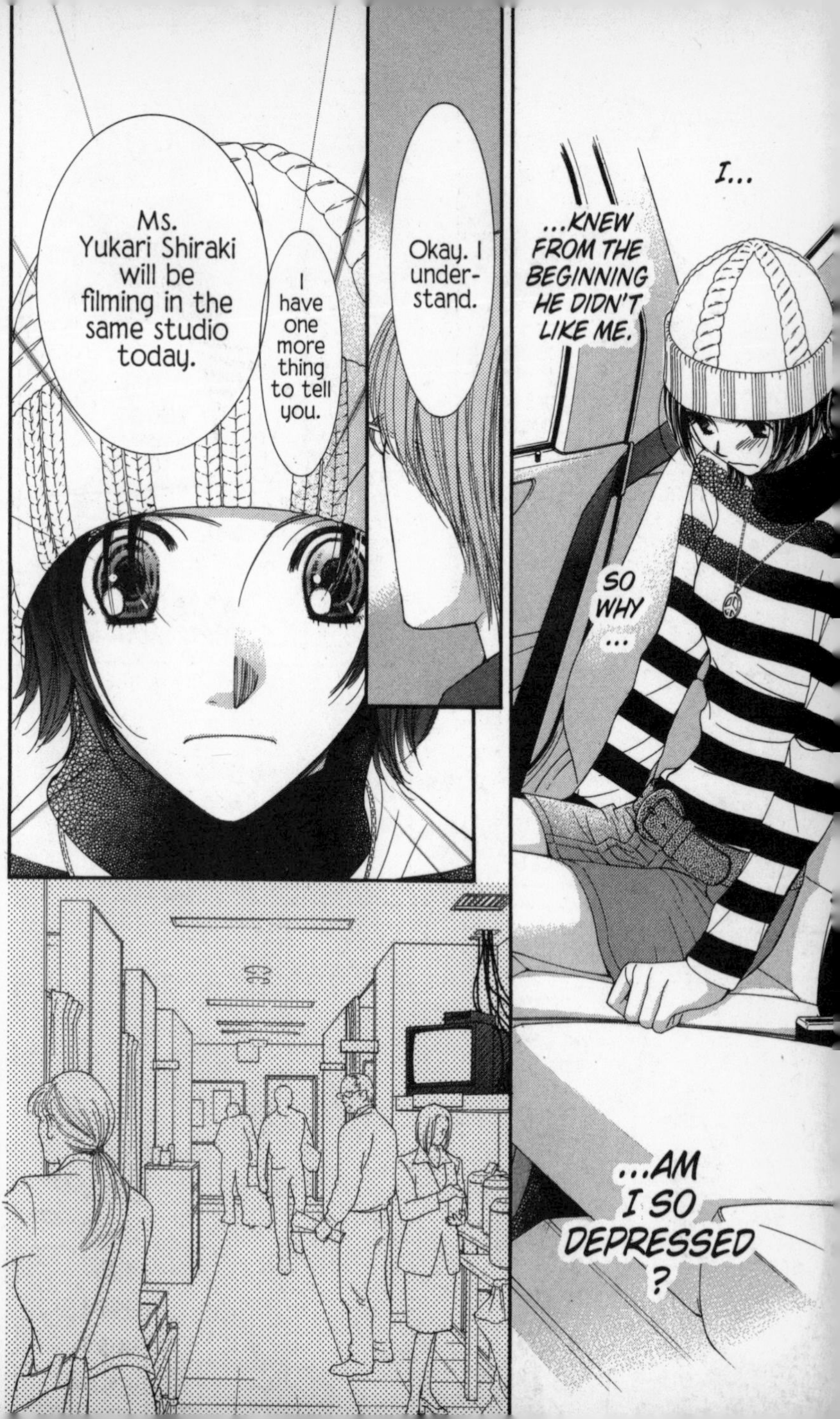

I...
...KNEW FROM THE BEGINNING HE DIDN'T LIKE ME.
SO WHY ...
...AM I SO DEPRESSED ?
Okay. I under-stand.
I have one more thing to tell you.
Ms. Yukari Shiraki will be filming in the same studio today.

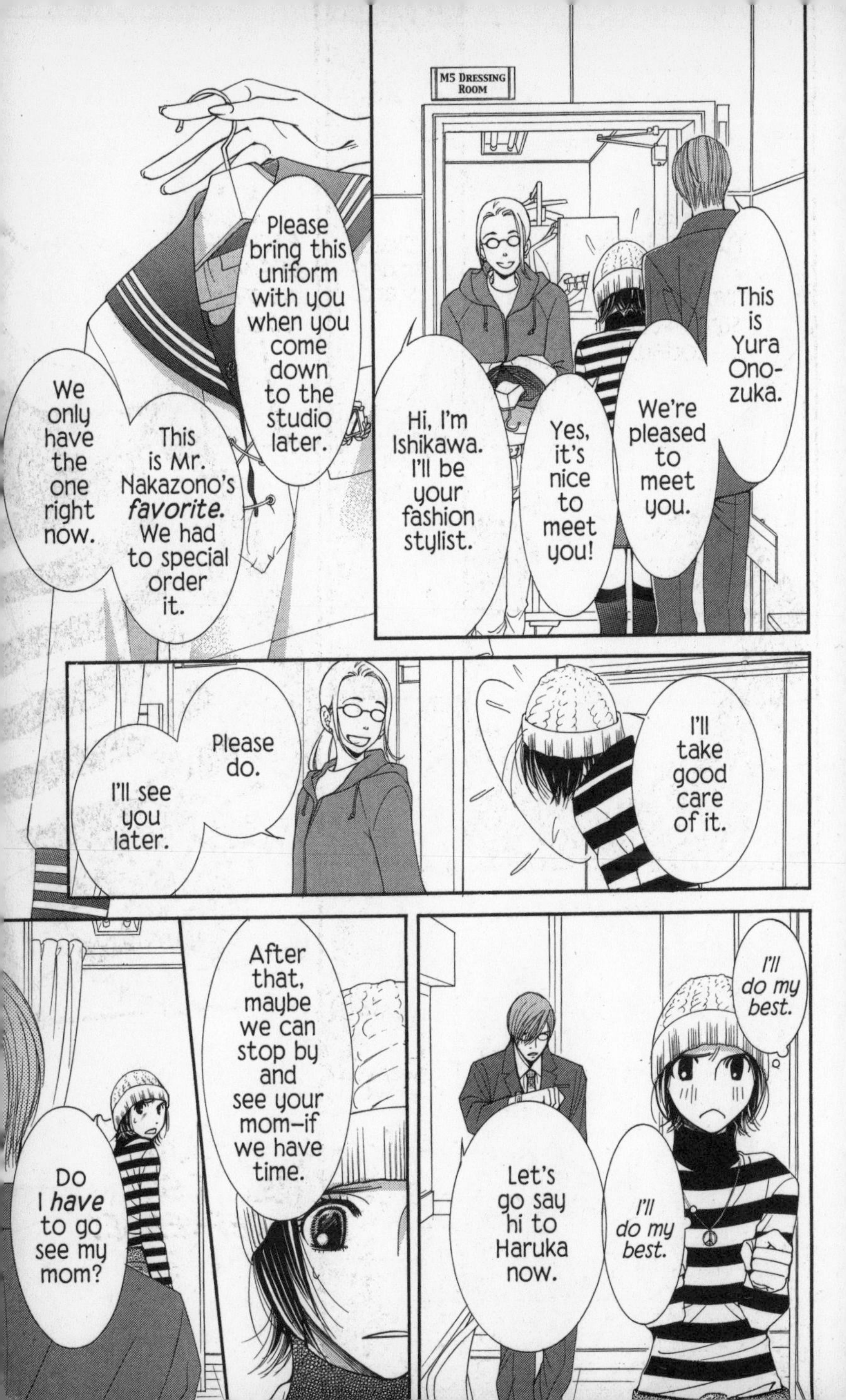
M5 DRESSING ROOM
This is Yura Onozuka.
We're pleased to meet you.
Yes, it's nice to meet you!
Hi, I'm Ishikawa. I'll be your fashion stylist.
Please bring this uniform with you when you come down to the studio later.
This is Mr. Nakazono's *favorite*. We had to special order it.
We only have the one right now.
I'll take good care of it.
Please do.
I'll see you later.
I'll do my best.
I'll do my best.
Let's go say hi to Haruka now.
After that, maybe we can stop by and see your mom—if we have time.
Do I *have* to go see my mom?

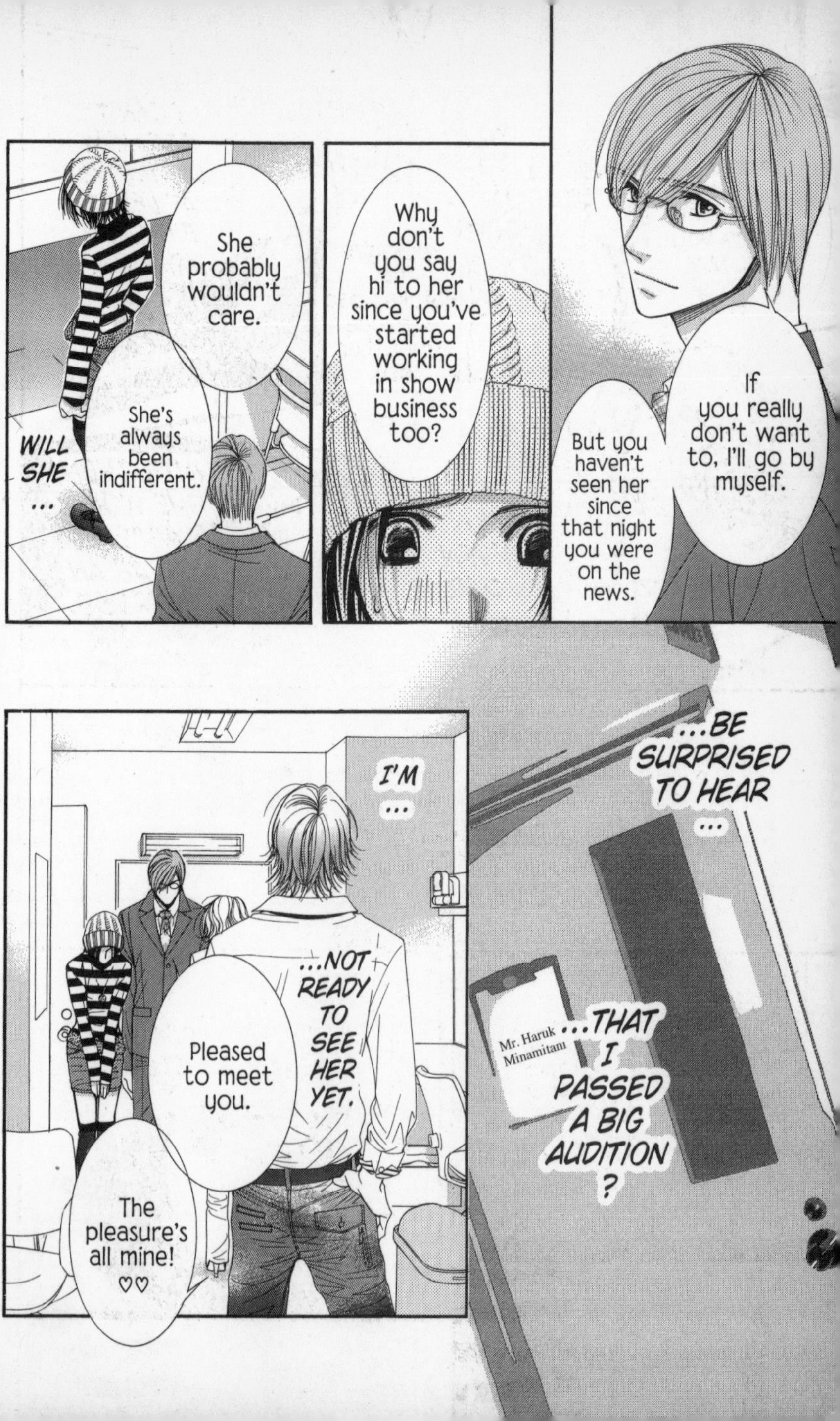
If you really don't want to, I'll go by myself.
But you haven't seen her since that night you were on the news.
Why don't you say hi to her since you've started working in show business too?
She probably wouldn't care.
She's always been indifferent.
WILL SHE ...
...BE SURPRISED TO HEAR ...
Mr. Haruk Minamitani
...THAT I PASSED A BIG AUDITION ?
I'M ...
...NOT READY TO SEE HER YET.
Pleased to meet you.
The pleasure's all mine! ♡♡

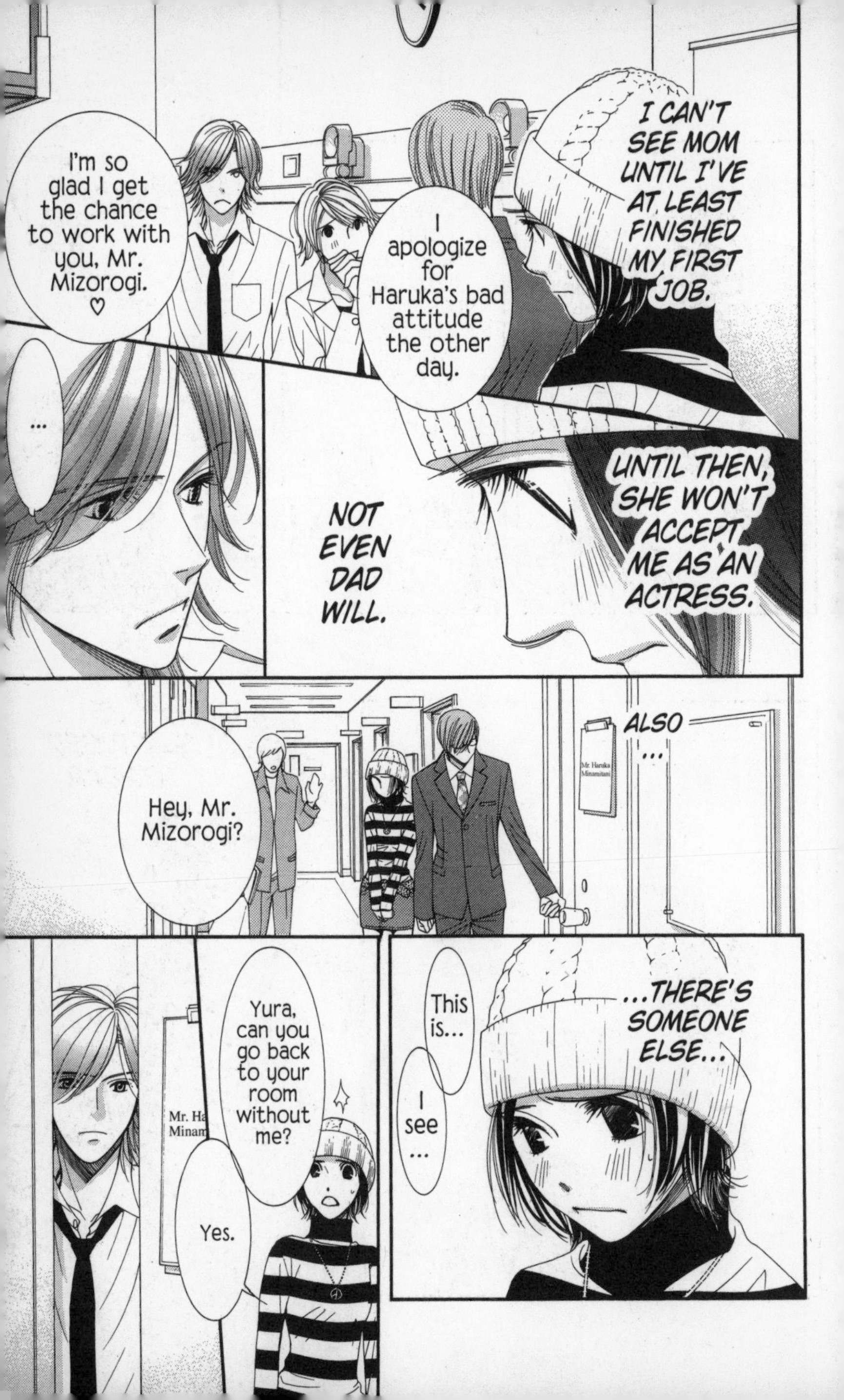
I CAN'T SEE MOM UNTIL I'VE AT LEAST FINISHED MY FIRST JOB.
I apologize for Haruka's bad attitude the other day.
I'm so glad I get the chance to work with you, Mr. Mizorogi. ♡
UNTIL THEN, SHE WON'T ACCEPT ME AS AN ACTRESS.
NOT EVEN DAD WILL.
...
ALSO...
Mr. Haruka Minamitani
Hey, Mr. Mizorogi?
...THERE'S SOMEONE ELSE...
This is...
I see...
Yura, can you go back to your room without me?
Yes.

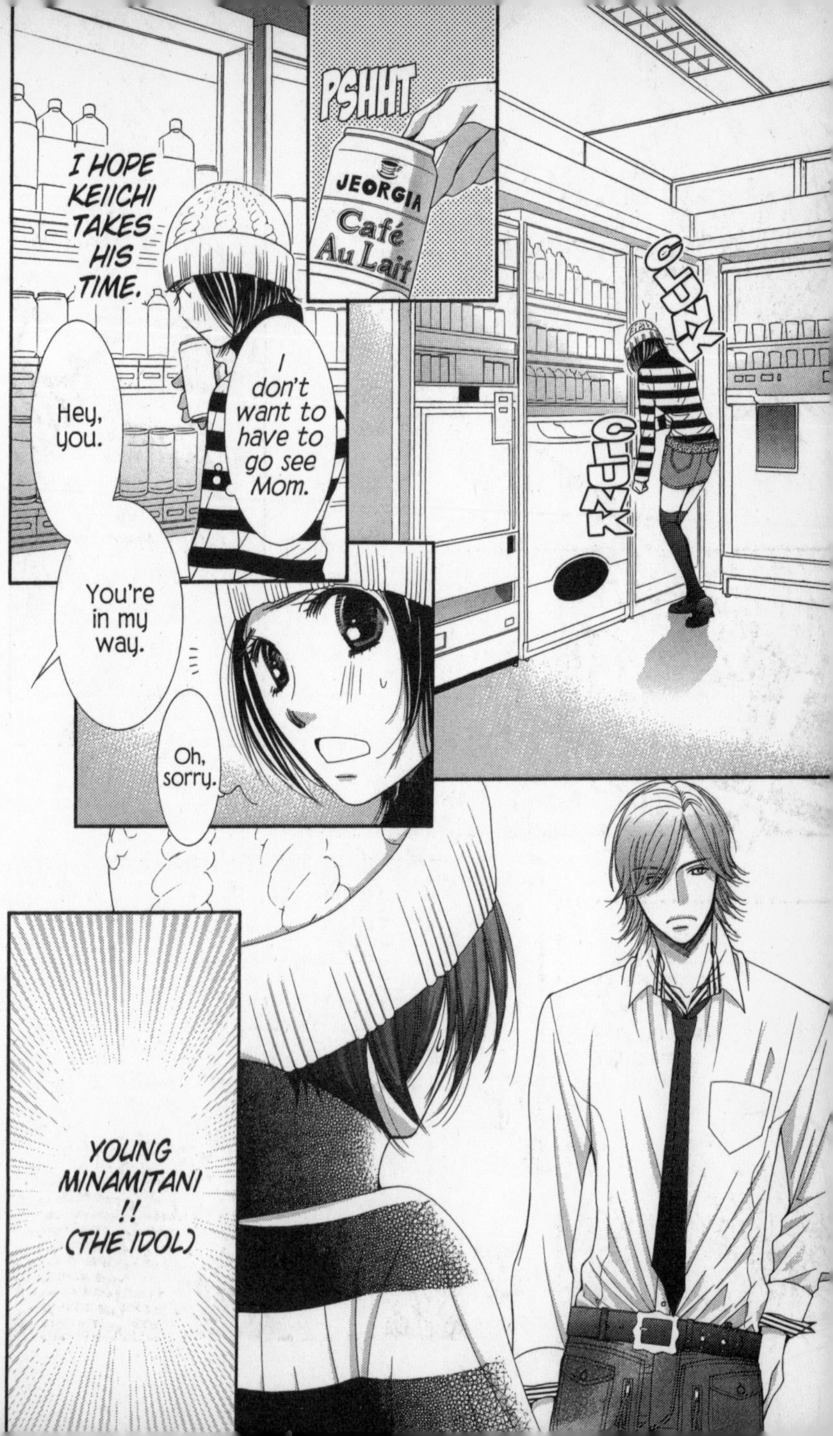

CLUNK
CLUNK
PSHHT
JEORGIA Café Au Lait
I HOPE KEIICHI TAKES HIS TIME.
I don't want to have to go see Mom.
Hey, you.
You're in my way.
Oh, sorry.
YOUNG MINAMITANI!! (THE IDOL)

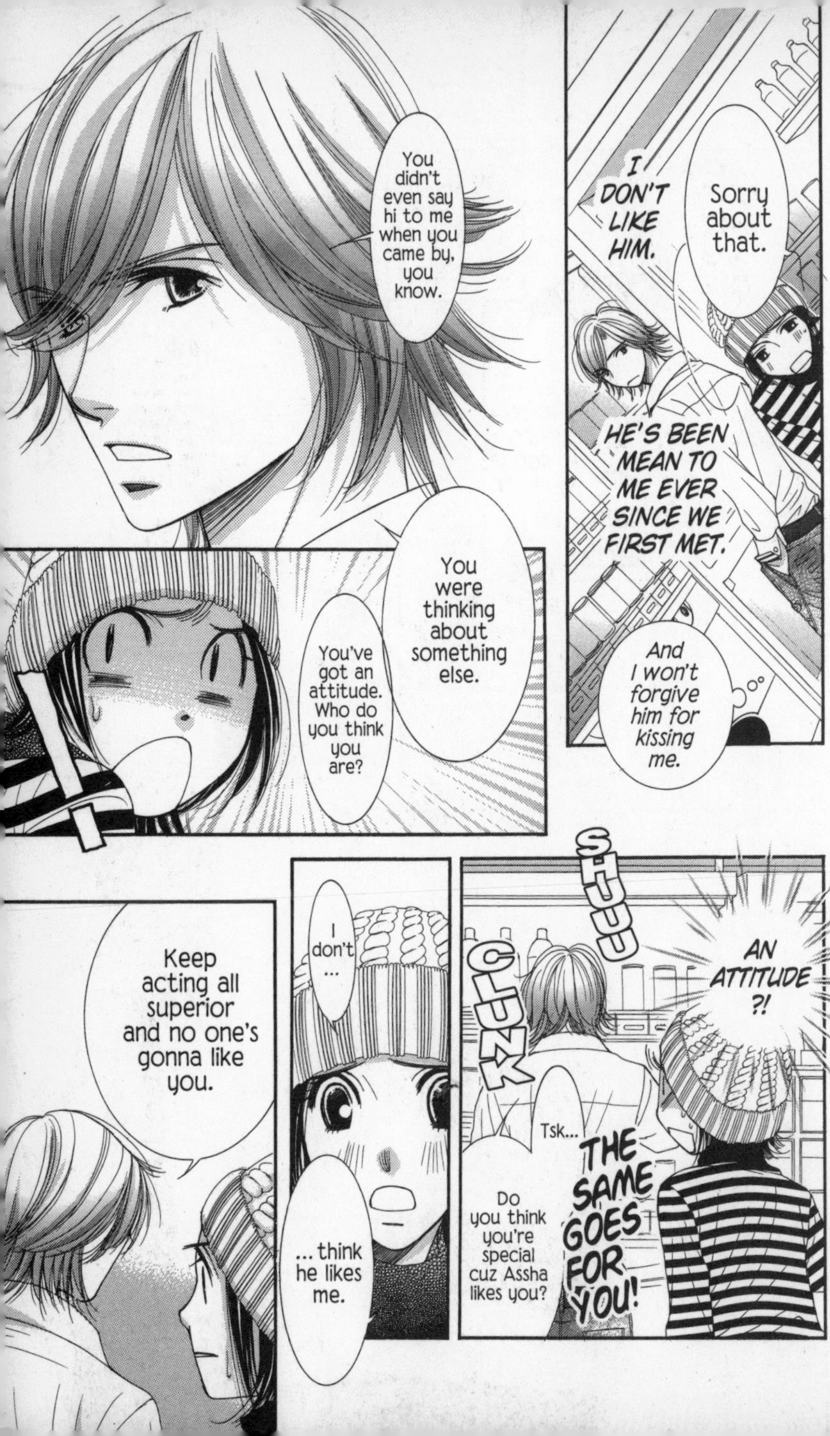
Sorry about that.
I DON'T LIKE HIM.
HE'S BEEN MEAN TO ME EVER SINCE WE FIRST MET.
And I won't forgive him for kissing me.
You didn't even say hi to me when you came by, you know.
You were thinking about something else.
You've got an attitude. Who do you think you are?
AN ATTITUDE?!
SHUUU
CLUNK
Tsk...
THE SAME GOES FOR YOU!
Do you think you're special cuz Assha likes you?
I don't...
...think he likes me.
Keep acting all superior and no one's gonna like you.

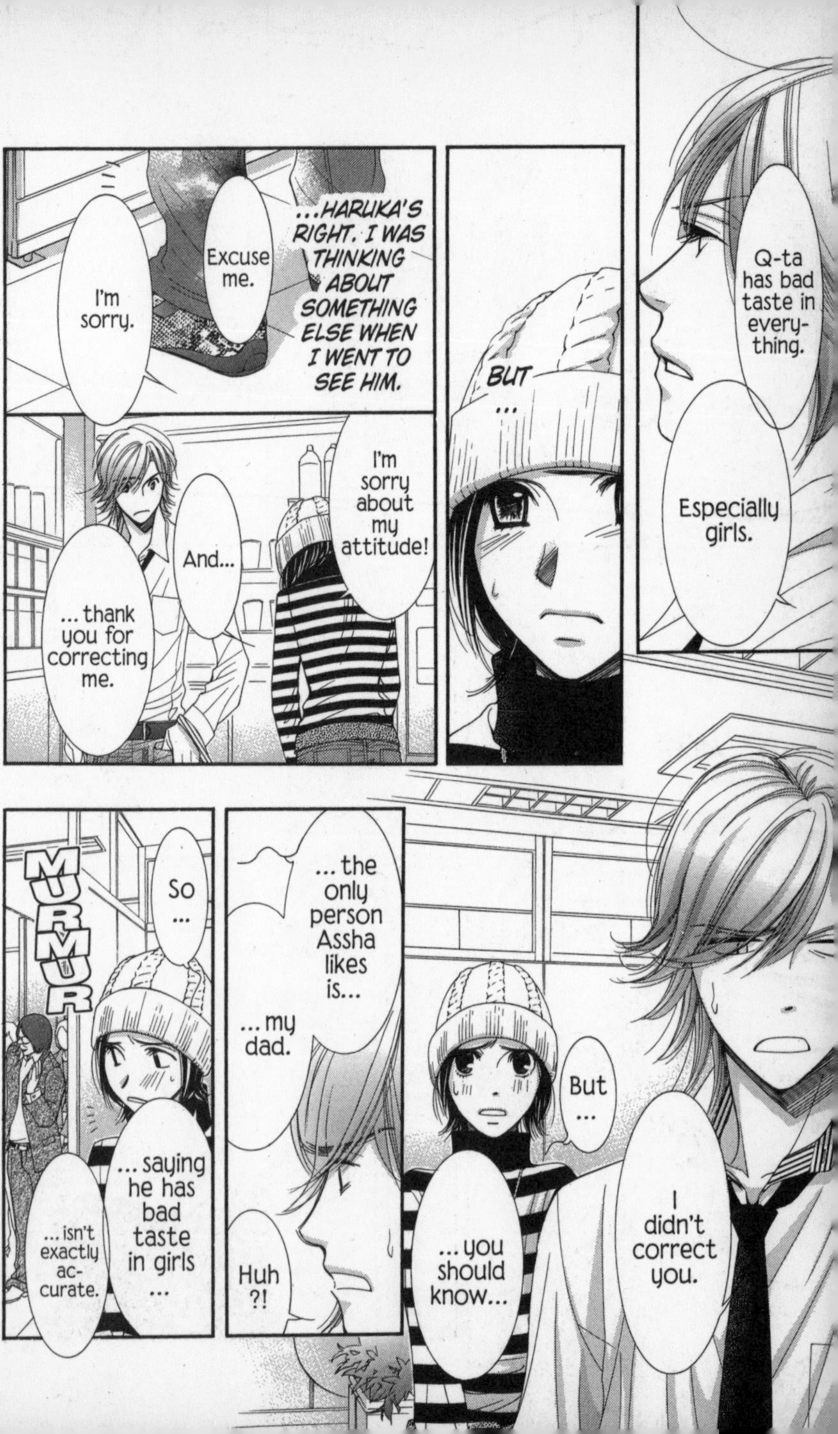
Q-ta has bad taste in every-thing.
Especially girls.
BUT ...
...HARUKA'S RIGHT. I WAS THINKING ABOUT SOMETHING ELSE WHEN I WENT TO SEE HIM.
Excuse me.
I'm sorry.
I'm sorry about my attitude!
And...
... thank you for correcting me.
I didn't correct you.
But ...
... you should know...
... the only person Assha likes is...
... my dad.
Huh ?!
MURMUR
So ...
... saying he has bad taste in girls ...
... isn't exactly ac-curate.

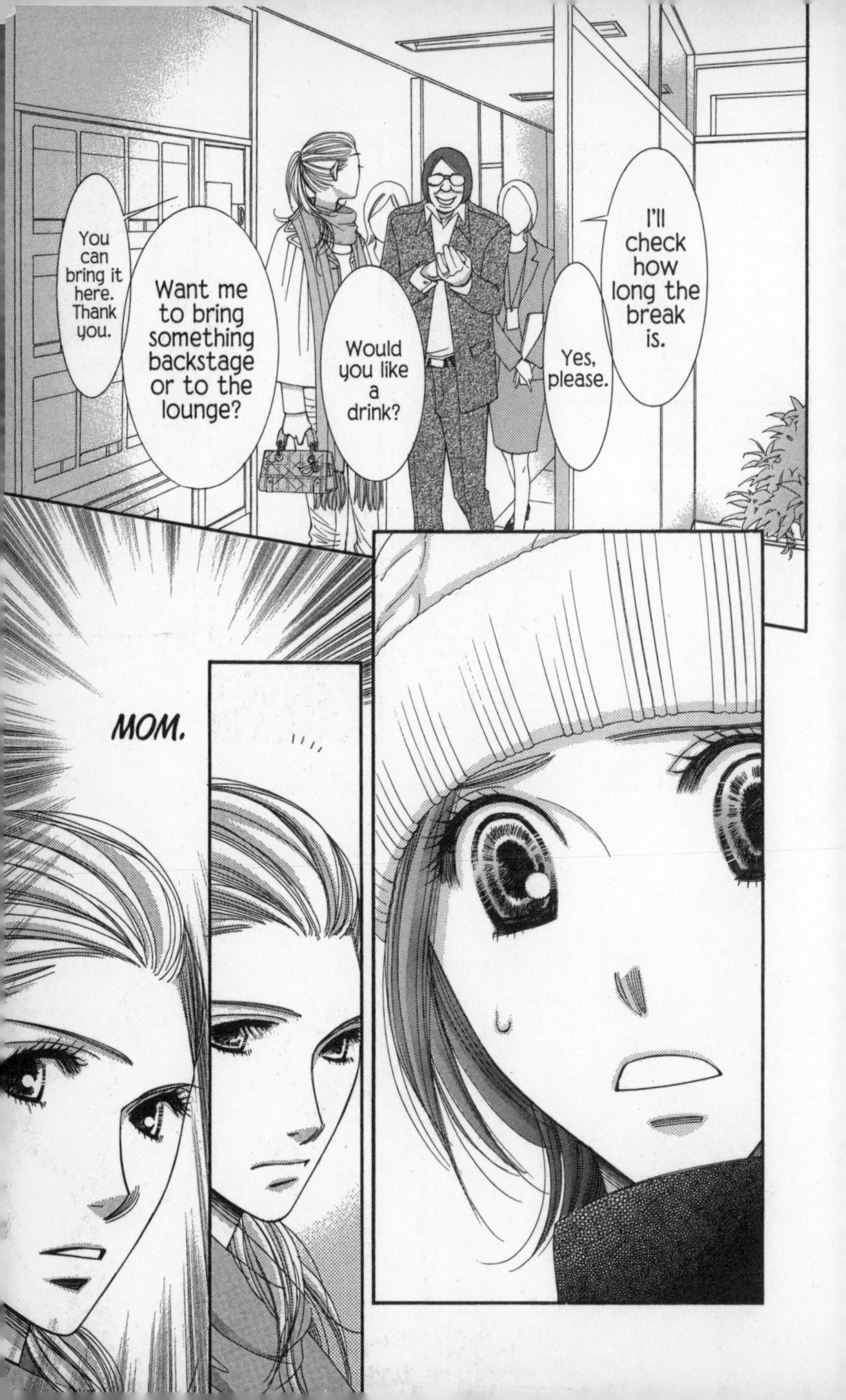
I'll check how long the break is.
Yes, please.
Would you like a drink?
Want me to bring something backstage or to the lounge?
You can bring it here. Thank you.
MOM.

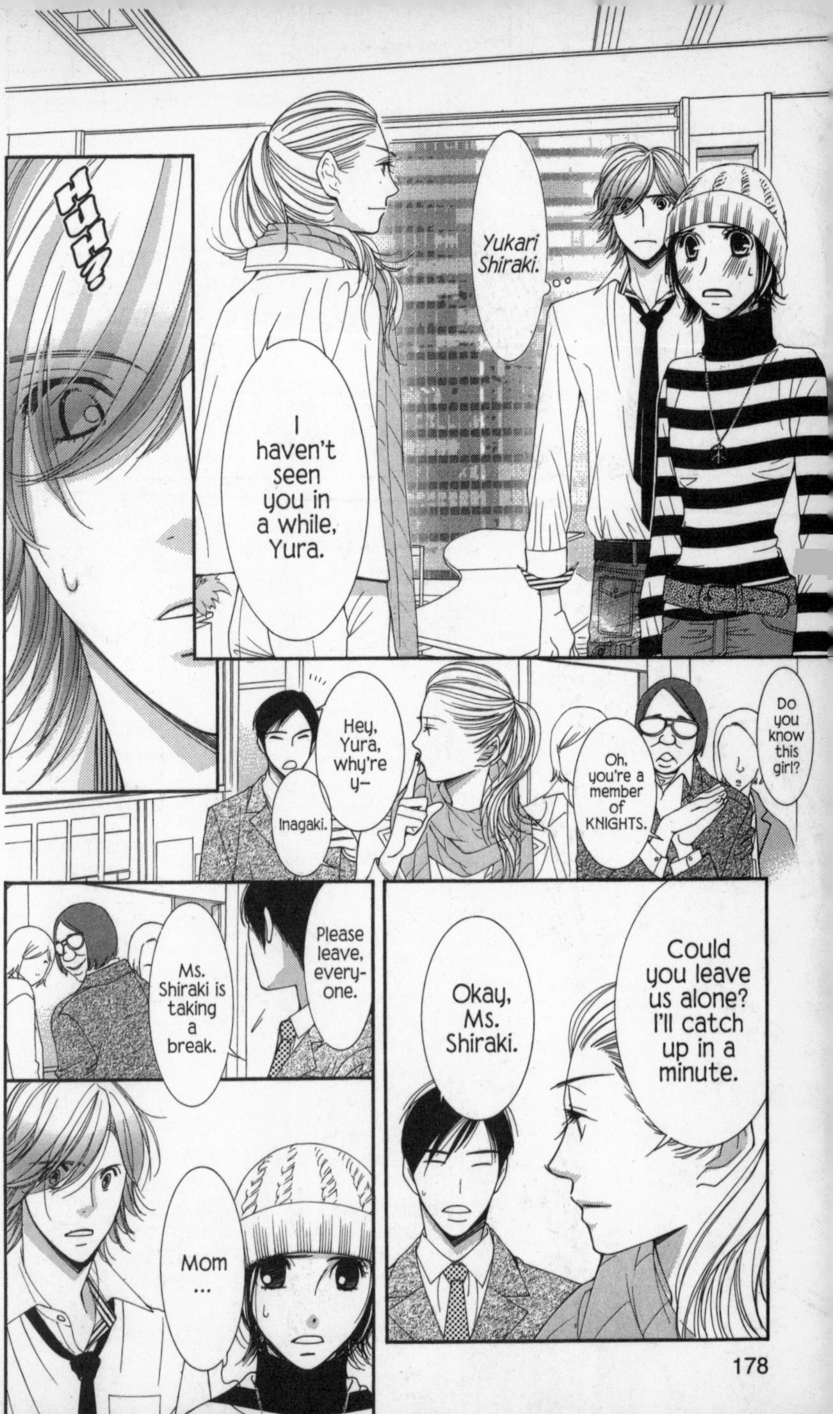
Yukari Shiraki.
I haven't seen you in a while, Yura.
Do you know this girl!?
Oh, you're a member of KNIGHTS.
Hey, Yura, why're y–
Inagaki.
HUH!?
Could you leave us alone? I'll catch up in a minute.
Okay, Ms. Shiraki.
Please leave, every-one.
Ms. Shiraki is taking a break.
Mom ...

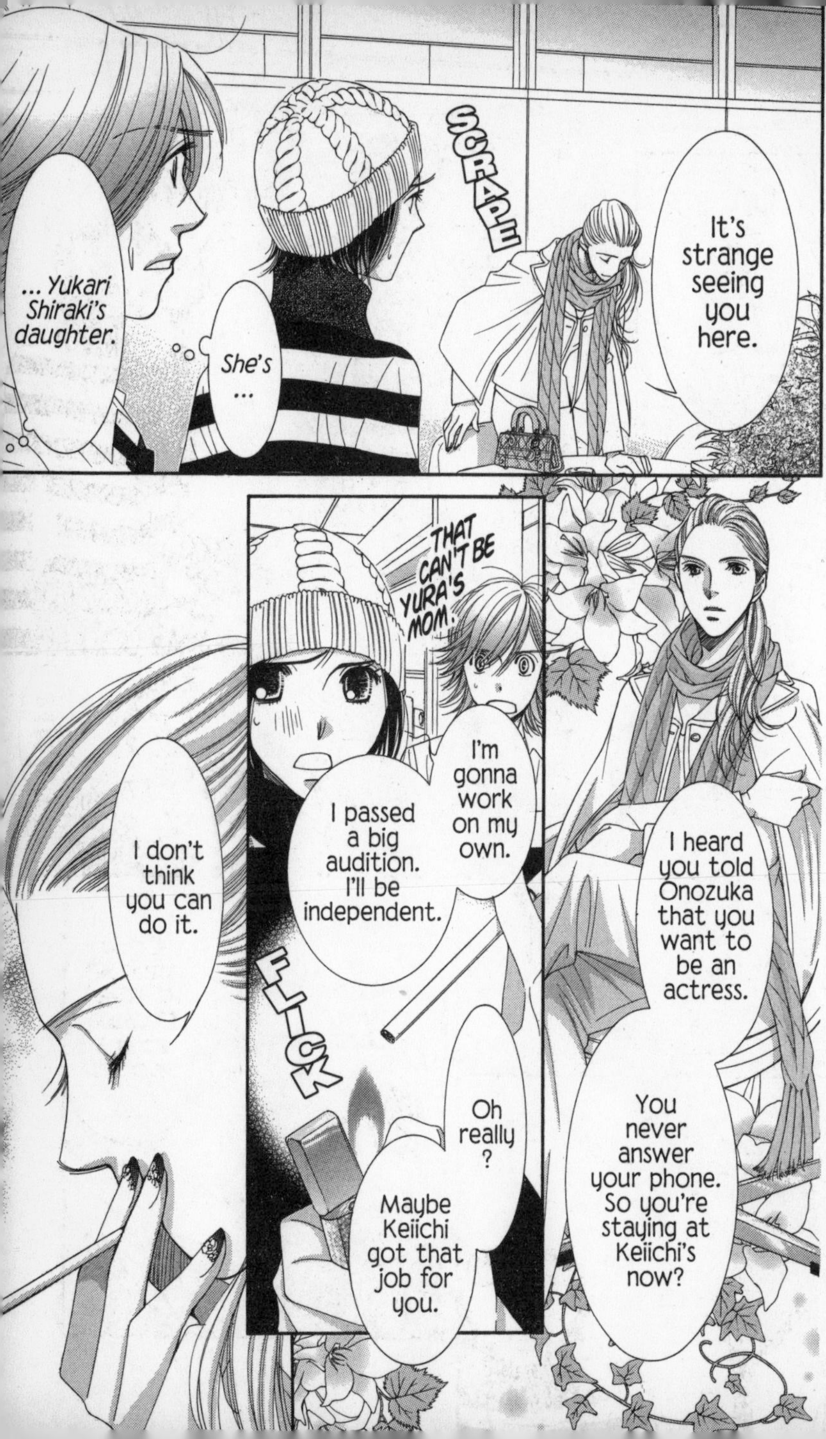
It's strange seeing you here.
SCRAPE
She's ...
... Yukari Shiraki's daughter.
I heard you told Onozuka that you want to be an actress.
You never answer your phone. So you're staying at Keiichi's now?
THAT CAN'T BE YURA'S MOM.
I'm gonna work on my own.
I passed a big audition. I'll be independent.
FLICK
Oh really?
Maybe Keiichi got that job for you.
I don't think you can do it.

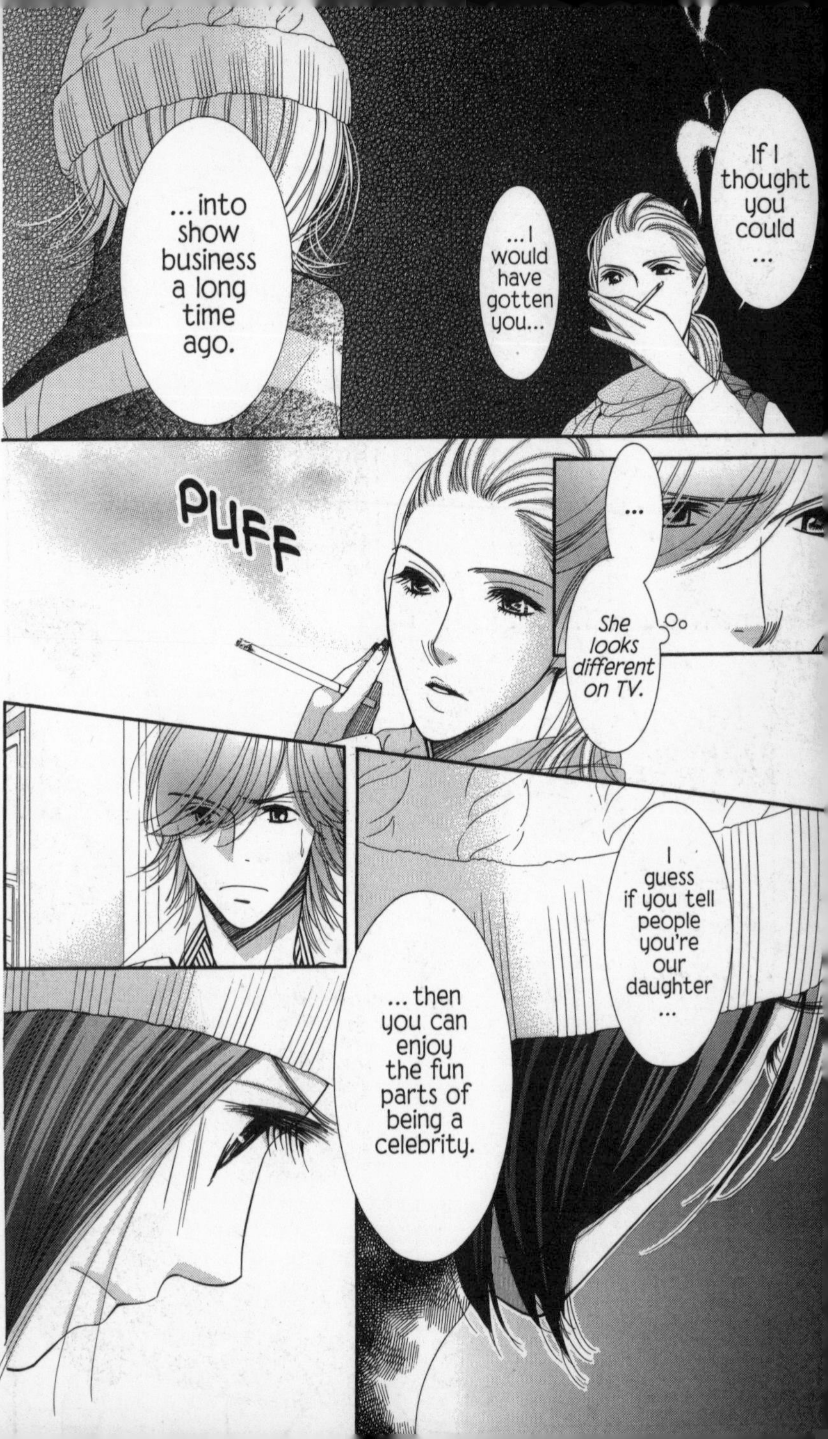
If I thought you could ...
...I would have gotten you...
...into show business a long time ago.
...
She looks different on TV.
PUFF
I guess if you tell people you're our daughter ...
...then you can enjoy the fun parts of being a celebrity.

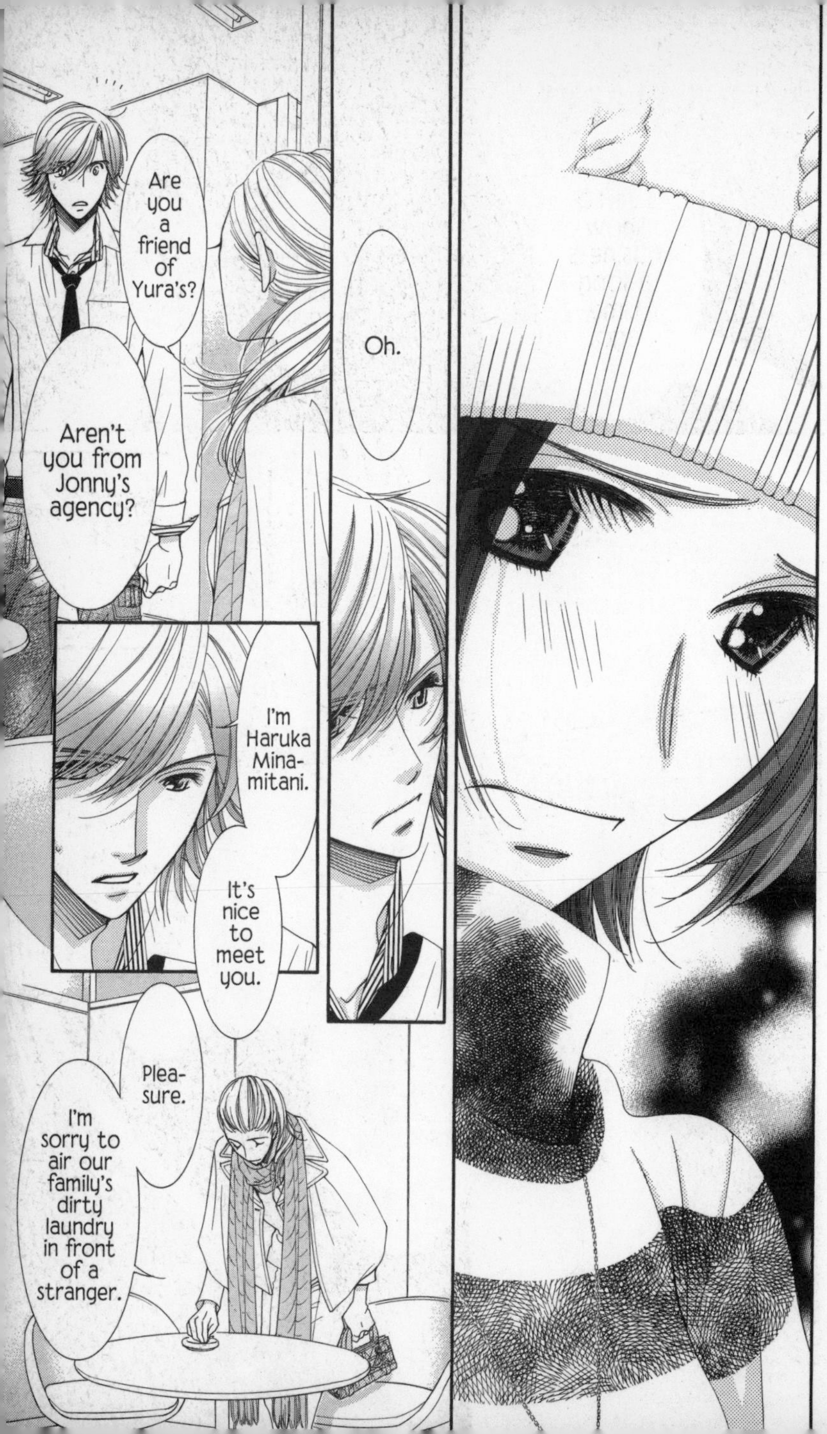

Are you a friend of Yura's?
Aren't you from Jonny's agency?
Oh.
I'm Haruka Mina-mitani.
It's nice to meet you.
Plea-sure.
I'm sorry to air our family's dirty laundry in front of a stranger.

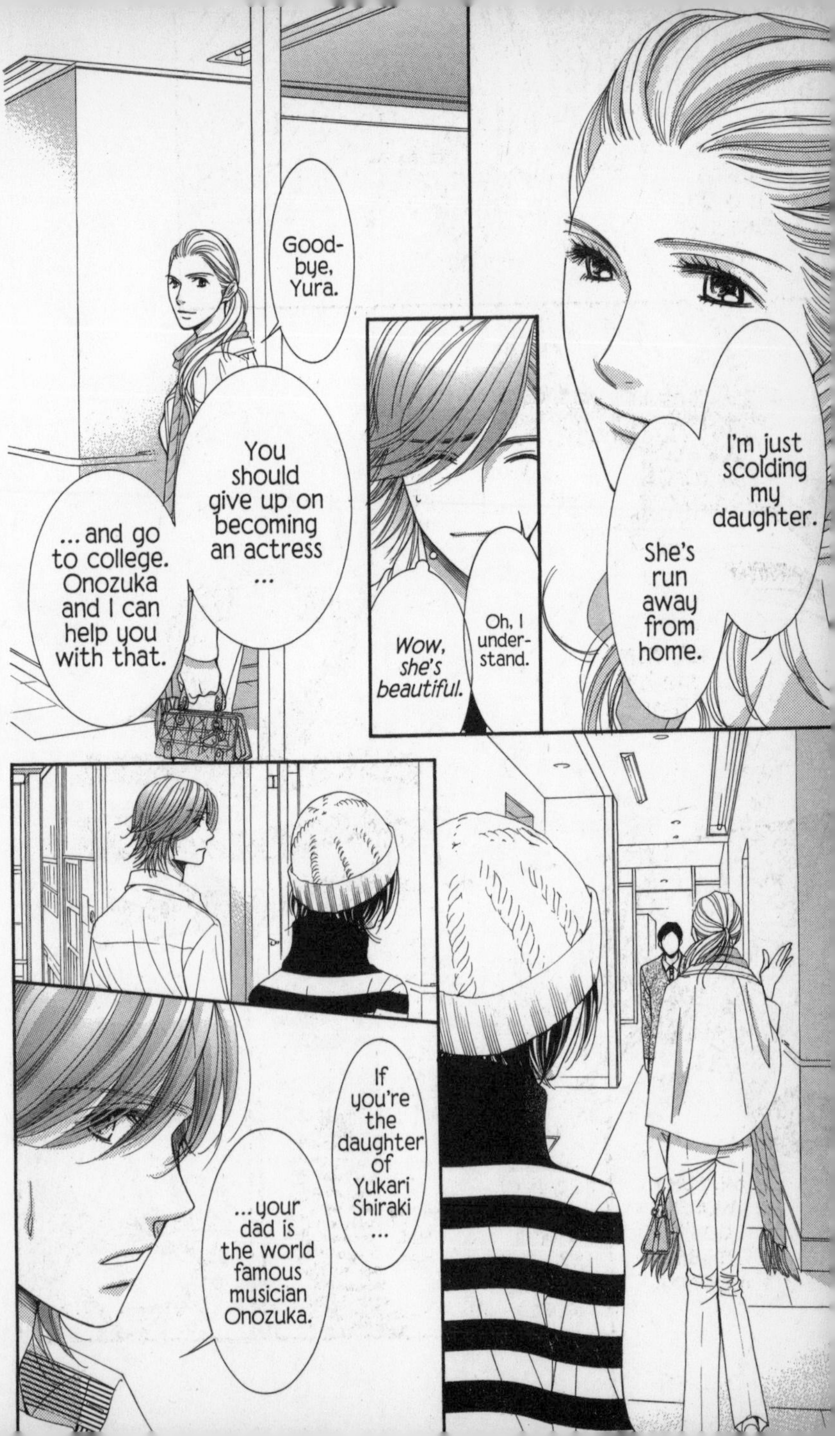
I'm just scolding my daughter.
She's run away from home.
Oh, I under-stand.
Wow, she's beautiful.
Good-bye, Yura.
You should give up on becoming an actress ...
... and go to college. Onozuka and I can help you with that.
If you're the daughter of Yukari Shiraki ...
... your dad is the world famous musician Onozuka.

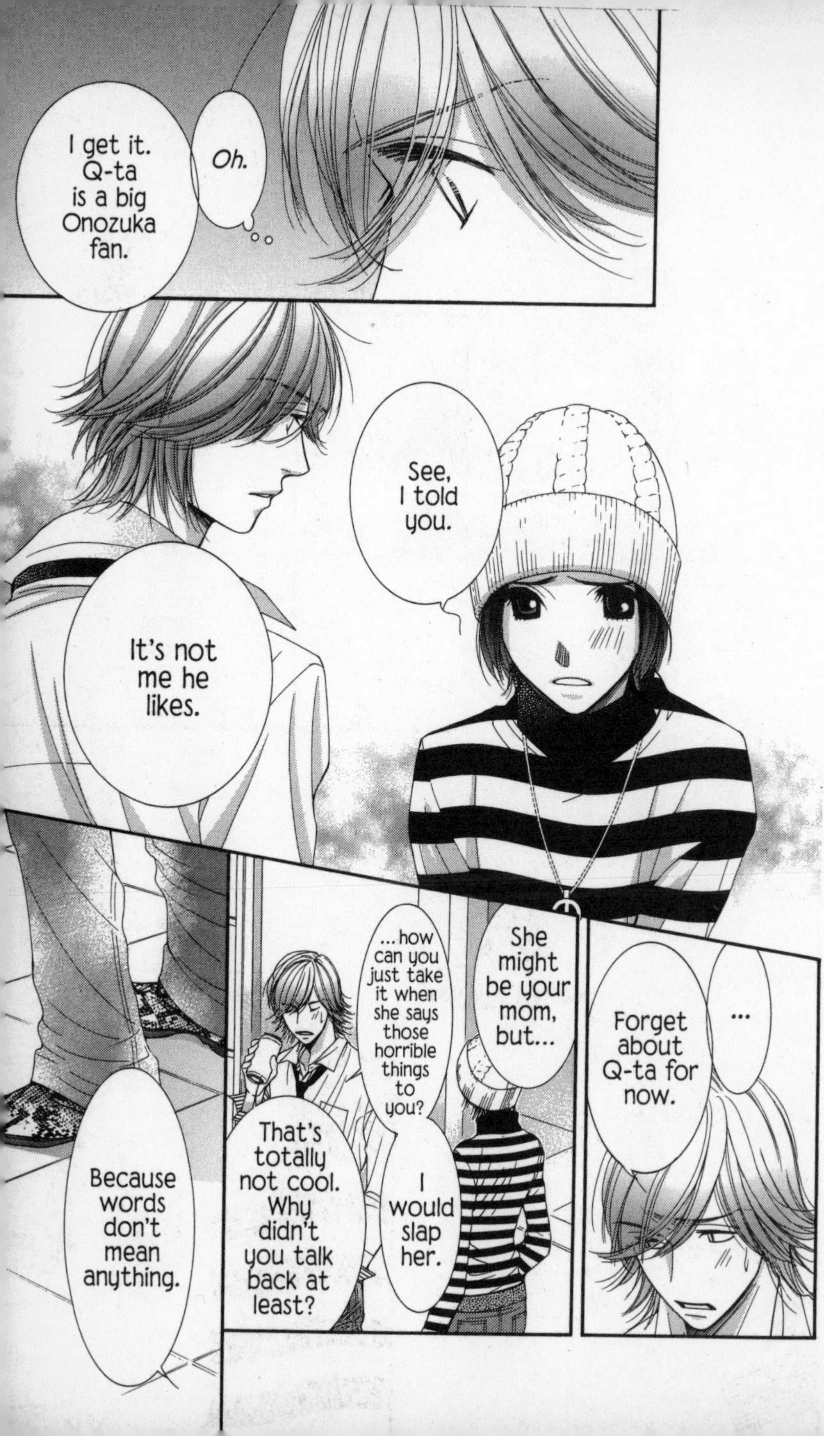
Oh.
I get it. Q-ta is a big Onozuka fan.
See, I told you.
It's not me he likes.
...
Forget about Q-ta for now.
She might be your mom, but...
...how can you just take it when she says those horrible things to you?
I would slap her.
That's totally not cool. Why didn't you talk back at least?
Because words don't mean anything.

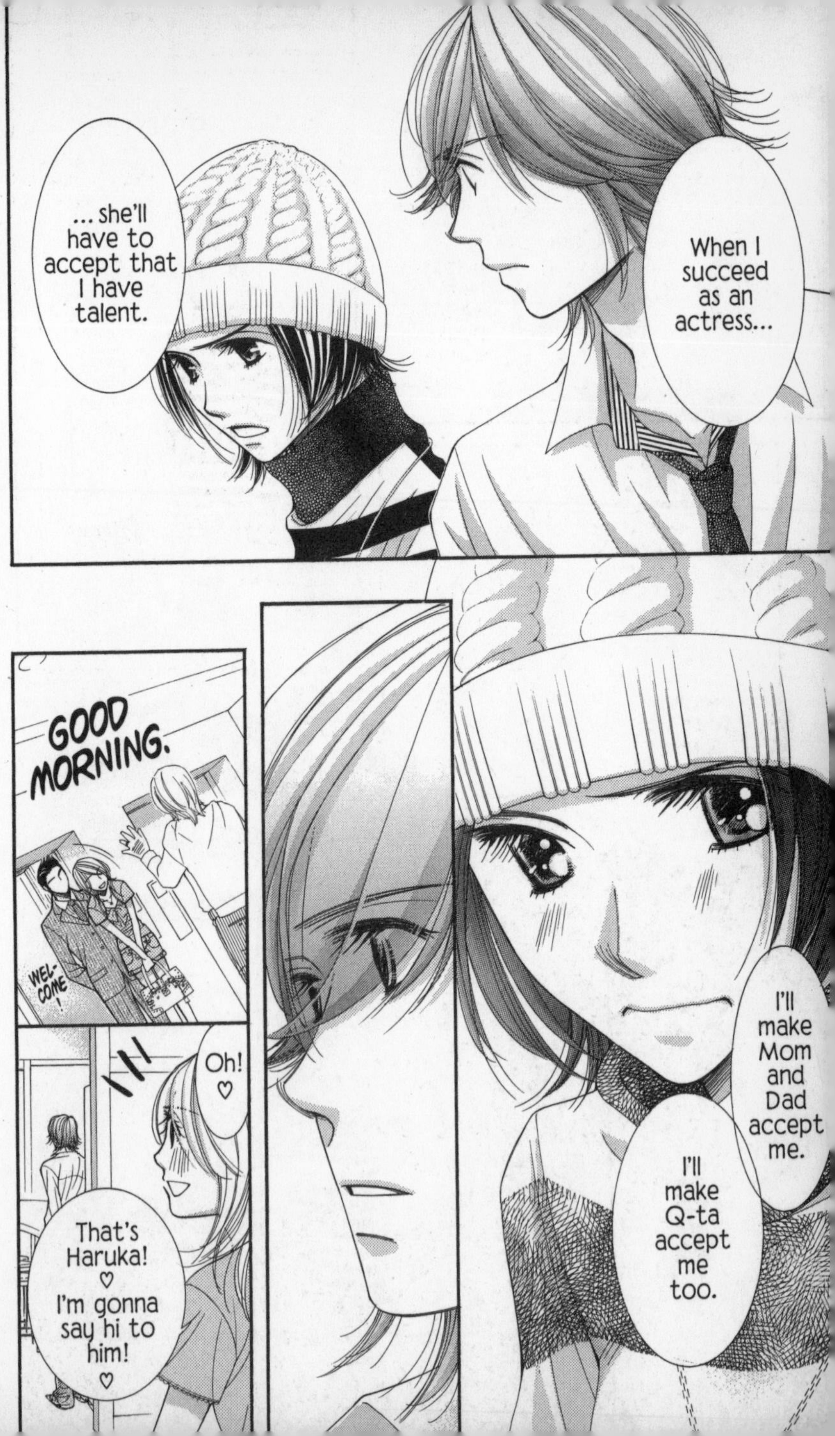
When I succeed as an actress...
... she'll have to accept that I have talent.
I'll make Mom and Dad accept me.
I'll make Q-ta accept me too.
GOOD MORNING.
WEL-COME!
Oh! ♡
That's Haruka! ♡ I'm gonna say hi to him! ♡

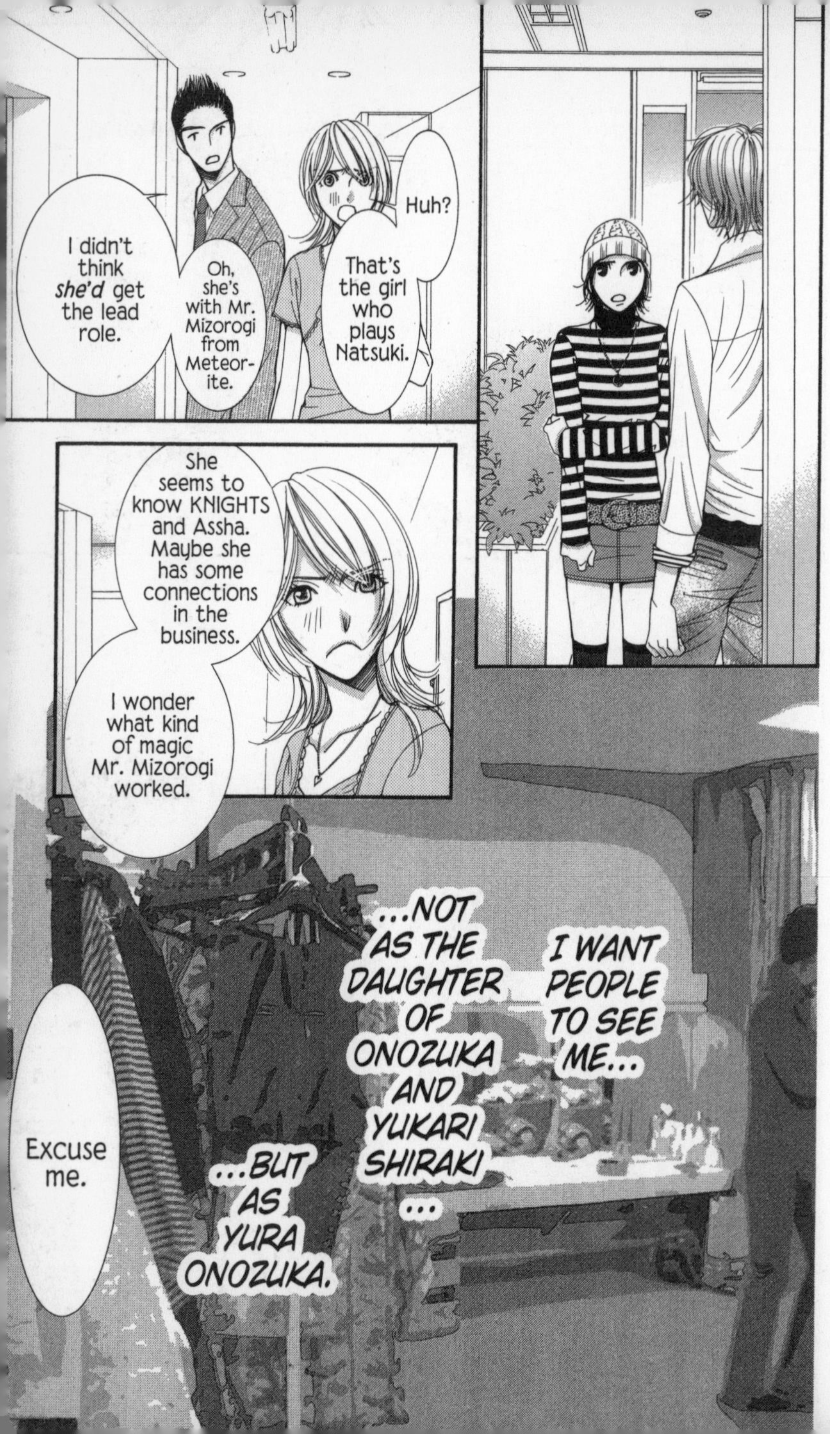
Huh?
That's the girl who plays Natsuki.
Oh, she's with Mr. Mizorogi from Meteor-ite.
I didn't think *she'd* get the lead role.
She seems to know KNIGHTS and Assha. Maybe she has some connections in the business.
I wonder what kind of magic Mr. Mizorogi worked.
I WANT PEOPLE TO SEE ME...
...NOT AS THE DAUGHTER OF ONOZUKA AND YUKARI SHIRAKI...
...BUT AS YURA ONOZUKA.
Excuse me.

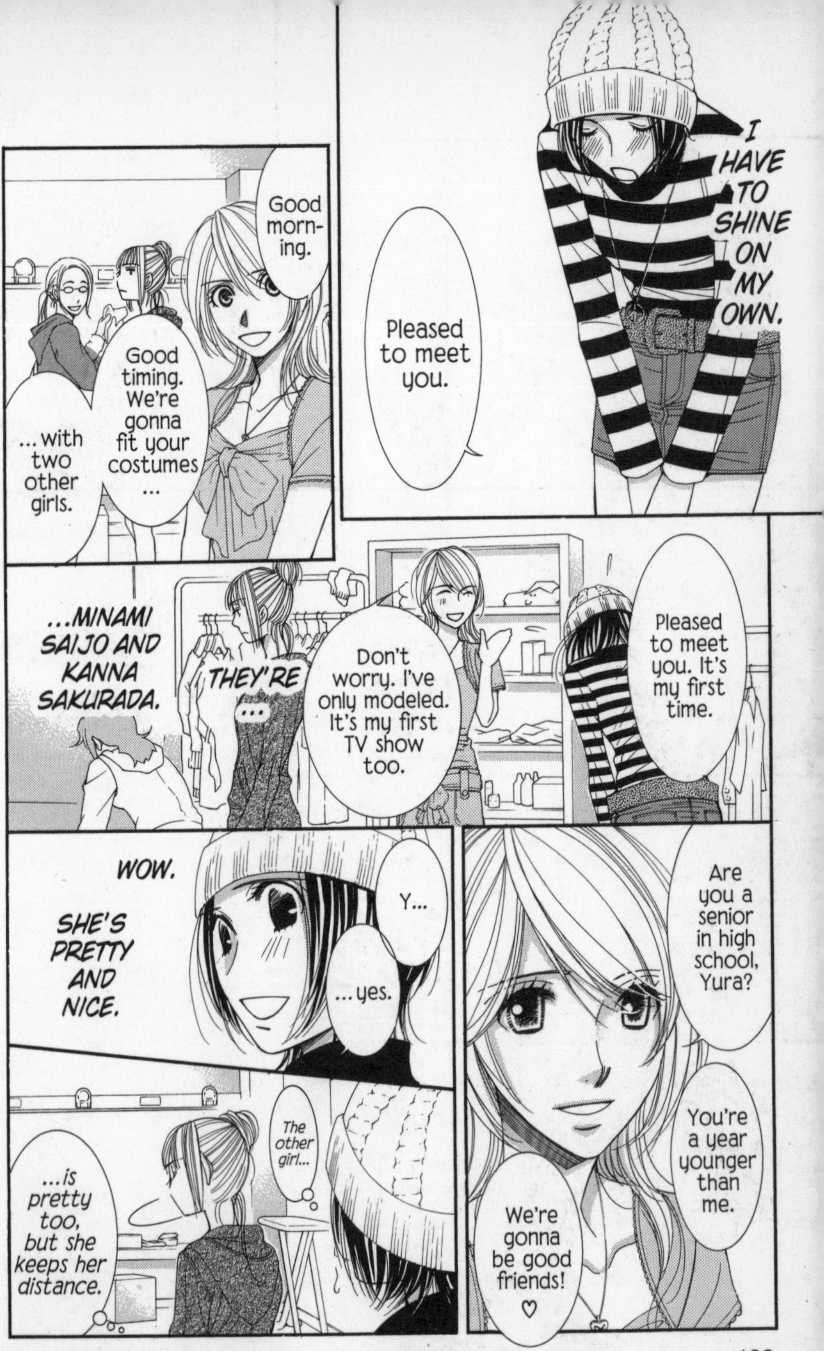
I HAVE TO SHINE ON MY OWN.
Pleased to meet you.
Good morning.
Good timing. We're gonna fit your costumes...
...with two other girls.
Pleased to meet you. It's my first time.
Don't worry. I've only modeled. It's my first TV show too.
THEY'RE ...
...MINAMI SAIJO AND KANNA SAKURADA.
Are you a senior in high school, Yura?
You're a year younger than me.
We're gonna be good friends! ♡
Y...
...yes.
WOW.
SHE'S PRETTY AND NICE.
The other girl...
...is pretty too, but she keeps her distance.

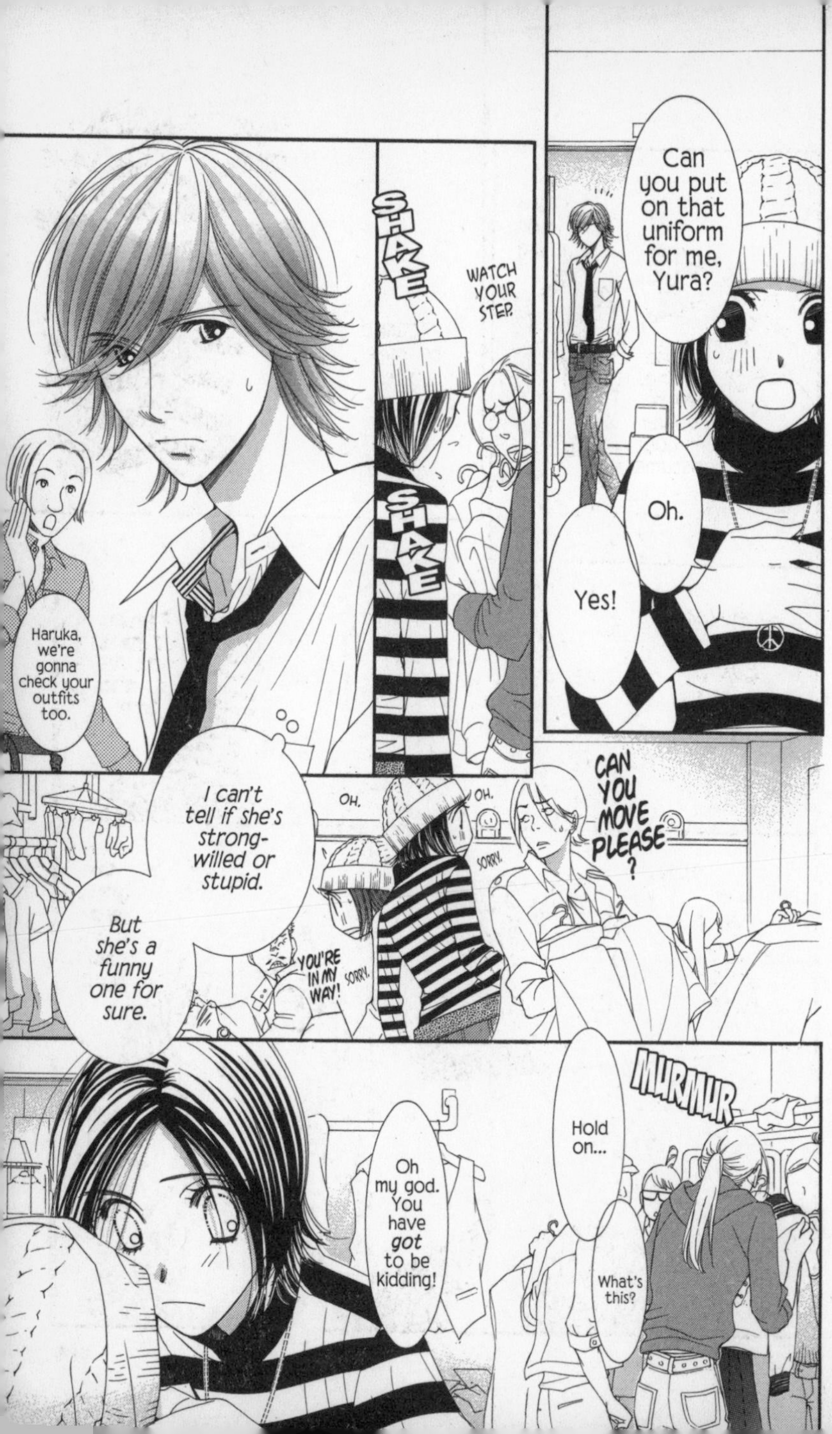

Can you put on that uniform for me, Yura?
Oh.
Yes!
SHAKE
WATCH YOUR STEP.
SHAKE
Haruka, we're gonna check your outfits too.
CAN YOU MOVE PLEASE?
OH.
SORRY.
OH.
YOU'RE IN MY WAY!
SORRY.
I can't tell if she's strong-willed or stupid.
But she's a funny one for sure.
MURMUR
Hold on...
What's this?
Oh my god. You have *got* to be kidding!

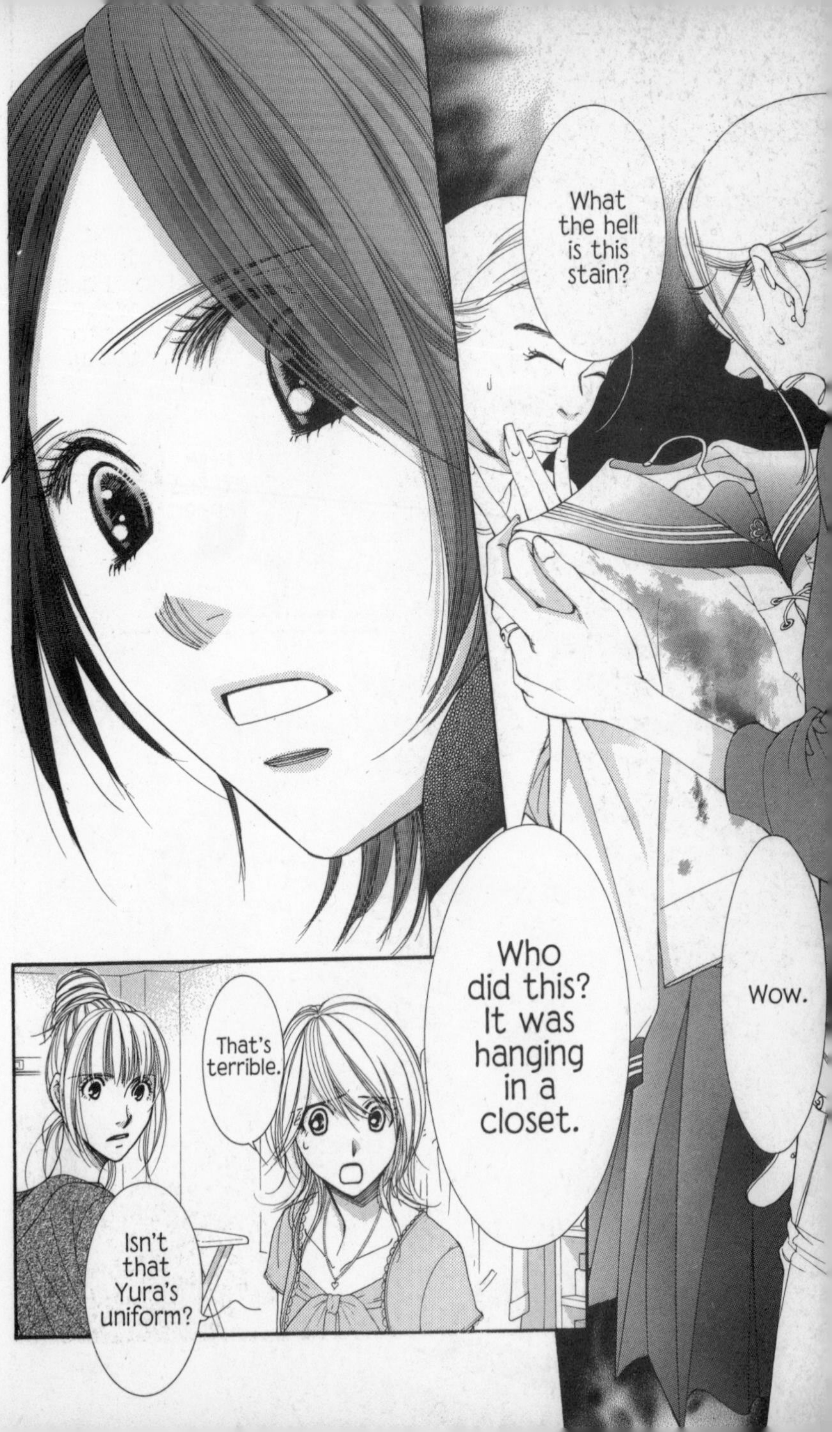
What the hell is this stain?
Wow.
Who did this? It was hanging in a closet.
That's terrible.
Isn't that Yura's uniform?

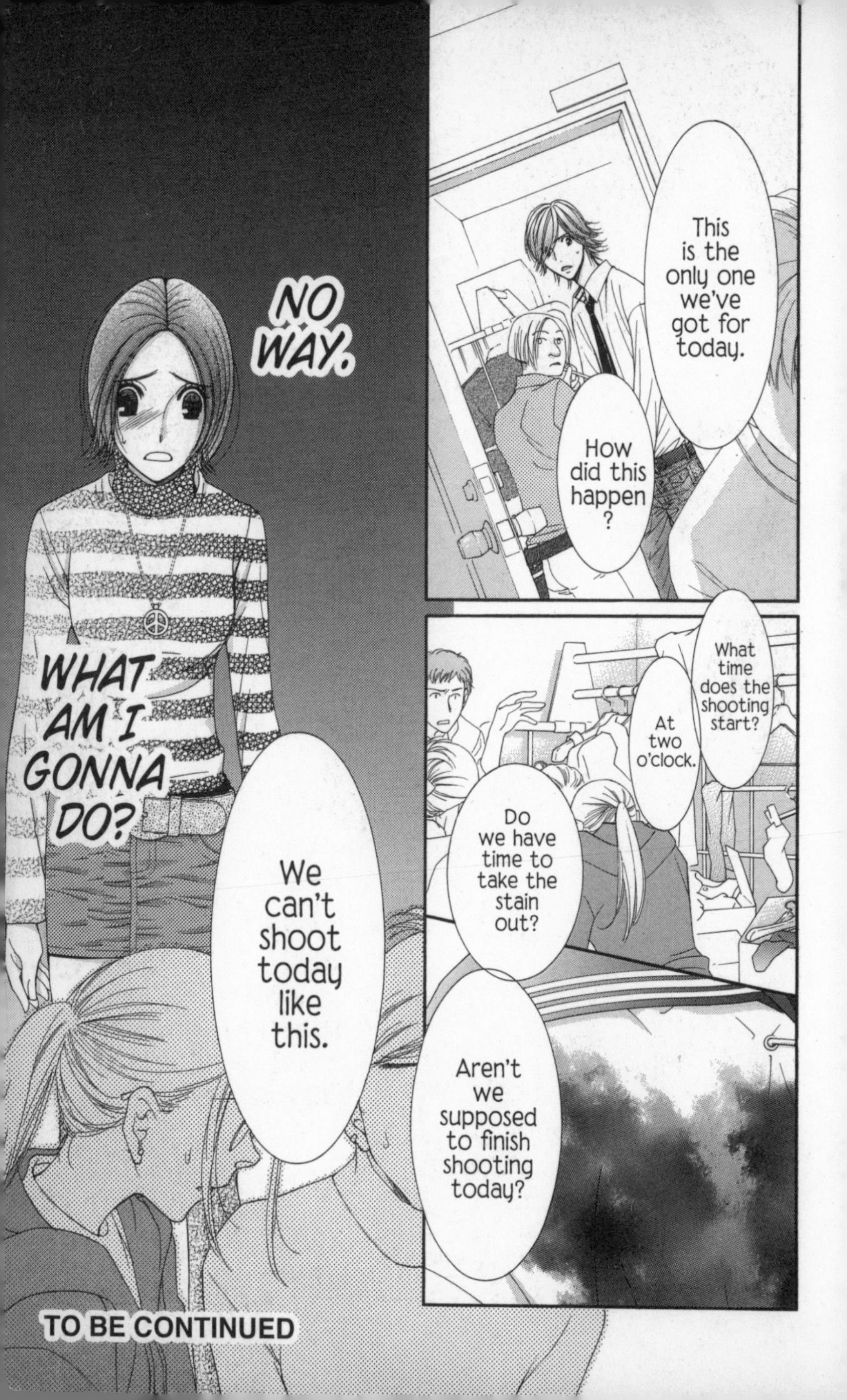
This is the only one we've got for today.
How did this happen?
What time does the shooting start?
At two o'clock.
Do we have time to take the stain out?
Aren't we supposed to finish shooting today?
NO WAY.
We can't shoot today like this.
WHAT AM I GONNA DO?
TO BE CONTINUED

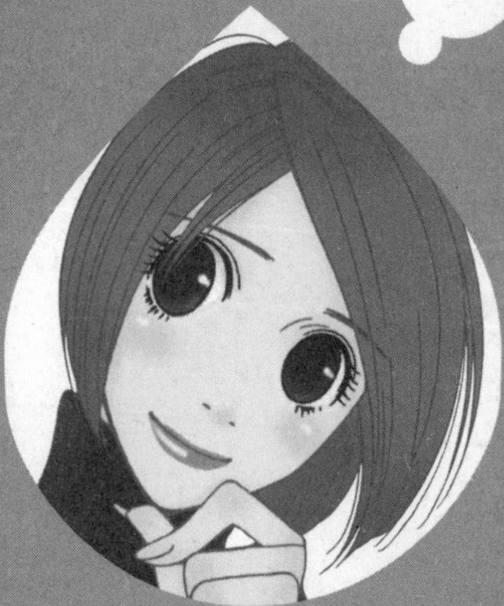

MIKI AIHARA

Miki Aihara, from Shizuoka Prefecture, is the creator of the manga series *Hot Gimmick*. She began her career with *Lip Conscious!*, which ran in *Bessatsu Shojo Comic*. Her other work includes *Seiten Taisei* (The Clear, Wide Blue Sky), *So Bad!*, and *Tokyo Boys & Girls*. She's a Gemini whose hobbies include movies and shopping.

Honey Hunt
VOL. 1

The Shojo Beat Manga Edition

This manga volume contains material that was originally published in English in *Shojo Beat* magazine, September 2008–January 2009 issues. Artwork in the magazine may have been altered slightly from what is presented in this volume.

STORY AND ART BY MIKI AIHARA

English Adaptation/Liz Forbes
Translation/Ari Yasuda, HC Language Solutions, Inc.
Touch-up Art & Lettering/Rina Mapa
Design/Ronnie Casson
Editor/Kit Fox

Editor in Chief, Books/Alvin Lu
Editor in Chief, Magazines/Marc Weidenbaum
VP, Publishing Licensing/Rika Inouye
VP, Sales & Product Marketing/Gonzalo Ferreyra
VP, Creative/Linda Espinosa
Publisher/Hyoe Narita

Printed in Canada

Published by VIZ Media, LLC
P.O. Box 77010
San Francisco, CA 94107

Shojo Beat Manga Edition
10 9 8 7 6 5 4 3 2 1
First printing, April 2009

store.viz.com

PARENTAL ADVISORY
HONEY HUNT is rated T+ for Older Teen and is recommended for ages 16 and up. This volume contains suggestive themes and adult situations.

RATED T+ FOR OLDER TEEN

ratings.viz.com

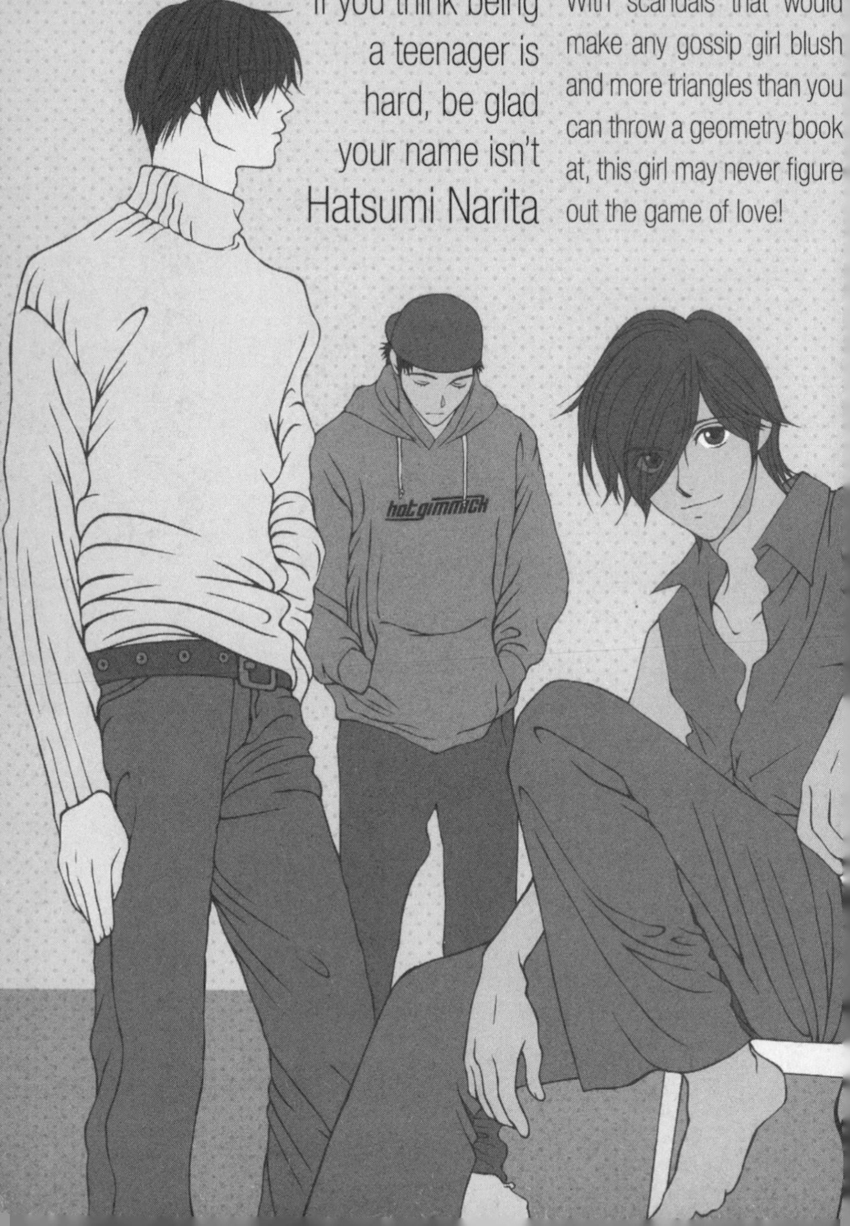

hot gimmick

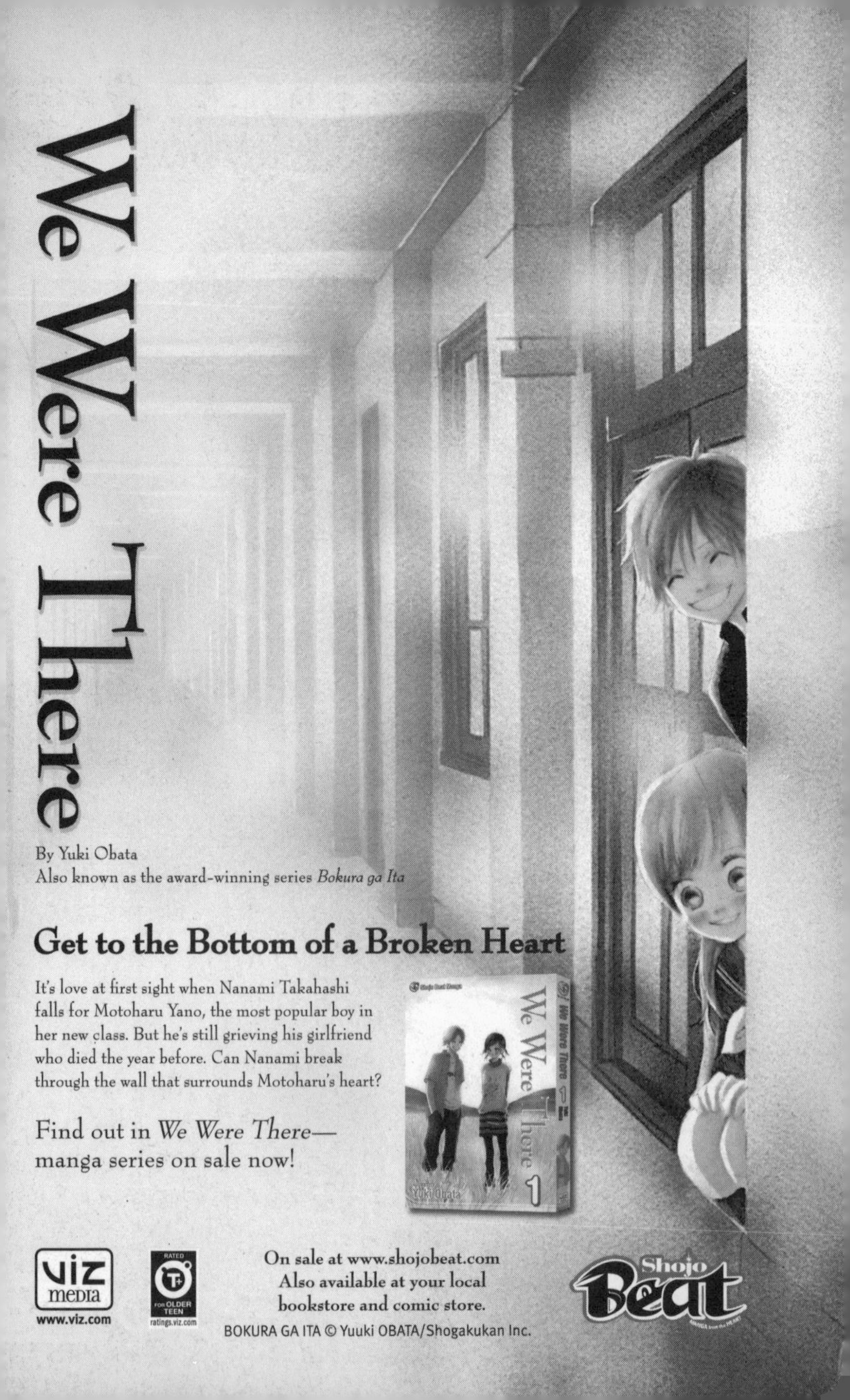
We Were There
By Yuki Obata
Also known as the award-winning series *Bokura ga Ita*
Get to the Bottom of a Broken Heart
It's love at first sight when Nanami Takahashi falls for Motoharu Yano, the most popular boy in her new class. But he's still grieving his girlfriend who died the year before. Can Nanami break through the wall that surrounds Motoharu's heart?
Find out in *We Were There*—manga series on sale now!
We Were There
Yuki Obata
1
viz media
www.viz.com
RATED T+ FOR OLDER TEEN
ratings.viz.com
On sale at www.shojobeat.com
Also available at your local bookstore and comic store.
BOKURA GA ITA © Yuuki OBATA/Shogakukan Inc.
Shojo Beat